"*The Journey Home* is a rare and intimate view on the initiation and process of becoming a swami through the fire of Bhakti and the extraordinary sacred landscape of India. An inspiring journey for all."
—SHIVA REA, AUTHOR, *YOGA WAVE*

"Here is an inspiring chapter of 'our story' of spiritual pilgrimage to the East. It shows the inner journey of awakening in a fascinating and spellbinding way."
—RAM DASS, AUTHOR, *BE HERE NOW*

"Radhanath's account invites baby-boomers to look a little deeper into how we found, lost, kept, gave away, and were given (back) the faith—how we managed to find the 1960s a time of grace and wonder. For this invitation, we can all be grateful to Swami Radhanath."
—FRANCIS X. CLOONEY, S.J.,
PROFESSOR OF COMPARATIVE THEOLOGY, HARVARD DIVINITY SCHOOL

"Radhanath's Swami's spiritual memoir is a model of modesty and candidness. He tells his story with remarkable honesty—the temptations of the 1970s, his doubts, hopes, and disappointments, the culture shock, and the friendships found and lost . . . Add a zest of danger, suspense, and surprise, and Radhanath Swami's story is a deep, genuine memoir that reads like a novel . . . Other readers will be moved by Radhanath Swami's spiritual saga and will find echoes of their own quest in his journey."
—BRIGITTE SION, ASSISTANT PROFESSOR OF RELIGIOUS STUDIES, NEW YORK UNIVERSITY

"Books like *The Journey Home* provide us with a profound opportunity to enter into presence—to have *satsang*—with spiritual seekers, saints, and holy beings through reading about their lives. This can cause a transformation of our whole being because we become like the company we keep."
—SHARON GANNON,
AUTHOR, *JIVAMUKTI YOGA* AND *YOGA AND VEGETARIANISM*

"From Malibu to Mumbai, Radhanath's search for enlightenment is a quest that you will never forget."
—NORMAN JEWISON,
DIRECTOR AND PRODUCER, *FIDDLER ON THE ROOF, IN THE HEAT OF THE NIGHT*, AND *THE HURRICANE*

"A sensitive, comprehensive, intuitive, and inspiring book, delving into one's soul and spirituality. His extensive commitment to achieve what he wanted to, how he learned his belief in reliance to God, and of hope are all written with utmost affection and in pure honesty by the author."
—YASH BIRLA, INDUSTRIALIST

"A generational journey to the East by one who found the real goal of all seeking, *The Journey Home* is one of the most remarkable and intimate portrayals of the life and adventure of an American swami, providing the reader the opportunity for a similar transformation."
—DAVID FRAWLEY,
AUTHOR, *YOGA: THE GREATER TRADITION* AND *YOGA AND AYURVEDA*

"It is a great joy to know that a saint like Radhanath Swami is now sharing his precious memories with the world through this long-awaited book. Having had the privilege to know him closely, I have no doubt that future generations will find these reminiscences fascinating and inspirational."
—ARVIND N. MAFATLAL, INDUSTRIALIST

"What is remarkable about this book is its transparent honesty . . . one marvels at Radhanath Swami's fearless description of his failings and shortcomings, fears, and anxieties as he went about from place to place looking for the ultimate purpose of life. In every chapter there is a glimpse of the great souls that have influences his thinking . . . This book is a must-read for all spiritual seekers."
—N. VAGHUL, CHAIRMAN, ICICI BANK

"*The Journey Home* is a stunning story worth reading. Radhanath Swami's journey from the external to the internal world is awe-inspiring. His quest to reach the spiritual kingdom of India is an unbelievable episode. His determination as an ardent seeker of truth is clear, for at last he savored seeing the soul face-to-face. I respect my friend Radhanath Swami for pursuing a pilgrimage where he experienced unity in diversity—part and parcel of India culture—and met various spiritual leads as he gained knowledge of *Adhyaatma Vidya* (Knowledge of the Soul). *The Journey Home* is the story of a seeker who became a seer. May many be inspired to experience what he has experienced."
—B. K. S. IYENGAR, AUTHOR, *YOGA: WISDOM & PRACTICE*

"This tale will reveal the love of God, which is dormant within everyone's heart. The reader is given a chance to change his life in the same way as the author."
—PEJAWAR SWAMI, PONTIFF OF MADHVA SAMSTA

"*The Journey Home* is an incredible account of tremendous determination in the face of seemingly insurmountable obstacles. Radhanath Swami has a gift of observing the smallest detail, and his amazing memory is able to recollect experiences occuring almost forty years ago. A must-read."
—HRISHIKESH MAFATLAL, INDUSTRIALIST

"*The Journey Home* is a spellbinding autobiographical narrative, permeated with the devotion and determination of Richard Slavin (aka Radhanath Swami) as he embarks on a courageous journey in search of the ultimate truths of life. It gives endearing glimpses into the kaleidoscope of Indian spirituality. An invaluable guidebook for all who are seeking the path home."
—PADMASHREE DR. VIJAY BHATKAR,
INDIAN SCIENTIST, DEVELOPER OF THE PARAM SUPERCOMPUTER

"This wonderful book shows how purity of heart can overcome all obstacles on the Spiritual Path. It sings to us of holding on to our dream of Real Love until it becomes Reality. Come take this journey with Radhanath Swami!"
—KRISHNA DAS, KIRTAN SINGER

"Radhanath Swami's life history is an inspirational road map for
an ordinary person. [His] profound vision, intellectual power,
strong determination, and extraordinary personality is embedded
in each page of the book."
—Venugopal N. Dhoot,
Chairman, Videacon group of companies

"What is particularly remarkable about Radhanath Swami's *The Journey
Home* is the striking detail of his descriptions of his daily existence
on the spiritual path . . . All of this is set forth in an elegantly clear
[language] that completely avoids ambiguity."
—Charles S. J. White, Ph.D.,
Professor Emeritus, American University, Washington, D.C.

"This book is a profound story of Radhanath Swami's journey
from the material world of temptation, attachment, and several
difficulties to the innermost innocent spiritual awakening.
One should learn from Swamiji's life story about the depth of dedication,
conviction, and total commitment to the inner search of truth.
His whole life flows like a river from mountain to valley,
from jungles to cities, till it merges into the ocean, where all running, flowing
comes to an end with the inner silence and bliss.
This book is a powerful guide for all those who
wish to have spiritual awakening and exploration of inner truth."
—Dr. Vasant Lad,
Author and Founder of the Ayurvedic Institute, Albuquerque New Mexico.

"I greatly enjoyed *The Journey Home*. It shows how a man of great spiritual energy can start his adult life as a typical young rock 'n' roller and open his heart, mind, and soul to great adventures and very great learning. The journey of Radhanath Swami is an inspiring and humanly touching one. Throughout this book the reader never loses the impression that he is 'one of us.' Unlike other 'holy men,' he is not posturing as one step removed. He is teaching us because he remembers how to be one of us. That is why the book is touching—because he himself has remained within close touching distance. We feel it is possible to take this journey."

—STEPHEN CHAN, PROFESSOR OF INTERNATIONAL RELATIONS, LONDON UNIVERSITY SCHOOL OF ORIENTAL AND AFRICAN STUDIES

"Shri Radhanath Maharaja's *The Journey Home* is like reading a modern-day rendering of stories that we find in exalted spiritual texts such as the Shrimad Bhagavatam. Truly, an opportunity to imbibe the accounts of God's lovers is the fruit of our spiritual endeavors!"

—SHYAMDAS, DEVOTIONAL BHAKTI YOGA PRACTITIONER. AUTHOR AND TRANSLATOR OF *THE PATH OF GRACE* AND MORE THAN 20 BOOKS ON BHAKTI YOGA

"*The Journey Home* is a generational classic. It portrays an American teenager's search for meaning and fulfillment in the turbulent world we live in. He travels across Europe, the Middle East, and into the mystical world of India. It's a tale of adventure, humor, and love. I recommend *The Journey Home* as a must-read for seekers of all sorts."

—SAURAV GANGULY, FORMER CAPTAIN OF THE INDIAN NATIONAL CRICKET TEAM

"Have you ever had the experience that when you start reading a book, you get so involved in it, you actually want to slow down because you don't want it to end. Well, this is that book. The freshness of this voice really struck me."

—PAM BINDER, PRESIDENT OF THE PACIFIC NORTHWEST WRITERS' ASSOCIATION

The Journey Home

AUTOBIOGRAPHY
of an AMERICAN SWAMI

MANDALA PUBLISHING
10 Paul Drive
San Rafael, CA 94903
www.mandalaeartheditions.com
800.688.2218

For more information on the subject matter of this book or the author go to
www.radhanathswami.com

Library of Congress Cataloging-in-Publication Data available.

ISBN: 978-1-60109-056-0

Mandala Publishing would like to thank Joshua Greene, Arjuna van der Kooij, and Rasikananda
Das for their valuable contributions, as well as Peter Simon, Lissa Nicolaus and Shankar
Maharaja of Rishikesh for the use of their photographs.

Photograph of J. Krishnamurti courtesy of the Krishnamurti Foundation Trust.

Photograph of Tat Wala Baba courtesy of Shankar Maharaja of Rishikesh, Himalayas.

Painting of Radha and Krishna with the gopis copyright © Indra Sharma.

Painting of Bhakti saints Rupa Goswami and Sanatana Goswami courtesy of Puskara Dasa.

Photograph of A.C. Bhaktivedanta Swami Prabhupada courtesy of the Bhaktivedanta Book
Trust, Inc. www.krishna.com. Used with permission.

All other images copyright © Mandala Publishing.

ROOTS of PEACE   REPLANTED PAPER

Roots of Peace is an internationally renowned humanitarian organization dedicated to eradicating
landmines worldwide and converting war-torn lands into productive farms and wildlife habitats.
Together, we will plant 2 million fruit and nut trees in Afghanistan and provide farmers there
with the skills and support necessary for sustainable land use.

Manufactured in China by Insight Editions
www.insighteditions.com

10 9 8

The Journey Home

AUTOBIOGRAPHY
of an AMERICAN SWAMI

RADHANATH SWAMI

MANDALA

San Rafael, California

To all my guides of various faiths, who extended their compassion and wisdom as I stumbled along on my journey home.

To my mother and father, who nourished me with selfless care and devotion. They never gave up on their wayward son.

To my guru, who transformed my life with his unconditional love.

To the many sincere souls, my brothers and sisters, who also seek the forgotten treasure of the heart.

tvayi me nanya-viṣaya
matir madhu-pate sakṛt
ratim udvahatad addha
gangevaugham udanvati

"My sweet Lord, as the river Ganges forever flows to the sea without hindrance, let my attraction be constantly drawn to you without being diverted to anything else."

Srimad Bhagavatam 1.8.42
—Spoken by Mother Kunti

TABLE OF CONTENTS

PROLOGUE

As I crawled out from the icy Himalayan water of the Bagmati River, I gazed at two heaps of ashes, one from a cremation pit and the other from a sacrificial fire. I was dressed in only a loincloth, and a cold wind chilled me to the bone. An intense longing gripped me. What was I doing here—shivering, alone, nearly starving, and so far from home? Was all my searching to be in vain? I stared up at stars that were shimmering through the branches of an ancient banyan tree. Birds of the night warbled a melancholy song. Sacred fires burned brightly along the riverbank, where holy men, their hair matted like ropes hanging down below their knees, threw offerings of pungent herbs into the flames. From the smoldering remains, they scooped out handfuls of ashes and smeared them over their flesh. Completing the ritual, they marched toward the sacred shrine that I yearned to enter.

It was the spring of 1971 in Pashupatinath, Nepal, where a flood of pilgrims had converged that night. Just out of my teens, I felt half a planet away from my home in suburban Chicago, and I ached for the solace of a holy place, a place where I might pray for direction. An hour earlier, I had approached an ancient temple, its towering gateway carved with mythical lions, serpents, gods, and goddesses. As I climbed the stone steps, thrilled with anticipation, a gatekeeper whipped his club into my chest. I sunk to my knees, gasping for breath. Flanked on both sides by police, the gatekeeper blocked my path and shouted, "You are foreigner! Get out!" Their chief, dressed in a turban and military attire, burst forward with burning eyes and smacked his rod across a sign that read: No Foreigners Allowed.

"Out from here!" he roared. "If you try again, you'll be severely beaten and thrown in prison. And I cannot say what the angry mobs will do." He ordered his charges to be vigilant. I had wandered to the bank of the river, crestfallen. My arduous quest for spiritual meaning had led me this far. I couldn't turn back.

Now, watching the holy men, an idea sprang into my mind. I kneeled down at one smoldering pit where a sacrificial fire had burned and sunk both my hands deep into the warm, powdery ashes, sifting out the lumps of glowing coals. Shuddering, I plastered the ashes across my skinny body from my matted hair to my calloused bare feet. The musty powder burned into my nostrils, choking my throat and parching my mouth. I wrapped two river-stained cotton sheets over my upper and lower body for robes and crept again toward the gate, my heart beating heavily in my chest.

The same sentinels stood guard with clubs in hand, but they did not recognize me and let me pass. As I entered a vast open courtyard surrounding the ancient altar I thought, *if I'm caught in here, I could be killed.* Several thousand people gathered in an unruly line and were waiting to see the altar. Only one person was allowed at a time. Patiently taking my place in the rear of the line, I inched forward. Suddenly, the same police chief who had stopped me earlier passed by. I gasped and turned my face away, my adrenaline surging. He stepped right in front of me, stared into my ash-covered face then barked a question in the local Hindi language. I didn't understand a word. If I spoke a single word of English here, I knew I would be finished. Receiving no reply, he stared at me and launched into a barrage of questions, this time much louder. My mind reeled with thoughts of years wasted in a filthy Nepali prison or worse. With a blank expression, I stood motionless, knowing he was trained to detect anything suspicious. Did he recognize me? I could only guess.

Another idea rose in my mind. Placing one palm over my mouth, I waved my other hand side to side. Those who vow never to speak, *mauni babas*, often expressed their vow in this way.

The chief gripped my arm and dragged me away. Where was he taking me? Was I under arrest? He yelled. Instantly, two police guards came running. Surrounded, I was yanked through the line of pilgrims until we reached the place of maximum congestion. Raising their clubs, my captors roared like thunder. Was this to be a public lashing? Would the mob tear me apart for defiling their sacred shrine? They shouted louder and louder as people scattered. I waited, terrified. The men dragged me through the bustling crowd until I found myself standing directly in front of the altar, a colorful pagoda with swirls of sandalwood incense pouring out. In front stood a massive stone bull. On the altar stood a stone figure of the deity Shiva, adorned with embroidered silks and glittering with gold and precious jewels. The chief lifted his stick and squeezed my arm. Would he pummel me right before the holy image?

Surrounded by his lieutenants, rod raised above his head, he shouted orders at a priest, who rushed back into the altar. I waited, trembling. From the inner sanctuary the high priest appeared dressed in robes of red silk. A striking red circle of powder marked his forehead and he wore a gold necklace and strand of dried *rudraksa* seeds around his neck. In a deep, hypnotic tone, he recited the mantra, *"Om Namah Shivaya."*

My captor, his stout body sweating profusely despite the chilly wind, yelled something to the priest that I again could not understand. The high priest listened intently. He nodded his head, closed his eyes and paused. Moments passed as the mass of pilgrims clamored impatiently. Then, straightening his posture, the high priest took a deep breath and began to recite incantations from ancient Sanskrit texts. He stunned me by wrapping a silk turban around my head. Then he draped a shawl over my shoulders, placed several jasmine and night queen garlands around my neck, anointed my forehead with sandalwood paste and offered me saffron-flavored water to drink. Standing in a daze, I realized that the police were holding the massive crowd back in order to grant me an exclusive opportunity to worship the Lord and be honored by the temple. Bowing low with humility, the police chief then begged with joined palms for my blessings and departed.

Did he not recognize me in my disguise or was he aware who I was and simply honoring my determination? This I will never know. Whatever the reason, I was deeply humbled. I had defied human law and deserved to be beaten, but God is merciful. Standing before the altar, my limbs covered with ashes, my drab ascetic robes, and tangled, matted hair awkwardly covered with silks and flowers, I squeezed my tearing eyes shut, joined my palms and prayed that I would be shown my true path as I continued my journey.

I returned to the riverbank and sat on the cold earth. It was a moonless night. Stars glittered in the dark sky, a breeze filled the forest with the scent of blooming jasmine, and the cooing of an owl emerged out of the silence. Gazing downstream, I wondered where the river of destiny would lead me next. How did I land into a life so foreign to my upbringing, but so familiar to my soul?

I

Journey to the East

MY BEST FRIEND DANNY AND I crept down the creaking stairway into his cool, damp cellar. Suddenly an intuition flashed through my mind—*I shouldn't be here.* My heart pounded. In the middle of the room, a barbell holding weights of two hundred and fifty pounds was propped on steel hooks. My classmate bragged, "My father lifts this every day." I was seven years old, small and skinny, with short black hair, brown eyes and a dark complexion. Touching the cold weights, I felt tiny.

Danny turned to me, "Richie, I'm going to show you a big secret." Putting his index finger across his lips, he whispered, "Promise you won't tell anyone?"

He climbed up a shelf, reached high into a rafter and came down with a brass key. Then, leading me to a wooden cabinet bigger than we were, he unlocked it and swung open the doors. He pointed to a stack of magazines.

"Go ahead." Danny smiled. "Look at one."

I did. It was filled with photos of naked women in amorous poses. My little body froze. Never before had I seen what was under a girl's clothing. It looked so strange and forbidden.

"Neat, huh?" Danny asked.

I nodded my head, unsure what to say. Flapping the magazine shut, I shoved it back into the cabinet.

"Wait till you see what's in the drawer." He pulled it open, exposing two pistols and several hand grenades. "My father always keeps the guns loaded and the grenades are real." He handed a grenade to me. "Here, hold it."

Holding the cold, heavy metal, I shivered. "This is pretty neat," I mumbled. Trying to hide my fear, I placed the weapon carefully back in the drawer.

"Richie, wait till you see this."

Danny pulled open two doors inside the cabinet, exposing a sort of altar. There, a framed photograph held a figure whose eyes stared ominously into mine. Horrified, I found myself face to face with Adolph Hitler. Two armbands embroidered with Nazi swastikas had been draped ceremoniously on either side of the photo and below hung a dagger with a shining swastika embossed in its handle. My heart sank. Hideous images flashed through my mind. I had often heard my elders speak about the recent slaughter of our relatives at the hands of the Nazis. My grandfather's family had never been heard from since 1941 when the Nazis occupied Lithuania, our ancestral home.

Danny whispered, "This is a secret, but my parents hate you."

A wave of heat rushed from my stomach to my throat. "Why? What did I do?"

"Because you're a Jew. They say you killed Jesus."

"What!" I stood paralyzed. What I was hearing just didn't make sense.

"My father says that even God hates you."

The heavy footsteps of his parents creaked through the ceiling above us. I didn't know if I should run, hide, or cry.

"Do *you* hate me, Danny?"

"No, you're my best friend. Because you're a Jew, I might hate you when I grow up. But I hope not."

My mind went blank.

Locking the cabinet, Danny led me upstairs to the kitchen table where his mother was waiting with two plates of vanilla cookies and two glasses of cold milk. She smiled tightly. A loud creak in the floor announced the entrance of Danny's father, a stocky man with a square jaw, graying crew cut, small piercing eyes, and a half smile that gave me chills. I felt utterly vulnerable in his presence.

Could the cookies be poisoned? I thought. But what could I do? I was afraid not to eat.

"Eat, Richie. What's wrong?" his mother challenged.

I struggled to hide my misery as I ate the cookies. With each bite I prayed to God to protect me.

Pale as a ghost, I walked home. At that age I had little power to reason. I was simply hurt, and badly.

My mother greeted me with a gentle smile. She was standing in the kitchen with an apron around her waist, rolling out dough across our circular dining table. "I'm making apple strudel for you, Richie. Your favorite."

"Mom," I asked, "does God hate me?"

"No, of course not. God loves you." Her eyebrows tensed as she placed her rolling pin on the table. "Why do you ask this question?"

I was afraid to tell her. "I don't know. I guess I'm just curious." To avoid further questions I ran upstairs to my bedroom.

I believed my mother. I believed that God loved me. Lying in my bed, staring at the ceiling, I struggled to come to grasp the contradiction of love and hate, both connected to the same God.

In the innocence of childhood, I secretly prayed in my thoughts or in a whisper. I'd mostly pray in bed, until I fell asleep. When I prayed, I felt a sense of shelter, and that someone was listening to me. I believed God heard me and was with me. Still, I had many questions about this divine being. *Who is this being called God?* I often wondered.

Is He like an enormous cloud or a shadow, nearly invisible? Or is he a friend who hears my every prayer, so real that I can almost touch Him with my thoughts?

My parents, Gerald and Idelle Slavin, were not particularly religious in a formal sense. Rather, they expressed their faith in God through their gratitude, generosity, kindness, and dedication to the family. They had grown up during the Depression, and ever since their childhoods had worked hard to support their families. While they wanted the best for their children, they were also careful not to spoil us, encouraging thankfulness for all we had and were given. In 1955, when I was four, they had moved us from Chicago to the village of Sherwood Forest in Highland Park, Illinois, so they could raise my two brothers and me in an environment free from the pollution and dangers of the big city. Our tranquil neighborhood was set on flat terrain with abundant grass and trees. Children played in the empty lots and the quiet streets lined with houses that were almost identical to each other.

"Our Little Richie is sweet, but so strange," my parents would often say. "Why is he like this?" I had odd habits. No one had any idea where they came from.

Until I was eight or nine years old, I refused to sit in chairs while eating and preferred to sit on the floor, which my parents forbade. As a compromise, I was allowed to stand at the dinner table, even in restaurants. It was a common occurrence for waitresses to ask if they could bring me a chair. "He doesn't believe in chairs," my mother would reply with a shrug of her shoulders.

While my parents took great care with their appearance, always dressing neatly and well, my mother had to wash my new clothes again and again until they looked old before I agreed to wear them. When they bought me new shoes, I scraped them with rocks till they looked worn. Whenever my parents had a new car, I squeezed onto the floor of the back seat until the car wasn't new anymore.

Having better things than others made me feel embarassed. I idolized the poor and downtrodden. Once, my father took the family to dinner at the local country club. I disrupted everything by suddenly rushing from the table and out the door because I couldn't bear to be served by the busboy who was a classmate of mine. When my Grandpa Bill found me sitting alone in our car, I explained my feelings. "It's all right, Little Richie," he said. "You did the right thing. I'm proud of you."

My father's father, William "Bill" Slavin, left a deep impression on my life. His loving nature reflected the deep-rooted belief he had in his religion. I was fascinated to observe the quiet, unassuming way he tried to harmonize his old-world traditions with life in America. Often, I'd catch him praying softly to himself at family mealtimes as the rest of us went about eating all around him.

When I reached the age to enter Hebrew School, my father could not afford to send me. Still, he strived to give me the best he could. When I turned thirteen, he approached Rabbi Lipis to ask for a simple Bar Mitzvah to bless me. The stately, silver-haired Rabbi readily tutored me in the basic prayers free of charge. One day I asked him, "Rabbi, could you explain to me the meaning of these prayers?"

Tears welled in his soft brown eyes and he embraced me with an affection I will never forget. In his old-world Yiddish accent, his voice cracked with emotion. He told me, "Little Richie, I'm satisfied with your sincerity to understand the meaning of this ceremony. It is becoming rare."

"Rabbi, how should I pray?"

A wide grin expanded across his square, slightly wrinkled face. I felt sheltered by his affection. Something, I believed, every child needed.

"In the Talmud," he said, "a book on Jewish law written by Rabbis thousands of years ago, it is taught that it is better to pray to God for the strength to overcome temptations, difficulties, and doubts in order to do His will, rather than to pray for Him to do our will."

On my thirteenth birthday, my older brother Marty gave me the debut record album of Peter Paul and Mary, the folk trio from Greenwich Village. Their songs protested war, prejudice, and social injustices, but it was their lyrics referring to God that most stirred my soul. Leaning back to listen, I would close my eyes, drawn like a magnet to every word. The album's opening song began, "Early in the morning, about the break of day—I ask the Lord to help me find my way." Again and again I listened, unaware that this simple prayer would guide the coming years of my life.

In my quest for meaning, folk musicians like Pete Seeger and Bob Dylan spurred the rebellion erupting within me. But if folk music left me spellbound with meaningful lyrics, the blues struck my heart with raw emotion. The blues is all about feeling and yearning, pouring the grief of your heart into every note played or word sung, discovering relief and joy in that expression. Listening to a blues singer cry for a lost love, I would cry along for my lost love, though I didn't know yet who this was.

While I was introspective, shy, and often worried about the feelings of others, my older brother Marty had a sixth sense for how to rile people. Wild like a monkey, he was called Monk for short. In 1965, when I was fourteen, I entered Deerfield High School, where Monk had just graduated. Seeing me, some teachers gasped, "Oh no, another Monk." From my first day of school I was labeled Little Monk. The name stuck, although the irony of it escaped me until many years later.

As a freshman, I was promoted to the varsity wrestling team. I cannot say that I was highly skilled, but when I applied my mind to something it was with intense absorption. The coach and teammates had great hope that in the coming years I could be a champion. At first I loved the challenge. Scholarships were mine if I pursued them. But something strange was happening to me. I had begun to crave a purpose in life beyond wealth, prestige, and the fads of society. How could I be content in the idyllic land of Highland Park when I knew that African Americans were imprisoned like slaves in the ghettos just miles away? How could I be satisfied with a wrestling medal when my older friends were being forced into the horrors of the Vietnam War? Haunted by such questions, I, along with my friends, questioned the very fabric of the life we knew.

On a hunt for purpose, I burned with a passion for the civil rights movement of Martin Luther King Jr., poring over the words of Malcolm X, and books on social reform. Along with my best friends Bassoon and Gary, whom I'd known since we were ten, I got a job at a carwash after school and worked there full time in the summer. It was hard work, but I loved it. Here we found ourselves working to the backdrop of soul music among older African American men from the ghettos of the South Side of Chicago, a world away from the security of Highland Park. In the company of these men, who were beaten down by poverty, racial discrimination, and alcoholism, hearing the raw cry of a blues or soul singer stirred my heart. I was fifteen years old and deeply troubled by unanswered questions.

Then, when a close friend, only sixteen, died after his car skidded on the winter ice and plummeted into the frigid waters of Lake Michigan, I found myself wondering, "Who am I and where am I going?" It seemed that the whole world was skidding on the ice of uncertainty.

In search of a sanctuary, I moved down to our basement and covered the walls with psychedelic posters that glowed under a black light. Fishing nets hung from the ceiling. Jasmine incense smoke hovered like a cloud. Sometimes I would switch on the flashing beam of a strobe light to heighten the dreamlike effect. In the privacy of my basement, I listened to the revolutionary music of the sixties. "A Day in the Life" by the Beatles churned my longing to seek a meaningful life beyond the superficial. When I laid back, closed my eyes, and listened to George Harrison sing, "Within You, Without You," I cried with the strings of his sitar for inner peace. Over and over again I played Ray Charles's soulful rendition of "Old Man River" as I sat motionless and grieved for the plight of the downtrodden. When I listened to B.B. King, the mournful notes bursting from his guitar pierced my heart, and I wondered why sad songs made me feel so good. One late night, in the turmoil of questioning everything around me, I heard Johnny Rivers through my stereo headphones singing, "Look to Your Soul for the Answer." I took a deep breath, looked up and exclaimed, "Yes, that's it!"

Incited by the times, my closest friends and I threw ourselves into the spirit of the counterculture of the 1960s. As the minority in a school where conservatives, jocks, and cheerleaders predominated, we began to wear our hair long, to experiment with marijuana and LSD, and to generally rebel against the values of our parents' generation.

But I was torn. I hated to disappoint anyone. I agonized over quitting the wrestling team and didn't have the heart to let my coach and teammates down. The school expected me to help lead the team to championships. The coach once declared to the team, "When Little Monk's determined to win, he's like a hungry tiger pacing the mat. He's champion material. But he seems to be getting distracted."

Confused, I prayed for a way out.

Soon after, in a prestigious tournament, I pulled my opponent down in the first five seconds of the match. The crowd roared, cheering me on, but I knelt as if paralyzed. My shoulder had been yanked out of its socket and the bone ripped through the muscles of my chest. Pain stabbed through my body. At that moment, with the dislocation of my shoulder, my life was dislocated from a passion that had already died. Trembling in agony as hundreds in the gymnasium looked on in shock, I silently thanked God. I was free.

What I didn't have the courage to give up myself had been cast aside, I felt, by the power of destiny.

Gary Liss, whose friendship would become a miracle in my life, was friendly, outgoing, and ever restless for the next adventure. Gary was a rebel who truly found himself when he found the counterculture. He and I had traveled to California together during the summer break of my junior year in high school. On the Sunset Strip and on Haight-Ashbury we reveled in the freedom we found. In these havens for flower children, we met many beautiful people, idealists like ourselves. As for the more outrageous characters we encountered there, people who seemed to value being destructive, rude, or just hedonistic—we steered clear.

In 1969, I attended Miami Dade College in Florida along with my close friends from high school, Bassoon, Steve, and Gary. I, like so many of my generation, was young, wild, and hungry for adventure, but it was at this time that I first noticed something taking precedent over everything else—a desire for spirituality that burned in my heart. It grew daily. Someone gave me a book entitled *The World's Great Religions*. I drank in every word and wanted to devour more and more. In further readings of other books I discovered an ancient Indian technique that taught silent meditation on the sacred syllable *Om*. Through my inner voyages, I uncovered a subtle reality so rich that I longed to go deeper.

One morning I saw a poster on my college campus advertising a lecture on transcendental meditation. Mike, a bearded, long-haired American, spoke on the science of consciousness as taught by Maharishi Mahesh Yogi. I was enthralled. Mike invited me to Hollywood, Florida, where, with no commitment, I could receive a personal meditation mantra. Once there, I placed a flower, handkerchief, and thirty-five dollars on an altar where a one-syllable mantra was whispered into my ear. Daily meditation became the most important part of my life.

The seed of my spiritual inclination was sprouting rapidly. But along with that seed grew a weed—my aversion toward bigotry and fanaticism. In those days, by growing my hair long in protest of the norms of the establishment, I became a target for those who hated hippies, including the police who used to pull me over, search me, and harass me on a regular basis. The truth was, I felt a sort of sad fulfillment when people hated me for my long hair, minority religion, or for what I believed. I felt it an honor to be persecuted for a noble ideal rather than "sell out" to popular opinions or fashions. At the same time, I was also beginning to understand that to hate those who hated me was to share the same disease. I longed to break through these sectarian barriers and discover the inner essence of all religions, the oneness of God.

While in college I studied psychology and humanities, but my meditation and music remained priorities. Near the college, in the town of Opa Locka, was a house called "The Ash Tray," where the dedicated musician James Harmon lived. Known to us as Jimmy the Bear, he was a stout, long-haired, bearded man, and the lead singer and harmonica player for the Burning Waters Blues Band.

The Bear loved me like a little brother. One day, with a proud smile, he slapped one of his harmonicas into my hand. "Brother, I'm going teach you to play the harp."

"But I don't know music," I responded shyly.

"That don't matter, man. Your heart's got deep feeling, and that's what the blues are all about." From that day on, my harmonica became my inseparable partner in life.

During this time I was befriended by some African American students, and through one of them, developed a special friendship with an older woman who had been a close associate of Dr. Martin Luther King Jr. A gentle but strong-willed woman, she too had dedicated her life to being a civil rights leader. As she was in her late forties and I only eighteen, I called her "mother" and she called me "son." We shared soul-searching discussions about Dr. King's vision and his sad assassination. A devout Baptist, she was kind and gracious, yet fearlessly determined. At one point she organized a civil rights march through a neighborhood of Miami and invited me to participate. Her face lit up with surprise when I actually showed up—a white boy in a black march in the Deep South. Proudly, she took me by the hand to walk beside her up front.

Onlookers were appalled to see me there. White racists threatened and jeered as we passed. Some threw stones or bottles as the police looked the other way. Mother smiled as over three hundred marchers sang Sam Cooke's anthem, "A Change Is Gonna Come," and "We Shall Overcome." The march culminated in a rally in the park. Here the marchers sat on folding chairs. I sat beside my friend until she stepped up to the microphone under a coconut tree. Denouncing the injustices inflicted on her people, she urged the audience toward "an uprising devoid of violence."

Her voice thundered with conviction. "Violence will degrade us to the evil ways of our persecutors. We must be fearless and stand together and demand our rights, not with weapons and fire, but with integrity and faith in the Almighty God. We must boycott wherever we smell the stench of bigotry. In the face of our oppressors we must never cower from the truth." Tears filled her eyes and her voice soared as she echoed her mentor. "This is America, the land of the free. We'll never give up until the chains of slavery are broken forever and we can shout into the heavens—*Free at last, free at last*. Reverend King had a dream. He died for his dream. We will live for his dream. Amen."

Cheers filled the park. Taking her seat, she whispered in my ear. "Did you like it, son?"

I nodded with conviction.

Next rose a speaker who screamed out for a revolution. "All hope for a nonviolent solution terminated when Reverend King was shot dead!" he said, his voice full of indignation and rage. "Brothers and sisters, rise from your slumber. We must fight fire with fire. The freedom of this nation was won by war, not peace. We must vow to exterminate our white oppressors and burn their cities." Half the crowd howled in support while others sighed in shame. Soaked with sweat, the man shook his fist in frenzy. "They plot to keep us forever in the back of their buses and prisoners of the ghettos." Hatred ignited in his eyes as he thrust his finger toward me, screaming. "Look here, brothers and sisters, see this insidious white man. Today, in *our* march, he shamelessly walks in front, leaving us black folk in the back." His supporters roared in fury.

The man went on to identify me as the symbol of everything they despised. He thundered on, inciting vengeance and retribution. My friend leaped up to defend me but her protest was muted by the man's fury as he now controlled the microphone and a majority of the crowd. Gripping my hand tenderly, she shook her head in dismay. "Son, I'm terribly sorry. I brought you to the front of the march and God knows that. You trusted me and now you're in jeopardy." She squeezed my hand and sighed. "You better leave now. And may God be with you."

I crept from tree to tree away from the rally. My friend watched carefully, ready to rise and defend me if required. I was struck by the way so many people, even as they are yearning for equality and justice, focused on difference to the point of violence. Still, with a deep breath of relief as I left the park, I realized that my admiration for Dr. King and his followers had been heightened by the day's experience. I felt that, faithful to their ideal, they fought oppression relentlessly from without and within. As I walked alone under the Florida sun, I recalled a passage that shed light on the experience: *If a person does not have an ideal he's ready to die for, he has nothing really meaningful to live for.* Then it came to me. Martin Luther King Jr. had a dream he lived and died for and that dream changed the world. Wasn't that power in all of us, if we pursued our calling?

I completed one year at Miami Dade. Summer break came and I found myself standing alone on the edge of a highway in rural Pennsylvania, my thumb stretched upward, my wavy black hair draped down my back. It was a humid day and I was headed to New York City to visit a friend. Just nineteen years old, only 5'6" and hardly 120 pounds, I felt frail and vulnerable whenever I hitchhiked. Three hours passed before a rusty '59 Plymouth slammed on its brakes and halted. I ran to the car and expressed my gratitude. "Thank you. Thank you very much, sir."

A single middle finger thrust out from the window and the sweating motorist inside scowled. "Get a job, you useless parasite." He shoved his stocky arm out of the window, grabbed a lank of my long hair and jerked my face close to his. The stench of beer and tobacco blasted me. Spitting on the ground, he cursed, "Punk, if I had my shotgun, I'd shoot you dead." He swerved away, tires squealing.

I coughed up the black smoke I'd inhaled from his exhaust pipes. Resentment swelled in my chest but I wrestled to curb it. I was seeking a spiritual life. On roadsides, I sometimes felt like an open target for anyone suffering from anger or negativity, but I hoped all these difficulties might help me to grow. I knew I needed to learn the value of patience, perseverance, and prayer to overcome obstacles.

In the summer of 1970, wearing one's hair long was not just a fashion, it was a statement of discontent—an aggressive challenge to mainstream values driven by money, power, and prejudice. It was a signal of what I believed. My friends and I were living out our beliefs. Protesting the war, we'd been tear-gassed the year before at the Democratic National Convention in Chicago, and conservative police often harassed us in our college town. All this, simply because we yearned for a meaningful life with ideals we could live and die for. Although in my heart I bore malice toward no one, my appearance invited hateful reactions.

Finally, after hours waiting for a ride, a friendly young man picked me up and brought me to his home near Gettysburg. There I sat alone in a forest on the bank of a creek. The song of the babbling stream soothed my heart. The flowing waters swirled around both wood and stone. The creek seemed to know a secret that could unfold the mysteries of life. *If only, like the running stream, I just follow my calling*, I thought, *nature may whisper her secrets and guide me to my destiny.*

Days later, after I had arrived in New York, my friend Hackett took me to the Randall's Island Rock Festival. An array of bands, from

Jimi Hendrix to Mountain, took the stage and played with abandon. I wandered away for a break and was approached by a young American with a shaved head. He wore white robes and I took him to be a strange sort of monk. With no explanation, he handed me a pamphlet and asked for a donation. I told him I had no money, and as we were talking another man approached, a pusher wanting to sell me hashish. When I repeated that I couldn't pay for anything, the two of them got into a debate together and wandered off. The monk forgot to take his pamphlet and, without giving it a second glance, I slipped it into my little bag.

The next day, at Hackett's home in Brooklyn, I got a telephone call from Gary asking me to come to Cherry Hill, New Jersey, to our friend Frank's house. When I got there, I found Gary and Frank kneeling over a map stretched out on the living room carpet. "We're going to Europe in a few days," Gary told me. "You've got to come."

I was completely broke and had plans to go back to Chicago as I had a job for the summer. But Frank assured me he had enough money for the three of us. "All right," I said, "I'll go."

All that remained was to explain my plans to my parents in Highland Park. No one in my family had ever ventured outside America. How would my protective mother and father react? I traveled back to my childhood home to find out.

Sitting at our round, glass-topped dining table, I stared down at the homemade dinner my mother had prepared. She would personally cook a feast for us every evening. Neatly arranged on my plate was succulent lasagna, crispy Italian bread lavished with a buttery garlic sauce, and buttered artichoke hearts. The aroma of sautéed herbs and spices wafted across the room. "I've decided to go on a trip to Europe with Gary," I announced. Blank faces stared back at me across the table as I nervously shook extra salt and pepper over my food. "It will be an education, don't you think?" No reply. I looked around the kitchen at the flowered wallpaper, and at the Hotpoint stove and refrigerator, both pink, my mother's favorite color. "We'll learn so many lessons. Don't worry. I'll be back in September for college. We're leaving in three days."

Silence. Mother looked as if she were receiving news of the death of a loved one. "Richie," she sobbed suddenly, "Why do you have to do this? How will you eat? Where will you sleep?" She anxiously shook her head and pleaded in a tender voice. "You're just a boy. Who will protect you?"

My father sighed. "My son, are you crazy? The world is a dangerous place. You're young and inexperienced. Anything could happen to you." Exhaling deeply, he added, "I'd forbid you if I thought you'd listen, but you won't." He stared, silently pleading for me to change my resolve, but I ignored him. His voice choked with emotion, he told me, "I'll worry day and night until the day you return."

My little brother Larry exclaimed, "Cool. I wish I could go." But seeing the torment of our parents, he grew sober. "Richie, please write sometimes."

Upper Left: The author's parents Idelle and Jerry Slavin
Upper right: Little Richie later known as Radhanath Swami, age eight
Below: In 1970 at age nineteen, author set out on a journey of self-discovery

Above: Catacombs in Rome where monks meditated
Bottom: A street band in Greece where the author played harmonica with lifelong friend Gary (far right)
Opposite Page: A mysterious and prophetic poster that the author discovered in New Delhi

Upper Left: Author in 1970 while living as a recluse in the Himalayas
Upper Right: Pashupatinath—a sacred shrine in Nepal
Below: A rock in the Ganges River that served as the author's seat for a month of solitary meditation

SAINTS AND YOGIS WHO INSPIRED THE AUTHOR ON HIS JOURNEY:
Upper left: Swami Rama—founder of the Himalayan Institute of Yoga
Upper right: Swami Satchidananda—founder of the Integral Yoga Institute
Lower left: J. Krishnamurti—renowned author and philosopher
Lower right: Swami Chidananda Saraswati—successor of Swami Sivananda of the Divine Life Mission

Upper left: Maharishi Mahesh Yogi—founder of Transcendental Meditation Programs
Upper right: Anandamayee Ma—renowned mystic and guru
Below: Tat Walla Baba—a cave dwelling Himalayan Yogi

Upper left: Mother Theresa of Calcutta and the author
Upper right: Swami Muktananda—founder of the Siddha Yoga Path
Lower left: S.N. Goenkaji—master of Buddhist Vipassana Meditation
Lower right: The Dalai Lama of Tibet and the author

Above: Dev Prayag, where the author met Kailash Baba who taught him how to live as a hermit in the jungle
Below: One of the Himalayan caves where the author dwelled

2

ON THE DAY OF MY DEPARTURE, I squeezed down the aisle of an airplane trying not to knock anyone in the head with my duffle bag. "Excuse me, ma'am," I said to a middle-aged American woman seated on the aisle. "Can I get to my window seat?"

She jerked her head up and frowned and I could hear her thinking: "Find another seat." I certainly preferred to do so, but the plane was full and the passengers in the aisle behind me were impatient. I carefully squeezed passed her to reach my assigned place. From beneath her bouffant she glowered at my long hair. I chose to keep my attention out the window.

Minutes later, I peeked from the corner of my eye only to be jolted by her unrelenting stare. A delay was announced; it was going to be a long flight.

Time passed, and again I peeked sideways, but this time, instead of the lady with the bouffant hairdo I saw a fascinating figure in black jeans, black boots, and a black sleeveless t-shirt. Silver bracelets circled his fair, thin arms. His long, straight hair was white as snow, as was his skin. His eyes were an albino pink, but his mischievous smile filled me with joy. This man looked so uncommon, yet familiar. I had seen him before. Yes, he was a legendary rock and roll star, one of my favorites, Johnny Winter.

"What's happening, brother? I'm Johnny."

"They call me Little Monk."

He greeted me with a soul brothers handshake.

"How did you to get this seat?" I asked him. "Someone else was here a minute ago."

Johnny chuckled and, in his trademark Texan drawl, replied, "Man, was that woman sitting next to you uptight. She came storming down the aisle and brewed up a big old hassle, demanding another seat. She don't like our kind, Little Monk. But, you know, that's all right, the stewardess swapped my seat to keep us brothers together."

We had plenty of time to talk. I shared with him my spiritual longing, and he shared with me candid stories of his life. I told him that I had recently seen a great show of his in Florida with Janis Joplin.

His slender body rocked with laughter, "Never was there a wilder, crazier woman on either side of the Mississippi River." He said Janis was confused, lusty, and stoned out, but a good kid. She was, he said, like a sister to him, but he worried for her. "Little Janis is burning her candle from both ends. I don't know how long she'll last." Waxing serious, his pinkish eyes gazed into mine, "You know Little Monk, money and fame can destroy people. Say a little prayer for her."

As the engine roared we zoomed down the runway and soared into the sky. Our hearts seemed to fly as we talked of the great blues legends from Chicago and the Mississippi Delta. Johnny was supercharged on this topic. "Soul brother, we can go on rapping forever. I ain't going to sweat if this old plane never lands." Suddenly he noticed the harmonica attached to my belt and shouted, "You play the harp. Let's jam, man." In an instant, he had his harmonica in hand. "Pick a song."

"Do you know 'Mother-In-Law Blues' by Little Junior Parker?" I asked.

"Right on man, Right on." His thumb shot up.

Thirty thousand feet in the sky and to my great amazement, the famous Johnny Winter began to perform with me as his partner. Older people stared in condemnation, while younger passengers smiled gleefully. The young airline hostesses, too, swayed in the aisle to a free concert. Absorbed in the blues, Johnny and I were oblivious.

The plane landed at JFK in New York, and Johnny and I strolled into the terminal. At the gate a beautiful Danish model was waiting for Johnny. Onlookers marveled. Thrilled to see me with Johnny Winter, Frank and Gary were impressed with my good luck. Gary stroked his wavy beard and beamed. "Hey, Monk," he joked, pointing at Johnny's girl, "don't you wish she was waiting for you instead of us?"

"Tonight," I replied, shaking their hands, "we'll begin our spiritual quest. I think I'll be less distracted with you guys."

We arrived in Europe. On our first night in Luxembourg we slept in a campground. Crammed into a single tent, the three of us lay in our sleeping bags full of anticipation for what the next day would bring. Finally, roosters crowed the arrival of dawn. Jumping out of the tent into the crisp morning air, Gary and I stretched, savoring our good fortune and breathing in the fragrance of evergreens and flowering trees.

Suddenly, a shriek rang out. "No! God damn it. No!" Frank emerged from the tent, pale and tormented. "I've been robbed. All my money's gone." Gary and I scrambled into the tent, searching everywhere. Frank had already given up. "I've searched. There's no use."

Gary placed his palm on Frank's shoulder and whispered, "It's all right, brother. We'll take care of you."

"Whatever we have is yours, Frank." I consoled him. "We don't need money. We have each other."

Frank cast his head down, shook it back and forth and announced that there was no way we could make it with what we had left. He was going home—immediately. "You guys coming?"

I had less than twenty dollars of my own. Still, Gary's eyes met mine, and I silently transmitted my resolve to stay. He agreed and we bid Frank, who spent only one night in Europe, a sad goodbye. As Frank slung his backpack over his shoulder and paced away back to the security of home, Gary and I pondered the mysteries that awaited us.

Later that day, I found a creek to sit beside. The high trees danced in the wind and the water flowed effortlessly. With Frank gone, I had almost nothing. But strangely, I felt free.

Quick enough, Gary and I were invited to breakfast with some hippies from Holland. After sharing their Muesli with us, Kosmos and Chooch offered us a ride to the Netherlands. Soon we were cruising through the countryside of Belgium and Holland in their Volkswagen van, gazing out our open windows at vast fields carpeted with hundreds of thousands of red, yellow, white, pink, and violet tulips, all in perfect rows blooming in the sunshine, as the cassette player boomed out Donovan, the Beatles, and the Rolling Stones.

After a stop at Abcoude, the idyllic home of one of our new friends, we arrived in Amsterdam, where we were led to an abandoned warehouse where dozens of hippies sprawled on the floor freely smoking marijuana. The lights were dim. Rats scampered here and there. A shaggy band played on an improvised stage of rotting plywood stretched across milk crates.

With hashish pipe in hand and a wild grin, Chooch blurted, "I'll see you guys, maybe on my pilgrimage to Haight-Ashbury, the Mecca for hippies." Then he waved goodbye and disappeared into the smoke.

In the days that followed, Gary and I learned to survive with practically no money at all. Early in the morning we'd spend a few cents on a loaf of bread, hot out of the baker's oven. Under a tree, we cut the loaf in half and relished it as our subsistence for the day. This shared loaf of dry bread was to become our daily diet wherever we traveled. On special occasions, we managed to procure a hunk of cheese too. We usually slept either as guests in the homes of people we met, under trees, inside abandoned buildings or in public crash pads. What little money we had, we tried to stretch for as long as possible.

The European counterculture flocked to Amsterdam. Dam Square was the social center. Hundreds of seekers congregated in venues like Fantasio, Paradisio, and Melkweg to hang out and hear music. Another popular place was Cosmos, a "spiritual nightclub." It was there one night that I met a tall American with a partly shaved head, ponytail, and white robes. "Do you want some spiritual food?" he inquired. I nodded meekly. "Cup your hands." When I did, he dumped a huge ladle of fruit salad mixed with runny yoghurt into them. As the concoction dripped down my arms, I stood there perplexed.

"What do I do now?" I asked.

"Eat it!" He laughed, taking his leave. Little did I know that destiny would have us meet again, thousands of miles away in a setting beyond my wildest imagination.

Gary and I were making friends from the world over. But pleasant as it was, I was distracted. Something I could not comprehend was calling me. I found myself retreating to museums to contemplate religious art or to Vondel Park to meditate and study spiritual books. But my favorite place was sitting over a canal. While the city might rage with a passion for power, wealth, and a multitude of pleasures, and while fashions and fads changed like the seasons, the cool water of the canals seemed at total peace as it flowed through it all. I would sit for hours watching the water, wondering where the current of my life was leading me.

We continued our expedition. Using a little bit of the money we had saved for boat fares, we hitchhiked to the Hook of Holland and took a huge ferry across the English Channel to the United Kingdom. Gray clouds discharged a misty drizzle. The ship surrendered to the movement of the waves below, slowly moving up and down. As we lunged forward, cutting into the choppy sea, I mused on where I was heading. At nineteen, I ought to be preparing for a career, but I had no inclination to do so. Where was I going? Why couldn't I focus seriously on anything besides the ideals that filled my head? I had a vague concept of spirituality but no hint of my future. I spotted a row of life preservers fastened to the side of the ferry and prayed to be thrown such a life preserver to rescue me from a sea of uncertainties. If a person does not have an ideal he's ready to die for, I recalled, he has nothing meaningful to live for. I left my homeland in search of that ideal but I was like a leaf careening in the wind not knowing where I was going.

Suddenly, the stunning White Cliffs of Dover appeared from behind a cloud of fog. The ferry soon docked at the coast and we were funneled through British immigration. The officials stared at us with suspicion. Gary was about 5'8" and lean, his flowing brown hair, beard, and striking face evoking the frequent comment that he resembled Jesus Christ. He wore blue jeans, a green T-shirt, and canvas shoes. A raggedy old U.S. Army surplus backpack and sleeping bag were strapped to his shoulders. As for me, despite my long hair, my childish face could not for the life of it grow a mustache or beard. I wore gray pinstriped jeans, a gray turtleneck, and a black vest. For those who knew me, this simple black vest had become my trademark; I wore it every day for well over a year. A faded brown duffle bag and sleeping bag were slung over my shoulder, and moccasins covered my feet.

Standing in line, we were the targets of unsavory stares and comments by government officials. When we reached the desk, we meekly held out our U.S. passports only to be pulled into a room. Minutes later, two customs officials and a bobby entered, staring us down. The leader wore a gray suit and brown tie. He commanded, "Search them for drugs." Dumping the contents of my bag on the table, the officer found nothing but one green T-shirt, a pair of underpants, a toothbrush, hairbrush, a bar of soap, the Bible, and the little pamphlet from Randall's Island.

The man grimaced. "That's all you have?"

Timidly I responded, "That's it, sir, besides this." I held out my harmonica.

Gary, too, was searched. Then came the loaded question. "How much money are you carrying?" When we showed them our meager funds, their disgust turned to wrath. The leader's face reddened. "We don't need animals like you in our country," he spewed. "We'll cut off all your bloody hair and throw you in jail." Turning to a bobby, he ordered, "Get the scissors and cut their hair to the scalp." They then stripped us of all clothes and scrutinized every inch of our belongings. Next they launched into a long interrogation that seared our minds. Finally, with the words, "You're in big trouble," they stormed out of the room.

Anxiety-stricken, Gary and I could not speak a word. We passed an hour in isolation, anxiously awaiting word of our fates. Eventually, two bobbies flung open the doors, grabbed us by the arms, and drove us down a corridor. When we reached customs, they shoved us through the gate. With the words, "One wrong move and you're in jail!" they stamped our passports and we were free.

Still shaken, we found ourselves on the roadside, grateful for the beauty of the English countryside, our thumbs out. A car stopped and we jumped in. A young girl and her boyfriend smiled while their Scottish terrier leaped on our legs. "Where are you going?" the girl asked.

"We're not sure," Gary answered.

The boy swigged from a bottle of beer and said, "We're traveling ahead to a rock festival at the Isle of Wight. It will be a jolly good time. Why not join us, mates?"

Gary and I smiled in agreement and we were off, the barking terrier licking at our faces. We crossed by ferry to the island and were soon cast into the swarming multitude of the counterculture. The enormous gathering was set amid green hills and valleys. At the fences, angry police with attack dogs battled against ticketless pilgrims as the bands played on. Three days and nights of sensational performances were in full swing. Marijuana smoke filled the air and people were dropping acid left and right. Men and women slid together down the hillsides in the mud and more half-naked bodies writhed in time to the music.

One night, while rains poured out of the sky, Gary and I were not far from the stage when Jimi Hendrix came on to perform. He wore an orange velvet suit with flowing sleeves, but seemed otherwise quite subdued. Gone was the guitar-burning showman I'd seen before. Tonight he was very much the serious musician.

He played his warped, woofing version of the Star Spangled Banner. Here was one of the icons of my generation, a prophet of the counterculture, delivering a message of freedom to express oneself without taboos—of rebellion against the establishment. To my mind, the message was to follow my heart regardless of popular opinion.

The music was thunderous and seemed to shake the hills, stir the sea, and scatter the clouds. But the silent call within me, one I couldn't yet name, seemed louder still.

After the concert, Gary and I were picked up by a van packed with rowdy travelers headed toward London. Seeking refuge, I looked through my bag and picked out the pamphlet the strange monk on Randall's Island had given me. On the back cover was a photograph of a man sitting under a tree. His large, almond-shaped eyes appeared to be glistening with ecstasy. Although he was very old, his expression shone with the innocence of a child. He was dressed in a turtleneck and his smile radiated peace. I did not know who he was or even where he was from but I was struck. *If anyone in this creation has spiritual bliss,* I thought, *it's this person.*

Sometime later, we were staying in a small apartment in a suburb of London with some brothers we'd met at the Isle of Wight. One of the brothers was reading the newspaper. His face turned pale as he looked up and groaned aloud. "What is it?" we asked him.

"I've got bloody bad news for you, mates. Jimi Hendrix is dead."

"No! What happened?" I asked

Our host placed the newspaper down as if in slow motion. "The London paper says that last night he overdosed on sleeping pills and choked on his vomit."

Gary dropped his head into his hands. I felt as if the wind had been knocked out of me.

What should I learn from this? I asked myself. Hendrix had everything the world craves and at such a young age: wealth, fame, and amazing talent. But he was dissatisfied. This idol for our generation became a victim of his own excesses. Thousands were proclaiming "sex, drugs, and rock and roll" as the progressive way to live. Freedom was their highest value, but were they really free? I thought of all the wonderful people I'd met who were part of the counterculture, but also of those who seemed merely wild and ungrateful. I thought of how gratitude had been the most important value my mother and father had taught my brothers and me. Did I really want to be a part of all this? I certainly didn't fit in with my parents' generation. Where would I fit in? Please, God, show me. With these thoughts, I offered a prayer for Jimi.

I was already beginning to feel disillusioned with the movement that I had rejected social and family norms to join. I'd once had a dream that the counterculture would create an enlightened world, but now I felt that the more destructive elements of the movement, such as "rebellion for rebellion's sake" and "for the sake of personal pleasure", had won out. With the useless, tragic death of Jimi Hendrix my dream had all but died. Still, like a man on the verge of death may struggle for one last chance to survive, I was about to dive into the excesses of my generation like never before.

In London, Gary and I explored Piccadilly Circus among acidheads, potheads, and seekers of peace, all dressed in flamboyant attire. Hippies rapped, drug pushers and prostitutes solicited, bobbies scrutinized, skinheads growled, and tourists snapped photos of the bizarre scene.

On Lambeth Road, across the river from the British Parliament, we met a Catholic priest who sympathized with young travelers. Each night at nine, he opened the stone basement of his church for young people to sleep on the floor for free. We had to leave at nine in the morning, and nothing was provided but the cold, hard floor. Still, it was a place to crash and travelers brought their own sleeping bags. Finding a spot on the floor every night, I maneuvered through this room, packed with unwashed bodies, the air thick with the smell of hashish. When the lights were put out, it got very dark. Soon I would begin to hear the sounds of couples having sex, moaning and rolling around. Sometimes, I caught sight of people lighting little candles in the far corners of the room, strapping off their arms, and shooting heroin in the candlelight.

Affected by this atmosphere, I smoked more hashish and marijuana than ever before and, on the surface, began to fit in more with the crowd. But while those around me socialized, I retreated within myself. I often found myself wondering why I was bothering to indulge at all. Often, after Gary had gone in to find his sleeping place, I would sit, sometimes for hours, on the bank of the river Thames. The massive sheet of flowing water had a hypnotic effect on my mind and I would question the life I was leading. I looked up at the relentless hands of Big Ben and wondered if I was just wasting my time.

Another part of me felt a dire need to prove to myself, once and for all, that I could break out of my shyness and just enjoy life like never before. For one thing, here I was, nineteen, and I had never had a girlfriend. In my shyness, I had always been more comfortable listening to music in my room or hanging out with friends than I was on dates. Many propositions had come to me but I shied away, fearing I might lose my freedom or even worse, break a nice girl's heart. But all around me now, other guys were bragging about their sexual conquests. I was sick of being different. I met some girls trying to "make the scene" and flirted more seriously than ever. Still, my efforts felt empty.

A force within me was dragging me away from it all. Battling against that inner force, I was determined to be victorious, to experience firsthand the unrestricted pleasures glorified by society. Was it the Lord in my heart I was fighting? *Yes*, I silently boasted, *and I'm winning the battle*. But late at night, when I came back to the river, gazing down into the current, I felt ashamed. I was winning but I felt lost.

One evening, I closed my eyes and sat in silent meditation among a sea of pigeons at Trafalgar Square. Circled by shouting children, chattering tourists, and the honking evening traffic, I felt I was connected to a universe within myself far more substantial than anything around me. Taking a deep breath, I smiled. My conception of my body seemed to evaporate and I felt my mind merging into an ocean of peace. By comparison, my attempts at gaining sensual pleasure or overcoming my natural introspection seemed irrelevant. Opening my eyes, I visualized downtown London transfiguring into a beautiful family made up of marble lions, Lord Nelson on his column, and all the pigeons, tourists, businessmen, shoppers, and beggars. I strolled across the street and was given a cup of barley soup and a bread slice from a church charity, which I relished along with the homeless. Then, with sincere reverence, I entered the church, St. Martin's of the Fields, where I sat on a wooden pew and absorbed myself in reading the Holy Bible. There, a particular passage struck my heart. Lord Jesus instructed his followers, "Come out from among men and be separate." I pondered this.

Why should I waste my life trying to fit in with the social fashions of my peers? Why not try to live on my own terms? And hopefully, someday, on God's terms?

Traveling by ferry across the English Channel, Gary and I disembarked in Calais, France. It was a sunny day with birds warbling in delicately formed trees. Fine grasses in lush pastures yielded to the gentle wind. We relished our freedom. Now we could go wherever we pleased.

"Hey, Monk, where to next? Your wish is my command." Gary's green eyes glistened with adventure as we stood on the side of a country road in western France. "The world is at your beck and call." From the back pocket of his jeans he pulled a tattered map of Western Europe and pointed to various places. "Morocco, Spain, Paris, Rome, Switzerland, Germany. Where?"

"Where would you like to go, Gary?"

"Everywhere! But in which order? That's the question."

Thinking for a moment, I remembered the streams I so often studied, and stretched my arms toward the sky. "We should surrender our destiny to the will of God."

Gary laughed, threw down his backpack and sat on it. Mimicking my gesture, he responded, "What does that mean?"

"What would you like it to mean?"

Gary mockingly joined his palms in prayer. "You spend your days studying scriptures and meditating while I'm hanging out." Again stretching his arms to the sky, he said, "You decide how we should surrender our destiny to the will of God."

Plucking a yellow wildflower from the ground, I declared, "Like this."

"You want us to sit here forever like that flower?"

"Look, Gary. From a small seed buried in the dirt, this flower has grown into what it is—a beautiful blossom, basking in the sunshine. How? By surrendering her destiny to the will of God."

"You win, brother, but how does your fancy poetry translate into a hitchhiker's language?"

I smelled the flower and had an idea. "Whenever a car stops for us, what are the first words they always ask? You play the role of the driver and I'll be us."

Gary shrugged his shoulders. "Hello, where are you going?"

"Where are *you* going?"

"To Casablanca," he said, pretending to steer a car.

I clapped my hands, "Perfect, that's exactly where we are going." Handing him the flower, I asked, "What do you think Gary? Every time we stand on the side of the road our destiny will be a mystery to be revealed by the next ride."

Leaping up, Gary patted me on the back and exclaimed, "That's it, wherever our ride is going, that's where we go." He cast the wildflower into the wind.

Days later, after passing through villages and towns, we found ourselves on the outskirts of Paris. As we came closer to the city, we burned with anticipation. The Louvre, the Eiffel Tower, magnificent monuments, palaces, and cafes were only a few miles away. But fate had other plans for us. The first ride we got took us to Geneva, Switzerland, where we were soon meditating at the shore of a placid, crescent shaped lake.

At a youth hostel, we shared a dormitory with about twenty-five others. One of our roommates, Jim, had recently been honorably discharged from the U.S. Army. Jim had a fascination for books on Eastern mysticism and we spent hours talking. He was lean, strong, and eager for adventure, having been cooped up in the army for several years.

One day, out of curiosity, Jim asked, "Monk, with the Vietnam War raging, how is it you never got drafted?"

I told him how the draft board had accidently typed the wrong birthdate onto my records. Later, when the draft lottery was held and the nation watched, sitting on pins and needles, they pulled out one birth date after another. The early draws were the first to be drafted. My actual birthdate came up at the beginning of the draft but the mistaken one was drawn near the end and those called later were never called to service.

Jim looked out into the sky, rubbed his chin, shook his head and mused for a minute, then remarked, "Maybe it wasn't the draft board's mistake. Maybe God has other plans for you."

Jim invited Gary and me to come with him through Italy on his way to Morocco and we agreed. Near Genoa, the city of Christopher

Columbus, we loaded into his Volkswagen Beetle with all the money he'd accumulated in the military, including electronics he planned to sell for profit in the U.S. Terraced hills gave way to the Mediterranean Sea, afternoon sunshine played on deep blue waters, and we took a break to swim. When we got back to the Beetle, to Jim's horror, everything inside was gone.

We went down to the police station to file a report, and matters got even worse. To our shock, the police, shouting and jabbing their fingers in our faces, shoved us into a prison cell. As the heavy steel door slammed shut, a chill ran up my spine.

Their chief approached us. "You have two choices," he barked, "remain in jail or get out of town and never return." Of course, we chose the latter. In the darkness of night, a squad car with red lights flashing on the roof escorted us up to the city limits. That was our first day in Italy.

We drove until morning when we reached a telegraph office. Jim contacted his comrades in Germany, who wired him gas fare to return to his military base. Again Gary and I were on our own. We stood on the roadside wondering what was next.

"Hey Monk, do you think we're bad luck? First Frank and now Jim. Whoever tries to help us loses everything."

"I don't know Gary, maybe there's a reason for all of this."

Gary looked back down the road from where we came, "Do you really think there's a reason for everything?"

"Yes, I believe there must be a beautiful plan behind it all."

Gary nodded. "I also believe."

With that, we stuck out our thumbs and waited to see what fate had planned for us next.

3

S ET LIKE A MAGNIFICENT JEWEL in the heart of Florence sits the Cathedral of Santa Maria del Fiore. Completed in 1367, its enormous dome and historical carvings attract throngs of tourists. While the bustling crowds snapped photographs on the steps outside, I sat alone in the pews of the inner sanctuary. I had visited churches throughout Europe and always felt at home in them. Now, in the presence of the holy altar, I prayed for spiritual direction. A stream of the faithful knelt down to pray as well. Aristocrats and peasants alike fell to their knees in appeal before the Almighty. I wondered what they were praying for. Were they begging the Lord for success in their endeavors or relief from misfortune? Were they petitioning money, fame, or vengeance? Or maybe they were begging for unconditional love. As for me, I questioned my own motivations for traveling. Was I neglecting my responsibility to society by not getting a job? Was I trying to escape it due to some inner weakness?

I searched my heart. At the beginning of my journey, I had hoped to break out of my shell, push past my inhibitions, and experience the joys the world promises, thinking that that would bring me closer to God. But I now felt the distractions of the trip dragging me away from my cherished goal. My heart yearned for a spiritual experience. Gazing up into the massive dome, I pressed my hands together and prayed, *I don't really know who you are, but I do believe you hear my prayers. I long for your presence.*

Feeling tiny, I looked up at the enormous stone arches and the towering walls. The sun shone through stained glass windows, illuminating the massive octagonal dome and casting a veil of soft light on the marble saints. Touched by the sun and surrounded by candles, the holy altar glowed. There, an almost life-sized figure of Lord Jesus, cast in bronze, hung from a wooden crucifix. Here was the symbol that true love and compassion brings with it a willingness to endure suffering for those we love. Above, in the dome, an enormous painting depicted the miseries of hell and the glories of heaven and was crowned by the risen Lord encircled by angels. While I gazed up at the holy crucifix, a passage I had memorized, the words of Jesus, spoke through my heart, "Seek ye first the Kingdom of God and all these things shall be added unto you… for where your treasure is, there will be your heart also."

A chill tingled up my spine, my limbs trembled, my cheeks quivered, and my head felt hollow and light. Gripped by both shame and sorrow, I suddenly felt lost and alone, like an orphan. I envisioned the pilgrims around me to be frozen still like the statues behind them. Those statues glowed; now they appeared to be breathing.

Then, another biblical passage echoed in my mind: "Blessed are the poor in spirit for theirs is the kingdom of God. Blessed are the meek for they shall inherit the earth." In these words, I felt a shower of forgiveness that seemed to bathe me with a new life. Emerging from the silence, a pipe organ filled the sanctuary with a song that lifted my heart beyond the peak of the dome. Feeling alone and naked in the presence of the Lord, I wept. I felt so free. The internal battle I fought in London was over. In that confluence of indecision I once and for all chose the river that flowed toward my spiritual aspiration. I knew that I would never turn back.

That night I wandered alone into a forest and sat on the low remnants of an ancient dividing wall. There, under the moonlight, I played my harmonica. I shared my deepest feelings with the instrument. Like a dear friend, it patiently listened, responding with a song that sent my mind deep within to find solace and wisdom. My joys, sorrows, and cravings were freely expressed as I played the blues. I was crying out for my lost love—God.

Hours passed as I played and played. Suddenly, I was startled by the figure of a young woman standing nearby in the silvery moonlight. Shyly, she stepped forward. "I'm Irene," she said, explaining that she'd been listening for hours. "Your music touches me. Can I sit close by as you play?"

"If you like," I replied. Timidly, I played on for some time, but it wasn't the same. Then, in my shyness I stole a glimpse at her. Irene was as beautiful as a girl could be, her every gesture expressed with modesty and grace.

Nervously pushing her long, light brown hair from her delicate face, she spoke softly, "I come from a village in Switzerland. I'm on holiday to seek spiritual friends." Tears welled in her hazel eyes. She spoke of her disappointment with the people she'd met, who were after selfish pleasures. She told me how she longed to be closer to God. "From your song, I believe you are also on a spiritual search. Please tell me."

We spoke for several hours about our lives and our longings. It was alarming how much we had in common. Her soft cheeks glistened with tears. She took a deep breath, highlighting her charming form. "I have been praying for a companion. Please take me with you wherever you go." I listened in awe as she proposed, in her sincere manner, that we share love as we searched for enlightenment. With a tender gaze she concluded, "Please consider my appeal." I told her I would.

We spent the next day together visiting museums, strolling through parks, and exchanging our thoughts. She was unlike any other woman I had met. I was enthralled. In the evening, as I shared bread with Gary on a grassy hill, another girl, a stranger to me, climbed up to where we ate, studied my eyes, and placed a letter in my hand. Retreating alone to the forest, I found that the letter was from Irene. She wrote that unless I accepted her plea, it would be too painful for her to ever see me again. "If I do not hear from you," she wrote, "I will understand." I spent that night walking alone through the forest. Was this a temptation to divert me from my spiritual path, or was it a once-in-a-lifetime opportunity to share my life with a gentle, beautiful angel? I pondered the strangeness of it all. Just hours before I'd met her, in the cathedral, I had the deepest spiritual experience of my life, committing myself before the altar of the Lord. If Irene had come a day before, how could I have resisted her? She was everything I could ever want in a girl, and I felt a deep affection and attraction for her. I could imagine her as an ideal partner in my life. I didn't know her well, but I knew that to say no would break her heart and mine.

Once again, I found myself at a confluence. There were two streams that could lead me to enlightenment; one that offered the pleasure of a beautiful companion and the other a path I would take alone, offering my whole energy for the Divine. I walked and walked that night in contemplation and prayer. Could I really give up such a chance at earthly love? Gazing into a sky full of stars, I considered Catholic saints,

Tibetan Lamas, and yogis of India, who all chose lives of renunciation in their passion for enlightenment. They forsook life's pleasures to answer the call of exclusive dedication. I longed to follow in their footsteps. I knew it would be difficult, but with God's help, I decided to try, at least for now.

Under the moonlight a tear fell on my address book as I scratched out Irene's name. I never told Gary about her. He would never know unless he could translate the song of my harmonica.

Although the summer was ending and the date was approaching for us to return to college, family, and friends back home, Gary and I recognized that we could not turn back. Our search for enlightenment was only beginning.

A few days later, we found ourselves in Rome. Just behind the hostel was a forested hill where Gary and I slept under the starlit sky.

Much of the day, I wandered away from my friend in search of solitude. One day, I came upon an ancient monastery and entered its small chapel. As I knelt down and prayed, an elderly monk tapped me from behind. "Can I help you?" he asked. His white hair was partially shaven on the top of his head. He was tall and wore a brown robe. Clean but tattered, it fell in one piece from his shoulders to his feet. A rope was tied around his waist and worn leather sandals covered his feet.

His appearance inspired my reverence. Speaking slowly, I said, "Please, your Holiness, if you think I am worthy, tell me about your spiritual path."

He sat down beside me in the pew and smiled with great serenity. "I was raised in an aristocratic family," he began in a soft and deep voice. "As a young man, I had too much wealth and was terribly affected by my peers. To gain their acceptance, I committed many sins, indulging in fine clothes, wine, and women." He paused for a moment, his voice full of regret. "While I studied in university my entire family met with tragic death, sinking in a ship while on holiday. Bereaved, I considered the futility of my avaricious life. That set me on a search for meaning that ultimately acquainted me with a monk of the Franciscan order. Under him, I studied the holy books." Tears welled in his eyes as he raised his palms toward the altar. "In the life and teachings of Jesus Christ, I found salvation from my sins and the fountain of eternal life. Inspired by the devotion of Saint Francis, I took monastic vows. That was almost fifty years ago."

I bowed my head slightly. "Thank you very much. Could I ask you a question troubling my mind?" A ceremony was beginning in the chapel and the gathering of people created a stir. With his soft blue eyes, he looked into mine. Deep wrinkles in his face showed a rigorous life of denial. But his semi-toothless smile radiated a subtle joy that was the mystery of his life. "The service is soon to begin. Please follow me."

He led me through a narrow corridor and down stone steps into pitch darkness. He lit a lantern and we edged forward into an underground tunnel, perhaps four feet in width. The walls of that tunnel were ancient stones, the ceiling low, and the smell, damp and musty. A bat screeched past my face. In the gloom, the monk murmured, "I am taking you to a place where I love to pray." His words echoed against the stone, as did our footsteps. We entered a secluded chamber. The dancing flame of the lantern dimly illuminated the eight by eight cell, which held only a wooden crucifix on the wall and a wooden bench. Smiling, he inquired, "Is this quiet enough for you?"

I felt blessed to be there and told him so. We sat down on the bench and the monk set the lantern down between us. Then I revealed something that had been on my mind since I'd arrived in Europe. "I'm from a Jewish family and I honor our faith. As a child my heart was affected by my Grandfather's devotion to Judaism. I gained inspiration and wisdom from my study of the Holy Torah and Kabbalah as I was traveling. At the same time, the life and teachings of Jesus move my heart to tears. His wisdom, compassion, and love for God deeply affect me." I became a little nervous as I had never openly spoken these thoughts to anyone, but the monk reassured me with gentle eyes. I continued, "History tells of the persecution of Jews at the hands of Christians. There are Christians who despise Jews as the killers of Jesus and I've personally had to bear the brunt of such sentiments. Yet there are some Jews who possess a condescending attitude toward Christians, dismissing Jesus as having little relevance." Flashbacks of my past interrupted my speech. Staring into the faint glow of the lantern, I appealed to him for answers. "Why is there such conflict among those who strive to love the same God? Am I betraying my Jewish ancestry by my heartfelt reverence for Jesus?"

The old monk placed his hand over mine. He looked toward heaven for words to speak, and then closed his eyes in silence. After a moment, he opened them. "My child, there is one God. All religions teach us to love and obey him. Due to shallow faith, ego or politics, people fight over superficial differences. In fifty years of meditation, prayer, and charity, I have discovered that God's love manifests in different ways to different people. There are saints in the various spiritual traditions who sacrifice their lives for the love of God and goodwill toward man." Stroking his chin, in deep thought, his voice faltered. "I believe in Jesus Christ as the Son of God and my personal Savior. Perhaps it is God's will to inspire devoted Jews with a different belief than my own." He went on to say that Moses and the prophets taught us to love God with all our mind, heart, and soul. Jesus taught the same, coming not to change this commandment, but to fulfill it. "Why should there be hatred and fighting?" he went on. "One path may appear in different forms, but the Kingdom of God is the goal we all share. It is the men of small minds who create confusion." He released my hand and affectionately patted my head. "Do not be troubled my son. You are sincere. God will guide you."

His words touched my heart.

Another day, Gary and I came upon a monastery wherein the monks meditated in catacombs filled with the skeletal bones of their predecessors. In some of these rooms, hundreds of human skulls or skeleton parts were piled high along the walls. In another, the skeleton parts were artistically assembled to make floral designs, furniture, and chandeliers. We asked an old monk sitting beside us to explain. "Here, we contemplate the impermanence of the body and its attachments. This helps us to overcome the temptations of the flesh and seek refuge in the Kingdom of God." We listened carefully. Deeper in the catacombs, a group of skeletons wearing monk robes pointed to a sign that read: "As you are now, we used to be. As we are now, you will be."

Despite these spiritual encounters, the material world continued to pull on me. One afternoon Gary and I wandered into a bookstore in Rome. We often visited bookstores and scanned books at random for inspirational passages. Today, one book caught my attention: *How to Play*

Blues Harmonica. Leafing through, I found lessons on the styles of the great masters of the field, and songs from all my favorites, Sonny Boy Williamson, Little Walter, Howlin' Wolf, Jimmy Reed, Slim Harpo, Sonny Terry, Junior Wells, John Mayall, Paul Butterfield, and others. It would be a perfect manual to travel with, but I couldn't afford it. Would I ever find such a book again? I didn't think so.

My lower nature overcame me. Cautiously, peering to both sides, I discreetly slipped the book under my vest and walked out. When we returned to our campsite on the forest hill, I revealed my treasure to Gary. He smiled in approval.

Days later, we visited the Basilica of Saint Peter on a day the Pope delivered a sermon. Hours passed as we wandered through Rome and came upon a beautiful church. Sitting on heavy wooden pews intricately carved long ago, we spent a grateful hour meditating and praying in a cavernous sanctuary softly lit by candles. Later, hitchhiking, we reached a busy Roman intersection and Gary proudly unveiled an intricately carved wooden crucifix of Jesus. I took it in my hands and marveled at its beauty. "Where did you get this?" I asked.

"From the confession booth of that church," Gary replied cheerfully.

"What?!" I thrust it back to him. "You stole this from the house of God? How could you do such a thing? I'm ashamed of you."

Gary's eyes flared. "Monk, who are you to preach to me? Didn't you steal that harmonica book? Don't be a hypocrite."

He was right. I felt ashamed and defeated. I had no right to criticize him but had to speak my mind. "Yes, I stole it, but from a money-making business not from a holy place."

Gary's passions were high. Above the noise of the traffic, he protested, "The Church is one of the biggest money-making businesses in the world. They make billions of dollars while that bookstore is probably owned by a religious man struggling to make ends meet." As we argued, a crowd of pedestrians circled around us and cars stopped to view the conflict.

I strained to speak over the roar of the buses. "Maybe you're right, but still we worshipped God in that church. I can't bear that you stole from that place of all places. Please, brother, bring it back. Do this for me."

Gary's rage melted into a calm smile. He embraced me and, apologizing, agreed to return the cross.

"I'm sorry, too, Gary. I know I'm wrong, but thank you very much."

Gary and I hitchhiked back to the Church to return the stolen crucifix. It wasn't until night that we returned to our camp in the woods. We laughed about our dispute, agreeing that it had deepened our connection and proved our loyalty to each other. While lying on my back, inside my sleeping bag, I gazed into the stars and fretted. *I'm a hypocrite. Was it not hypocrites that nailed Jesus to that crucifix? How dishonest it is to preach but not practice.* Breaking the silence, as if reading my mind, Gary said, "Monk, please don't return that harmonica book. Everyone likes the new songs you're playing."

I kept the book for as long as it took to learn as much as I could from it. Just before we left Rome, I went back to the bookstore and slipped the book back on the shelf I'd taken it from.

In Rome, as I had in so many other places, I found refuge on a riverbank. Looking across into the Tiber, I reflected on how this river had flowed through the rise and fall of the Roman Empire and ever since. Generations and civilizations had perished and the magnificent buildings of Rome had become ruins. But all the while the Tiber flowed on, carrying wisdom I longed to know. Observing the current, I pondered my joys, sorrows, and trials while in Italy. I saw the robbery of poor Jim, our benefactor soldier. I remembered the priceless blessing I received in the Cathedral of Santa Maria del Fiore. My thoughts then flowed back to Irene, that sweet angel whom I had deemed an obstacle to my path. In the swishing currents of the Tiber, I heard the words of wisdom spoken by the Franciscan monk in that dark underground chamber. Then with shame, I recalled my hypocrisy in stealing and then condemning my best friend for doing the same. Through it all, I had felt a divine hand guiding me to invaluable lessons. As the water flowed, I began to contemplate the life of St. Francis. In his youth he despised the sight of lepers. But when touched by God's grace, he kissed the hand of a leper in sympathy, with a will to serve. A calling awoke in my mind to visit Assisi.

Separating from Gary for some days, I made the pilgrimage. Once there, I read stories of St. Francis's life in the very places they were enacted. The son of a wealthy merchant, Francis had served as a soldier as a young man, but in 1205, while praying in the Convent of Saint Damiano, Lord Jesus, from the church crucifix, called upon Francis to "restore the church in decay." It was a moment of transformation. Committed to a life of self-imposed poverty, humility, and devotion, he attracted many to follow. In Saint Damiano's I passed several days in contemplation on the transformation of St. Francis. Visiting his childhood home, I saw the closet where his father had imprisoned him for fear that he would renounce the world, and from which Francis tricked his mother into releasing him. I saw the Cathedral of Angels where he began his ministry and where, years later, he breathed his last breath. I returned to Gary in Rome, taking with me in my heart the inspiration of St. Francis's renunciation, compassion, and ecstasies of spiritual love.

From Rome we hitched to Naples, then on to the legendary city of Pompeii. I was struck by the fact that it had been a thriving township until Mount Vesuvius erupted. Now, centuries later, we walked through the ruins of the ancient civilization, marveling at all that had been excavated from layers of solidified lava. Perfect molds of human bodies were formed in the ashes. Animals, buildings, roads, and hundreds of artifacts were preserved in the hardened lava. I found myself lost in thought. What could we learn from the tragedy of Pompeii? At any moment disaster can come upon anyone. In our complacency, we fail to grasp the impermanence of all that is material. I thought of the bubonic plague that had ravaged Europe, the atomic bomb that leveled Hiroshima, the earthquakes and fires that had destroyed cities in America. Through the history of mankind, the powers of nature take everything away from us. Why put off seeking the eternal jewel of enlightenment? *Now is the time.*

As Mount Vesuvius had erupted, leaving a civilization in ashes, there had erupted from my heart an exclusive commitment to the path of spirituality, to leave all else in the ashes of my past.

4

From Pompeii, we hitchhiked to the port town of Brindisi and, using the very last of the cash we had managed to hold on to, sailed to the Greek island of Corfu, the ancient Corcyra written about by Homer in *The Odyssey*. Each day there, I would wander alone onto a mountainside that bloomed with olive and fig trees. Looking out over the Ionian Sea, I sat under a pomegranate tree and read the book of *Tao*, the Bhagavad Gita, and the Bible, eager to learn as much as possible from various teachers. Breathing the fresh Mediterranean air inspired contemplation.

We crossed to the mainland and hitchhiked toward Athens. As we soared along the roadways, I marveled at the unique terrain, language, and customs of Europe. I had come from the American Midwest, and the varieties were mind expanding to me. I gazed through the window and found myself lost in contemplation. All my life I had been conditioned to interpret reality a certain way, according to the culture in which I was raised. Why was it that we humans seemed to have a deep-rooted proclivity to feel superior to others, particularly in regard to nationality, race, religion, or social position? We think that our condition is normal and others are strange or inferior. This judgmental pride degenerates us into bigotry or sectarianism, generating hatred, fear, exploitation, and even war. I prayed that my travels would open my mind and provide sympathy for how other cultures viewed life, the world, and God.

After reaching Athens I wrote a letter to my family in suburban Chicago, telling them where I was, of how much the trip had meant to me, and how close I felt to them. I did not have the heart to tell them yet that I didn't want to return to school that fall, that I did not know when I would return.

In Athens, Gary and I were shocked to see the police waving automatic machine guns while patrolling the streets. We knew we should sleep at the youth hostel rather than under a tree, but there was a problem—our meager finances were exhausted. Although youth hostels were cheap, we still could not afford one. So we turned to the practice of many hardcore travelers of the time—donating blood at the government blood bank. The primitive process used then was painful. They strapped us to a table and then drew the blood in large syringes. We almost blacked out. It was a rule that each donor was given a cup of orange juice and had to sit in a waiting room for half an hour after giving blood. Only after seeing that the donor was in stable health did they pay. In the waiting room, biding our time, Gary and I endured the pain in our arms. He grimaced, lamenting, "There must be a better way to make money than this." We looked around the room and noticed a Frenchman with a guitar case in the same agony. A few seats down sat a Swiss boy with a violin case, he too holding his arm. As usual, I carried my harmonica strapped to my belt. We musicians looked at one other and smiled, having the same inspiration.

The Swiss boy, it turned out, was trained from childhood as a classical violinist, but as a teen, opted to play rock and blues. The French guitarist was likewise trained in classical flamenco but converted to folk music. After collecting our blood money, we streamed out into the street and, forming a makeshift band, began to play a wild improvisation of twleve-bar blues. A dozen people gathered around and danced. Soon it grew to dozens more. Gary became our rhythm section by dropping a few coins into a borrowed hat and shaking it. So pleased was the audience with our performance that they continually tossed *drachmas*, the Greek currency, into Gary's hat. As the enthusiasm mounted, we formed a musical procession down the streets of Athens playing one long song. The crowd skipped along behind. When we stopped at a corner, dozens assembled and the hat overflowed with drachmas.

At the end of the first day, we divided our earnings and checked into the youth hostel. By the next morning, we were famous. Wherever we went, crowds of smiling, clapping Greeks gathered around us in a circle. They loved us. We joyously played on, thinking it too good to be true. At one plaza, our music filled the air, old folks clapped, teenagers danced, children jumped, and mothers swung their babies to the rhythm. Everyone smiled on that sunny afternoon and the hat overflowed until, all of a sudden, the crowd abruptly dispersed. The music stopped as machine guns were thrust into our faces. We were arrested and hauled off to the station. There, the police confiscated all the money from the hat and warned us never to commit this crime again. That was the beginning and the end of my career as a professional musician.

With some funds we'd managed to hide from the police, feeling it was time to find a more peaceful place to cultivate our spirituality, Gary and I paid our fare on a boat to the Isle of Crete. Arriving at the port of Iraklion on the Aegean Sea, we rode a bus to the southern coast. There we found a place of wild and rugged beauty, a steep and rocky coastline inaccessible to ships and resplendent with natural springs, gorges, sandy beaches, mountain goats, and abundant sunshine. We had never seen so many caves. Amazed, we chose one that overlooked the Mediterranean Sea for our residence. This island paradise was a perfect sanctuary for fasting, meditation, and prayer. Before sunrise every morning, I climbed a mountain where I would meditate and pray until sunset. As I looked out over the clear waters of the sea, my thirst for enlightenment intensified like never before. Meanwhile, Gary was down at the seaside, also meditating. After sunset, we would meet back at the cave and break our daylong fast with some plain bread. As we settled down to rest on the stone floor, we shared our realizations of the day.

Weeks of contemplation passed in this way. By now, my prayers and meditations had kindled the spark of my spiritual craving into a blazing fire. From that lonely mountaintop, I witnessed everything in my life evaporating into that fire. It felt like I was being consumed by my yearning for God like one possessed.

But fate was leading me to a crossroads. One road would allow me to remain the person I thought I was, an American boy from a particular family, expected to go to college and get a degree, who had joined the counterculture. Another road would lead me into a realm where everything had to change.

I was afraid. I knew I was making a choice that would completely change my life, but nothing could stop me. I didn't know where destiny was leading me, but I knew that if I were to move forward in my journey, I would find a whole new life, with a whole new identity. I had to leave everything else behind.

The day was ending, the soft red orb of the sun dropping into the mouth of the sea. It cast a veil of golden light over the waves, which swayed and danced to its touch. The mountains of the coast radiated gold. The dome of sky above me glowed pink, tangerine, and lilac. And then, from my heart, a sweet but commanding voice called, "Go to India."

Why India? I thought. *It's another world, so far away. I know so little about it.* I had next to no money and little idea of what to expect, but I believed this was the voice of my Lord calling for me. At other times I had felt the presence of God, or felt guilt that I had behaved in ways to separate myself from God. But this was different. This was a silent voice that resonated from my heart. I was convinced that it wasn't my voice or my mind. No, this was God, answering my prayers for direction.

In the twilight, I descended from the mountaintop toward the Mediterranean, immersed in my own sea of introspection. I felt each step I took was bringing me closer to my destination. As I climbed into our cave, I found Gary there in meditation. A lone candle flame flickered, shedding yellow light on the walls and ceiling of our shelter.

I sat on the stone floor at the mouth of the cave and gazed into the darkening sky, then broke the silence, "Gary, something amazing happened to me today."

His eyes widened. He exclaimed, "Really, Monk? Something amazing happened to me, too."

"Tell me."

Gary gazed out at the stars. "At sunset, a voice spoke to me."

"Incredible. What did the voice say?"

"It said," he whispered, "go to Israel."

My mouth dropped. "What?" Shivering in suspense, I leaned closer. I couldn't believe what I'd heard. "Where?"

"It said, 'Go to Israel.' Don't you believe me?"

I braced myself on the cave floor. "I also heard a voice as the sun was setting."

Gary burst out, "Amazing! We'll go to Israel together."

"But Gary," I whispered, my heart pounding, "the voice told me, 'Go to India.'"

"India?" Gary yelped. He fell silent.

Neither of us could speak a word.

Silence rose between us and I looked into the galaxy of stars. To the heavens, I whispered, "Yes, I'm willing."

The cave was now dark except for the flicker of a single candle. I turned to my dearest friend. "Tomorrow I'll be gone. Maybe forever."

Neither of us spoke for a long moment, and then Gary broke the silence. "India is separated by the deserts of the Middle East by thousands of miles." Agitated shadows from the candle flame danced on the walls. "The passage is dangerous, even deadly. You have nothing, Monk. This is not a spiritual quest—this is suicide. Please wait. Why not come with me to Israel and make some money, then we'll go to India together?"

Minutes passed. I considered, but that inner call would not relent.

"Gary, I believe this to be the calling of God. I can't delay."

Worry washed across his face. "How will you get there, Monk?"

"I believe if I just hitchhike toward the east, someday I'll reach that land where the answer to my prayers awaits me."

He understood my heart. A tear trickled down his cheek, wetting his beard. "You have to follow your destiny," he whispered. "I'll pray for you."

As the candle flickered its last light, I lay on the cave's floor for rest. In the quiet of the night I gazed out into the limitless stars, my mind swirling in anticipation.

The sun came up and I prepared to leave. Gary came to the bus stop on the side of a country road to see me off. We stood among a few farmers waiting for the bus, feeling the sadness of separation beginning. The brotherly love we shared was rare. From childhood, we had passed together through the mysterious transitions of life. Together we had gazed up at the stars from our homes in Highland Park, from the hippie havens of California, from our college in Florida, and from many places in Europe. We had pondered why humans hate and kill, and opposed the Vietnam War and the treatment of African Americans. We dreamed of civil rights, of a world free of hatred and full of music. In our recent travels, we grew even more dependent on each other's friendship and support. But now the fateful moment had come. As the rickety bus approached, I wished to give Gary a gift, the most meaningful thing I had. Contemplating how best to express my feelings, an idea flashed through my mind. I took off my old black vest and handed it to him. I had worn it every day for years. To those who knew me, it was an inseparable part of my identity. It was also my most precious possession.

"The vest!" Gary exclaimed.

The two of us were like leaves carried by the wind, neither knowing where or how the wind would blow us. We shook hands, and then embraced. With emotion climbing in my throat, I said, "Someday, if it's God's will, maybe we'll meet again."

I found a seat on the bus and as it crawled forward, jostling over ditches and potholes, I looked back. Gary stood alone. I knew that giving him my vest signaled the shedding of my identity, past and present. I decided also to relinquish the nickname "Monk" and use my given name, Richard, from that point on. The journey to unknown India, I felt, would be a journey to reclaim my eternal identity.

5

AT Iraklion, the northern port in Crete, I found a fisherman willing to take me by boat to Athens. Once aboard, I sat apart to gaze into the sea. My mind tossed like the waves. I could not fathom what the days ahead would bring. Here I was, nineteen years old, and I had never even met a person from India. Aside from knowing that India lay to the east, I had no real idea where it was or how far. I didn't even have a map. According to what I had learned in school, India was a sprawling mass of poverty, disease, overpopulation, and snake charmers. Later, while searching for clues that might unravel life's deepest mysteries, I learned that many regarded it as the land of religion, a place of yogis, and great holy people. Would I live to meet these *rishis*? And not as a tourist or sightseer, but as a seeker of truth?

Once back in Athens, I found myself in an avalanche of negativity. To get to India, I learned, I had to pass through Turkey. Travelers who had been to Turkey warned me about Istanbul. "The Istanbul black market is bloodthirsty. They'll promise you a high price for a blood donation, but in reality they'll tie you down, drain all the blood from your body, and then throw your corpse into the Black Sea." Another chimed in, "The ghettos of Istanbul are havens for criminals so vicious they'll think nothing of killing you for a *lira*." Determined to go, I stopped my ears against these grisly tales.

At the youth hostel I inquired about the overland route to India. Once again, a group of Europeans gathered around to dissuade me. "Don't you read the papers? Are you mad?" Someone else shook an English newspaper in my face. Turkey stricken by cholera epidemic, the headline read. "You can't reach India without traveling across Turkey." Yes, Turkey was being ravaged by an epidemic of cholera. It was the news all over Europe. And to think I wanted to hitchhike across that country? Maybe I was mad.

Among these doomsayers, I met two young men who, like me, intended to travel overland to India. Jeff, an American from San Diego, was in his early twenties, tall, and athletically built with a square jaw and sturdy nose. His blond hair, neatly parted on the side, reached almost to his shoulders, and his blue eyes peered from behind black-rimmed spectacles. Although his features were rugged, he was a peace-loving soul. Like me, he was traveling to India on a spiritual search. Unassuming and fun loving, he was one of the most likable people I had encountered. Ramsey, an Australian with a ruddy complexion and rust-colored hair, in his mid-thirties, was a seasoned traveler. Although streetwise and tough, he too was a gentle soul and, having already hitchhiked across Europe and Asia, had maturity and wisdom that we lacked. Although I introduced myself as Richard, the band of travelers was tight enough that I was already known as Monk, and that's what Jeff and Ramsey called me.

Among us, only Jeff had any money. Breaking into a huge smile, he said, "Hey guys, there ain't much here, but whatever I have is yours." He swung his arm into his backpack and pulled out some bread, sesame butter, spinach, tomatoes, olives, and feta cheese. With the excitement of an overgrown child, he prepared a delicious feast for us and served it out into three equal portions. Sinking his teeth into the sandwich, he took a huge bite and, chewing, said, "After this, we'll have to really rough it guys, all right?"

Ramsey and I nodded, savoring the sandwiches.

It was there in the lobby of the youth hostel that the three of us solemnized our pact to traverse the overland trail to India. We went to the Turkish Embassy to see if the borders were closed. "Borders open," they boasted. We returned the next day to pick up our visas.

To reach Turkey, we hitchhiked north up the coast of Greece to the biblical city of Thessalonica and then east to Kipi, the northeastern point in Greece. Days went by without a single ride. Still, we managed to draw closer to the border, which was the bridge between Europe and Asia and the major gateway to Europe for smugglers of cannabis and heroin from the Middle East and Southeast Asia. The border post sat far from any town. We walked for hours to a desolate, dusty outpost where the road ended. A foreboding steel fence blocked our path. Topped by swirls of barbed wire, it stretched as far as my eyes could see. Greek soldiers stood in front, armed with automatic weapons. Approaching a nearby soldier, Ramsey asked, "Where is immigration?" The soldier pointed to a simple shack near the wall of fencing. No one was there, and evening was approaching. Now what?

We had already resolved to press ahead. Even so, the only responses to our repeated inquiries were indifference, irritation, or incomprehension. Finally, one young soldier who had been watching us disappeared. A few moments later, the Greek immigration official came out from a tea stall that, until then, we had not noticed. He was a stout, round-bellied man with a thick mustache, and his military shirt looked to be a size too small for him. Wiping the corner of his mouth with a towel, he handed it to the young informant and peered at us.

"What do you want?" he asked.

Ramsey coolly responded. "We want to cross the border to Turkey."

The round-bellied man looked at us in disbelief. "Not possible. Borders are closed. Cholera is raging like fire in Turkey. No sane man will go there now."

"But the embassy told us it was open," Jeff blurted out. "We want to—"

"Do you know what a cholera epidemic is?" the official, his face bristling with anger, shouted. "If I let you through that gate, you cannot return. This border is closed for entrance." He pointed east toward the darkening sky. "Out there is a no-man's land." Narrowing his eyes, he added, "Do you know what you'll find there? A wilderness filled with poisonous snakes and hungry wolves. A desert with no food or water."

Before he could say another word, Jeff cut in again, "But why would the embassy in Athens tell us it's open? We already paid and were promised entry."

The veins of the officer's neck bulged. Pointing his finger, he shouted, "The Turkish border is closed. If you walk through that gate, you'll never return. Do you hear me? I advise you to go back to where you came from. I'm leaving in two minutes. Make up your mind now."

The sun was about to set. We had struggled for days to reach the border. Hastily, we blurted out, "We'll go to Turkey."

Outraged, the man ordered the military to swing open the gate. As we passed through it, he shouted his prediction, "Fools, you'll never return!" Soldiers stood with rifles in hand as the steel gate slammed shut behind us.

We inched forward. The "no-man's land" was indeed the most desolate place I had ever seen, a deserted wilderness used as a buffer between two inimical countries. The sun was setting. At a distance I saw a snake slithering across the parched soil. A few leafless trees stood like sentinels marking our passage. It became darker and darker. Ordinarily this was a somewhat common passage for travelers, but on that night, thanks to the epidemic and the Greek border being closed, it was utterly deserted. We were especially vulnerable as it was dark and we were traveling by foot. I noticed the dry bones of some sort of a skeleton lying about thirty feet to our left but dared not bring this sight to my companions' attention.

Anxiety gnawed at my insides. What if the Turkish border really was closed? The embassy told us it was open, but that had been a week ago. Would we be trapped in this no-man's land to die? The darkness and the cold intensified. Wolves howled intermittently, piercing the silence, and we crept ahead. I remembered how a shopkeeper in Athens had warned me that this stretch of land was full of unexploded mines buried during the time of the Greek Civil War. "Mines that can rip your leg right off," he had said, "and plant pieces of your shoe right in the stump." I shuddered and stepped gingerly ahead, praying at every step. None of us dared speak a word.

The four-kilometer trek through pitch darkness was like a walk through the valley of death. Shivering, I felt hopeless and sick. Just as it seemed the night would never end, a glimmer of light appeared in the distance. Hastening forward, we made out a fence of steel beams topped by barbed wire. In the center, bolted on the gate, was a Turkish flag made of metal. We quickened our pace. An armed soldier stood guard inside, puffing on a filterless cigarette. Ever cool-headed, Ramsey whispered, "Let me handle this." He drew his passport from his pouch and coughed to draw the attention of the guard. When the guard looked up, Ramsey displayed his passport, pointing to us and then to the grounds beyond.

The man was disinterested. He shouted two words, "Border closed."

"But sir, you have to let us in or we'll die. The Greeks won't let us back."

"Border closed." A cloudy vapor burst from his mouth accentuating the two harsh words.

With nowhere to go, we felt like prisoners pleading for mercy. But there would be no mercy from this gatekeeper. His entire English vocabulary consisted of two words: *border closed*. He crushed the stub of his cigarette under his boot heel and stomped away into the darkness.

Twenty minutes later, he returned to find us still standing like refugees outside the gate. Gesticulating, he exploded into a litany of banishments: "Border closed. Border closed. Border closed." I wondered if he might shoot us. Just then, his superior officer came to the scene. Apparently he had been educated in the same school: "Border closed." Silently, we held our ground. Finally, our desperation and unwillingness to turn back convinced the second gatekeeper and he relented. Corralling us into a wooden shack, he confiscated our belongings including our passports, money, and even the clothes off our backs, then locked the door and abandoned us. Standing nearly naked in the freezing cold, we wondered if we were any better off than we had been moments before in no-man's land. What now? Had he left us there to die?

For about half an hour, we stood shivering in our underpants, as much from suspense as from the cold in that makeshift prison. Finally, our jailor returned. He peered into our faces, returned our clothes, stamped our passports, and broke into a smile. "Welcome to the great country of Turkey," he said.

Deeply shaken, we crossed over into a whole new world.

6

WHEN WE ASKED THE BORDER GUARD THE WAY to Istanbul, he pointed to a lonely country road. It stretched out into the darkness of the hilly, fertile country of Eastern Thrace. As we walked, I saw for the first time the minaret of a stone mosque. The mosque's dome and spires fascinated me and I was thrilled to see a place of God. There was no traffic on the road and Istanbul was still 150 miles away. What now? As we stood wondering how we would ever reach our destination, an old flatbed truck rattled down the road and pulled up next to us. Strangely, it was covered with wooden benches upon which sat a dozen or so cheerless policemen. We clambered aboard. All wore shabby uniforms. All were silent, except for one who wore no uniform. He whispered in my ear.

"I want to buy hashish from you. Sell to me. I am not a policeman."

"I don't have any," I answered. He demanded again and again. Later, he jumped down from the truck, put on a police hat, and strutted away.

In the middle of the night, we arrived in Istanbul. When the leader of the police asked us where we would stay, Ramsey told him that we were looking for an inexpensive place. The leader peered at us over his spectacles and then walked off to speak privately with a junior officer. When he returned, he told us to follow his assistant policeman.

The assistant's uniform was faded and torn. His expression was stoic and he didn't speak a single word or ever look in our direction. We followed behind him through the deserted streets of Istanbul, the poverty increasing with every block. It became obvious to us that he was taking us into the heart of the ghetto, one of the very places where the cholera epidemic was raging. The scene was demoralizing. Poverty and disease surrounded us on all sides.

Jeff trembled. "We've made a big mistake. That no-man's land was safer than this place."

Even Ramsey sighed aloud, "Mates, in my years of travel, I've never seen a place as depressing as this."

I tried to pray but my mind only reeled in confusion. Where was this man taking us?

The unnerving darkness was pierced by the shrieks and moans of people in agony. The contagion was taking a severe toll in this filthy slum. I was afraid to breathe. Cholera ravages swiftly, bringing about severe intestinal misery and death. We were lost and alone and—led by this strange man—we couldn't turn back.

An ominous medieval building made of stone loomed before us. An eerie sensation seized me. All my intuitions told me to run. But our guide, smiling, led us inside. We entered a dimly lit room that served as a billiard hall. Inside, a dozen men puffed on cigarettes and shot pool. They looked like the sleaziest gangsters of the underworld. As they sized us up with icy stares, I couldn't help but think that these thugs were the kind who would think nothing of killing someone over a gambling debt. The leader, short but formidable, leaned against a wall. His muscles bulged from a skin-tight black T-shirt as he scraped dirt from under his fingernails with a switchblade. When he saw our guide, he slipped the knife into his pocket, slid his hand across his oily black hair, and came over to speak with him.

The two seemed to strike up some kind of an agreement and motioned for us to follow to the back of the pool hall and up a dark, steep stairway made of uneven slabs of solid stone. To one side was a stone wall and on the other side a steep drop into a deep cellar with no railing. It was pitch black. We lost our breath climbing. Once at the top, we passed through an unlit hallway that led to the room where we were to stay.

There was no question of a hospitable welcome. Rather, our "hosts" insisted that we pay them cash up front. Their aggression was so startling that it began to dawn on us that we had seriously blundered. Had we just walked into a trap? We'd wanted cheap accommodations, not end-of-the-line. Ramsey spoke up, telling them that we didn't have any Turkish *lira* and asking them to tell the exchange rate for dollars. "Then we can discuss paying you. But for one night only." They shocked us by offering only half the official bank rate. Ramsey objected and politely tried to bargain for a higher rate.

But the head shark would have none of it, as we were now in his turf. With a scowl deforming his face, he flung his smoking cigarette at the wall. He sliced the air between us with his switchblade and exploded into a tirade. Small though he was, the power of his cruelty terrified us. His piercing black eyes raged. Lips quivering, he screamed insanely, pointing his finger into our faces. Anger personified seethed before us. The other thugs looked on with cold expressions. By this time, even our erstwhile friend, the policeman, shuddered and winced in fear. We were on our own. Taking our money, the men left us in the prison of our room.

What if they come back to rob or kill us? We looked for an escape route, but there was none. Other than the door, there was only one window with a long straight drop to the cobblestone alley below.

We were trapped.

"Jeff, lock the door," Ramsey whispered, "and, Monk, help me push this double bed against it. This way, those goons can't get in here while we're sleeping." Sleep was the last thing on any of our minds, but it seemed wise to do what we could to protect ourselves.

As quietly as we could, we lifted and pushed the bed into place and tied the steel bedpost to the doorknob with a rope for added security. Ramsey and Jeff lay on this bed, while I took a smaller cot against a wall. The room was a dump. A single light bulb hung from the ceiling. Green paint and plaster peeled on the walls. Cobwebs dangled from every corner and a stale stench turned our stomachs. Gasping for fresh air, I wrestled with a large window, six feet high and three feet wide, until it finally opened. I fell back into the bed, but within minutes bedbugs attacked. Rest was out of the question. The three of us lay in the dark waiting.

An hour or so later, we heard a key slowly turning in the lock. Silently, the door opened then hit the bed. The intruders pushed gently at first, not realizing that the three of us were squatting on the floor at the other end of the bed, heaving all of our weight into it. They pushed harder. Soon they understood that we were blocking them and howled in rage, slamming their bodies against the door. It flung open, but we pushed all our weight against the bed and shut it again. By now, both sides in this life and death tug-of-war were frantic. I jumped on to the bed to again tie the doorknob to the bedpost when, through the crack in the door, one of the attackers stabbed a knife in my direction. My mind screamed. *They want to kill us.*

The battle continued. They cracked their bodies against the door and it slammed again and again into the bed. They screamed threats and curses as we bashed ourselves into the bed. Unable to force the door open, they abruptly retreated. A heavy silence fell.

To rest before the inevitable next siege, I retreated to my bug-ridden bed. My mind was full of ghastly thoughts. *What was I doing here trapped in the cholera-infested ghettos of Istanbul, a target for the underworld?* Tossing over and over, I called to mind the life I had left in Highland Park.

I'm a simple boy with a loving family and friends. Why did I leave the shelter of such a peaceful home? Now I'm helpless and alone. I prayed. *I came here in search of enlightenment; is this the path I have to tread in order to learn surrender?*

A thought emerged. *If so, let it be. In our predicament, only God can save us.*

My prayers were interrupted by the door smashing into the bed. Round two of the battle began. Our would-be assassins shouted in wrath, pounding ferociously. A moment of inattention and we would be dead. Despite the biting cold, sweat flooded from our pores. We gasped in exhaustion and our limbs were battered, but our predators did not tire. Their roars terrorized us. By this time, I felt as if my bladder were about to burst. The only toilet was in the hallway outside the door. Three formidable battles raged simultaneously within me: the battle to keep the assassins out, the battle to keep my urine in, and the battle to make sense of it all.

Unable to bear it any longer, I deserted Ramsey and Jeff and climbed up to the windowsill. There I relieved myself into the alley below. Suddenly, a woman's scream blasted my ears. The alley was about fifteen feet wide. Straight across from me was a window where an old Muslim woman dressed in a traditional black veil had been watching. In my desperation I had not seen her, but she stared straight at me. Outraged by my obscenity, she screamed in revulsion. This was too much. I stood helplessly on the window ledge with my pants down, urinating, face to face with her and begging for pity.

Cursing me, she threw a shoe into my face. It was a direct hit. I shut the window, jumped down, and wiped blood from my nose and mouth. But I had not finished. My bladder was still bursting, Meanwhile Ramsey was crying out, "Monk, get back here. We can't hold them off." I was losing all three battles. *I can't survive this*, I thought, *God help me!* Just then, I saw the answer, and finished where I'd left off in the shoe. Putting it in a desk drawer, I reentered the battle. Pressing firmly, we held them off.

But we were trapped with neither food nor water. It was only a matter of time before they broke in. As the gray light of the dawn appeared, we agreed that our only hope was to quietly escape through the door between attacks.

We decided to risk our lives on the tiny chance of escape. We had no idea whether a guard was standing post outside our door, but if so, we were dead. It was a chance we had to take. Slowly, and as quietly as possible, we swung the door open into the pitch darkness. I could not see my hand before my face. As we tiptoed forward, the aged wooden floor creaked with every step, each creak like a scream. In this darkness, would we blunder right into one of them? My heart was pounding. We made it to the gothic staircase. Still unable to see, we groped the outside wall, terrified of falling over the other side. In this way, we crept down the staircase toward the dimly lit pool hall where, to our horror, the guard lay sleeping on a pool table. Holding our breath, we stole across the room to the door.

It was locked. The latch would not budge. We had never seen a lock like this. Frantically, each one of us tried to open it. Finally our attempts roused the guard from his stupor and he shouted to the others. From another set of stairs came the horrifying sound of their stampede.

"Oh my God," I gasped. "Open the lock quick, Ramsey, open the lock!"

"I'm trying. I'm trying."

He jiggled the lock in every possible way to no avail. The stomping of boots as our captors came closer made me sick. Just as they were almost upon us, all at once the lock popped open and we burst into the street, running as we had never run before, backpacks and all. Behind us, we could hear the screams of our adversaries. Not looking back, we dove into a taxi. We knew of only one place in Istanbul. "Blue Mosque, Blue Mosque," we chanted in unison.

But, scanning through the rear view mirror at the gang of men approaching us, the taxi driver did not move. He saw an opportunity.

"Two hundred dollars," he demanded. "What? Two hundred dollars?" Jeff cried.

The driver shouted loudly, "Two hundred dollars, Two hundred dollars."

Hastily, we agreed, "Yes two hundred dollars, two hundred dollars."

He zoomed off. But were we safe?

Jeff, the keeper of the wallet, was concerned. "We can't give him two hundred dollars," he whispered. "Will he be the one to kill us?"

We didn't want to find out. At the first stoplight, we bolted from the taxi. The driver howled, "Two hundred dollars, two hundred dollars." But we were gone.

EAGER TO LEAVE ISTANBUL, we boarded a ferry to cross the Bosporus Strait. From the crowded deck we watched, weary but relieved, as the sun rose in the hazy, overcast sky. Birds soared and I bowed my head in gratitude. As the ferry sailed through the sea, I looked back at the grand city as it was slowly swallowed by the horizon. Last night, I thought, our death seemed sealed, but we struggled and took an unimaginable risk to escape. It was possible because we had hope. Hope in the divine can empower a human being to overcome unimaginable obstacles. In a terrible predicament, when our hearts embraced hope, we attracted a power beyond ourselves to guide us, purify us and, ultimately, liberate us. My hands were still trembling and my adrenaline rushing, but in my heart I thanked that gang of murderers who had served as instruments to teach me an essential lesson and prepare me for the pilgrimage ahead.

Nothing about our hostile reception in Istanbul could have prepared us for the cordiality of the people we met as we traveled east across Turkey. Some invited us into their homes and shops to eat with them. Their meals were simple, usually traditional flat bread and tea, but we were touched by their hospitality and always satisfied. I was also fascinated by the exotic designs of the many mosques we passed and whenever possible, spent time visiting these beautiful houses of God.

Our methods of travel reflected our lack of finances. Either we hitchhiked or caught rides, jammed in with the local people, their gear, and their livestock on jalopy buses or on the backs of trucks. We traveled across the arid, windswept highlands of central Turkey, stopping briefly in Ankara, where cattle grazed on the bare and spacious hills. After a couple of weeks on the road, we reached the more rugged and mountainous terrain of the eastern highlands where the nights grew colder. We had traveled about 800 miles beyond Istanbul when calamity struck again.

I was afflicted with severe dysentery. Travel was no longer possible, so we stopped in the town of Erzerum and inquired of the local people for the cheapest possible place to stay. They led us to a tea stall on the outskirts of town and gave us a room on the third floor of the time-beaten edifice. My burning concern was the toilet room. To reach it, I had to climb down a steep staircase of about thirty stone steps. In a hallway to the left of the stairway was a hole in the floor. That was the toilet. Human waste was left to pile up in the hole until it was shoveled out, which, from what I could tell, was infrequently. A partition of rotted wooden planks provided privacy. The stench made me dizzy, the air so thick I felt as if I were drowning. Still, I practically lived in that latrine for days. After finishing my business and hauling my body to the top of the stone steps, I would be forced down again to evacuate. Intense nausea, vomiting, and constant loose movements ravaged my body. My friends, meanwhile, patiently waiting for my recovery, would go out each day to explore the town.

One day, alone in the room, I was surprised to see a strange man enter and begin to rummage through Jeff's backpack. Discovering his Swiss Army knife, he plucked it out and announced to no one in particular, "One *lira!*" Then he plunked down a *lira* on the table and hurried away with his new possession. *But the knife is worth much more than that,* I thought. Despite my precarious condition, I felt it my duty to defend my friend, so I struggled up from my sickbed and chased the man down. I returned his one *lira* and politely insisted he give back the knife, which he reluctantly did. "Please come back later and discuss with Jeff," I said wobbling on my legs. He said nothing and left.

Not five minutes later, a mob rushed up the steps. Dehydrated, feverish, and barely able to sit up, I was in no shape for a confrontation. They barged in through the door. Leading the mob was the intruder who had just moments before stolen the knife. He pointed his finger at me shouting, "Pakistani, Pakistani! He is Pakistani." The mob was outraged. They circled my bed brandishing clubs and daggers. In a rage, they shouted, "You Pakistani, you die. You Pakistani, you die." I was alone and bewildered. What else could I do but pray to God?

Hastily I seized my U.S. passport and held it up for them to see, "Look, I'm American."

An elderly leader of the mob stepped forward. He took my passport and examined it like a self-proclaimed immigration agent, then looked up and spoke quietly, "So. You are not Pakistani?"

"No."

"You are American?"

"Yes," I replied.

He smiled and reached down toward the bed to shake my hand, "Very good, we like Americans. You give Turkey weapons." Everyone offered respect and left.

Before I could recover, I heard the mob racing up the stairs once again. I prayed for shelter. Again the mob burst into my room, more than a dozen of them, and surrounded my bed. This time, though, they came in peace, offering me flat bread and tea.

The eldest spoke. "You American. This is very good. We sorry. Now you eat."

Overcome with nausea, I had no appetite; In fact, I gagged from the smell of food. I knew that eating that bread and tea would force me into the horrible latrine for the rest of the day and night. But what could I do? To refuse their gifts would be an insult. This type of hospitality was hard to refuse. I forced a smile and ate the entire plate and more until they were satisfied. Soon after, I did pay the price.

My health began to slowly improve. One evening I roamed along the dusty road, astounded by the poverty in the district. Families crowded in decrepit shacks with few possessions and wore raggedy clothes. People crouched down along the dusty road looking hungry and discontent. It was poverty of a type difficult to comprehend in the West. Even though it was only October, the night air was frigid, a sign of the long, bitter, cold winters in that region of Turkey.

To return to our room I had to enter through the small teashop on the ground floor of the building. One evening, inside the teashop, a powerfully built man in his thirties with glossy black hair and a thin mustache grabbed my arm and pushed me into a chair. I could tell by the way people regarded him that he was highly respected. Sliding a small glass of tea toward me, his smoldering black eyes riveted to my own, his lips and body trembled. I was sitting face to face with intensity personified. He spoke no English. Pointing to an Arabic inscription on the golden ring he wore, he roared like an angry lion, "Allaah!" Then he thrust a finger at my face and with that gesture demanded that I say the name of God.

I couldn't bear to look at him. My eyes gazed at the transparent glass of tea on the table. It had no milk or cream, only a cube of sugar slowly dissolving on the bottom.

Yanking my chin up, he forced me to meet his intimidating stare. I was dissolving faster than the sugar. He again thrust a finger in my face and screamed, "Allaah!"

It seemed crucial to my wellbeing to satisfy him, so I murmured, with much reverence, "Allah."

He squinted as if he wanted to burn me to ashes, and shook with rage. When he could contain it no longer, he smashed his fist on the table. "No! Allaah!" As the tea glasses crashed to the floor, everyone circled around us. Ratcheting up the volume, again he thundered, "No! Allaah!" Again he thrust his finger into my face.

Much louder this time, I cried out, "Allah."

But it was not loud enough. By now his rage was white hot. I was petrified. He again smashed his fist into the table, and for the fourth time roared at the top of his lungs, "No! Allaah!" Every pair of eyes in that crowded shop glowered at me as if I had been apprehended while desecrating their holiest shrine. He jabbed his powerful finger into my chest, forcing my chair back to the wall and demanding that I say God's name in a way that matched his fervor.

Not for the first time on my journey, I felt certain that the angel of death had found me and was hovering just inches from my head. What else could I do but pray to Almighty Allah to save me? I stood up, raised my arms and with all my energy, I cried out from my heart, "Allaaaaah!"

He gazed into my eyes for a long time as the teashop fell silent. Nodding his head in grave approval, he walked out. As the rest of the crowd returned to their tables, I sat stunned. No one before had ever preached to me like that.

8

AFTER I RECOVERED, RAMSEY, Jeff and I resumed our journey eastward. In those days, there was a whole counterculture of world travelers who endured the hardships of a very low budget. Most were adventurous and many were spiritually inclined. At times we met in the most unexpected places. In Erzeram, Ramsey and Jeff met some traveling brothers who had convinced a bus driver to let them ride for free on a company bus traveling to Tehran. The bus was only half filled with supplies, so there was plenty of room for a few passengers. In this way, joining them, we crossed the border of Turkey and entered Iran.

Once inside the impressive immigration building on the border, we took note of the wall-sized photograph of the Shah. Even more sobering was a sign posted by the U.S. State Department. In big letters it warned American citizens that in Iran the penalty for possession, transportation, or selling of hashish or opium products was death. If one was arrested the State Department had little influence to help.

The bus driver was delayed by immigration formalities, so we went to wait inside the bus. It was evening. Soon, a crowd of children gathered to see the strange foreigners through the bus window. Although they wore ragged clothing, they were beautiful children. I smiled at a small boy of about four years old. But he glared back at me with such intense hatred in his eyes that I lost my breath. How was it possible for such a small child to possess such hate? I was to be haunted by repeated nightmares of his stare. I thought how frightening it was to see how impressionable children are. By family and surroundings, they can be conditioned to love, fear, or hate before they are even able to reason.

We arrived at the ancient city of Tabriz. As I explored the streets on my own one day, one kind family invited me into their home—a two-room abode made of brick. The women of the family had been working painstakingly for several years on a single Persian rug. Mother and daughters sat on the floor of their simple hut creating precious art. The intricate designs might have up to 250 handmade knots per square inch. Naturally dyed wool shone with dazzling colors, each one with a life of its own. Red, blue, green, orange, yellow, white, and violet, these were but a few of the colorful yarns they stitched so meticulously.

So simple and gracious was their hospitality that I felt like part of the family. They didn't speak a word of English, but that didn't matter. For dinner, all the men of the family sat on the floor and invited me to join them. They first recited a beautiful prayer of thanksgiving before enjoying the flatbread and tea. As we munched happily on the homemade food, their ten-year-old son entered the door smiling proudly. He held a great surprise in his clenched hands—dates from their tree. Moving toward me, he placed the sumptuous fruit on my plate. Everyone laughed and exclaimed my good fortune.

Five times a day the family abandoned whatever they were doing to offer prayers to Allah and the Holy City of Mecca. The natural devotion of these humble souls moved my heart. I thanked God for this experience and I thanked this family for their kindness towards a wayward stranger.

Our bus cruised through the mystical terrain of Iran. As far as the eyes could see, the flat, arid desert expanded in all directions. Hours passed with no sign of life. From time to time, sandy hills or villages of tiny clay houses appeared in the distance. We drove during the cool parts of the day and all night long. One night, the moonless sky filled with a multitude of stars that sparkled beyond the horizons on all sides. Fascinated by the beauty, we stared through the bus windows. My fellow travelers urged me to play my harmonica. Gazing into the ocean of stars, I played a spontaneous song of my sincere yearning for God. I poured my heart into that instrument. As my tearful song played, the bus fell silent. When it ended, everyone exclaimed. I looked around and saw more than a few passengers weeping. Smiling, Jeff patted my shoulder from the seat behind while in front Ramsey flicked his thumb up in approval. I was humbled. Knowing that I really didn't know how to play the instrument well, I thanked God and Jimmy the Bear back in Opa Locka.

It was while traveling across the Iranian deserts that concern for my mother and father flooded my heart. They had expected me home several weeks earlier and had not heard from me since Athens. They must be suffering miserably. Why, then, did I not write to them? The truth was I didn't know how to compose the letter. Whatever words I might use to try to explain my resolve to travel overland to India, their hearts would shatter. What could I do? My search for God had become the only thing I was living for. If I neglected it, I knew I would be a hollow shell.

Mother and father had dedicated their lives and souls to the welfare of their three children. Both came from poor Jewish families whose immigrant parents fled from Lithuania, Romania, Russia, and Poland to escape religious persecution. As far as we knew, all the relatives who'd remained were later murdered by the Nazis.

My mother had lived through a difficult childhood. As a small girl she suffered her father's early death, then soon after, her elder sister was attacked in an alley and left traumatized for life. As a teenager, my mother had to work to support her ailing mother, her now handicapped elder sister, and her younger sister. But she was always cheerful and grateful for what God had given her. Later in life, she served her husband and children faithfully twenty-four hours a day, but she never abandoned her first family, quietly scrimping and saving to send relief.

While raising three sons, she single-handedly did all the chores of the household, including cleaning, washing and ironing clothes, shopping, and cooking an amazing feast every evening. She was slender, radiant, and dressed meticulously. The parents of all my friends marveled at my mother's beauty and grace.

Her willingness to help others extended beyond her family. As long as I could remember, she joyfully volunteered to serve in various charitable organizations, performing in fundraising dances in particular. And my brothers and I were always on guard lest she suddenly give our used toys or clothes away to Goodwill. Throughout our lives she had emphasized the virtue of gratitude. She was sure to ask if I had thanked the parents of my friends if I ate at their houses, sure that I offered thanks to whomever showed kindness to me. Of all the displeasing traits children could exhibit, ingratitude disturbed her the most. Consequently, she was sure not to spoil us by satisfying our whims, and whenever we were given a gift, she stressed, "It's the thought that counts." She led by example. Whether she received a gift of precious jewelry or a simple flower, she was equally thrilled. In this, she taught me that happiness comes not from the material thing, but from the love with which it is given.

She took immense pride in seeing whatever good we did. Whether the results were big or small, she was happy as long as our efforts were honest. Time and again, she revealed her selfless service to us. When I had suffered my dislocated shoulder, she was there within moments to drive me to the hospital. After surgery, the first person I saw at my bedside was mother. I coughed and pleaded, "Mom, your cigarette is making me sick." As was the fashion for American women at that time, she had been smoking two packs of cigarettes every day for over fifteen years. But the thought that she caused me pain greatly affected her heart. As she frantically extinguished the cigarette, tears welled in her brown eyes. Ashamed, she came to my bedside and stroked my cheek. "Darling Richie, if my smoking causes you pain, I promise you to never touch another cigarette for the rest of my life." She never smoked again.

My father shared much in common with my mother. He had to leave school at fifteen due to shortage of food at home and labored to assist his parents in the time of the Great Depression. Later, as a married man, he worked hard to financially maintain his aging parents and sickly mother-in-law, along with his own family. Financial challenges seemed to follow him like a shadow. In 1958, when I was seven years old, he and my Uncle Irving invested everything they had in a promising business venture. They became the largest automobile dealership in the Chicago area for a brand-new line by Ford, the Edsel. But Edsel sales plummeted, becoming infamous as one of the greatest failures in automobile history. Consequently, my father sunk into bankruptcy and lost everything. I watched as he struggled, working long hours to protect us from poverty.

Besides providing for the welfare of his children, my father loved to play sports and games with us and, when he had time, took me to football and baseball games. Later, he opened a shop for auto repairs and in time, with hard work, became quite wealthy. Still, from the age of fifteen, I worked various jobs after school hours and during school vacations. I never wanted to add to the burden on my parents, a value I had absorbed by their example.

The day before I was to leave home for college, my father was especially emotional. "Richie," he said, "let's take a ride together." We drove along the tranquil streets of Highland Park's Sherwood Forest, surrounded by the sounds of children laughing and playing. "Son," he began, "as long as I'm alive, I'm always here for you." Stopping the car, he held my hand as his voice quivered, "As your father, I expect you to do your best, but whether you succeed or fail, do good or bad deeds, or even betray me, as long as I'm alive, I'll love you and I'm here for you. This is a promise I will live and die to keep. Please, never forget this." Overwhelmed, I listened. I knew that he meant every word he spoke. Sure enough, he remained true to his promise, though I was to test him beyond his farthest expectations.

The bus stopped on a hill outside a village and I was lifted out of my reminiscence. I lifted my duffle bag off the floor, untied the strings, and pulled out a pen and an Iranian aerogram. The moment had come to explain my resolve to my parents.

My dear family,

Everything has been going well with me. Roads get bumpy at times but they are fine roads. I have been doing much thinking and have found that now is the time when I will do something I have been longing to do. Much thought and much contemplation has gone into making it clear that this is the right way.

Throughout the world, people look at life through different windows. For almost twenty years I have been seeing through the eyes of a western man. I have seen and experienced the laws, philosophies, religions, arts, and overall ways of life of the west. Now I will see how life is lived in the east. I do this not to escape my previous life, but to see another. It is something I cannot see through schools because schools can only tell me about this through slanted points of view. So I will go to the east myself. What greater education is there than that? I am not doing this to worry you, so please don't hurt yourselves by worrying. It is impossible to write as often as you would like. Sometimes I simply cannot find a post office. Gary is no longer traveling with me. He is in Israel. I always have companions. Give my love to all friends and relatives.

Richard

The letter was postmarked Iran and had no return address.

Upper left: George Harrison with his friend and guide Shyamsundar
Upper right: The author's lifelong friend Gary (right) with traveling companion Hackett
Lower left: Baba Ram Dass—founder of the Seva and Hanuman Foundations and the author of *Be Here Now*
Lower right: Neem Karoli Baba—renowned mystic yogi and guru.

Above: Madan Mohan temple, Vrindavan
Below: Asim Krishna Das (right) and the author (left) just after his "fateful haircut"

Upper left: Swami Bon Maharaja—founder of the Institute of Oriental Philosophy
Upper right: Krishnadas Babaji—a God intoxicated devotee in Vrindavan
Lower left: Sripad Baba—founder of the Vraja Academy
Lower right: Visakha Sharan—Vrindavan devotee and scholar

Above: Ghanashyam in his closet temple in Vrindavan
Lower left: Ramesh Baba—an ascetic devotee of Sri Radha dwelling in Her home in Barsana
Lower right: Yamuna River, Keshighat, Vrindavan

Above: Sri Radha's mountain temple in Barsana
Below: The Samadhi (sacred tomb) of sixteenth century saint Rupa Goswami, Vrindavan

Above: Painting of Radha and Krishna with the gopis (cowherd women) of Vrindavan
Below left: Bhakti saints Rupa Goswami and Sanatana Goswami   *Below right:* Chaitanya
Mahaprabhu (1486–1533), the Supreme Lord who incarnated as the avatar of divine love
Opposite Page: Bhaktisiddhanta Saraswati Thakur—Founder-Acarya of the Gaudiya Mission
Following Page: A.C. Bhaktivedanta Swami Prabhupada—Founder-Acarya of the International
Society for Krishna Consciousness and the author's guru

9

OUR BUS PASSED THROUGH A VAST DESERT spotted with villages of earthen huts. We watched caravans of camels winding across the plain. The camels carried heavy bundles, but strutted forward effortlessly, their long necks moving slowly back and forth in perfect sync with every other limb. In the heat of the sun, nomads, their heads wrapped in turbans stained white by sun and sand, rode on the camels or paced alongside their trusted animals. Here, under the clear skies of the Iranian desert, was a lifestyle completely foreign to my own. I felt I had gone back in time. As the sun rested in the western horizon, the starlit Persian night made its entrance, so still and quiet that I dozed into a dream.

Opening my eyes minutes later, I was blinded by a flash of light. Neon signs outshone the stars: Mobil, Shell, Exxon, Texaco. It seemed we had accelerated through centuries in mere minutes, as if the bus had become a time machine. Everyone but the driver and I were fast asleep. We had reached the outskirts of Tehran where the Shah of Iran had rolled out the red carpet to welcome foreign oil companies. From where I sat, the city appeared as a neon-lit island floating in a sea of ancient desert.

In Tehran, some traveling companions brought Jeff, Ramsey, and me to a hotel frequented by the western youth. With each step we climbed toward our room, the pungent scent of hashish grew. Hippies from England, Germany, and California were passed out in their beds while others sprawled on the floor. The Iron Butterfly's "In-A-Gadda-Da-Vida" blasted through stereo speakers. Everyone was stoned. One young man, his scraggly blonde hair scattered over his face, staggered up to us. "Hey brothers, welcome home," he slurred with half-shut bloodshot eyes. "Get hip and get high, man. Just be cool and blow your mind." He sucked heavily from a hashish pipe and held it out, "Take a toke." On the tables lay several balls of hashish the size of softballs. People in the room continually tore off chunks to smoke or eat. Although we were open to such experiences, this was too much.

Ramsey expressed our shock. "Egad, there's capital punishment for possession of a gram of hashish, yet you mates have kilos lying around in the open."

Jeff chimed in. "Are you guys crazy? Smoke is bellowing out your door into the hallway. You could be killed for this."

A hippie sprawled out on the floor turned and yelled, "You're a bummer, man, get out of here."

A disheveled blonde girl shoving potato chips into her mouth and chewing wildly, chided, "What's with you? Are you straight or something?"

"Don't be paranoid, man," slurred our host, puffing his pipe. "Either be cool or get off of my cloud."

The three of us looked at one another in disbelief. Jeff muttered, "We've got to get out of this place."

The warning of the U.S. State Department was etched in our minds. As we hurried down the stairs, we ran right into three policemen on the way up. It struck me that these hippies really were on a cloud and it appeared there might be some thunder and lightning coming their way.

It was in Tehran that I quietly studied the followers of Islam. Religion was so much a part of their everyday lives and seemed to inspire such beauty in their spirits. I was inspired to see the spiritual integrity of ordinary God-loving Muslims, but shook with trepidation on encountering those who practiced extremism in the name of that religion. Seeking the essence of the world's religions, I hoped to better understand.

Journeying on across the Iranian countryside, we came to Meshed, a place of pilgrimage for Shiite Muslims. Here I expressed my wish to spend some time alone, so Jeff and Ramsey agreed to travel ahead and meet me in Kabul, Afghanistan.

I must have been a peculiar sight, a young American with hair draped down his back, wearing a turtleneck and pin striped jeans and sitting alone in front of a mosque intermittently reading the Koran and meditating. One man observed me from a distance and, taking interest, wandered over to where I sat. A tall fellow of about forty, he had clear brown eyes and a fair complexion and wore a spotless white robe and turban.

He bowed his head respectfully. "Sir, allow me to introduce myself. My name is Ibraham. I am a resident of the holy city of Meshed."

I extended my hand to him. "You appear to be interested in my religion, may I speak with you?" After inquiring about my life, he agreed to teach me about Islam. Just outside the magnificent tomb of a saint, we sat on two small rugs to study. He looked to the sky and spoke in a deep voice, "Almighty Allah has sent you to me at this sacred time and place. Within this shrine is the burial place of the saints Imam Reza and Harun al-Rashid. And thousands of pilgrims are now in Masshad to observe the holy month of Ramadan, the ninth month of the Islamic calendar." He paused and smiled gently, then talked about how the Prophet Mohammed had received his first revelations of the Holy Koran during the month of Ramadan. "In a cave, Gabriel the merciful messenger of Almighty Allah revealed the Holy Koran to the Prophet, to bring peace to all sentient beings." He pressed his palms and fingers together, and then touched the tips of his index fingers to his forehead.

"Islam means submitting to the will of Allah, the Almighty God of creation. Please hear as I explain our teachings and practices." Soon a crowd of staring pilgrims encircled us. I was no ordinary sight in this neighborhood.

Ibraham kindly escorted me to the library room in his home. I found him to be a liberal-minded scholar of scripture and he seemed to practice the tenets of his faith sincerely, with generosity and kindness. He removed the Holy Koran from a shelf filled with old Arabic and Persian manuscripts and recited a passage of invocation. Then, raising his outstretched palm to the heavens, he began, "Islam teaches that there is no god but the One God and Muhammad is the messenger of God. God revealed His word for mankind to Muhammad and other prophets, including Adam, Noah, Abraham, Moses, and Jesus. Muhammad is the last, or the seal, of the prophets. Thus, his preaching for humankind will last until Qiyamah, the Day of the Resurrection." He went on to explain how Almighty Allah had sent angels to the earth to help prepare the faithful for the Day of Judgment when they would meet their fate in either heaven or hell. He said that Muslims believed that the main written record of revelation to humankind was the Koran, the final revelation of God to humanity. He also told me of the five obligations Muslims have to fulfill in their lives: to believe in Allah as the one true God, to offer *namaz* or prayer five times every day, to fast during the month of Ramadan, to give in charity to the deprived, and to perform *Hajji*—the pilgrimage to Mecca—at least once in life.

In this way, Ibraham spoke for hours about the history and teachings of his faith. He was a refined gentleman, so different from the man who had forced me to scream the name of God in the teashop of Erzeram. I was gaining striking lessons on how every religion has so many levels of practitioners and how shallow it would be to generalize about an entire religion from a few of its followers.

As the sun set, casting a golden veil over Meshed, Ibraham gave me a decorated box of dried fruits and bid me farewell to join his family as they broke the Ramadan fast.

10

O
N THE BACK OF A TRUCK PILED HIGH WITH BURLAP sacks of grain, I reached the border of Afghanistan. The shabbiness of the immigration post signaled the poverty of the nation, yet the immigration officials offered a cordial welcome, quite different from most other border guards I'd experienced. My first stop in Afghanistan was Herat. The people here were charming and friendly. In the stark desert terrain they wore raggedy, dusty clothing, and lived in shambled dwellings. Although they were the poorest people I had seen in my travels yet, everyone I passed offered a smile and no one asked me for anything. On the contrary, they were eager to share what little they had. Each day in Herat, I was invited into their homes.

Usually, a family lived in a hut of one small room. They joyfully shared their flat bread with me. My hosts could neither read nor write. Yet so many of them struck me as both humble and wise, living with dignity through the tribulations of their lives. Although they spoke not a word of English, the communication of the heart that we shared was especially satisfying to me.

On a winter day in 1970, in a small tea stall in Herat, I wrote a letter home.

Hello my family,

How is life? I am now in Herat, Afghanistan. It is amazing to be here in a country with people that are naturally friendly and humble, poor but peaceful.

I know it is late but I will still wish happy birthday to Dad and Larry

I wish you the very best of everything.

With love,
Richard

Early one morning, I innocently set out to explore the town of Herat and stumbled into a neighborhood unlike any I had ever experienced. It was late morning as I stood on a dusty roadside and observed my surroundings, at first enjoying the sights. Looking around, I was transported into a realm of timeless simplicity. My heart pounded. Camel after camel sauntered by. There were no sounds of horns or modern vehicles, only camel hooves clacking on an earthen road. Families were crowded into tiny one-story houses made of dried mud. A pungent taste of arid dust dried my mouth and the smell of camel excrement and burning wood assaulted my nose. People chatted while squatting on the roadside, dressed in their traditional Afghani clothing. Their loosely fitting garments were elegant though faded and tattered with wear. Men wrapped long sheets of cloth around their heads as turbans and many had faces riddled with deep blotches, scars made by small pox. Like aged leather, their skin was dried and toughened by the elements, and huge, spontaneous smiles revealed rotting or missing teeth. Baggy shirts extended below their knees as they performed their chores apparently with no concern for the time. Women covered their faces with a fine mesh and wore blue or black gowns that reached from the top of their heads down to the ground, leaving no trace of their bodies visible. A blind man sat on the road singing religious songs in a high voice as he thumped the skin of a drum.

It was cold, but smoke from cooking fires filled the air. Suddenly, quite unexpectedly, I was literally brought to my knees by culture shock. My eyes burned from the smoke. I felt dizzy and nauseated, deeply disoriented and afraid. All at once, I found it impossible to identify with anything my five senses perceived. Utterly alienated, my ego succumbed to a painful breakdown. On my knees, sweating with emotion, I struggled to connect something to the world that I knew. I failed. I felt totally disconnected. Although the dire poverty was disheartening, the people of Herat appeared to be the happiest, most carefree people I'd ever seen. This surreal combination of poverty and happiness short-circuited my intellect.

Old men sat on the roadside smoking from large water pipes. The scent of the arid desert dust blended with the acrid aroma of hashish. The sights, smells, and sounds were disconcertingly foreign to my senses. I was alone in a culture where nothing existed that I could relate to.

As I sat motionless on that roadside, a lonely alien in a distant universe, I prayed to be spared from this confusion. What was happening to me? What was the cause of this bewilderment? Why was I so affected? I grappled to find myself. From birth, I'd identified with my external surroundings. Not until this moment could I fathom the extent to which I had been conditioned. Just as wearing green-colored glasses tinges everything we see as green, so according to our surroundings and experiences, we have a particular perception of reality. The conceptions perceived by my body and mind had become my identity. Now those familiar conceptions had evaporated, casting me into a void. *God please help me. Who am I? Who am I? Who, really, am I?*

The world around me seemed to disappear as my prayer and meditation transported me into a state where a silent inner presence predominated over the phenomenal world. There I discovered a precious truth, a truth that awakened a sense of shelter and freedom: *I am the soul, distinct from the world of externals, a child of God.* The blaze of culture shock had acted like the rays of the sun to dissipate the fog of misconception. I felt liberated. Flooded with gratitude, I knew that Herat would forever remain a sacred place on the map of my heart.

Whenever I look back to that day, I am reminded how prayers may be answered in ways we never expect. To grow may require that we be shaken right to our core. While kneeling on that roadside in Herat, something died within me, giving birth to a realization necessary for me to move forward on my path. With each step, a camel lifts its hoof from a stable place on earth in order to move forward. And to reach the sea, each ripple of the river must let go of its present state to surrender to the current.

As I walked back to my room, I came upon an aged man slumped on the roadside. Beneath his head-wrap was a face defined with deep crevices and sagging with wrinkles. His toothless smile was radiant as he waved for me to share the hashish in his *hookah*. Smiling, I politely declined. His culture had already given me a high I prayed never to forget.

I n Herat, I was offered a ride by camel to a place where I could take a bus to Kandahar in central Afghanistan. The dilapidated bus was filled with poor farmers and no one seemed to care if they paid the few cents for the ride or not. In the center aisle were sacks of produce, a half dozen chickens, two sheep, and a goat. The straining, unmuffled motor, the laughter of men and women, and wailing of babies provided the soundtrack for this amazing show. Suddenly, the bus stopped in the midst of a vast desert. In a moment everyone got off. Was this an emergency? No, not at all. The passengers carefully unrolled their prayer rugs on the sand and faced the direction of the Holy City of Mecca, performing their *Namaz*, or offering of prostrations and salutations to Allah and his Prophet Mohammed. Every few hours this ritual was repeated with no consideration of where we were. The religion of these tribal people was their life. They were not mullahs, priests, yogis, or monks, but ordinary family people. Yet in all situations and places it impressed me how their devotion to Allah took priority.

In Kandahar, the people greeted me warmly. One man in particular, Hariz, took a special interest in me. Tall and well groomed, he was an educated man who had acquired wealth and respect in the trading business. Through his economic ventures and holidays, he frequently traveled abroad. After guiding me on a tour of Kandahar, he invited me into his spacious home. One quiet night while we sat on his rooftop terrace engaged in a philosophical discussion, he calmly said, "Mr. Richard, please excuse me for a brief moment, I have an obligation to attend to." Suddenly, he jumped up from his chair, cocked his head to the moon and began to howl like a wolf, "Aaauuuwwww, aaauuuwwww, aaauuuwwww." What was going on? Had this distinguished gentleman gone mad? He grabbed a long rope with a loop at the end, raced to the edge of his rooftop and hurled it down to the road. What in the world was he doing? With rapt attention, he slowly reeled the rope in. To my amazement, he had fished up a wriggling rodent the size and shape of a ferret. I watched in wonder. This was a mongoose, which, it turned out, wandered the town by day, and each evening, responded to Hariz's howl, by crawling into the loop of the rope, where he was hoisted up, and spent the night on the roof. As my friend and I resumed speaking, I felt the mongoose scaling up my back with his sharp pointed claws. He crawled under my long hair until he reached my head. There, he burrowed himself in my thick locks, making his nest, and went to sleep. Feeling his warm body deeply breathing on my head, I experienced another kind of culture shock.

I looked to my host for help. "What do I do now?"

My friend laughed. "Mr. Richard, he found a good nest in your hair."

My neck felt as if it were breaking from his weight. "Please take him off."

Hariz became serious. Under the starlit night, he sipped his tea and narrowed his eyes, warning me, "There is an ancient truth: Never wake a sleeping mongoose." He set the teacup on the table and told me that the animal was sacred to the ancient Egyptians. "The mongoose is a ferocious killer when angered. In battle, a mongoose will slay the cobra, the deadliest of serpents and symbol of death." Hariz sipped his tea again and leaned back, "If you suddenly wake him, he may tear your head to shreds. Mr. Richard, do not even slightly move until he leaves on his own."

Hours passed as I sat motionless, fearing for my life. From time to time, the mongoose moved, digging his claws into my scalp. Hariz could no longer stay awake, so with many apologies, he left to sleep. I sat alone now. That dark sleepless night in Kandahar seemed never to end. My neck throbbed with pain, but I was too terrified to move. The mongoose on my head was like a time bomb that could explode at any second. I was quickly losing the attachment I had to my long hair. If only the immigration officers in England had acted on their threat to shave my head, life would be so much safer tonight.

I tried to console myself. At least someone appreciated my hair! But the mongoose had not come alone. Ravenous insects started biting into my scalp, obliterating these noble thoughts. Why was this happening to me? Feeling my vulnerability, I strained to control my emotions. Then, contemplating, I tried to make sense of it all. I realized that our free will could convert a curse into a blessing or a blessing into a curse. Yes, ludicrous as it was, this mongoose may have been sent to teach me the sacred virtue of patience and forbearance. To bear difficulty and turn to God was a priceless blessing. To transform a crisis into an opportunity was true wisdom.

The rest of the night was spent in an unusual state of gratitude. Little did I know that what the mongoose taught me about crisis would give me strength in the hard times that awaited me. By the time the sun finally rose, my uninvited guest had enjoyed a good six hours of sound sleep. He awoke, crawled down my back, and jumped to the floor. He then did something that moved my heart: the mongoose stared at me with an innocent affection as if thanking me for my hospitality. Turning from me, he crawled into the loop of the rope where Hariz, who had just awakened, lowered him down to the street for another day.

Hariz smiled at me. "Mr. Richard, I beg forgiveness for the inconvenience you suffered. Nothing like that ever happened in my home before. But please be happy to know that in our culture it is a pious deed to offer hospitality to an uninvited guest. You gave good hospitality to one of our mongooses and you did so without any of the mechanical formalities. This morning he looked so happy and well rested."

My aching neck numb from strain and sleeplessness, I considered his words. Had I heard him say mongooses, in the plural? I decided I really didn't want to be around the next time he cocked his head toward the sky and howled like a wolf. Scratching my bug bitten head and itching to move on, I sighed, "Hariz, thank you very much. You've already done so much for me. But I think I best be on my way."

One evening as I walked alone down a quiet side street in Kandahar, a small man with one eye and one arm grabbed me by the hand. Pulling me through an alley some distance, he yanked me down a winding stairway. It was pitch dark. As we descended the crude stone steps, I pondered the mysteries that might unfold. Once underground, I was pushed into a dark, chilly dungeon. As my eyes adjusted to the darkness, I saw a tarnished lantern shedding meager light. Its flame flickered on a crumbling stone ceiling and walls, where cobwebs and iron chains hung ominously. There was not a single window or piece of furniture. On the dirt floor squatted a dozen barefoot old men in soiled, tattered robes and turbans. They were huddled around a shadowy mound. What could it be? As my eyes adjusted to the darkness, I saw it was a mountain of Afghani Black Hashish, perhaps a couple hundred kilos. Back in Europe, I had been told this was among the most expensive and powerful hashish in the world. The poor old men were continuously tearing chunks from the mountain and forming palm-sized paddies for easy smuggling. My escort abandoned me to a corner as he joined the others in making hashish paddies.

How strange, I thought, *what am I doing here?* I probably couldn't find my way out even if I tried. Someone then rose to his feet and lit a flaming torch. Like a high priest on procession to the altar, he marched to one side of the room. There stood what appeared to be the venerable deity: a massive hookah. The man proceeded to feed the giant mouth of the pipe with kilos of hashish and ceremoniously lit it with the torch. Just then, another man rose, approached the long upward curving spout, and with all of his strength, inhaled long and forcefully until his lungs were filled to the brim. Then, removing his mouth from the spout, he exhaled, only to inhale another dose. Again and again, he forcefully sucked in great volumes of hashish smoke. It was beyond belief. Soon, on its own, a thick stream of smoke was gushing out of the spout, yet he kept puffing and puffing. It was superhuman. When he reached the point beyond even super human limits, his lungs revolted. Tumbling to the ground he lurched uncontrollably, coughing so severely I expected his guts to come pouring out.

Meanwhile, everyone else was nonchalantly rolling his hashish paddies. Then, the next man stepped up to the ominous hookah and repeated the same ritual. He sucked and sucked, perhaps twenty times. The smoke poured out of the spout, and finally, reaching the climax, he collapsed to the earthen floor. Tossing and turning, he too coughed incessantly. Everyone in the room repeated this same unbelievable spectacle. When he'd gained control of his coughing, each man would calmly join his brothers in making paddies while squatting around the hashish pile, giving way to the next victim of the hookah. Each man took his turn in rotation several times as the all-devouring hookah consumed kilo after kilo and smoker after smoker. *These old Afghanis are certainly post-graduates in the art of getting high*, I thought. *In comparison, the proud hippies of the west are hardly toddlers in the nursery school.*

A dense cloud of hashish smoke hung in the airless dungeon. My eyes burned. Simply by breathing the air down here, I had become higher than ever before in my life. My turn had come. They pulled me up to the hookah. Was I to be the next sacrificial offering to their deity? A dense stream of hashish smoke was pouring out of the wide spout. How to approach it? I wobbled forward. I hadn't even reached the spout to begin sucking when the stream of smoke attacked my lungs like a serpent rushing into a mouse hole. To the ground I collapsed, rolling violently back and forth. Tears sprang from my eyes as I coughed so severely that I thought my lungs and throat would be ripped to shreds.

Meanwhile, the veteran smokers slapped their knees, shook, and howled with laughter. For here I was, a young American, one-third their age, and I couldn't even reach the spout.

This was their nightly recreation, but it was too much for me. I crawled back into my corner, slumping against the wall. Rushes of energy paralyzed my every limb while strange visions appeared in the immense cloud of smoke. All sound was a strange music, and my mind seemed to be whirling and whirling, beyond time and space. I could not move and there was no place to go. My eyes burned with tears. Hallucinating, I watched the billows of smoke rising from the hookah taking the forms of ghostly demons coming to devour me.

I reflected on the times I'd sought relief, happiness, or meaning through intoxication. What had I gained? My mind wandered back to the sight of the drug addicts and alcoholics I encountered on the skid rows of American cities. Acquaintances in college had succumbed to drugs, becoming helpless slaves to their addiction. I remembered a dear soul who went insane from too much LSD. An intelligent college student, she started chirping like a bird. Everyone was amused until she tried to fly out of a second story window. A year later she still believed she was a bird, but now chirped in the cage of a mental asylum. I too, had at times, sought peace through intoxicants. I was led to believe that chemical or herbal stimulants could induce higher spiritual perceptions, but I had quickly realized their limitations. It was an artificial state that drew me farther from my heart's longing. I had to move on.

Swallowed by a cloud of torment in that hashish dungeon of Kandahar, a vow sprung from my heart: *Dear Lord, I will never again indulge in intoxicants.*

I stumbled out of the room and onto the street, still reeling.

One last evening in Kandahar, while in a dim crowded tea stall, I squatted on the floor with the locals. Suddenly everyone's attention focused on a blind boy who stumbled in carrying a rustic wooden instrument with a single string nailed across it. He was perhaps sixteen years old, and like the others, wore soiled rags that loosely covered his emaciated body. My heart quaked—nothing covered his blinded, disfigured eyes. Despite his extreme poverty, he smiled radiantly as he poured his heart into singing songs in praise of Almighty Allah as he thumped that one-stringed instrument. His sweet voice and sincere emotion hypnotized all six of us crowded in the tiny shack. An hour passed as the spontaneous joy of that blind boy lit up the room with a supernatural joy. He plucked upon his one string and cried in praise of God.

I was moved. He was homeless, blind, illiterate, and poverty stricken. Yet, even in his humbled state, he sang of the vast treasure of joy he had found within his heart: his love of God.

Kandahar had been extraordinary. From a mongoose, I had learned patience; from a den of hashish addicts, temperance; and from a blind boy, spiritual joy. Grateful for all I had learned in the city, I bade it farewell.

11

O N A BUS TO KABUL, I squeezed in with my fellow passengers. Two wooden benches extended across the length of the bus to provide seating. In the middle, dozens of chickens flapped their wings scattering feathers in the air and clucking loudly. Roosters called out, flapping their wings and expanding their chests. Goats poked about for something to eat while a few sheep clustered around their owner bleating wildly. The animals brought with them swarming flies and other exotic insects. A sociable goat stared me right in the eyes as if pleading for charity. Then with great enthusiasm, he chewed on the cuff of my pants, which must have been delicious as another goat soon joined him to chew the other cuff, a chicken then jumped onto my lap and pecked on my thighs.

This portable barnyard was a daily affair for the passengers who stared at me and offered smiles. Perhaps they were experiencing a type of culture shock, too, seeing a strange creature like me dressed in gray pinstripe jeans, my gray turtleneck, and long wavy hair. The bus stopped and all the human passengers poured out into the desert where they laid down their prayer rugs and offered prayers toward the holy city of Mecca. Only the animals and I remained on the bus.

I had once read that humans without a spiritual path are like two-legged animals. Though I had been exploring and learning about many different religions, I still felt I had no one clear path. While the devout Muslims prayed outside, I felt I was among my colleagues in the bus.

Once the imperial capital of the Mughal Empire, Kabul was a beautiful city. High on a mountainous plateau surrounded by snow-covered peaks, I knew it was the capital and most important city of Afghanistan. Here, I reunited with Jeff and Ramsey. They had already been in Kabul for about a week and were eager to continue the journey down the famous Grand Trunk Road to India. We planned to travel across the Khyber Pass together into Pakistan. Early one morning, we set out for the bus stand where Jeff bought our tickets. Before boarding, however, all passengers were required to present their documents to immigration officials who stood outside the bus. Jeff and Ramsey stood before me in line, and after passing through the formalities, they boarded the bus. But when my turn came, there was a stir of confusion. One official snatched my passport and dragged me into the immigration office. To my dismay, the bus driver revved the engine and roared off, taking my ticket with him. Jeff and Ramsey had carried it on the bus, not realizing I'd been left behind. Another immigration official, it turned out, had mistakenly written the wrong date for my departure. Realizing their mistake, they released me.

Stranded alone in Kabul, I wondered how to proceed. It was unthinkable to hitchhike alone through the Khyber Pass, infamous as one of the most lawless lands on earth. I had heard frightening stories during my travels about this borderland between Afghanistan and Pakistan, stories of foreboding cliffs and warlike tribes who accepted no law. Like the denizens of the Old West of America, they settled disputes with loaded rifles and shoot-outs, and accepted killing and banditry as a way of life. I had heard stories of tourist buses being stopped at gunpoint, passengers being robbed and sometimes killed, and how bus companies had to pay the tribal leaders to protect their buses from such violence. I did not know how true these stories were, but certainly this was no place to find out. What was I to do now? I had no money to purchase a bus ticket. Alone, I walked the streets of Kabul wondering about my destiny.

The day passed in this way. With the night came the freezing cold. I had no warm clothes and nowhere to go. The full moon was like a block of ice. Trembling, I sat down on a lonely roadside, closed my eyes in meditation, lifted my harmonica to my lips, and poured out a song from my heart. Some time later when I opened my eyes, a shapely young woman stood in front of me, her dark blond hair flying on the cold wind. She looked upon me with pity. "Aren't you freezing here in the middle of the night without proper clothing?" she asked. She shivered as she gazed at me with sparkling blue eyes and I told her what had happened to me.

"I'm from Holland," she answered tenderly, "but I have been living in Kabul for several years. You may come to my home and keep warm tonight." Grateful, I followed her.

From the frigid street outside, she escorted me through a door into a warm, beautiful room. Bedecked with gold and green curtains, it contained a white sofa and a fine dining table with chairs. She welcomed me to sit on the soft sofa. This was like nothing I had experienced since leaving my family home in Highland Park, which seemed like ages ago. The Dutch woman invited me to the dinner table where she served warm bread with butter, baked vegetables, and chocolate cake for dessert. I considered how it might have been a hidden blessing that I'd missed the bus.

After some casual discussion, she invited me to sleep. "You must be terribly tired after sitting in the cold for so long." She led me across the room where there were two beds. "Here's your bed. I'll sleep in my bedroom."

Suddenly, from another room, a giant of a man appeared. My hostess introduced him. "This is my bodyguard. He's an Afghani warrior, obedient to me." I looked upon this gargantuan figure standing before me. He was about 6'4" with a body like a mountain, each limb bulging muscles like boulders. His long, oily hair was black as coal and an unkempt beard covered his face. I sat down on my bed and the Afghani warrior sat down on the other. Squinting, his pitch black eyes pierced mine. He then stretched his fists above his head with a prolonged growling yawn, his body radiating with the stench of sweat. My hostess continued, "He is my protector. I have seen him crush a man's skull with one blow of his fist. You may now sleep." She crossed the room to an adjoining room. Before disappearing through a beaded curtain, she switched off the light. "I will go into my bedroom now."

The Afghani warrior was my roommate and oddly enough I felt safe with him by my side. The house was so warm and comfortable that as I lay my weary body in bed I felt fortunate. How would I have survived the freezing night if this friendly woman had not taken pity on me? Pulling up the soft blanket, I savored the experience as I drifted into sleep.

Minutes later I woke to my hostess parting the beaded curtain between our rooms. She was wearing only a transparent silk nightgown. Incense burned and soft music played. She approached my bed and spoke sweet words into my ear. "You are so young and good." Her eyes were glazed with passion. Slipping off her gown, she presented to me her naked body, and then wrapping her arms around me, she laid her perfumed body over mine. Bewildered, I struggled to focus on the purpose of my journey.

"I'm sorry, I don't want this. Please let me sleep," I pleaded. Undaunted, she tried to arouse me in various ways. "Please leave me alone," was all I could say. Tormented, I lay there like a dead, cold fish.

In a frenzy of passion, she whispered in my ear, "If you don't satisfy my desire, my bodyguard will crush your skull. You can't escape."

Scorned, she cried for his help. The warrior sprang from his bed, bounded across the room, and stood over us. "Submit, submit or die," he growled.

My mind was reeling. As my seductress continued her efforts to overcome me, I lay under her trembling. Meanwhile, the Afghani warrior towered over us. He yanked my hair and roared, "Submit or die. Submit or die." The words were like bombs exploding in my head. Questions rushed through my mind. Was this a nightmare? Must I surrender to her or die? Why was this happening to me?

In a flash, with all my strength, I heaved the woman off me, grabbed my bag and shoes and raced to the door, leaving my sleeping bag behind. She screamed. The bodyguard roared and lunged to capture me but I dodged him. With all my might, I bolted through that door and burst into the street. The warrior was close behind. Seething with wrath, he wailed. I ran without once turning back, terrorized by the thought of his mammoth fist crushing through my fragile skull. I ran and ran and ran. Somehow, I escaped.

Once again, I was alone with nowhere to go, in the middle of the night. As I wandered the deserted streets of Kabul, I realized that the freezing cold night that I previously dreaded was now providing me shelter. The icy moon that had chilled me to the bone was radiating warmth that nourished my weary mind. Walking with no direction, I was free. Gazing into the stars, I contemplated on the powers of passion. Sex could be a gift of God, but when it becomes an obsession, it plunders all intelligence and people are driven to abominable acts to satisfy their lust. When passion is frustrated, people lose all good sense. I thought about the fact that throughout history there had been saints in all traditions who raised beautiful families utilizing sex as a divine offering. Then I began to wonder why, throughout the same history, many saints took the vow of celibacy. The more I pondered, the more

I tried to answer my own question. Maybe they realized the charm of the opposite sex to be a distraction from their exclusive dedication to God. Maybe they were determined to direct that powerful energy toward prayer and devotion. Maybe this was what I, too, was looking for. Certainly, it would explain why I had turned my back on Irene in Italy. *Love is the offering of the heart,* I thought. *Pure love must be selfless, without selfish motives.* As the full moon rose higher over Kabul casting rays on the mountains, a vow arose in my heart to remain celibate for the remainder of my life. Embraced by the bitter, cold wind, I prayed to God to help me to keep my commitment.

As the sun rose above the panoramic mountains of Kabul, I hurried to the bus stand wondering what the future would hold. To my relief Jeff had sent my ticket back with the returning bus driver. He included a little money as well. Before boarding the bus, I turned to look upon the city of Kabul one final time. On this mountainous plateau of Afghanistan, I had taken a significant step on my internal journey toward enlightenment, praying to accept a difficult vow that I was determined to follow. I felt deeply thankful.

Through my window, steep cliffs rose in an arid land. On the slopes, poor farmers toiled to grow a few sparse crops. Clearly, the rugged desert mountains secluded these people of the Khyber Pass in their own world. The local people toted rifles on their shoulders and some slung straps of bullets around their chests for protection. As the bus jounced along, we passed ammunition factories where primitive rifles were made available to all. At a distance I saw long caravans of camels with cargo strapped to their backs, sauntering along the dusty paths.

The bus jerked and rattled over potholes, straining forward through the Khyber Pass. As I peered out the window I could picture Alexander the Great on his march to invade India in the fourth century BC, Genghis Khan's bloody Mongol invasions here in the thirteenth century, massive Mughal armies led by their emperors marching through to conquer and plunder the subcontinent, and British soldiers being slaughtered by the tribesmen. For generations, bloodshed and death had been daily affairs for the local Pashtun tribes.

Although the struggle for survival took its toll on tribal members' faces, they appeared also to be stamped with a type of austere grace.

Remembering all the ghastly tales about them, I now felt happy to honor these people, albeit through my bus window.

In the evening, the bus let us out in Peshawar, Pakistan. My curiosity led me to a tranquil old woman in a black veil sitting on the footpath. In front of her she'd spread a piece of burlap cloth on which she displayed varieties of trinkets. I stepped closer to see what this grandmotherly soul was selling.

Brass knuckles. She was selling brass knuckles.

Studded with razor-sharp spikes designed to penetrate flesh and rip it apart on extraction, these weapons of cruelty were ornamented with semi-precious jewels. She directed me to press a hidden button on the brass knuckles, and when I did, *whoosh*—a blade shot out. My head reeled. The old woman insisted that I bargain with her, but I politely went on my way.

India was only one country away now. I eagerly continued my travel overland to the ancient city of Lahore to receive my Indian visa. On the way, I met some kind people who extended themselves to make me feel at home in Pakistan, providing meals and rides in trucks or buses. Early one morning, I waited outside of the Indian embassy in Lahore. Large hawks circled overhead in the clear sky. When the embassy doors finally opened, I entered and timidly presented my passport to the official. When he stamped it, my heart rejoiced. I felt as if it were a visa to God's kingdom. India was a step away now. The land of yogis, lamas, and sages was waiting.

12

T HE SUN SHONE CLEAR AND BRIGHT in the fresh winter air. I had set out from Lahore at sunrise, walking and hitchhiking fifty-five kilometers down a single-lane dirt road that cut through stretches of wheat, cotton, and yellow fields of flowering mustard. Acacia trees lined the roadside and sometimes a few rose between fields as markers. Otherwise, trees were scarce. More scarce still was the traffic along this road. The few vehicles that did occasionally pass were as exciting to my senses as the traditional turbans and robes of the people in them. Decrepit trucks rumbled by, each as brightly and intricately painted as a wealthy rock star's psychedelic mobile. An occasional bullock cart, hay-lined and piled high with wheat, livestock, and whole families, creaked along. It was on conveyances such as these, and my own feet, that I reached the Hussainiwala border crossing into North India.

My heart was swelling with anticipation as I approached the immigration officials. I felt that I had aged thirty years during the six months I'd spent crossing Europe and the Middle East, but I knew that the trials I underwent were necessary purifications for entering sacred India. I was now so close, only steps away.

Only a stout woman seated alone behind an immigration desk stood between my destiny and me. Her stern glance was not at all inviting. In drab military attire, she sat under the Punjab sun. I stood before her full of hope and covered in dust. I handed her my passport. India's Border Security Forces flanked her on both sides, rifles slung across their shoulders. While she was examining each page of the document, my thoughts whisked me back to the moment on the mountaintop in Crete that set my feet to follow my heart to India. Something had happened to me on that mountaintop. Some, I knew, would dismiss it as an aberration of the mind brought on by hours of solitary prayer or some kind of hallucination brought on by fasting. But I felt that God had appeared to me in my heart, and I had heard His words loud and clear: "Go to India." From that moment on, I'd believed that the Lord was calling me to Him in India.

Three months and over three thousand miles had passed since then on my journey through the Middle East, each moment unlike any I had ever imagined as a boy seeing the world through the ill-fitting lenses lent him by suburban America. And with each mile, my heart was flying toward the sacred soils of India and a rendezvous I knew I could not live without.

I longed for India. There my heart's deepest desire might become real. My heart and soul was already with the yogis in their mountaintop ashrams. For months and through unimaginable hazards, I had pressed forward to reunite with them. Now, a step from my goal, I stood waiting before the border guard who gripped my passport to India in her bureaucratic hand.

She looked up after some minutes of scrutinizing it, her face expressionless. "Show me how much money you have."

As I reached nervously into my cloth bag, she leaned forward in her chair. There were only a few coins to show her.

Disgust crept across her face. "You require two hundred dollars minimum to enter." She leaned back and folded her uniformed arms across her chest, eyeing me with suspicion. "Where is your money?"

Looking at the ground, I stammered, "This is all I have now."

"You cannot enter then." She slapped the passport down on the table that now stood like a wall between us. "Go back to your own country."

Her words were like arrows that pierced my heart. "But I've traveled overland for months, risking my life to see your country. I burn with a desire to study your religions from the holy people." From far away, I heard my voice pleading with her. "I have abandoned the comforts of an American home out of love for India. Please, give me a chance."

She glared at me now. "We have beggars enough in India. We don't want another one." She motioned to one of the guards, and he raised his rifle. "You will not enter India. You are rejected. Now go back to where you came from."

"But—"

"That is final. No more discussion." She stood up from the table, turned her back on me, and marched over to a small barracks.

I followed her, trying to change her mind, but she shut me out. Her final edict, "You cannot enter India," lacerated my heart. Her colleagues, who until that moment had seemed stiff and impassive, suddenly, upon her declaration, hoisted their rifles and ordered me to leave at once. Shaken, I walked back some distance along the road behind me and sat in the shade of a large neem tree. As I gazed out across the flat green Punjabi countryside, my mind reeled. Where to go? What to do?

How long I sat there stunned, I do not know. But when awareness of my surroundings broke through again, I knew that I would not turn back. If that gatekeeper would not grant me entry into the land of my heart's desire, I resolved to remain in the dust under that tree. Never once did I dream that entry to India would be denied me.

Ignorant as I was of politics, how could I have known then that India and Pakistan were on the eve of their third war since the Partition of India? How could I have guessed that one year later in December of 1971, bloody war would break out along this very border where I now found myself? No one had warned me that I was hazarding one of the tensest borders in the world, second in notoriety only to Berlin's Checkpoint Charlie. At Hussainiwala two armies stood poised, one in Pakistan and one in India, each facing the other in military standoff across the divide.

All this was unknown to me on that sunny winter afternoon as I trudged along the road back toward Pakistan. There, from a seat on the dusty ground, I could see my frustrated antagonist pacing beyond the window of her small barracks. Was she expecting a bribe from me, a soul she had mistaken for one possessed of the affluence derived from a Western birth and white skin? Could she even guess all I'd been through to reach this lonely border post? *Will I ever get to India?* I wondered. After hitchhiking all the way from London, could it really be possible that I would be turned back at the Indian border for want of money? Feeling like an exile, my thoughts turned to my best friend and traveling companion. At our parting Gary, too, had looked like an exile. Where was he now? What had become of him? Did he ever make it to Israel? As I sat in the dust of that Punjabi plain watching the breeze ripple through a stand of blooming mustard nearby, I missed my old friend.

Over a period of hours, I kept getting up from beneath my tree and returning to the border, but each time, the official ignored me. Finally, as a last resort, I pleaded with her again. She stomped the ground with her military boot. "You are testing my patience." She jabbed her stubby finger toward my face, her lips trembling. "You are rejected. Do you hear me? This is my last warning. Don't disturb me again."

I turned back to my tree and passed the day in turbulent thought. As the sun was setting, I observed that a shift was about to take place at the immigration desk. An elderly man had come to relieve the woman from her duty. He was a tall Sikh in an elegantly wrapped turban the same drab beige color as his military uniform. The female official pointed to me, making sure he understood that I was not to enter India. Then an army jeep carried her away.

Not knowing what else to do, I meekly approached the new officer, praying in my heart of hearts. I handed him my passport and pleaded, "Please allow me entrance into your great country."

His voice was cold and disinterested. "I was warned that you are a nuisance. I have been given strict orders to reject your entry. Now show me sufficient money or go back."

Tears sprang to my eyes as I explained my life and my spiritual aspirations. "I have left behind the comforts of America to search for India's spiritual treasures. Risking my life, I've hitchhiked all the way from London to reach your homeland. I yearn to find the way to God. Please be kind to me. Someday, I promise, to do something good for the people of India. Honestly, sir, I will help your people. Please give me a chance."

Tears filled his eyes. "Give me your passport." As the light of day was fading, he thumbed through my document then gazed into my eyes and said, "Sometimes a man must follow his heart. I believe in your words." Reaching down to the table, he lifted the stamping tool by its wooden handle. Then he pressed the rubber script into an ink pad and with a *thump*, stamped my legal entrance into India.

"It is done," he said, closing the passport and handing it back to me. With an affectionate smile, he placed his hand on my head, "Son, I give you my blessings. May you find the truth you are crying for. Welcome to India."

II

Mother India

1

A S I WALKED DEEPER AND DEEPER into the Indian countryside, the feeling that I had finally arrived overwhelmed me. Evening was falling. In my heart, I embraced every leaf in the trees, every star in the sky, and every plant in the fields. Everything was thrillingly new, yet profoundly familiar. As the twilight faded, a deep stillness covered green fields that stretched out into the distant horizon. Birds warbled and frogs and crickets chirped. I knew that on my own I could never have survived my arduous journey to this point. By the grace of God, I had come home.

I walked for some time before flagging down a car. The driver greeted me warmly and conveyed me to Firozepur, a town in the Punjab state of North India. After a pleasant discussion, we arrived at the railway station where he offered me passage to Old Delhi. In the course of my entire journey, I had never traveled on a train, always hitchhiking or riding on the backs of trucks, in poor people's buses, once on a camel, and on overcrowded ferries. Now a railway passage was being offered. How could I refuse? Looking forward to a restful trip, I walked along the platform with my new friend.

Up and down the platform, vendors wheeled carts filled with full meals, snacks, fruits, biscuits, souvenirs, magazines, medicines, tea, and clothes. Food I had never seen before were being cooked right on the carts. Someone was deep-frying vegetables dipped in a thick, yellow batter in a vat of hot oil. On another cart, flat dough was tossed into smoking hot oil, instantly expanding like a balloon. Nearby, a wood fire burned under an iron wok filled with sand. The cook stirred, roasting peanuts. The smell of pungent spices fried in cooking oils mixed with the scents of diesel fumes and incense.

Hundreds of people conversed noisily as they waited for the next train. Many families picnicked along the railway tracks. Porters balanced heavy trunks on the tops of their heads with only a small piece of red cloth separating their skulls from the heavy luggage. Beggars pleaded for charity, displaying their deformities. Some were blind or lame; some had missing arms or legs, burnt faces, or mangled limbs. One man suffering leprosy put his rotting fingers in peoples' faces, begging. Mothers in rags carried babies whose eyes oozed with pus and were swarmed by flies. Each of these unfortunates moved from person to person. Overhead, the speaker system crackled non-stop announcements. Underfoot, human spit dotted the platform. In spite of the clamor and hubbub, dozens of people peacefully slept on the ground amid it all.

When the announcer blared the arrival of our train, all passengers suddenly rose to their feet. The whistle blew. Black smoke poured from the engine's chimney and steam hissed. As the locomotive approached the platform, hundreds of people suddenly began running full speed alongside the moving train. My host also ran as fast as he could. "Follow me," he yelled. All at once, when the train slowed to a reasonable speed, everyone began diving in the windows. My friend, while sprinting, tossed his bag in through a window and leaped in behind it. I was running as fast as I could. He screamed at me from inside the train, "Jump now, before it's too late." Diving into the window of a moving train looked incredibly dangerous, but everyone was doing it. Finally, after a few cars had passed, I took my leap, grabbing onto the ledge of a window. But I was losing my grip. Looking down, I shrieked. The huge steel wheels rolled steadily along the track below me. I felt so frail. Struggling and confused, I somehow pulled myself up and squeezed through the window and onto the moving train. Within seconds, two others squeezed in through the same window behind me.

Inside the moving train, I looked around to see people diving and crawling in through every window. By the time the train had come to a halt, every compartment was so jam-packed that no one else could possibly squeeze in. There was no question of a seat. On the wall, a sign read "maximum 60 passengers." I couldn't count, but there were perhaps 200 people crammed in all around me. There was no possibility of a conductor even attempting to check for tickets. My host had dived into another compartment several cars ahead of mine and I never saw him again.

Everyone rode for free. This was often the system, I later learned, for third-class compartments in the Indian Railways. There was a price to pay, but not in rupees. Inside the train, the crowd pushed and shoved, yet everybody appeared surprisingly peaceful. This was, after all, their routine mode of travel. As the train stormed ahead, people were still hanging partially outside, yet they seemed quite composed. Looking up to the ceiling, I saw metal bars used for baggage storage. Instead of bags, dozens of people had crushed themselves on the racks. I spotted an empty space of about three feet and climbed up. Somehow, by tightly curling my body, I, too, squeezed in with the rest. From the shelter of a baggage rack I looked down at the densely packed crowd and felt as if I were riding in luxury. I was thrilled to be in India.

That old steam engine hissed and whistled through the night until, in the first gray light of the morning, it pulled into the station at Old Delhi. Not knowing where to go, I disembarked and walked aimlessly along the railway platform.

Suddenly, somebody called out my name. "Monk, Monk! I can't believe it's you." I turned around to find two Frenchmen I had met in Switzerland. We had discussed *The Tibetan Book of the Dead* on the shores of Lake Geneva. After a joyful reunion, they invited me to shower and rest at their place. By rickshaw, we arrived at a low budget traveler's haven, the New Crown Hotel. I took a shower and then rested on a veranda floor until a long, furry tail wagged against my face and interrupted my sleep. I opened my eyes only to see a brown monkey sitting at my side. His green eyes stared at me from his pink face. I looked back. Never had I imagined that wild monkeys could roam freely in a crowded metropolitan city. Twenty or thirty more jumped from rooftop to rooftop playing or scouting for food. Down below, shopkeepers were just opening, and they used sticks to scare the pests away.

My stay with the Frenchmen was brief since they were leaving for Nepal. Saying good-bye, I left the New Crown Hotel behind and stepped into the street.

Excitement filled me. What would unfold next in my spiritual quest? I was just turning twenty and Mother India, my cherished destination, was now spread out before me. Coming out of the hotel, I found myself in Chandni Chowk, a crowded bazaar. The street was lined with endless shops. Music blared, incense burned, and monkeys frolicked. I saw brightly colored saris, turbans, and decorations in all directions. Children played with their cricket bats while cows strolled gracefully by. After spending months in the grave and stoic culture of the Middle East, I found this atmosphere to be a celebration of life. I walked through the crowded street observing and absorbing everything I could.

Suddenly a man blocked my path, greeting me with a barrage of questions. "What is your name? From what country have you come? What are your educational qualifications? What is your purpose for coming to India? How do you like my country?" We walked together as he listened to my answers. "Would you like a refreshment?" he asked.

"Please," I replied, excited.

He led me out of the bustling street into an empty stall where a bare-chested man with only a skimpy cloth wrapped around his waist took the order. Flicking aside the homemade cigarette he was smoking, the shopkeeper picked up a block of some resin and rubbed it against a stone slab until it became a pale green paste. With his index finger, he then scraped the paste into an iron vessel and mixed it with water, shaking it vigorously. Pouring the preparation into a glass, he tossed in some powdered spices, stirred it with a spoon and slammed it down on a table. I looked to my host, who was wearing a peculiar smile. "Drink this," he said, "It is a natural beverage, non-alcoholic and very healthy."

Not having had food or drink for over a day, I drained the cup. "Would you like another glass?" he inquired. I gratefully accepted a second glass of the green concoction and then a third and a fourth. Its astringent taste was unrecognizable.

"What is it called?" I inquired.

Still smiling, he replied, "Bhang."

I had never heard this word before.

He said goodbye, and I continued to walk down the bustling street. Suddenly, my mind exploded into a state of intoxication. Strange colors, sounds, and countless people spun around me. My body trembled as waves of disorientation washed over me. I was walking right into people. Paranoid, I grew convinced that everyone was staring only at me. How could I have known that *bhang* is an intoxicating drink derived from the cannabis plant? Thinking it harmless, I had innocently drunk four glasses of it in a very short time. Horror overcame me as I realized that I must have unwittingly broken my vow never to take intoxicants. Now I walked alone in this strange, unpleasant state, struggling to reach the end of the road where I might escape the intimidating crowds. The road seemed to never end. I helplessly bumped into humans, cows, hogs, and rickshaws.

I reached the end of the road and stared through an intoxicated blur at the massive stone walls that guarded the Red Fort. The immense proportions of what, in the seventeenth century, had been the royal palace for the Mughal Emperor Shah Jahan were overwhelming. In the front was a large open area where a crowd had gathered. In my delirium, I went to see what was going on. An old man in a white turban was sitting and blowing through the two bamboo reeds of an exotic musical instrument. A foot and a half long, it was made out of dried pumpkin. This snake charmer played a haunting drone all the while swaying from side to side. Surrounding him were about a dozen hand-woven baskets with lids. A big, bearded man wearing black robes and a red turban opened each basket. The crowd gasped. As the charmer played his hypnotic song, poisonous cobras appeared, raising their fearsome hoods. Forked tongues slithered in and out of their mouths. They swayed from side to side as if dancing to the music. The bearded man then opened other baskets, revealing different varieties of snakes until finally he lifted out a huge serpent about twelve feet long and three inches thick. The crowd stepped back.

Before I could blink, he darted toward me and wrapped the monstrous serpent around my hips. Slowly, the serpent crept upward, encircling my waist and chest in its cold, strong coils and locking my arms against my trunk. Its face was only inches from mine and I could practically feel and smell its breath. Its slitted eyes stared into mine, its forked tongue flitting in and out. My heart pounded and my limbs trembled as the snake tightened its grip. The intoxicating bhang was still at a peak. Nightmarish hallucinations, spinning, and paranoia seized me. Meanwhile a growing crowd of onlookers encircled me, keeping at a safe distance.

Suddenly, a man stepped forward and spoke in English. "What is your name, sir? What country are you from? Why are you in the coils of this dangerous snake?"

"Please help me," I gasped. My captor tightened its grip as soon as I spoke. It was as if the serpent jealously demanded my total attention.

The big, bearded man in the red turban came up and stared me in the eyes as if I were a foreign invader. Waving his hands like weapons, he shouted at me, "50 rupees. 50 rupees." Finally, someone in the crowd explained to me in English. "He will only take the snake off if you give him 50 rupees."

Straining, I somehow spoke, "But I have no rupees."

The onlooker warned, "Then you will remain like this," and nonchalantly departed.

My mind went blank, and fear and humiliation rushed through me. Everyone stared at me, a strange foreigner encircled by a snake. Perhaps they thought I was part of the act. A painfully long half hour passed with the snake licking its lips and from time to time staring into my eyes. All the while, the old snake charmer played his hypnotic song and the cobras swayed.

Thoughts seared my consciousness. It was only my first day in India. Gazing at the teeth of the snake I wondered, *Is this the place I risked my life for? What would my mother and father think to see their son so far from home in this condition?* With no other recourse, I closed my eyes and prayed. *If you have something for me to do in this world, Lord, please help me.* As I offered this simple prayer I felt a small burst of inner peace.

Finally, a lone man emerged from the crowd with prayer beads in his wrinkled hands. Sympathetic to me, he bargained with the snake man and donated ten rupees toward my release. To my relief, the snake man chanted mantras, inviting the serpent into his hands again. The crowd cheered as the snake released me. Thanking the donor, I quickly fled across the street.

There I saw some men sitting on wooden chairs and popping what looked to me to be red candy into their mouths. They asked if I wanted some. Still curious to experience the customs and foods of India, I ate one. My mouth erupted into flames. Drenched in sweat, tears flowing from my eyes, I grabbed for water and drank, but water had the effect of kerosene on fire, increasing the pain. I had just eaten a red-hot chili pepper, the first one I had ever seen or tasted. Again a crowd of curious onlookers circled around me. I politely thanked the men and went on my way. I thought of the saying, "One man's food is another man's poison." That saying had come alive for me as a burning message. I thought of my studies and observations of Judaism, Christianity, and Islam, and my explorations of Buddhism, and some of the philosophies of India. What is enjoyed by one person creates suffering for another. What we experience of the world is so relative, so conditioned by our subjective experience. In the same way, God, who is absolute, reveals himself to different people in different ways. My mouth still burning, I realized it would be very narrow to think there was only one way to God.

As evening approached, the effects of the bhang and the pepper at last subsided. Returning to the Chandni Chowk Road, I strolled aimlessly amid the fervor of the bustling bazaar. I had nowhere to go. Among the throngs of pedestrians a man emerged with a welcoming smile. Thrilled to discover that I had come from so far to understand his traditions, he invited me to dinner at a roadside restaurant. Our outdoor table was just inches from the road. As he told me about his family customs, a white cow nuzzling its calf strolled by. So gentle was their demeanor, so graceful their movements, and so innocent their large, beautiful eyes that my heart melted. This mother doted on every movement of her child. While the calf was suckling her milk, she licked her offspring tenderly. Lying down just inches from our table, she played with her little calf. In all of my life, I had never been so close to a cow, having only seen them in distant pastures as we raced by on the highways. Now I was struck by how these animals shared loving exchanges so similar to those of a human mother and her child.

A waiter rushed by and slapped down our plates. I was famished, as all I had eaten all day was some bhang and a chili pepper. Struggling with the serpent, too, had stirred my appetite. I delved into the food. Halfway through the meal, my gracious host asked, "Mr. Richard, would you care for me to explain what all this is?"

"Please."

Pointing to each item he described, "This is *chaval*, or rice. This thing that looks like wheat bread is called *roti*. These vegetables are called *subji*. This soup over here is made with lentils, and we call it *dhal*. Here is our condiment, or *chutney*." Then he pointed to some small chunks on the rice. "And this is meat."

His last three words exploded in my mind. I stared first at the meat chunks and then at the cows. At that moment, the mother cow leaned over to lick my leg. My heart cried. Why should a beautiful life be slaughtered to eat some meat? She loves her child. And this innocent calf loves its mother. Why had I blindly participated in this? Why are we all so blind and deaf to the horror in every slaughterhouse? How has human society become so insensitive to the cruelties inflicted upon these children of God? Although the meat I had been eating was not cow meat, this was the first time I had made the connection between my diet and the suffering of animals. Thinking of the thousands of animals killed every day in America, I lost my composure and dissolved into tears.

My poor host didn't know what was happening. "Is something wrong, sir? Why are you so disturbed?"

I could barely speak. "Thank you for everything, sir." I stood up and pushed my chair back. "Please excuse me, but I'm feeling ill." On my way out, I patted the mother and her calf and she reciprocated with a slow lick to my hand.

Thousands of people crowded the street. In the midst of this bustle, and to my delight and surprise, Ramsey and Jeff walked right into me, not noticing me at first. I had not seen them since that day we were separated in Kabul.

"Monk, it's you!" exclaimed Jeff. "What a relief to see you. I can't believe it."

"Hey, mate," exclaimed Ramsey, "We've been worried about you since that day you were lost."

Shaking hands and embracing, we were together again.

They brought me to stay with them on the roof of a cheap hotel. As I was dozing off on a bed of twine under the starlit winter sky, the mother and baby cow appeared in my dream. Their gentle, tearful eyes looked helplessly into mine while the blade of a butcher ruthlessly slaughtered them for meat. From my heart burst the biblical commandment: "Thou shalt not kill." I awoke from the nightmare in a state of unbearable nausea and rushed to the toilet for relief.

The toilet consisted of a cement hole on the roof, surrounded by crumbling brick walls and a sheet of aluminum for the ceiling. It was pitch dark in there with no plumbing except for the *bhangis* or street sweepers who emptied the toilet by shovel. Digging out the waste into a bucket, they would carry it away on their heads. But this toilet was overdue for a cleaning. Stool soaked with urine had piled up above the floor level. With no control over my vomiting, I was trapped inside that latrine. Insects buzzed and bit and I felt something moving over my feet. All I could do was heave with nausea and shiver in a cold sweat. All the while, in my mind's eye, I could see only those two cows gazing at me with their innocent eyes. In that dark, rooftop latrine in Old Delhi, I offered another vow before my Lord. *I will never again eat meat.*

This concluded my first day in India.

The next morning, Jeff and Ramsey appealed to me. "We've been a great traveling team. Let's stay together and tour India."

"We've passed through a lot together," I said, "and bonded as brothers. I can never repay both of you for your kindness and friendship. But I want to travel the Himalayas as a hermit. Please bless me to do so."

Jeff spoke first, and kindly. "We understand. In fact, we were expecting you to do something like this." He placed his large hand on my small shoulder. "May you find what you're seeking. We'll really miss you."

A cloud of worry veiled Ramsey's face, as I was like his little brother. His eyes reddened. "How are you going to survive that kind of life?" But seeing my resolve, he forced a smile and exclaimed in his Australian accent, "It's been a great journey, mate. Cheers."

Before we parted, Jeff handed me a small note that read: "It's kind of sad in a way, we are each going his own way—in search of himself. I'm sure you'll find it."

ON A COLD DECEMBER MORNING IN OLD DELHI, while planning my journey to seek the yogis and sages in the Himalayas, I happened to look up at a sign plastered on an old Victorian building. "The World Yoga Conference" was to be held in New Delhi beginning that very day at 9:00 A.M. Excited, I rushed to the site. A British Yogi, Christopher Hills, impelled by his love for India, had organized this huge and prestigious event. The coming four days promised a bazaar of gurus, yogis, lamas, pundits, and sages sharing their gifts with the world. Some, after decades of seclusion in the jungles, promised to show their faces to civilization. From morning to night, darshans, or spiritual meetings, were conducted simultaneously in seven locations. Later, I would learn that 800 yogis had assembled for the event. I couldn't believe my good fortune.

On the first day, in a large tent, I first met with one of the greatest masters of yoga–Sri B.K.S. Iyengar. He lucidly explained the science of Hatha Yoga while his students demonstrated various *asanas*, or physical poses meant to harmonize body, mind, and soul. One of Sri Iyengar's students sat with his legs wrapped behind his neck. Another balanced on his forearms with his legs bowing backward touching his head with his feet. Yet another stood motionless on his head, while another balanced on one foot, arched his back, and pulled the other foot over his head. Another yogi swallowed a long strip of cloth, then pulled it back out as an internal cleanse. Another student, to clean his sinus, fed a thin rope up through his nose and pulled it out through the mouth, pulling it back and forth.

I marveled at how easily they had accomplished these practices due to their early training from an accomplished master. All the while Sri Iyengar explained the benefits of each technique to the audience. I was deeply inspired by the conviction and compassion in which he taught. I could feel his burning desire to share the gift of yoga with all of the world. In the years to come, Sri Iyengar was to become a dear friend and well-wisher.

As I came out of the tent, I was approached by an older man, a small, thin Buddhist monk from Southeast Asia. He had a shaved head and wore bright orange robes. Beaming a bright smile, he introduced himself as Bhikku Vivekananda. He was fascinated by me, a young American seeking God, and we became close companions at the conference. Bhikku was the spiritual leader for thousands of monks in a monastery in Thailand. He had traveled a great distance to attend the conference. Although over fifty, he was as exuberant as a teenager. He explained the Buddhist philosophy with his sweet Thai accent as we explored the yoga conference together.

It was also at this conference that I first met Swami Rama, who has since become renowned as the founder of the Himalayan Institute. A towering man with a regal stride, pristine robes, and a dignified aura, he commanded awe. His eyes were deep and dark and his head was framed by silver hair brushed straight back to his shoulders. I was eager to learn more about him, as I would be about many participants in the conference. In addition to asking his disciples to tell me about him, I read everything I could get my hands on about his background.

Born in 1925 in a village in the Himalayan Mountains, Swami Rama had wandered since childhood living among *rishis*, or holy men, in the jungles. With a booming voice, he told of how his Guru had instructed him to bring the ancient wisdom of the Himalayan sages to the west. "Try your best," Swami Rama's master had told him, "but whenever you feed your ego or try to do anything selfish, you will not succeed. This is my blessing to you, that whenever you want to become selfless, loving and without ego, you will find a great force behind you, and you will never fail to achieve some good."

To exhibit the powers of yoga, Swami Rama brought several American doctors. While he entered into yogic trance, they connected his body with modern diagnostic devices. He demonstrated, among other things, that he could consciously raise the temperature of a spot on the left side of his hand 10 degrees, slow his heart rate from 74 beats per minute to 52 in just 50 seconds, produce specific brain wave patterns on demand, consciously move a physical object half way across the room, and even stop his heart altogether. Coming out of trance, Swami Rama explained, "All of the body is in the mind. Mind over matter is developed by control of consciousness. You really do not need to know many things, but you definitely need to practice what you know." Placing his palms together he added, "I did this not to show that I am superhuman, but to demonstrate the science of yoga." He went on to explain that although yoga had been practiced since the most ancient times, it was the greatest of all sciences. Based neither on superstition nor sectarianism, yoga could achieve what modern scientists cannot explain. "It is," he said, "the science by which one realizes the enlightened state within."

I was sincerely impressed with Swami Rama. When I appealed for his blessings, he said in his deep voice, "The foundation of your spiritual path will be to keep the company of holy people." He raised his open palm to me. "The blessings of sages will carry you across all obstacles on the path."

Each night I slept alone on the ground under a banyan tree near the conference center. In the morning I awoke to the calling of a hawk as it spread its wings from the nest overhead and soared high into the sky. While waiting for the doors to open, I meditated under that tree in the brisk Delhi air. The closing session of the conference was held in the Vigyan Bhavan, New Delhi's largest concert hall. Three thousand people assembled that evening seeking knowledge and blessings from the assembly of yogis. Christopher Hills, the organizer, reminded us of our fortune to be in one room with so many spiritual masters. Then, to our surprise, he announced that the program must conclude punctually at 7:00 P.M. (unbeknownst to us at the time, he had been informed that he and other swamis would be shot by fanatics at 8). But how could a program of so many swamis and yogis, especially in India, possibly end on time?

When it became clear that not all would be given the chance to speak, one yogi jumped to his feet and attacked Hills with a barrage of insults. Christopher endeavored to satisfy everyone present, but an underlying tension was brewing.

Minutes before seven, Christopher Hills nervously took the microphone in his hand and stood in silence for a moment before announcing that the time had come for the conference to end. A swami began chanting the closing *Om*, which I knew to be a divine vibration meant to put our consciousness in harmony with God. This punctual ending outraged some of those who were deprived the chance to speak.

Even while the *Om* was being sounded, an uproar ensued as some yogis grappled to grab the microphone. One of them got hold of the mike and rambled on like a politician with flaming eyes. Aghast, the audience watched a battle of yogis on stage. Were these the men who were supposed to bring peace and harmony to the world? Nobody knew what to say or do.

Bhikku Vivekananda and I just shook our heads. My innocent expectations were disappointed. Finally, Christopher Hills heroically seized the microphone and wrenched the wire out of its socket. Then he disappeared behind the stage. The conference was over.

After the program, in a solitary hall near the chaotic auditorium, I came upon a tall, thin man with long white hair, flowing beard and saffron robes, a person of venerable presence who looked like an ancient sage right out of the Holy Scriptures. Swami Satchidananda welcomed me with a jolly smile and entrancing gaze. As a disciple of the famous Himalayan saint Swami Shivananda, Swami Satchidananda had taken the ancient science of yoga to the West and had followers from around the world. His interfaith work would always seek to bring people of various religions together under the "oneness of the spirit." In his first meeting with the Pope, Swami Satchidananda praised the Pope for working to unite Christians worldwide and then quickly added, "Now, why don't you come forward to bring the whole world together? Not only Christians should come together, but all people in the name of religious harmony."

An appearance at the legendary Woodstock Rock Festival had given him overnight national fame as the "Woodstock Guru." The promoters of the event asked that he give the opening address, hoping he would create a peaceful mood. After being flown in by helicopter, he faced hundreds of thousands of hippies and spoke about how sound controls the universe and America leads the world. He urged the American youth to use their sound of music to create peace and joy. "Let us not fight for peace," he said, "but let us find peace within ourselves first."

During the World Yoga Conference I had carefully observed how he maintained grace and dignity through the recent chaos. Now, in a tender voice, he said to me, "I am sorry that you had to see this fighting. Please understand that each person is on his or her own level of progress. Even among practitioners, we cannot expect everyone to be perfect. If we judge others for their faults, we fall into a trap. It will be better to put your faith in those of good character and cultivate your own yoga practice."

His disposition was calm and poised, and his slow and powerful way of speaking moved me. He instructed me that we are beings of happiness, love, and light, but that we have forgotten this because we identified too much with our bodies and minds. "We were fine originally and lost that fine-ness. That's when we became defined." The essence of yoga and religion, he said, was to enable us to align with our forgotten nature as spirit. "Yoga is the process of re-finement." He stressed that we overcome our mind's tendency towards self-centered concerns in order to realize our essential nature. "There is only one cause for all our worries and anxieties. Selfishness." The process he taught for attaining this realization of essential nature became known to the world as Integral Yoga, a synthesis of six yoga disciplines. Swami Satchidananda presented spirituality in a down-to-earth, insightful, and often humorous manner.

With gratitude, I took my leave. Standing erect, the Swami spoke with a graceful wave of his slender hand. "Be sincere and disciplined in your practice. A true yogi is one who lives with the highest human conduct." He closed his eyes, took a deep breath, and opened his palm to me in blessing. "Richard, you have come a long way. May you discover the treasure of your heart."

That night Bhikku Vivekananda and I attended an independent lecture by the world-renowned author and orator J. Krishnamurti. We entered a large tent, or *pandal*, and took seats in the second row of chairs. As the pandal rapidly filled, a man of about sixty sat beside us. His name was Dilip. "Would you like to hear something about the life of J. Krishnamurti?" he asked. "He's my teacher."

"Please," we responded.

He crossed his legs, leaned back in his chair, and began. He told us that Krishnamurti was born in South India in 1895 and, as a child, was discovered by the renowned clairvoyant Charles Leadbeater. Both Leadbeater and Annie Besant, who was the leader of the Theosophical Society, proclaimed that the child was the "vehicle" of the same World

Teacher who spoke through Christ. Annie Besant educated the boy in England and brought him around the world where thousands received him as the next Messiah and formed the "Order of The Star" around him. When he was twenty-seven, he formally accepted the role as the enlightened master and was soon worshipped by over 60,000 members.

Dilip leaned forward, "But in 1929 he rejected his position as Master, dissolved his religious movement and—"

Suddenly everyone rose as J. Krishnamurti appeared on the stage. An elderly man of seventy-five, he was small and slender and impeccably dressed in a Nehru jacket and loose pants. His smooth-shaven face was worn by the lines of age and his predominantly white hair gave him a scholarly distinction. His soft eyes glistened with enthusiasm as he welcomed the assembly graciously in a British accent.

Soon enough, though, he launched into a call for revolution. Shaking his clenched fist, he declared, "You have too many gurus in this country. They have told you what to do, what to think, what to practice. They are the dictators." Pin-drop silence filled the tent. "Truth is a pathless land, but yoga, with its breathing and postures, is nothing more than psychosomatic acrobatics. Ashrams and monasteries are concentration camps of the mind." He paused and looked right into my eyes. "When you have a system of meditation, it is no longer meditation but is utterly futile and has no meaning whatsoever."

He told a story about the devil who was walking with a friend. They witnessed a man ahead of them on the road picking up a brilliant object. The devil's friend turned and asked what the man had found. The devil answered, "He has picked up the truth."

"That's a bad business for you," the friend said.

"Not at all," the devil replied. "I am going to help him organize it."

To make his point more emphatic, Krishnamurti closed his eyes and slowed down his speech. "We must bring about a revolution in ourselves. But how can this take place when our lives are superficial? Spending years in the office, living a shallow, empty existence..."

He leaned forward, "Man cannot be enlightened through any organization, creed, dogma, priest, or ritual, nor through any philosophic knowledge or psychological technique. He has to find it through understanding the contents of his own mind, through *observation*, not through intellectual analysis or introspective dissection."

I shuddered to think of how this discourse would affect my dear Bhikku Vivekananda. After all, he was the guru of thousands of monks in an organized monastery teaching meditation and ritual. I turned to him and whispered, "Bhikku, he is attacking everything you have dedicated your life to. What do you feel?"

Bhikku's eyes widened in wonder and he exclaimed, "What he says is true."

Taken aback, I asked, "What are you going to do now, Bhikku?"

His features turned grave. "I will have to think seriously about this."

For the next few days we attended a series of talks given by Krishnamurti where he demonstrated an amazing power of logic and conviction. Even though he was renowned as one who could answer any question and defeat any argument, on a personal level he was gentle, kind, and humorous. I pondered his teachings. Eastern literature was filled with histories of enlightened saints who carefully followed their religion or their particular Guru. How could I disregard them all on the basis of one man's realizations? However, Krishnamurti had impressed upon me that superficiality had no place in spiritual life. We must take personal responsibility. If we become overly attached to the externals, we may forget their very purpose: to purify the heart.

One day while sitting under the shade of a peepal tree with Bhikku, I asked if he knew what he was going to do. He ran his finger along the edge of his begging bowl. "Yes, Richard, I do," he said. "I will return to my monastery in Thailand."

"Really?" I responded, "So what is your opinion of Krishnamurti's teachings?"

He stared off into the middle distance in thought, and then spoke. "I will follow Mr. J. Krishnamurti." A mischievous little smile played on his lips. "Shall I tell you how?"

"Yes, please."

"I will reject the teachings of the teacher who teaches us to reject teachers and teachings," he jested in his sweet Thai accent.

Later that day, I bid farewell to Bhikku and wandered on foot to Connaught Circus, the commercial center of the city. Here I sat beneath an ashoka tree and wrote these words to my family in America:

The way India is affecting me is beyond words. This is all that could be said. Deep love lies in my heart for all of you. I pray that you are well.

Richard
New Delhi, India
December, 1970

Designed by the British, Connaught Circus was laid out in an immense circle surrounding a spacious park. Exploring the enclosed walkway, my attention was drawn to a hand-painted sign that read, "S.S. Brijabasi and Sons Religious Artwork." Stacked on the sidewalk were hundreds of 8 x 10 prints. I was lured to look closer. The prints, full of marvelous figures that struck me as very odd, yet very beautiful, were like windows into a world of colors, mysteries, and magic. I wanted to keep one as an object for meditation. Looking into my small bag, I saw that I had barely enough change to buy a single image. For about an hour I sat on the sidewalk searching the selection. Among the pictures was a beautiful woman with eight arms holding swords, choppers, and spears and riding on a lion, then a fantastical, somewhat pudgy man with the head of an elephant who was sitting on a mouse. Flipping through them I found the picture of a handsome blue person with four arms decorated with elegant ornaments lying on a multi-headed serpent, next was a tranquil yogi immersed in meditation with snakes wrapped around his limbs, the moon resting on his head and water gushing up from his hair, and then there was a heroic boy holding a spear while riding on a peacock. I came across a magnificent monkey, wearing a crown, whose eyes shone with devotion. Smiling, he flew through the sky effortlessly carrying a mountain in the palm of his hand. As I rummaged deeper through the stack of prints, I discovered a person with a dozen heads, each of a different species and multiple arms. Gruesome people were flying into and being devoured by his flaming mouths. This art was beyond description, the figures unbelievable. Were they from fairy tales or mythology? I didn't know. But I felt that the art was inspired.

I wondered how I could possibly choose only one.

Suddenly, from out of the stack of prints appeared a personality that attracted me like no other. He had a bluish complexion, wore a peacock feather in his crown, and played a flute while posing gracefully beside a river. Behind him a white cow stared lovingly and a full moon bathed an enchanted forest in pearly light. Spontaneous tears filled my eyes. The person in the picture seemed to fill my very soul. Why was this happening to me? I felt him calling me. But how? It was only a painting, and of a fantastical person I didn't even know. His name was written on the bottom in an ancient alphabet I couldn't read.

I gave whatever money I had to the shopkeeper, but it was not enough. He smiled and gave me the picture anyway, a picture that I would not part with during the rest of my travels. Who was this person in the image? For a long time, that was to remain a mystery.

3

THE YEAR 1970 WAS SOON TO CONCLUDE. I had just turned twenty and dreams of the Himalayas were luring me north. I did not know much about where I was going. I only knew that this part of the world was home to many great sages and holy people I longed to meet and learn from. I was so excited to be in India, on the precipice of great discovery, that I had little time to miss my family. They didn't know where to reach me so I had had no letters from them since arriving. Still, before making the journey to the Himalayas, I wrote the following message to my home, so far away.

My Dear Family,
Today I am leaving Delhi to go to the mountains to study. I do not know if I will be able to write often where I am going. Please do not worry if I do not write for a while. With God on my side, what can harm me?

With love and thought,
Richard

I secured free passage on a third-class train and headed to Rishikesh, a holy town in the Himalayas known for its many ashrams. As the steam engine chugged forward, leaving Delhi behind in a billowing trail of black smoke, I watched the sunrise from my window and prayed that my pilgrimage to the Himalayas would inaugurate a new day in my spiritual quest.

Hours later, I arrived in Haridwar, a holy place on the bank of the Ganges about 140 miles northwest of New Delhi. From there, I commenced the remaining fifteen miles to Rishikesh on foot. By now in my readings I had devoured page after page about the spiritual legends of the Himalayas. Being here was a dream come true.

My first sight of the Himalayan foothills thrilled me beyond imagination. The foothills were covered with dense green forests;

I saw each tree as a conduit emitting tranquility. A solitary pilgrim, I trekked along an earthen footpath swooning with anticipation. From a distance, I caught sight of something that, like a spark, detonated an explosion of emotions—the river Ganges. I hurried forward and pressed my fingers into the cool, rushing blue waters. I shivered.

After sitting for an hour in that lonely place, I walked along the riverbank and came upon "The Divine Life Mission," which is the ashram of the renowned Himalayan saint, Swami Sivananda. This was the ashram where he performed his meditation and established his teachings. This was the guru of Swami Satchidananda, the regal Woodstock guru I had met in Delhi. Sivananda's prolific writings, humanitarian efforts, and personal example had attracted world fame. I had already read some of his writings and was delighted to come across this place. Entering, I learned from some of his followers that before Swami Sivananda left this world in 1963, he chose as his successor Swami Cidananda Saraswati from among his accomplished disciples. Swami Cidananda happened to be at the ashram when I arrived. For a couple of days, I simply soaked in the peaceful atmosphere of the ashram. I learned that ashrams, so prevalent throughout India, were supported by their gurus' followers, who maintained ties to the everyday world of business and commerce. After the fourth day there, I asked if I could meet Swami Cidananda. I was led into a simple room where I was greeted by the Swami, an extremely friendly, respectful, and humble man who invited me to sit on the floor with him.

Swami Cidananda, I had learned from disciples, was born in South India in 1916 as the eldest son of a fabulously wealthy landowner. Around the age of twenty he heard a calling to live as a renounced monk, giving up all material comforts to serve God. It was at that time that he began to serve lepers, building huts for them on the vast lawns of his home and looking after them personally. In 1943 he finally left his home and moved into the Ashram of Swami Sivananda in Rishikesh where he was quickly recognized as a brilliant lecturer.

Each morning I attended his lectures. He was a thin man with a shaved head and saffron robes who was revered by both Himalayan ascetics and seekers from the West. Swamiji sat in a cross-legged yogic pose, speaking eloquent English, with precise hand gestures. "Life is meant for the realization of God," he emphasized. "If you die without attaining

God-realization, your life is in vain. You have wasted away this precious gift of human birth given to you by God."

He identified a common problem among spiritual practitioners— that one can do meditation in the morning and evening, but during the activities and dealings of the day, show petty-mindedness and selfishness. This, the Swami explained confidently, undid whatever one accomplished in the hours of meditation.

He placed a great emphasis on the cultivation of virtue as a fundamental part of one's spiritual evolution. He compared this cultivation of virtue to the work of removing stones, pebbles, weeds, and brambles, therein making the soil fertile so that one could plant a garden. Throughout the day, he taught, one must sacrifice for others. Morality and high ethics, he said, were like roots on the tree of yoga.

He stressed that the disciple should have complete faith that in this age one could achieve God-realization through mantra *japa*, the recitation of God's holy names. "You should practice chanting the Lord's name," he said, "until you reach a state in which the *japa* goes on uninterruptedly in the mind even while sitting or standing, eating or drinking, walking or working, waking or sleeping."

I didn't know how to chant the Lord's name, but I was very impressed by Cidananda's teaching. One evening, while he and I sat on the floor of his lantern-lit room overlooking the Ganges and the Himalayan valley, the Swami enthusiastically described the details of my travels with uncanny accuracy and even voiced my most intimate thoughts. He told me how I had left home and discovered a burning passion to journey to India, risking my life along the way to get here. I had never told him these things, but he knew everything so perfectly. While he poured his blessings upon me, I sat in awe. It was rare to encounter someone with such power and fame who could remain so simple and kind.

Longing to be in seclusion and purify myself, I thanked Swami Cidananda and left the ashram. The next morning, while sitting on the banks of the Ganges River, I composed a short letter to my mother.

My Beloved Mother,
I am doing just what I think I should be doing here.
Rishikesh is a holy city on the banks of the Ganges River.

I feel there is much to be learned in the peace and tranquility I have found here. It is quite difficult for me to tell you what I have been doing. I am not so much a tourist or a sightseer. I am more a seeker of my own soul. Living in the East is an entirely different way of life than living in America or Europe. Everything is completely different. It is very difficult to say when I will return. But I will say this: I deeply miss all of my family and all of my friends and I long to see all of you. But you must understand that I must carry out what I set East to do, find the true meaning of life.

Your loving son,
Richard
Rishikesh, Himalayas, India
January, 1971

I boarded a crowded boat to cross to the eastern side of Ganges. Large fish swarmed around the small vessel as we sailed across the sparkling aqua current. A cool breeze swept over me. With deep breaths, I drank it in, listening to the hypnotic chant of students reciting the Vedas, or holy scriptures, on the riverbank. Reaching the other side, I walked alone southward along the bank of the Ganges in search of solitude. Finding a quiet place, I meditated, feeling myself millions of miles from the world I knew. Hours later, I spotted someone approaching. Pacing slowly, with eyes fixed to the riverbank, was a holy man with a golden complexion, gray beard, hair draped down his shoulders, and robes that rippled in the mountain breeze. He radiated tranquility.

I stood to receive him. Raising his soft wide eyes, he spoke. "You do not know who I am, but I know you. I have been observing your determination. Now, offer the clothes you wear to the river Ganges, and today, I will award you the cloth of a *sadhu*."

"What is a sadhu?" I asked.

"A sadhu is a wandering mendicant who has forsaken worldly attachments to pursue a divine life. Or you may just say, a monk."

On the bank of that holy river, he presented to me two pieces of unstitched white cloth made of thin cotton. He showed me how to wrap one piece around the lower part of my body to form a *lunghi* and one piece around the upper part to form a *chaddar*. Then he gave me a loincloth of two strips of cotton called a *kaupin*. Honored to receive this gift from such a kind soul, I placed my western clothes into the river's sweeping current and offered a prayer. My turtleneck and jeans were gone forever.

Before departing, the man whispered something in my ear. Given the letter I'd just written home, I found it uncanny. "The Ganges will be your mother," he said. "She will reveal this to you in time."

A few days later, I came upon Veda Niketan, a small, lonely, one-story ashram made up of about a dozen austere rooms. The residents, like many people I was meeting, were preparing to go to Kumbha Mela, the biggest religious festival in all of India. When I heard twenty million people were going to be there, I decided to stay behind. Not far behind Veda Niketan, I found a cave in the forest where I made my residence. Each morning before sunrise, I walked to the bank of Mother Ganges and looked out into her swift current. She was perhaps a hundred yards wide at this spot, her riverbank covered with soft, silvery sand. Like jeweled ornaments of multi-colors, smooth rocks ranging from tiny pebbles to boulders weighing thousands of pounds lined her banks. Feeling unworthy of the treasures I sought, I felt a desperate need for purification.

Then and there I resolved that for one month I would sit in silence and prayer from sunrise to sunset. I prayed to have a spot revealed. Just then, before my eyes, I noticed a series of small rocks in the river. They formed a natural bridge to a much larger, somewhat flat rock about twenty-five feet from the bank. This rock was to become my cherished place. I would sit on it every day from sunrise to sunset, surrounded on all sides by the forceful current of the Ganges. In that incredible panorama I felt so tiny. At dusk, as I returned to the cave, I passed an old man who sat on the ground selling miniature carrots displayed on a piece of old burlap. As I passed, he would offer me one. Ganges water and one carrot a day, I decided, would be my only food for thirty days.

The solitude of that rock became my shelter. I sat from dawn to dusk facing upstream. To my left, on the opposite bank, I could see in the distance an occasional yogi sitting in meditation. To my right stretched the beautiful Himalayan foothills. The closest mountain took the shape of a heart at its very top. I gazed on it for hours thinking of how it symbolized for me the heart of God, a heart that is unlimited, giving ultimate shelter to all beings; a heart that is majestic and beautiful. Just as in climbing a mountain we leave behind the earth where we stand, to reach the heart of God we have to leave behind unfavorable earthly attachments. Sincere spiritual practice is an uphill climb, and no matter how many difficulties we face, we have to continue looking upward with hope. The mountain provides all support for those who strive to reach its top. Similarly, if we are sincere, the Lord will provide us with the means to reach his supremely merciful heart.

Spread out around me on all sides was Mother Ganges in her winter dress of sparkling, undulating aqua. Her waves rippled and swirled as if intoxicated by her own beauty. No human artist could capture even a moment of this unending display. And, just as her art was created, it simultaneously disappeared. I took from this a lesson. All beautiful forms of this world are in the process of transformation. Nothing is stable. With every moment, our reality is changing. Mother Ganges, like nature, is constant, but no manifestation of hers remains. Likewise, all that we hold dear in this world is imperceptibly vanishing. We cannot cling to anything. But if we can appreciate the beauty of the underlying current of truth, we can enjoy a reality deeper than the fickle waves of joy and sorrow. I sat, a submissive student, trying to learn from my teacher. She begins her course from high in the Himalayas and flows without cease to the sea. Innumerable obstacles—huge rocks, fallen trees, or even mountains—block her way, but nothing will stop her journey to the sea. Gracefully she flows over, under, or around all obstructions. Mother Ganges teaches us that if we want to attain the sea of our aspiration, we must persevere in our goal and never be discouraged by the inevitable obstacles that come on our path. All impediments are like rocks in the river of life. We should flow around them and never give up. With the Lord's help, there is always a way.

As I sat on that rock, I imagined that watching the flow of the river was like watching the passing of life. If one is inside the river, one is greatly affected by it, but if one sits on the bank, one can observe it with detachment. Mother Ganges teaches that if we learn to be detached from our ego and the flurry of the mind, senses, and the world around us, and observe life with a sober disposition, we gain wisdom. After the sunset each evening, I returned to my cave in the forest and contemplated the gifts of the day.

One day I thought about how millions of years of history had been enacted on these banks. During the Age of the Aryans, spirituality flourished. Alexander the Great came and went. Then the Mughals, conquering North India, ruled for centuries only to be vanquished by the British Empire, which was eventually driven away by Mahatma Gandhi, Subhash Chandra Bose, and the Indian freedom movement. Slavery and freedom, war and peace, political conquest and defeat— like the seasons they had all come and gone. Through it all, timeless Mother Ganges patiently flowed toward the sea. Truth, too, was unchanging. Whatever may happen in this world, however dramatic, it could not disturb the flow of truth.

Many objects, I observed, were swept along in the current, among them leaves, flowers, uprooted trees, a dead buffalo, and even human corpses. If an object remained in the river's flow, I reflected, it would eventually be carried to the sea. But in the course of time, most things would be diverted to the banks and their progress halted. The spiritual path and the spiritual teacher are like the current of Mother Ganges and the students are like the objects carried along on the river. If the follower remains faithfully in the current of the holy teachings, he or she will be carried to the ocean of spiritual truth. But many temptations and diversions appear along the banks, promising comfort and happiness, tempting the follower to come out from the current that leads to one's heart's aspiration. Not all aspirants will remain faithful, but those who do can reach the ocean of enlightenment. I wondered, *Who will be my teachers? And can I remain faithful?*

Early one morning, just before sunrise, as I looked downstream into the current that never slept, I considered her thousand-mile journey. The sea was calling and each drop of water patiently flowed in the current to her ultimate destination, so far away. *Mother Ganges is teaching me that patience and steadfastness are required to follow my calling.*

I never really stopped to think why I had left behind the promises of the world to sit alone on a rock in the Ganges and endure a rigorous, self-imposed fast. Why did I act in such extreme ways, like a person obsessed? At the time, I did not feel that these were *my* choices. I felt the mysterious hand of destiny leading me forward.

One brisk winter day, while absorbed in meditation, sweet harmonica melodies began to play in my mind, drawing my attention away from anything else. My consciousness flowed irresistibly toward that imaginary music. Concert after concert was performed within the theater of my mind. A longing impelled me to reunite with my beloved harmonica, which I had not played since arriving in India. Every day from before sunrise until after sunset, I had remained faithfully on my cherished rock. But this day would be different. An urge pulled me away, and leaving behind the rock and river, I returned to my cave to play.

As I lifted the harmonica to my lips, something strange came upon me. An invisible force induced me to return to the river. With each step, my impatient senses burned to play my instrument. Wading across Mother Ganges' stream, I crawled onto my rock. There, as on all other days, I sat on the cold coarse surface. But today I held the harmonica, and my heart surged with a wave of affection that made my whole body shiver. How could a piece of metal and wood induce such an emotional state? This harmonica had been my dear friend into whom I poured the intimate feelings of my heart. So confidential was our relationship that I whispered to it secrets that no one but God and I would ever know. It translated my inner joys, sorrows, and aspirations into sweet music. Over time, there had evolved between us the natural dialogue of the player and the played. In many ways, we were like lovers.

As if jealous, my harp seemed to demand my full attention now. I wondered what it was I truly desired in my life. Gazing upstream into the distant mountains, a quiet sadness touched my heart. I understood that my trusted companion was now distracting me from my path. Standing on that rock, I peered into the deep blue waters of the Ganges. Then I gazed on my harmonica, knowing there was no other like it within a thousand miles. Moved, I revealed my heart to my comrade, not in song this time, but in simple words. "My dear friend, I thank you for being my faithful companion all these days. In times of pain and loneliness, you have always been there to give me solace and joy. How patiently you heard my innermost thoughts and transformed the words I was unable to speak into songs that touched people's hearts." I wept.

Next, I turned my eyes to the holy river and prayed. "Mother Ganges, in offering to you what I hold so dear, I wish to offer my unworthy heart to God. Please accept it."

With both hands I pressed the harmonica to my heart and then cast it into the Himalayan breeze. The instrument floated upward, as if in slow motion, and then descended. My heart shivered on hearing the "plop" as my dear companion disappeared forever in the current of the Ganges.

Often the most precious gifts of life come in ways we neither plan nor expect. Some say it is due to chance, others cite karmic destiny, and yet others believe the Lord may intervene in our lives at any moment. One afternoon, as my awareness drifted away from my meditation toward the hymn of Mother Ganges' rushing current, her powerful, gentle waves seemed to be singing an anthem of wisdom and love. Held captive by that sweet song, I listened effortlessly. This became my meditation. From dawn to dusk, I simply meditated on the song of the river.

Days later, while sitting in the crisp winter breeze I gazed up at the Himalayan sky; puffs of milky white clouds hovered from a limitless sapphire dome. Below me, the current swirled, rippled, and foamed. The sound of the river was a symphony that released me from the shackles of my thoughts. From the river's song emerged thousands of celestial voices, all chanting in unison the sacred syllable *Om*. The sound captured my mind.

Another evening as the sun was setting, I observed golden winter clouds floating in the deepening blue sky. The mountains were cloaked in a gown of purple and appeared so alive I felt them to be breathing. Flocks of white cranes, black nightingales, green parrots, and birds of vibrant blues, reds, and oranges soared across the sky, each chirping, warbling, or trilling its own sweet song. Except for the birdsong, that evening the Ganges valley was still with an almost mythical silence. My mind floated, recalling how God had taken from me so little and given me so much. For a moment I contemplated that to the degree one feels unworthy of grace, one will be grateful when it comes. It is gratitude that makes the heart receptive to receive the Lord's blessings. Closing my eyes, I merged again in the endless chant of *Om*, the river's song. It was just so beautiful. I felt on the verge of something extraordinary. Then I heard something that seemed to ascend from the depths of

Mother Ganges' heart. The choir of thousands of celestial voices sang a slow, entrancing song that seemed to reverberate throughout the river valley:

"Hare Krishna, Hare Krishna
Krishna Krishna, Hare Hare
Hare Rama, Hare Rama
Rama Rama, Hare Hare."

Through the song of the river, I felt, God had whispered this beautiful mantra into my ears. It was a mystical rite of passage, carrying me on a wave that lifted me closer to my aspiration. My heart soared with gratitude. Inadvertently, I found myself breaking my long silence and singing these words aloud with the river. No intoxication on earth could come close to that experience. The meaning of the song was unknown to me, but it stole my heart. What *did* it mean? I believed that this mystery, like the mystery of the picture of the blue boy, would be revealed in time. In sacrificing the song of my harmonica, I had inherited the song of the Ganges.

4

A T THE MONTH'S END, I WAS MORE THAN READY to end my fast. Remembering a peanut vendor in a shop near the Choti Walla Restaurant at the Swargashram, I ventured there with one rupee that a pilgrim had donated to me, then the equivalent of approximately twelve U.S. cents, expecting a handful of peanuts in return. But when the shopkeeper saw one rupee, his eyes lit up and he quickly patched together some old newspapers to form a large shopping bag and filled it with peanuts. "Today I will feast!" I rejoiced as I walked along the jungle path back to my cave.

Deeper into the forest, I found myself face to face with a huge brown monkey who blocked the path like a customs agent. Growling and baring his pointed teeth, he sized up his victim with small, piercing green eyes. Thick brown fur clothed his muscular form. He had a bright pink face, scarred from past battles, gnarled pink fingers, and shiny pink buttocks. Suddenly, he sprang on me. In one motion, he seized the bag of peanuts, swiftly kicking my chest to catapult away. Gasping, I stumbled back a few steps. When I regained my footing, I smiled, seeing that he had disappeared instantly into the jungle with the whole bag. Some of the peanuts, though, had fallen on the ground during the scuffle. *Oh well*, I thought, *these will have to suffice for breaking my fast.* As I stooped to pick them up, another monkey leaped from a tree, scooped up every peanut and disappeared. I was not spared a single nut.

As I proceeded to my cave for the night, my stomach rumbled. *Compared to the treasure of spiritual experience, worldly acquisition is like those peanuts,* I thought to myself.

People lie, cry, and die for a few of these peanuts. They fight and struggle for a handful. Wars are raged over them. But at any moment, a monkey, another's greed, or even the inevitable march of time may plunder from us our cherished peanuts.

The next morning I traveled by foot to the far end of the Ganges bank in Rishikesh. Climbing up a mountain, I arrived at Sankaracarya Nagar, the ashram of Maharishi Mahesh Yogi. In this hermitage, earthen pathways wound through ancient trees, fragrant bushes, and flowering vines, leading to quaint huts for meditation. Further on, I found myself at the brink of a steep cliff that offered a spectacular view of the river Ganges. Near the edge of the cliff was the simple home of Maharishi. Entering, I found myself in a room with a flower-adorned altar. On it was a picture of the Maharishi's Guru, Brahmananda Saraswati. He had a white beard. His long white hair was combed back from his clear brow, and he was sitting on a tiger skin. An esteemed yogi, he was the first in over 150 years to be awarded the post of Shankaracarya of the Himalayan region Jyotirmath, a role similar to a pope's.

In the morning and evening, the residents of the ashram came together in Maharishi's *puja* room to chant hymns, offer articles of worship, and conclude the ceremony with group meditation. Somebody told me that Maharishi preferred to meditate in the basement—a dark, cave-like cellar into which few descended. The cool, silent cellar turned out to be my favorite place to meditate also. It was here that I especially felt the Maharishi's presence as a deep peace and serenity permeated my mind and body.

Maharishi was born in 1917 in central India and graduated with a physics degree from Allahabad University. For thirteen years, he served his guru, Brahmananda Saraswati, in the position of secretary. Before departing from the world, his guru gave him this order: "What I have taught you also contains knowledge of the technique for the householder, which has been misinterpreted and forgotten over the centuries. Don't think of money for traveling here and there. Don't worry and don't be afraid of being alone. Don't be anxious about anything. Begin working and everything will go by itself." To prepare for his mission, Maharishi entered the caves of Uttar Kashi for two years of solitary meditation. Then in 1955, he began teaching Transcendental Meditation (TM) and established his hillside ashram at Rishikesh. From 1957 on he began his travels across the world.

The Maharishi Mahesh Yogi taught that, by practicing TM, our consciousness enters into finer and more subtle states. The goal is to enter a state more subtle than our ordinary states of wakefulness, sleep, and deep sleep. To meditate, then, is to experience a consciousness beyond the subtle existence of the mind and ego, for it is in that liberated state of pure being that we experience the eternal self. Maharishi was especially creative in harmonizing modern scientific technology with the ancient sciences of yoga. Although the Maharishi was abroad while I was there, under his inspiration in the sanctuary of his ashram, I read his books, *The Science of Being* and *Art of Living*, and six chapters of the Bhagavad Gita.

Every evening at Sankaracarya Nagar, I spent time with an Australian sadhu named Bevin, a leader of the ashram and one of Maharishi's closest disciples. Together we met in his hut where we listened to reel-to-reel tapes of the Maharishi and discussed his teachings. I remember hearing the Maharishi say in his high pitched and often giggling voice, "Here we make no empty promise of Heaven after death but the positive experience of 'Heavenly Bliss' during lifetime. Come, whoever desires it."

His technique was simple—only fifteen to twenty minutes of "effort-less" meditation in the morning and evening, and no need for lifestyle changes or religious and philosophical adjustments. He taught that life is essentially bliss, that we are essentially beings of bliss, and that TM can bring us into contact with this blissful state of being by gently directing our mind's natural tendency to seek after happiness toward the inherent happiness of our being. He would sometimes refer to this as "watering the root and enjoying the fruit."

It was winter, and quiet. Hardly another foreigner besides Bevin and I turned up at the ashram. Bevin told me how only a couple of years earlier, the Beatles, Donovan, and Mia Farrow and her sister Prudence had visited and stayed with Maharishi. Since that time, the influence of yoga and meditation was spreading throughout the world.

Meditating in that sanctified forest and sleeping on that mountaintop were priceless gifts. On three occasions, Maharishi Mahesh Yogi appeared in my dreams. He sat cross-legged, holding a flower, his long graying hair and beard merging with his flowing white robes. Soft light emitted from his rounded face. Although a physically small man, his presence was immense. His soft but penetrating gaze seemed to be calling me into a realm of timeless peace. He did not speak, but simply smiled upon me, closed his eyes, then disappeared.

In time I returned to the solitude of my forest cave, where I asked myself why I left the Maharishi's ashram. After all, I had only enlightening experiences there. Obviously, the Maharishi was a powerful, loving force and everybody had been so kind. *Why did I move about like this?* Again and again in the months to come, I would ask myself this question and each time I would conclude that I wished to learn from many paths and teachers before I committed myself to one. *Until I gain the faith to dedicate my life to a path and a master,* I reflected, *I will remain a wandering pilgrim.*

One morning, while walking along a forest trail, a sadhu with a curious smile plastered across his face stepped right in front of me, refusing to let me pass. His almond shaped eyes squinted into mine. He had a tiny nose, flat face, cropped hair, and copper complexion. Who was this man? What did he want from me?

"I have been sent for you," he said, "but you do not recognize me."

Surprised but silent, I wondered what was about to transpire. He gripped my hand. "The greatest of saints lives in a cave nearby. My mission is to bring you to him."

"How do you know me?" I asked.

"That you do not need to know. Follow me."

Intrigued, I followed this sadhu, who told me he hailed from Nepal, into the depths of the forest where we walked along a stream on an overgrown path. As we passed, we crunched the twigs and trampled the foliage beneath our feet while rustling through the bushes. To our left, wild boar scuttled into the brush. We approached a clearing where my guide pointed up to a mountaintop. There I could see the smoke-blackened entrances to three caves. The sadhu led me up a set of narrow stone steps that were more like a thirty-foot ladder carved into the steep rock. After climbing to the top, we entered one of the caves where a fog of smoke burned our eyes.

There, in the lotus posture with back erect, sat an amazing being. His thickly matted hair extended beyond his back and several feet onto the ground behind him. About six feet tall, his physique was powerful. He wore only a rope around his waist and a loincloth covering his groin. His eyes were closed in meditation. He seemed to have entered into another world, a world far beyond time or space. An aura of indescribable tranquility emanated from his motionless form. This was Mahavirdas Tat Walla Baba.

We sat beside him, waiting patiently. The scent of smoldering wood from his sacred fire blended with the earthiness of the ancient cave. Holy Sanskrit scriptures lay on a stone shelf. His wardrobe, a wrapper of old burlap, was folded beside him. The Nepalese sadhu told me that he often meditated all night long. "Let us wait patiently," he said, "until he comes out of his spiritual trance." Finally, the yogi opened his dark shining eyes and stared into mine with the intensity of laser beams. My guide served as a translator. In a deep, compelling voice, the Baba spoke.

"God is one, and everything originates only from Him." Lifting his palm, he touched his index finger to his thumb. "The cause of all suffering is when we forget our identity with God. That is called *Maya*, or illusion. God is everywhere. You need not search to find Him. If you call Him with sincerity, He will reveal Himself to you. God sees within the heart not the externals. There must be no duplicity. You may wander through the jungles your whole life, but God is within your heart. When you meet Him there, you will see that He is everywhere."

I was struck that he seemed to address my deepest concerns. I was a wanderer, looking for God in my heart.

The Baba's hands then rested on his knees. His dark eyes emitted power and vibrancy and seemed to read my mind. "People are chasing the temporary. Do you not see that they are on the road to death?" His every word seemed like a sword cutting my own selfish conditionings. "You have renounced worldly life. This is good. Do not go back. Meditation will bring you supreme peace." We spent the hour listening to him. I left with the promise that we would return the next day.

After climbing back down the ladder of stone, the sadhu and I were greeted by an ascetic woman in a simple white sari with a long, black braid down her back. Mirabai and her husband lived in the forest and they cooked meals for all of Tat Walla Baba's followers. She promptly invited us to her home. "Would you like to hear about Baba?" she asked, as we followed behind her.

"Yes," I replied. The Nepalese sadhu nodded.

"Well," she began, "Baba was from the state of Punjab. From early childhood, questions burned in his mind. When he saw the suppression of the Indians under British rule, he wondered why a country with so many saints and scriptures did not have a solution for this suffering condition. Burning with the thirst for enlightenment, as a child he abandoned his home to search for a guru. First he went to Ayodhya, which is Lord Rama's birthplace, and then entered into the forests of the Himalayas, where he met with his Guru. At the feet of his Master, he learned the path of enlightenment." The three of us approached a hut made of clay and straw. Mirabai graciously opened the wooden door and invited us in. Offering us a mat to sit on and a clay cup of water, she asked, "Shall I tell you more?"

"Please," I urged, savoring the cool water she'd collected from the stream.

"Since the age of about sixteen, Baba has remained in these caves. He subsists on only wild herbs and fruits, and wraps a worthless burlap cloth, which we call *tat,* around himself for clothes. That is why he was given the name Tat Walla Baba, meaning a Baba, or holy man, who is clothed with burlap cloth." She went on to say that for fifteen years he lived in seclusion perfecting the practice of *asthanga* yoga. Gradually people recognized his enlightened state and started coming to him. He never allowed anyone to touch his body or cook for him. She took a deep breath and opened her eyes wide in awe. "With my own eyes, I have witnessed his power to read people's minds, see into the future, and heal the sick. In fact, when a yogi had unbearable migraine headaches, Baba came to him in a dream, removed a white fluid from his head by mantra, and cured him forever."

I felt so privileged to be there. She directed our gaze to a photo she kept of the Baba on her small altar and with folded palms she asked, "Would you like to hear more?" We nodded eagerly. "Baba meditates for long hours and sometimes for days. He keeps the sacred fire always burning and daily ponders upon the scriptures." Then she turned to me. "You have come all the way from America to become a sadhu. I honor your bravery. I will pray that you achieve your goal."

Before saying goodbye, she placed in my palm an unusual sweet made of translucent green pumpkin cooked with crystallized sugar. It immediately melted in my mouth, bursting with flavor. I had never tasted anything like it. Seeing my reaction, she said softly, "This sweet is called *petha.* Do you like it?"

"This is my very first sweet in India," I replied, "It's amazing. But do ascetic yogis eat these?"

She smiled like a mother toward her curious child. "You will be surprised to see what yogis may eat."

The next day I returned to the Baba's cave. After some time, my Nepalese friend left me alone with Tat Walla Baba, who sat immersed in his meditation. The whole night passed, yet he did not move. Absorbing his peace, I meditated close by. The sun rose, gently illuminating the green Himalayan jungles with a veil of gold, exposing the higher mountains in the distance, considered by many to be the abode of God. Far off, I could see Mother Ganges winding her way down from the heights to the plains, through forests and valleys spotted with sages performing their worship on her banks. From my place on a straw mat, I gazed below into the lush foliage and as time passed, I began to notice large, colorful snakes coiling through the jungle looking for prey. I saw wild elephants grazing on the trees and even the occasional spotted leopard moving through the green.

A picture flashed through my mind of my neighborhood in the Chicago suburb of Highland Park, with its flat manicured terrain, children boarding the bus to school, and parents driving off to work. I couldn't believe where I was. Nearby to the Baba's cave were other caves where several of his ascetic disciples resided and where I lived for some days.

Inside Baba's cave, inhaling the astringent smoke from the sacred fire that burned through day and night, I felt purified. As he sat with his back erect, Baba would read from scripture for about three to five hours. The rest of his time, he was immersed in meditation. If he rested at night, he woke several hours before sunrise to meditate, study, and perform yogic *asanas*. In mid morning, he wrapped his matted hair into a huge coil on the top of his head and took me to bathe in a stream and collect a pot of water. On the way back he collected herbs and fruits for subsistence and wood for the fire. Once I saw him effortlessly lift a huge log and carry it back to the cave.

On one early evening, as the trilling of birds filled the forest, Baba, through our Nepalese translator, gave me a good jolt. "I welcome you to spend the rest of your life in our caves. This is my invitation to you." He then closed his eyes, entering into a trance.

His words reverberated in my mind while I pondered the seriousness of the decision I had to make. One morning, I came out of my meditation and thought:

It would be a blessing to live under the guidance of such a holy man in this sanctified forest. Still, if I dedicate myself to following a guru, I should never disgrace him by changing my mind later in life. I wish to find a master and a path that I can dedicate my life to.

I asked myself whether I was certain that he was my master and this, my path. Moments of thought passed, then the answer came. I had experienced great inner awareness and inner joy while meditating with Tat Walla Baba. Still, I was uncertain. There was a pulling in my heart to meet the holy people of India and visit the sacred places, to experience the many varieties of spiritual paths. Then and only then would I feel I could make the most crucial decision of my life.

My mind rested, feeling that this was an honest approach. But I had to be careful about how I revealed my decision to Tat Walla Baba, for I was not dealing with an ordinary human but an extraordinary man with supernatural powers. Several days passed in this way. In his company, my meditation brought indescribable experiences. Finally, when I was about to reveal my thoughts to him, he already knew. Before I could open my mouth, he spoke the words I planned to speak. Soberly, he gazed into my eyes and extended his palm. "Good-bye. May God be with you. *Om tat sat.*"

5

DEPARTING FROM THE CAVES of Mahavirdas Tat Walla Baba, I lived again as a wandering mendicant. The winter was coming to a close. As the sun shone warmer, the days grew longer and spring buds appeared in the trees and bushes. One day, as I walked along a jungle pathway headed north, I came to the Laxman Jhulan, a long suspension bridge that crosses high over the river Ganges. Standing in the gently swaying middle, I beheld the Ganges descending from the Himalayas, ornamented on either side by temples, ashrams, and *rishis* performing their rituals. I crossed the bridge and walked along a dirt pathway and into the forest. Suddenly I froze, unable to bear the chilling sight before me.

Dying people, some naked, others in filthy rags, were wailing in agony, their faces shriveled and deformed, their noses melted away, their hands and feet mangled with bloody stubs instead of fingers or toes. Emaciated from starvation, people lay in holes in the ground that served as beds and buried their bodies with blankets of dirt against the cold. All of them were pleading to me through desperate eyes. I was horrified. I had stumbled into a leper colony.

Dozens of lepers surrounded me, crying out, "Baksheesh! Baksheesh! Baksheesh!" Pressing their bodies against mine, they stuck their mangled, bloody hands into my face and demanded charity. But I had nothing to give and, imprisoned by a wall of putrefied flesh, couldn't move a single step. They refused to leave me be. "Baksheesh! Baksheesh! Baksheesh!" The mob shoved so tightly around me that I was being smothered. I could not escape the stench of their breath and oozing, rotting flesh. "Baksheesh," they screamed. My mind reeled in confusion, struck by ambivalence. On the one hand, I was outraged to be so accosted. On the other hand, I pitied them, granting that their misery justified their behavior.

An endless twenty minutes passed. Agonizing, I tried to come to grips with what was happening. *Leprosy is contagious*, I thought.

Will I be afflicted to suffer and die with them? Will this mob ever release me?

Screaming "Baksheesh," the lepers tugged and shoved one another in a desperate skirmish. Their eyes seared mine with stares of anguish. Finally, they patted me down for valuables. What I didn't give, they were determined to take by force. When they realized that I didn't have anything, they dispersed.

Taking a deep breath, I took a few steps, but was stopped in my tracks. I saw an old woman in rags, her nose melted into the decaying flesh of her deformed face, lying on the ground in misery. Our eyes locked. In her teary eyes I felt the tender love of a mother, an affection real and rare. She wanted nothing from me but to open my heart to receive the love she so longed to give someone. She was beautiful. Folding her fingerless hands in a gesture of respect, she then extended her disease-smitten hand to bless me. All my fear of contamination was slain by her affection. I rushed to her side and placed my head under her palm to receive her blessing. "May God bless you, my child," she prayed. "May God bless you." I looked up and saw that now her face was lit with a supernatural joy, the joy of giving. I wept, feeling the whole ordeal to be a small price for this unforgettable blessing.

Walking on, I found a spot by the river and gazed down into the rushing current. I tried to glimpse beneath the swirling waves, but was unable to see below the surface into its mysterious depths. Although that woman was plagued with a despicable disease, beneath the surface she was a beautiful soul who only wanted to love and be loved. In my contemplation, I extended the analogy.

Today the river is exposing how we have the tendency to judge others by their surface appearance, and to find only their negative qualities. But if we search beneath the surface we discover that a myriad of strains mix together to create a particular person's nature. The faults we perceive are likely to be the effect of circumstances, the psychological response to trauma, abuse, rejection, heartbreak, insecurity, pain, confusion, or disease.

I thought of the people who had nearly killed me in Istanbul, the racists that hated the Blacks during the civil rights movement, the people who had mistreated me because of my long hair, and even myself, how I had judged the generation I'd rebelled against, thinking older Americans wrong to be so concerned with money and security when, in fact, they had lived through the Great Depression, a hardship I couldn't fathom.

If we understand the underlying cause of what we think of as bad in someone, instead of being hateful, we will be compassionate. For is not every soul inherently good? A saintly person will hate the disease but love the diseased.

I decided to leave Rishikesh and traveled north into the higher elevations of the Himalayas. In Dev Prayag, I came upon a man whose character is forever engraved in the slate of my memory. On a chilly morning, as the stars were fading and the new day's sun about to emerge, I scrambled down a mountain to the place the rivers Bhagirathi and Alaknanda converge. From the point of this confluence the river is called the Ganges. The river's song there was tumultuous. I submerged myself for a bath, ignorant of the power of the current.

As I took a step forward, the rushing current yanked my feet from under me and swept me toward the treacherous rapids. At that moment, a powerfully built man who happened to be bathing beside me seized my arm with a vice-like grip and pulled me toward him and then onto the riverbank. My rescuer then placed his right palm on my head and, with great feeling, chanted a series of mantras for my protection. This was how I first met Kailash Baba.

A holy man who appeared well into his sixties, he had a powerful build and matted, graying hair that he coiled around his head. When unwrapped, I would learn, it extended to the ground. Decades passed since he had cut any hair from his body. He had a square face, large brown eyes, high cheekbones, and a full mouth of teeth, something quite rare among old sadhus. All he wore was a single quilt garment that extended from his shoulders to his feet. In his hand, he carried an iron trident with a huge *damaru* drum tied to the top. This drum had two heads, each about twelve inches in diameter on opposite ends of a hollow wooden drum base. Between the heads a ball hung on a string. When the Baba shook it, the ball bounced back and forth, beating loudly on the drums. A metal begging bowl and an old blanket were his only other possessions.

Kailash Baba was the first to instruct me in how to survive as a wandering ascetic. On cold nights, we slept on hillsides often overlooking a river. One night, he offered me his blanket, and although I at first refused to take it, he insisted. For many nights, we slept together under the one blanket. He taught me how to procure food and medicine by identifying the edible roots, fruits, and leaves in the forest.

Taking me into a village, he instructed me on the proper behavior in which a sadhu respectfully begs alms. Unlike in the West, the begging of religious mendicants in rural India is considered an honorable way of life because the people receive so much in return from the sadhus they serve by giving alms. And as Kailash Baba was such an exalted person, I, too, felt that this was an exalted thing to do. He educated me in surviving on dried, flat, chipped rice. Because it is the cheapest food, any grain merchant will gladly offer it, and because it does not spoil, it can sustain one in the jungle for weeks. All that is required for a meal is to add some stream water to a portion of it. He taught me also how to clean my body by brushing my teeth with the twig of the neem tree and washing my skin with mud from the riverbed. Beyond lessons in how to eat and clean myself, he taught me how to respect not just sacred rivers, temples, trees, the sun, the moon, and the sacred fire, but also snakes, scorpions, and wild animals. He did not speak English, but seemed to have a mystical ability to transmit ideas to me, particularly the idea that God was in the heart of all creatures. He taught me to see the soul within the heart of a poisonous snake, for example, and to show my honor and respect for the creature by giving it its space. And when among other sadhus, he trained me in the etiquette of how to address different denominations and how to eat with them.

As we traveled alone together, he became more and more like a father to me and he lavished affection on me as if I were his own son. Although we never talked, where there is affection of the heart, communication transcends all language barriers. By a simple gesture, pointing of the finger, smile, or frown, he taught me whatever I was to learn. To an onlooker he appeared to be a fearsome, unkempt mountain of a man hardened by austerities and carrying an iron trident. But I found in him one of the kindest, gentlest men I ever met. Whatever simple food we collected, he always fed me to my satisfaction before he would take anything. When I resisted taking first, he easily defeated me by his innocent glance. In fact, every time he looked at me, affectionate tears filled his eyes. This man, a mountain of affection, drew a love from my heart like a lifelong friend.

From him and the other people I was meeting, I had begun to learn more about the different manifestations of God, or deities that made up the pantheon of Hindu religions. I wasn't sure how I felt about all of these deities and the many forms they took; it was all quite foreign to me. But I could see the deep love and devotion these manifestations inspired. My mind was open and I was eager to understand.

A worshipper of Shiva, the aspect of God presiding over material existence and its destruction, Kailash Baba constantly chanted the mantra *"Om Namah Shivaya."* As we walked along the forest pathways, he would call out the names of Lord Shiva, "Jai Sankar," "Hey Vishwananth," "Hey Kedarnathji," and "Hey Uma Mata." Whenever we were with other the worshippers of Shiva, or Shivaites, we chanted together. When the chant reached its crescendo, Kailash Baba would enter into a trance and wildly play on his *damaru* drum. It resounded almost to a deafening volume. That drum made the sadhus wild with joy. Madly, they shook their heads, their matted hair whipping from side to side. Some clapped, while others sprang to their feet to perform a mystical dance.

Among these homeless sadhus, Kailash Baba was highly revered. One aged ascetic in the forest confided to me that Kailash Baba could be several hundred years old. No one really knew his age. He possessed supernatural yogic powers to heal the sick and perform extraordinary feats. "About thirty years ago, I witnessed his miracles," this man said. "Crowds of people flocked to him, worshipping him as a God. But," he told me, "Baba realized that divine life is not about powers or fame. He vowed to never speak of his powers or make a show of them. He had neither disciples nor an ashram, but roamed alone in the forests of the Himalayas." I was not surprised to learn that Kailash Baba possessed great yogic powers, and I was impressed, but it was his character and devotion to his spiritual path that impressed me most.

As the days passed, I began to sense that Kailash Baba wished to enter into seclusion. I didn't want to impose myself on him and

I knew that it was time to move on. Bowing at his feet, I begged for his blessing. Baba laughed heartily and, with tearful eyes, hugged me with the strength of a bear then offered his blessings with the recitation of a mantra. I was touched both by the unyielding quality of his detachment and the softness of his heart as he bid me farewell. Like a father and son we loved each other, but as roaming sadhus, we sensed that we would never meet again.

This bittersweet experience of developing dear relationships, then moving on to never again see the people I was meeting was part of the life I had chosen. It was difficult for me, but the pain of separation kept the joy of our relationship alive in my heart. As I turned and walked away from Kailash Baba, I prayed never to forget him. And I never have.

I t was about this time that I shared my realizations in a letter to my family.

> *Dear Family,*
>
> *Better to live in poverty than to sell one's soul for an empty palace of gold. Better to live unknown than to sell one's soul for the empty and futile pleasures of admiration, name, and fame. Where there is no inner freedom, there is no life. Better to die at once than to be deprived of seeking the ideal of one's life.*
>
> *I have been doing what I consider to be invaluable studies with great men and places of the East. Such study, please understand, takes much time. I have barely started to even approach the beginning of such a vast study. I am selfish and egotistical. I am ignorant and blind of truth. I am perhaps the farthest away from knowing God. So it is that such a fool as me needs much time to see the blissful light of supreme truth that shines within you and me.*
>
> *Love,*
> *Richard*

A spark of spiritual longing, ignited in my childhood, had been fanned into a flame while praying in a cathedral of Florence. It was kindled into a blaze while meditating on the Isle of Crete and fueled higher and hotter by my challenges in the Middle East. Roaming the Himalayas in the company of holy men, that sacred fire in me now blazed furiously. Resigning my life to this purpose alone, I prayed to the Lord to help me.

I was now twenty years old. My arduous lifestyle had reduced my weight to about a hundred and ten pounds. The one set of robes I wore were tainted gray by the silt of the rivers, ponds, and streams where I washed them. My skin had become coarse and toughened by the elements, my lips chapped with cracks, and my hair matted. I wore cheap rubber sandals and my feet were dyed brown by soil and cracks formed around the border of my heels. The life I'd chosen was taking some toll on my health, but I showed little concern—my yearning for enlightenment now burned more brightly than ever. I loved my life as a homeless sadhu and I rejoiced in anticipation of the next adventure and in being in the presence of magnificent souls who were advanced in their spiritual paths. Roaming through the forest, I often asked myself, *Will I ever find the one path I should tread, the teacher I should follow?*

One day, while in Dev Prayag, I was invited to a nearby ashram for a meal among the sadhus. While there, a yogi emerged from the jungle. Nobody knew him. He advertised for the doctors of the town to assemble that evening. After several doctors arrived, the yogi made his appearance and then, with a thunderous voice, challenged, "Materially infected, you have more faith in modern science than your own heritage. God has brought me out of the forest to crush your foolish pride. By yogic power I will shut down all my life systems and die. You test me with your medical instruments. In exactly thirty minutes, I will rise from the dead."

With his back erect, sitting in a lotus position, he inhaled and exhaled with great force about twenty times. Then fully inhaling, he stopped breathing and sat motionless. Each doctor went to work with stethoscopes and other devices, but not one could detect a heartbeat, breath, or pulse. They were astonished. "He is clinically dead," one doctor announced. Skeptical, I also stepped forward and borrowed a stethoscope to check his pulse and heart beat, but there was none.

In New Delhi, Swami Rama had given me a spellbinding preview of the powers of yoga. During my time in the Himalayas, I had practiced *pranayam*, or breathing exercises and *asanas*, physical postures and silent meditation to better attune my mind and body with the divine force of God. I had seen the incredible effects of these practices, the great benefits to health, and the ability of practitioners to modulate their physical realities. But this scene was truly amazing.

Exactly thirty minutes later, to the second, the yogi exhaled, opened his eyes, stood up, and marched back into the jungles. He didn't ask anything from anyone. He simply wanted to show these skeptics the power of yoga. Both the doctors and myself gazed in amazement at his departing form returning to the wilds.

Wherever I traveled, people spoke reverentially of a woman saint named Anandamayi Ma. I myself had read of her extraordinary qualities in the classic *Autobiography of a Yogi* by Paramahamsa Yogananda in the chapter entitled "The Joy-Permeated Mother." On the bank of the Ganges at Dev Prayag, a sadhu informed me that she was living in the Himalayan town of Dehra Dun. "I'm going by bus to visit the holy mother today," he said. "You're welcome to join me."

Upon arrival, I entered into a quaint courtyard filled with the mother's followers. All were eager to see her. My companion disappeared. A small crowd gathered around me to share stories of their guru's life.

I was told that Anandamayi Ma, who was the guru of Prime Minister Indira Gandhi, was born in an obscure village in East Bengal at the dusk of the nineteenth century. From childhood she was indifferent to the trappings of the world and at times she bewildered her family by her spiritual trances. As her followers spoke to me about her ecstasies, miracles, and compassion, I became more enthralled than ever. Just then, everyone rose to their feet as a petite lady appeared in the assembly wearing a simple white sari. Greeting us with folded palms, her eyes glistened with joy and she sat on a chair. Thin and frail, she nonetheless emanated an unearthly power. Although the lines of time were drawn upon her wrinkled face, it shone like a playful child's. She appeared wise and sober, like a universal mother, and yet she also radiated the exuberance of an innocent little girl. Although her demeanor was as soft as the flower she held in her hand, one could feel that she possessed an indomitable willpower.

Smiling upon us, she led everyone in chanting God's names, all the while clapping her hands. Then, after several moments of silence, she spoke words of love, wisdom, and selflessness. "Love is everlasting forgiveness," she began. "Wisdom is to see everything in relation to the whole. If you understand that everything belongs to Him, you will be free of all burdens." Gracefully touching her hand to her heart, she closed her eyes. "All sorrow comes from the sense of I and mine. All sorrow is due to one's keeping apart from God. When you are with Him all pain disappears. By sorrow does the Lord dispel sorrow and by adversity does He destroy adversity. When this is done He sends no more suffering, no more adversity. This must be remembered at all times."

My heart was deeply moved by the affectionate exchange between the Mother and her children. A breeze rustled the leaves of the surrounding trees. Looking up, Anandamayi Ma paused from speaking and gazed on a chirping sparrow. With glances and smiles, everyone relished her tender mood. "The world oscillates endlessly between pleasure and pain," she continued. "There can be no security, no stability here. These are to be found in God alone. Suffering is sent to remind us to turn our thoughts toward God, who will give us solace. Whenever you possibly can, sustain the flow of the sacred Name. To repeat His Name is to be in His presence. If you associate with the Supreme Friend, He will reveal His true Being to you."

Her gentle glance awakened faith and hope, and her simple, unassuming nature brought peace to my heart. Although she considered herself no more than a child, everyone present accepted her as Mother. In the time I spent with her, I saw renounced sadhus, yogis, and swamis, who typically keep a distance from women, sit at her feet seeking her blessings.

One day, as I sat alone in a courtyard, Anandamayi Ma gracefully appeared. To show my reverence, I knelt down and touched her feet. Hopping backward, her face tensed with humility, she appeared embarrassed. Guilt rushed through me like a whirlwind. In her gentle presence, attempting to show my reverence and respect, I nonetheless felt that I had acted barbarically. What had I done? I understood that, though she was an exalted being, she must humbly prefer followers not touch her feet.

Taking pity on me in my mortification, she sat on a nearby chair. With a childlike smile, her eyes rolled upward into her head as her eyelids fluttered and then closed. In the silence of that moment she entered into a trance. I felt an aura of motherly affection beaming from her motionless form. Mystically, her face shone like an angelic child. An intimate silence prevailed as she came out of her trance, smiled, and motioned for me to come closer. Her eyes sparkled with affection, yet as I looked deeper into them, they appeared utterly blank from desires. Silently touching a lotus flower to her nose and lips, she placed it in my hand, and then, rising from her seat, departed.

Enshrining this experience in my heart, I carried on with my pilgrimage. Living as a sadhu, I was coming to appreciate, was a serious life—enduring the cold winter with no warm clothes or shelter other than the bare earth of a riverbank, jungle, or cave, being vulnerable to insects and animals both while awake and asleep, having no help in sickness, and primarily being all alone. Still, I would not give it up. From Dehra Dun, I traveled northwest, higher into the Himalayas, to Uttar Kashi known by many as the Valley of the Saints. Since ancient times, yogis have taken shelter of this forest for solitude and meditation. Wandering about, I discovered a cave high on a mountain. From there, I gazed down into the forest.

Over the course of days, I saw a leopard intently hunting through the foliage. One day, he poised for an attack and sprang on an unsuspecting deer who sunk to the ground under the grip of the leopard's jaws. There were also nomadic packs of brown and white monkeys sparring with one another, swinging from branch to branch in search of fruits and berries. Spotted deer chewed on green leaves, grass, and shrubs, while anxiously glancing from side to side in fear of predators. Birds of extraordinary colors flew about seeking buds, insects, or berries, while a King Cobra slithered on the ground and up trees to devour prey, unaware that a nearby mongoose was slinking behind, poised to tear it apart. These were my neighbors, and I, a guest in their homeland. Remembering how Kailash Baba taught me to cultivate the proper attitude around such creatures, I prayed to be fearless. Everyone in all species must struggle for survival as the strong exploit the weak. But in human life, I thought, there is something so much greater to pursue.

Here in my forest dwelling, I would often take out from my bag and meditate on the picture of the blue boy who'd found me in New Delhi. I was increasingly drawn to this beautiful person playing the flute and wondered who he could be. Still, I asked no one. I felt his identity would be revealed according to God's plan.

One spring day, sitting alone in the courtyard of a Himalayan temple, I listened to the stillness of the morning. Every so often, I could hear the low hum of a black bee drifting from flower to flower, seeking nectar. Observing it, I realized that I had adopted a similar life, moving from place to place, seeking to collect the nectar of spiritual wisdom and inspiration but not clear enough about my desires to choose one place, one path, one teacher.

Suddenly, in the distance, a baby cried for its mother. I also felt like a baby spiritually, though I lacked the spontaneous ability to cry so genuinely. *When,* I wondered, *will the day come when I will cry like that baby for my beloved Lord?*

Later, as a Himalayan breeze whistled through the courtyard, rustling the sprouting leaves, I reflected on what it took to see the essence of life and shared my thoughts in a letter to my family.

> *How is everything on that side of Mother Earth? I think maybe the more kind we are, the more kindness we will find everywhere, and the more good we are, the more good we will see everywhere.*

> *Richard*

Suddenly, gongs resounded and a few villagers gathered in the temple courtyard, which was nothing but a small clearing within a dense forest of huge banyan, neem, and tamarind trees with wild animals slinking about in the crisp mountain air. The villagers worshipped a deity that stood in the form of a stone statue in a one-room brick temple. After bowing on the ground, the villagers gazed fervently at the deity while offering prayers, candles, and flowers. Due to my background with Judaism and my studies of Christianity and Islam, I felt a certain discomfort with this and did not participate. Was this idol worship? I didn't really know. Trying to restrain my judgmental tendencies, I hoped, in the future, to better understand.

A fascinating soul came upon me that day, a wandering sadhu named Balashiva Yogi. Perhaps in his early forties, he was small and pudgy. He had wavy black hair, a small nose that twitched repeatedly along with his eyebrows, and twinkling eyes. He behaved like a restless juvenile. Frivolous and talkative, he told jokes and moved about in a nervous fashion. When begging for alms, he insisted on being given sweets, a trait I hadn't yet come across in a Himalayan mendicant. But when it came time for him to execute his yoga practices, he transformed into a pillar of intensity. His multi-faceted personality made him charming company. Together, we passed a few days of close friendship until I felt a calling to enter the higher Himalayas.

When I said goodbye, Balashiva Yogi clasped my arm. "No," he said, "I insist you come to my lecture this evening. Please?" The more I declined, the more he pleaded. I finally relented. Once at the lecture hall, I looked out over a crowd of several hundred people who had gathered before a raised platform on which Balashiva Yogi stood. I sat on a chair to the left of the stage. He began the program by opening his empty hand for all to see, closed it again, went into a meditative state, and, to the crowd's astonishment opened his hand to reveal a long black stone. It was a Shiva *lingam*, a deity form of Lord Shiva. It appeared that the stone had grown right out of his hand. The crowd was transfixed. As far as I could see, this was not a magic trick, but real magic. He placed the Shiva lingam on the podium. Then, chanting mantras, he induced ashes to materialize from his hand. These mystical ashes poured constantly from his bare palm, showering the lingam. In about a minute, the stone was buried under a hill of ashes. The audience, myself included, was spellbound.

An elderly man stood and praised the yogi while an old woman gazed at him as if he were a god. As the demonstration concluded, the crowd came forward to worship him. Moving back, I marveled at how such a simple, restless man could possess such powers. Raising his open palms, Balashiva Yogi addressed the assembly in a thundering voice. "Ladies and gentlemen, what you have just seen is called *prapti siddhi*, a yogic art. It is only viewed as supernatural if you do not understand the science. Through yogic discipline, a person can learn to manipulate the gross elements of nature by controlling the subtle elements with the mind." Tensing his eyebrows, he warned, "But do not be fooled. What you saw is not spiritual, rather it is a material skill attained through meditation and austerities. I am not God nor is anyone else who performs such supernatural feats. I am just an ordinary man with some yogic powers." With both hands he threw some of the ashes into the air and declared, "I can create ashes. God can create universes." He paused for a moment and, staring into the audience, bellowed out his final message. "True spiritual life is to know that you are beyond the body, mind, and ego and realize the soul within and to realize God and be godly. This alone will bring peace."

As the crowd lined up to receive his blessings, Balashiva Yogi came to where I stood. "Are you happy you stayed?" he asked.

"Yes, thank you," I said. I had been deeply impressed by his powers, of course, but more than that, I appreciated his honesty about what was truly important. I understood that if I stayed and studied with any one of these accomplished yogis that I, too, might learn to perform certain feats. But I also understood that this was not at all the goal of spiritual life. "Please bless me to realize your words," I said.

Laughing aloud, he embraced me like an old friend. Then he held open his hand to bless me, closed it, and opened it again to reveal a sacred rudraksa bead, a raw, reddish seed, covered with ashes. He placed it in my hand as the gift of his *vibhuti*, or blessing.

As I roamed back into the forest, I thought about what I had just seen. It was incredible, but after my time in the Himalayas, not shocking. What was most incredible in what Balashiva Yogi had done is that those people were about to worship him as a god, but he stopped them. In America, athletes are worshipped for their speed and power, entertainers for their beauty and talents, scientists for their theories and inventions, politicians for their speeches and influence, scholars for their intellectual skills, and business men and women for their wealth. In India, yogis are worshipped for their mastery over subtle energies. Balashiva Yogi's honesty impressed me. True spirituality is to realize God and be godly, not to show off one's powers. Because they don't appreciate God's power, people are fascinated by these kinds of feats. Taking a seat under a sprawling banyan tree, I reflected on why people were so anxious to see such things. Everywhere we look, we witness the unsurpassable miracles of God, but because we see them constantly, we take them for granted. Picking up a seed, I examined it. God has put a gigantic banyan tree in this tiny seed and each tree produces thousands more seeds. That's a miracle. And in a single cloud, so light it floats in the air, He stores enough water to flood an entire city. When a male and female come together to procreate, they have no engineering plan on how the child will develop at each stage. It just happens. What a miracle. Every species of life is empowered with amazing talents, to fly, swim, run, climb trees, walk up walls, or create civilizations. Could all of this be happening by random chance? Creation is nothing but one amazing miracle after another. It was hard not to feel awed that a human could move the material world in such ways. But Balashiva Yogi had rightly challenged his spellbound audience, "I can create ashes. God can create universes."

6

I WAS SITTING ON A LONELY HIMALAYAN FOOTPATH one day when a fearsome tribe of perhaps twenty men approached. They were holding iron tridents crowned with human skulls, and each held their trident like a processional flag. Heavy coils of matted hair were piled on their heads and their knotted beards swung in rhythm to their march. From their dreadlocks to their bare feet, a thick covering of ashes covered their flesh, and strands of rudraksa beads hung from their necks. On their foreheads, they smeared the three-line symbol of Shiva, and around their waists they wrapped iron chains draped with bright red loincloths to cover their groins. Except for the loincloths, they were naked even in the biting cold. Some remained completely naked.

These were the Naga Babas. Avowed to celibacy for life, the Nagas often perform tantric methods to kill sexual desire or mystically transform it into psychic powers. Ignoring social conventions, many roam naked as a discipline. Their unshorn hair was but one act of diverting attention away from the body completely, a form of renunciation. The Naga Baba sect has existed since the prehistoric past, and some Naga sects have fought as armies against Mughal and British conquerors, Buddhists, and even other sects of Hindus.

My mind burned with eagerness to understand why anyone would choose such a severe life. I mustered my courage and asked to travel with them. One among them who spoke English asked the others. They displayed their approval by raising their tridents high above their heads, shouting "Jai Shankar," and dragging me by the arm into their entourage. I was quickly accepted as a brother. After walking many miles, we stopped on the bank of a river to set up camp where a priest named the Dhooni Baba gathered wood and lit a sacred fire. All the Naga Babas sat around it. I, too, approached the fire to sit among them.

A horrifying shriek jolted my wits. Turning, I saw Dhooni Baba screaming in rage, bolting toward me with his trident raised over his head. His eyes blazed red, lips quivered, and limbs trembled as he waved the trident over my head. Shouting curses, the assembly of Nagas unleashed furious stares at me. I was utterly bewildered. What had I done? Was my life to end by the trident of the Naga Babas? I prayed. One of the babas, his face contorted with disgust, pointed to my rubber sandals. I yanked them off and hurled them far into the jungle. The Nagas stared. Everything was still as I held my breath.

The Nagas erupted into hearty laughter and welcomed me to sit among them. As the tension broke, I exhaled and drew in a breath of mountain air, taking my seat on the cold ground but still quite bewildered. The one Naga who spoke some English explained, "The sacred fire is our temple. No shoes are allowed. Actually, we were not angry. This is our method to teach you a lesson you will never forget. Dhooni Baba has given you much kindness today."

I solemnly promised him that I would never forget this lesson. Dhooni Baba grinned.

In the center of the sacrificial fire, they planted an upright trident representing Shiva. Then, chanting mantras, they offered oblations of clarified butter and at a certain point in the ceremony, presented a clay pipe called a *chillum* before their altar. Still chanting mantras, they ceremoniously filled the chillum with a type of marijuana called ganja and gave the first honors to a senior Naga. He reverentially held the chillum to his forehead and chanted incantations before puffing it. Then they passed the pipe around the fire, each Naga chanting mantras before smoking. When it was passed to me, I hesitated. My mind flashed back to that smoke-filled cellar in Kandahar, Afghanistan, where I made a promise before the Lord. As respectfully as I could, I declined. A hush fell over the Nagas. They stared at me with discontent and then erupted into shouts of, "Mahaprasad, Mahaprasad, Shankar Mahaprasad." The English speaking Naga translated, "This is Shiva's Mercy. You must honor it with us. It will help you to meditate on the Infinite. If you refuse, it is a punishable offense." The rest of them stared at me like a vengeful mob.

"I vowed to never take intoxicants," I said softly.

He translated my words to the Nagas and they fell into an eerie silence. Then one of them stood up to gather wood and fed it into the sacred fire. Pausing, he stared at me and shook his head in disapproval. My head swirled. *Is this fire going to be my funeral pyre?*

Suddenly all the Nagas smiled at me. Dhooni Baba affectionately rubbed my head and laughed. They honored my vow to abstain from ganja.

To my relief, an iron pot was placed on the fire for cooking dinner. When the cooking of the rice and dhal was complete, Dhooni Baba offered part of it into the fire while chanting mantras. The remainder became the sanctified food called *prasad* and was served to the assembled Nagas. That night, we all slept near the fire and in the morning, after bathing in the chilly river, I watched as they smeared their bodies with the ashes of the sacred fire, which they did whenever crematorium ashes were not close by. Perhaps because of the bitter cold, the fire was the most popular place to be. Some of them smoked ganja while other Nagas meditated or chanted mantras on their rudraksa beads.

Then, before my eyes an elder Naga, sitting motionless in the lotus posture, slowly levitated about a foot above the ground. Another Baba near the fire did the same. I pinched myself to be sure I wasn't dreaming. No, I was awake, just in another world, a world of rough and rowdy mendicants aloof to everything but their own reality.

> *Everywhere there are outlaws who break the law and here, retreating in their forest hideout, are these Naga Babas who effortlessly break the laws of gravity. They are so much in harmony with the natural laws that they are free to play with them as they like.*

While the two Nagas floated in the air, I looked around to see the others' reaction. The rest of the Nagas paid no attention; levitating was common practice to them.

The next morning, we received a summons from the Naga tribe's guru. We traveled to the forest where, I was told, their guru was performing his severe yogic meditation while sitting for days in the lotus posture without movement, food, or water. As we strode through the bushes, the English-speaking Naga who had become my translator enlightened me about their leader. "He abandoned his home at the age of twelve to become a Naga Baba. Strict in yogic discipline, he never indulges in smoking ganja or any intoxication like many of us. Nor does he engage in any sensual pleasure. Meditating almost constantly, he has attained supernatural powers that are a wonder to see. He seldom speaks, but when he does everybody listens."

It took six hours until we came to a clearing in the forest where the Nagas' guru presided. His enormous body was folded in the lotus posture and his form pulsated with power. Perhaps in his seventies, his gray, matted hair extended down his back and stretched several feet on the ground. Naked and covered with a thick layer of ashes, his eyes were shut in meditation. One Naga Baba beat a primitive kettledrum with a tree branch, while another blew a buffalo horn to rouse the guru and announce our arrival. The guru slowly opened his eyes.

Without blinking, he stared at me. I shivered. All the Nagas gathered around to witness the event; there was pin drop silence. A deep growling voice emerged from the guru's mouth as he bellowed out, "Why waste your life? You become Naga." Smashing his fist against his massive bare chest, he boomed out, "Naga will conquer illusion. Naga is MAN." Aiming his finger into my face, he slowly shook his head and blasted, "You become Naga Baba. Now. Not tomorrow. Now!"

The Guru's stare sizzled right through me. Feeling like a tiny mouse in the presence of a roaring lion, I wondered if his mere glance would reduce me to ashes. He waited for my answer, as did they all. What should I say? What was to come? I had to follow my heart. I stood in silence. Long seconds passed. The Naga guru seemed to be staring right into my mind. In that silence, I now felt confident that he would understand me, would understand that, while I appreciated his path, it was not my own.

With a gaze of acknowledgment he raised his thick powerful hand, and, closing his eyes in meditation, he offered me his blessings. "Yes, God will help you," he said. The Naga Babas praised my good fortune and went back to their activities.

Through yogic discipline, this Naga Guru radiated an unearthly power that invoked both awe and fear, and his determination seemed as unshakable as the Himalayas. I was honored to meet him, but felt I had better move on.

The next day I bowed to the leader, asking for blessings to carry on my pilgrimage. The Nagas all raised their tridents and shouted their blessing, "Jai Shankar!" Turning around, I walked alone through the forest path, barefoot. This particular sect of Naga Babas shared a rare camaraderie. Their loyalty to the sect and to each other was real and for life. Wherever they roamed, onlookers often shook with fear, for they were wild, rough, and lived severely, but in their own way it was all in the search for God.

I set out to visit Badrinath, high in the Himalayas. Traditionally, when a man was in the last stage of life, he would trek to Badrinath and never return. But it proved an impossible journey for me as the paths were impassable due to snow and avalanches. Returning to Rishikesh, I found myself at one of its most prominent ashrams, Swargashram, where to my delight I was invited to a special feast for all sadhus. All of the sadhus sat on the ground together in lines, one line facing another to honor the spiritual food, or *prasad*, that had been prepared for us. Watching how much these old sadhus could eat on such occasions, I was amazed and promptly followed suit. When we finished, we washed our hands and many of us lay left side down on the ground, a traditional method for aiding digestion.

After resting, I set out to explore the area. While meandering along a footpath, I met with some wealthy pilgrims who were fascinated to see a western boy living among the sadhus. We spent the rest of the afternoon conversing on a veranda. Toward early evening, a yogi in his late thirties begged for charity, but my hosts ignored him. Irate, he fixed his mind to teach them a good lesson. First he stood on a chair and reached up to unscrew a glowing light bulb from its socket. Standing before the pilgrims, he crushed the hot bulb with his bare hand. When he opened his fist, he showed us how he had ground it into a fine powder. Amazingly, there was not a trace of blood or single cut on his hand. And this was only the beginning of his performance. He then poured all the fine glass powder into his mouth, and drinking a cup of Ganges water, swallowed it all. The wealthy pilgrims were astounded. Reaching into their pockets, they each gave him a generous donation and asked if he would show them more of his powers.

For his next feat, the yogi went to a nearby construction site to claim a long pole of steel rebar. Covering one eye with a thin patch of cloth, he balanced one end of the metal pole on this eye socket and the other against a wall. Then, he slowly walked forward toward the wall. The metal pole bent more and more with each step until he actually reached the wall, bending the two ends of the pole together with his bare eye. Tossing the now u-shaped rod aside, he removed the cloth to reveal an eye that was bright red with irritation but undamaged.

I had seen so many of these powers among yogis it had become quite ordinary to me. But the pilgrims now lavished more money on him, asking how he gained his powers. While massaging his eye with his palm, he explained, "For twenty years I lived with my guru in a Himalayan cave. Guruji took note that I was using the powers he taught me for prestige and monetary gain. Rejecting me, he exiled me from the ashram and cursed me to go back into the society." Dropping the people's money into his cloth pouch, he continued, "Now, I am raising money to get married. Having been trained as a yogi, this is the only way I know to make a living."

Although I had been learning from everyone—from Swami Rama, who altered his heartbeat and moved objects with his mind, to my energetic friend who'd materialized the rudraksa bead—that such feats were not to be revered above simple devotion to God, it wasn't until this moment that I realized mystic powers were not necessarily spiritual at all. Those who were able to counteract the apparent laws of nature had naturally impressed me. So much of what I'd seen seemed miraculous. Now I saw that such feats unconnected to a meaningful search for God were truly insubstantial. I was looking for more.

The Himalayas had given me much. But I did not yet know what form my own worship would take and sought to expose myself to the rich variety of worship in India as a whole. The promise of visiting Varanasi, a highly spiritual city praised in Indian literature, and learning more about Buddhism and its practitioners at Bodh Gaya, lured me to travel southeast into the plains.

I was about to descend from the Himalayas, but I knew I would be back. These four months had seemed like a lifetime, and had given me much to digest. Returning to my cherished rock in the Ganges, I listened to the river's song. There, my Himalayan experiences flashed across the screen of my mind. There was the sadhu who instructed me to submerge my western clothes in the river and granted me the robes of a mendicant, the jewels of wisdom I collected while watching the river, offering my harmonica into the Ganges and receiving her sweet song, Swami Cidananda's simplicity and wisdom, Maharishi's blessings in dreams, Tat Walla Baba's absorption in meditation, the leper woman's blessing, Kailash Baba's fatherly kindness, Anandamayi

Ma's motherly compassion, Balashiva Yogi's yogic powers, the Naga Babas' unique teaching techniques, and the lessons I learned from the rivers, mountains, trees, sky, and wild animals. As I bade farewell to the Himalayan Mountains and all of the people there, it seemed as though I had been living in these forests for the better part of my life.

7

To reach Varanasi, I boarded a train to Delhi. Through my window I watched as the plains of India spread out before me. Expansive fields, some barren and others lush, were plowed by pairs of oxen or buffalo and followed by barefoot men clinging to plows. Gradually the scenery turned to villages, then towns and then, accosted by the smell and taste of diesel fumes, we entered New Delhi. Horns blared, truck engines roared, and people crowded everywhere. Hawkers yelled, children shouted, and moneychangers struck deals. The Himalayan forests were now far away, replaced by a polluted city teeming with a population of millions.

Wandering near the fountain at Connaught Circus, I heard a shout. "Monk! I can't believe it." A moment later, a blonde traveler ran up and grabbed my hand. It was Sean, a traveling friend who kept a small Canadian flag plastered to his backpack. We had met at Piccadilly Circus in London amid the counterculture. Happy to see him, I was nonetheless coming from a whole other world, and was ill-prepared for the encounter to come. As we spoke, Sean's language, mannerisms, and interests seemed so crude and uninteresting. What was happening? I politely listened as he gossiped about people we knew, his views of world politics, places where he got high, and his bouts with dysentery, even down to the details of the texture of his stool. I wanted to run away. Less than a year ago, I enjoyed his company. Why was it so different now? Had he changed? I took a deep breath and suddenly realized that it was I who had changed. Until this meeting with an old friend, I couldn't fathom the degree I had changed. In Sean's company, it felt as if I had transformed into a totally different person. For a moment it was startling. I felt dizzy and my limbs trembled. I realized that I had to be more balanced in dealing with a world that had been so familiar, yet was now so foreign to me.

As Sean rambled on, I looked within; there I saw again how the association and environment we choose can mold our character down to the fundamental views of life. Nearby, the massive fountain gushed a constant stream of water high into the air. Reaching its peak, each drop of the water fell down and splashed into the pond. Watching, I prayed not to fall into the vicious trap of becoming judgmental. Because of my unconventional choices in life, I had been on the receiving end of judgmental attitudes time and again and couldn't live with myself if I did the same to others. Still, that tendency to criticize was so strong. I might no longer agree with Sean's ideas or ways, but why shouldn't I respect him as a soul that originated from the same Divine source, and carry on with the life I now held as sacred? All these thoughts flowed through my mind as I carried on the conversation. After some time, Sean invited me to join him for lunch. I politely excused myself.

"It's been great meeting with you, Monk," he said, with an enthusiastic handshake.

"It's been enlightening meeting with you, Sean."

From that day on, whenever I passed through New Delhi, I stayed at the Hanuman Temple near Connaught Place in the company of sadhus.

Continuing my journey to Varanasi, my train stopped in Agra, home of the Taj Mahal. One of the luxuries of riding third class was that one could impulsively get down anywhere and later jump into yet another train heading towards your destination. How could a person stop in Agra and not visit this seventeenth-century tomb glorified as one of the wonders of the world? Entering the massive outer gate, I beheld a long pool of water lined with cypress trees. On both sides were flower-filled Persian gardens. At the distant end of the pools stood the Taj Mahal with a backdrop of blue sky and the river Yamuna. Moving closer, I admired the hand-carved white marble inlaid with semi-precious jewels both inside and out.

While resting in a garden, I read a booklet on its history and learned that a Mogul king had the monument built when his favorite wife died, and that it was meant to be her tomb. Taking twenty-two years to complete and twenty thousand workmen and craftsmen, the monument was finally completed in 1648. Legend told that the hands of the gifted craftsmen were then severed to assure that there could be no duplication. In his later life, one of the king's own sons usurped the kingdom, exiled or killed his brothers, and imprisoned his own father. Looking up from the book, I tried to make sense of it all. After constructing magnificent palaces, forts, mosques, and the Taj Mahal, this king was conquered and imprisoned by his own son. In the confines of prison, he suffered miserably while his family battled and murdered one another.

Such is the pitiful consequence of greed for power. In the heart that harbors the weed of selfish greed, the flower of love cannot survive. To conquer one's envy, lust, and greed, now that is truly monumental.

I continued my journey to the ancient city of Varanasi—named Benares by the British. Glorified throughout the Holy Scriptures of India by the name Kashi and considered by millions of Hindus to be the holiest of all cities, it was especially dear to those who worship God as Lord Shiva. I wandered over to the Ganges. The sun was rising. Ancient stone steps, called *ghats*, extended in both directions leading down to the river as far as my eyes could see. Tens of thousands of residents and pilgrims were gathered to perform their ritualistic bath. Clouds of incense smoke wafted toward the heavens. Cymbals chimed, bells rang, horns trumpeted, drums beat rhythmically, flutes emitted sweet melodies, and stringed instruments droned sacred *ragas*. Countless flowers and garlands were offered into the river's current. In all directions people chanted songs, hymns, and mantras, which merged together in tribute to the Lord. The worshippers wore their most colorful saris, turbans, and garments to honor Mother Ganges. Merchants set up hills of bright red, yellow, green, orange, and blue powders along the steps with dozens of large umbrellas shading them from the day's sun. Devotees offered incense, flaming lamps, conch shells, cloths, jewels, and fans. In the river, throngs of worshippers offered prayers, oblations, and rituals, as men, women, children, cows, buffaloes, goats, monkeys, and elephants took their baths. Sacred food was given freely. Carts everywhere sold snacks and religious articles. It was a grand festival of religious fervor. Entering into the contagious enthusiasm of the crowds, I took my morning bath.

Afterwards, I visited the Temple of Kashi Vishwanath, an ancient temple at the heart of Varanasi. According to scriptures, Lord Shiva and his consort Goddess Parvati once resided there. Throughout history, saints, kings, and common people made pilgrimages to this temple, which so outraged a Mogul conqueror that he destroyed it and built a huge mosque in its place. At that time, however, the Hindus had hidden the deity of Lord Shiva and later they established it in a new temple. Now, once again, tens of thousands came to worship each day.

One day while exploring Varanasi, I heard the sound of wailing women. A funeral procession was passing through the narrow alleyways leading to the river. The corpse lay on a bamboo stretcher decorated with flowers and was carried on the shoulders of loved ones. Walking behind the body, men were soberly restraining their emotions, and behind were women sobbing uncontrollably. Seeing their suffering, I was affected. I followed along behind and approached the funeral pyre to observe the final rights. It was so different from anything I had witnessed in the West. There on the burning ghats of Varanasi, I contemplated the mystery of death, the same mystery that philosophers have struggled to comprehend for millennia. Praying to gain deeper insight, I made a decision. From sunrise to sunset, I would sit on the bank of the Manikarnika burning ghat to meditate on the inevitable reality of death.

Many Hindus believe that it is a great fortune to die in Varanasi near the Ganges, for it is said that Lord Shiva comes and whispers the name of Rama, the supreme Lord and source of eternal pleasure, in the ear of the dying, thus assuring liberation from the cycle of birth and death. For this reason, many pilgrims come to Varanasi at the end of life. Sitting in a place just overlooking the burning bodies, I observed the relatives and friends as they were forced to see the reality of death face to face. After a chanting and crying procession through the streets, the body was placed on a pyre of wooden logs, and then decorated with sacred objects to the recitation of prayers, mantras and sacred texts. To conclude the last rites, the eldest son or closest relative walked around the body while sprinkling it with Ganges water, then touched a flaming torch to the pyre. The burning of a dead body signified the release of the spirit and the flames represented Brahma, the creator. The fire then began its work. Its flames raged higher and higher as black smoke drifted toward the heavens. At this point, many of the mourners offered a final prayer, bathed in the river, and departed. But I remained, carefully observing the final moments of the corpse. The hair sizzled into nothingness. The flesh shriveled away, organs melted and bones crumbled. Gradually, the flames devoured the entire body. In the end, nothing remained but a pile of ashes. These were then carefully swept into the current of Mother Ganges, the final resting place.

Such was the grand finale of a person's life. In the background of it all was the sweet song of Mother Ganges calling us back to an eternal reality. At times in her song arose the Hare Krishna mantra, which I chanted while reflecting on death. In the course of time, the body would be placed in the earth or fire. If the body is really what friends and family members love, then why do they destroy it?

It's not the body that people love, but the soul. The body is a temporary vehicle. Without the soul, the body is like a car without a driver. I see through my eyes, smell through my nose, taste through my tongue, hear through my ears, feel through my skin, think through my brain, and love through my heart. But who am I? Who is the witness, enjoyer, and sufferer that activates my body?

I contemplated this question while witnessing body after body preparing to enter into the holy river. Regardless of race, sex, nationality, education, wealth, or religion, in due course, all bodies will be carried away by the river of time, the ultimate equalizer.

Sleeping on riverbanks or under trees and begging for some cheap grains to eat—this was the life I had chosen. Except for the times I succumbed to dysentery, I was in fair health. The cloth given to me in Rishikesh, which I still wore, had gradually faded and tattered. My hair had grown longer. My feet were calloused and scarred from roaming the jungles, fields, villages, and cities barefoot. All I carried now was a wooden begging bowl, a walking stick, a cloth bag filled with books, and the religious picture I had bought with my last money. But my heart soared with joy because I believed so deeply in the goal I pursued. Life was a school and I had become its eager student. Something inside pushed me forward to see more and learn more. Something inside probed me to wander from place to place and person to person, not letting me settle down. Who or what was that something?

I believed it was God, the presence who, throughout my life, had always been with me. Whom I prayed to as a child, feeling him so distant but so close, whom I shamefully betrayed again and again as a teenager and whom I now longed to know and to love.

In Varanasi, I heard of another holy place of Shiva, Pashupatinath, where it was said that, on one particular night, one's prayers are sure to be fulfilled. Both the promise and adventure thrilled me. I traveled about two hundred and fifty miles northeast by train and on the rears of trucks to the Kathmandu Valley in Nepal where thousands of pilgrims flocked to the temple of Pashupatinath. Being a foreigner, I was rejected entry. But I had come so far and was determined to worship that night and pray for a blessing, to find my way to God's love. At much risk, I covered myself with sacrificial ashes and entered. It was a profound experience that also had me questioning the foundations of my faith and my direction in life.

The next morning I set out to cross back into India. I was heading about two hundred miles south of Pashupatinath in the state of Bihar to Bodh Gaya, the holiest place on earth for Buddhists. Two thousand five hundred years ago, Prince Siddhartha Gautama escaped the luxuries of his royal palace to seek a solution to the sufferings of birth, old age, disease, and death. For six years, he lived as an ascetic, enduring self-inflicted pain, starvation, and exposure to the elements, all in pursuit of liberation. Realizing the limitations of that path, he ultimately came to Gaya where he sat in the meditative lotus posture under a peepal tree and vowed not to move until his goal of enlightenment was attained. Like Satan's temptations to Jesus in the wilderness, Maya, the power of illusion, tempted Siddhartha with every possible pleasure, but he remained fixed in his resolve. Under this sacred peepal tree in Bodh Gaya, he became the Buddha, the Enlightened One. From that time on, the tree has been worshipped as the Bodhi Tree, or the tree of enlightenment.

Under the Bodhi Tree, I studied books on Lord Buddha's teachings and gratefully meditated from sunrise to sunset. Meditating under the Bodhi Tree, I felt that a flow of dynamic energy was lifting me out of my body and mind into space.

In the 1960s, authors like D.T. Suzuki and Alan Watts were pop-ularizing Zen Buddhism in the West. I had studied some of their writings and found its simplicity and directness appealing. When it came to my attention that a Zen Master from Japan was teaching the way of Zen in Bodh Gaya, I was excited to have the chance to attend his lectures. About fifteen students, half Indian and half Western, assembled in the meditation room, eagerly anticipating our first sight of the Master. A bell rang, and the revered Japanese teacher entered. His head was shaven and he wore long, flowing black robes. Carrying a bamboo rod in hand, he slowly sat on the floor, back erect. A shaft of sunlight highlighted his striking features as he addressed us. "I will be your master. Your master will teach you the original way of Zen as it has been passed down from a long tradition." The rhythmic way he spoke had a hypnotic effect. "The source of all suffering is desire," he began. "And desire arises from the mind's attachments to the senses. Freedom is to empty the mind of all thoughts. To have no mind or thought is *satori,* the liberated state." His eyes shut tightly in concentration as he explained that Zen is to understand the meaning of life directly, without being distracted by logical thought or words. "You are Buddha," he said, "but you must discover it yourself. All beings are Buddha as ice in essence is water." He recalled, "The great D.T. Suzuki has written that the practice of Zen means a life of humility; a life of labor; a life of service; a life of prayer and gratitude; and a life of meditation."

He then described his method of discipline. "Your Master will be strict and you must obey his every word and observe silence at all times. Yes?" Everyone nodded. He began to lay down the law. "You must pay no tribute to the senses. No sex, no intoxicants, no games, and no music. You will eat only when and what your master gives you." The new students began to squirm while the seniors reassured them. He continued, "Your master will teach you with *koans,* paradoxical puzzles that will liberate you from rational thought. Your master will teach you *kinhin,* walking meditation, and *zazen,* sitting meditation. There will be three sessions of group meditation or *zazen* a day, one to two hours each. You will be absolutely still. Any motion will be corrected by the punishment of your master's rod."

Folding his hands on his lap, he then taught us a technique to empty our minds by sitting and concentrating on the intersection of the floor and wall, nothing else. "When your master rings the bell, you begin. You will end only when your master rings the second bell."

In the first evening session, my shoulder ached, so I moved it slightly. *Whack!* The bamboo stick lashed my shoulder. I never moved again. Anyone who moved was disciplined with the bamboo rod of chastisement. As our limbs ached and mosquitoes feasted on our blood, the whack of wood against flesh was quite common. Finally, we were saved by the master's bell.

All the students surrendered to the point of shaving their heads—everyone but me. I did not have the heart to commit my life like the others. I just didn't have the conviction or will to do so. When the fourteen-day course ended, I thanked the Master and departed. I felt the regimented lifestyle he demanded and the almost constant meditation to be a good experience. But there was something I couldn't name in the experience that made me suspicious.

Some days later, just coming out of meditation under the Bodhi tree, I met a young American couple, two of Master's faithful followers. When I asked how they were, the woman began to cry. "You won't believe what happened after you left the ashram," she said.

"I can't imagine." Under the Bodhi tree, I braced myself.

With a long, heavy sigh she sat down next to me and began her story. "Late at night, Jonathan went outside to use the toilet. He happened to see something very, very strange." Rubbing her eyes, she paused to collect her emotions. "Do you remember Pam, one of his American disciples?" I nodded. "Well, she was entering the Master's quarters. She came out nervously hours later. The next few nights, Jonathan hid in the banana grove to watch. To his dismay, he observed the same thing. When he broke the news to us, well, we felt that we just had to interrogate her. Pam admitted the truth. Master was having a full-on affair with her every night." The young woman sobbed into a handkerchief and looked up at me again. "We were betrayed."

A sinking feeling came over me.

She continued, relating how they had tested Master by secretly putting LSD in his tea. Under the influence, he revealed himself for what he was. "You should have heard him. He went berserk, on a complete ego trip." She deepened her voice and shook her finger in my face in imitation of the Master. "You must obey only me. I am the enlightened one. All others are frauds. If you dare to question my words or actions, you are doomed."

She finished by saying that all his disciples had left him.

My heart pained, I lamented hearing such news about one of my teachers. After my American friends departed, I tried to make sense of it. The Zen Master had been extremely strict with his students, but not with himself. He had misrepresented a long tradition of sincere teachers. Unfortunately, such hypocrisy stains the image of all the world's great traditions.

An irresponsible leader can break the hearts and faith of his followers and raise suspicion even toward those who are genuine. What pain his hypocrisy caused to those who trusted him and just see what it has done to his own life. How essential it is to live what we believe. How vital it is to practice what we preach.

Throughout the scenic terrain of Bodh Gaya were scattered temples representing the various Buddhist nations of Asia. I wandered the countryside visiting these sanctuaries. In the peaceful setting of the Burmese *vihar*, or temple, I met Satya Narayana Goenka. A year or so before, this teacher had come from Burma to share an ancient technique of meditation. He invited me to attend a ten-day course beginning the next day. Moved by his sincerity, I became his student, along with a dozen others. Goenkaji, as we called him, became like an affectionate father to all of us. His silvering hair was neatly parted to the side and his clean-shaven face radiated peace. A blue-checkered cloth called a *lunghi* was wrapped around his waist extending to his ankles and he wore a white button-down shirt.

As he sat in a cross-legged position, Goenkaji shared with us the story of his own life. Born in 1924, he was from an Indian family that settled in Burma to pursue business. Although he attained great wealth and prestige, he was quite miserable, suffering migraine headaches and mental anxieties. He told us, "In 1955, I came in contact with my revered teacher Sayagyi U Ba Khin. The experience changed my life and I learned from him for the next fourteen years. His teachings represent a tradition that is traced back to the Buddha." He explained, "The Buddha never taught a sectarian religion, rather, he taught Dhamma or dharma, the way to liberation." He taught us that *vipassana*, which means to see things as they really are, was one of India's most ancient techniques of meditation. "It was rediscovered by Gautama Buddha more than 2,500 years ago and was taught by him as a universal remedy for universal ills." Goenkaji spoke about his teacher with immense gratitude. "Although U Ba Khin was a householder and not a monk, he mastered the art of practicing and teaching vipassana. To fulfill a great dream, he blessed me to bring vipassana meditation back to India, the country of its origin."

In Goenkaji, I found a man of honesty and integrity. He was easy to trust. His teachings were simple and direct. Three times a day, we had group meditation and each evening he lectured. "Through this meditation," he said, "you will learn to observe life within and without, to witness it with neutrality, detached from the conceptions of pleasure or pain, success or failure, and happiness or distress. In this way, the mind gradually finds more and more subtle states of peace, and, from peace, compassion awakens."

Each day in the mid morning, I had private discussions with Goenkaji and we became very close. With sincere concern he extended himself to each of his students, and he asked nothing in return. His powerful presence and conviction sheltered his small following. At the conclusion of the ten-day course, he invited me to attend his upcoming courses in Bombay. I agreed to meet him there. For several days, I practiced vipassana under the sacred Bodhi Tree from sunrise to sunset and prayed to the temple's golden Buddha for blessings.

From Bodh Gaya, I traveled northwest to Sarnath. It was in the Deer Park that Buddha inaugurated his preaching mission. There I studied the Bodhi Sattva vow, in which one follows in the Buddha's footsteps by making one's life a sacrifice of compassion for those who are suffering in the illusions of the world. While contemplating this virtue, I decided to travel to Calcutta to seek the blessings of a selfless soul of whom I had heard so much about, Mother Theresa.

I traveled east by train to the Howrah station in Calcutta. Struggling through the crowds, I wandered on to Kali Ghat on the bank of the Ganges. It was early morning as I walked to the temple of Goddess Kali, a form of the compassionate energy of Lord Siva who in particular destroys evil. Swarms of people crowded on the entrance lane. Shops displayed pictures of the sword-wielding Goddess with Her long tongue hanging down. Shopkeepers yelled out, "jaba mala," while holding up blood red garlands of hibiscus flowers. Each trumpet-shaped red flower, which was dear to the Goddess, had five petals and a long, drooping red stamen protruding from the center, resembling the pictures of Kali's tongue. Incense and jewelry were stacked up in overcrowded stalls, while piles of milk sweets, flowers, coconuts, and red powder were aggressively sold as offerings to the Goddess. Deafening music blared from speakers as pilgrims, shopkeepers, and beggars collided. Lines of lepers, widows, and the lame sat staring at the passersby with hands stretched out, crying for charity. I wanted to give them something to alleviate their misery, yet I had nothing to offer but a sad smile and my prayers. At the entrance gate, amid shoving and chattering, hundreds of people were streaming in and out of Kali's Temple. I was not prepared for what I was about to witness.

Across from the Goddess's altar were sacrificial altars stained with blood and flesh. Squealing frantically, a black goat was being lifted by the legs as its head was inserted between the bloody staves. Bare-chested and chanting mantras, a priest swung a large, wide, curved knife down and—*swack*—severed the head of the goat. Blood spurted from its neck. A lifeless head, its eyes looking into nothingness, fell with an eerie thump to the ground while its body was immediately taken away for cooking to feed the poor.

Nauseated, I rushed outside to the bank of the Ganges, struggling to make sense of it all. *What a striking contrast,* I thought, *between the bloodshed I see here and the peaceful sages I lived among who follow the same Hindu religion.* I grappled to understand the apparent contradiction. Approaching an old sadhu who was reading a book and leaning back against a jackfruit tree, I revealed my dilemma. "Years ago," he began, "I was a priest in such a temple. With the sacrificial sword I severed the heads of many animals. But repeated nightmares began to haunt my sleep."

"Can you tell me about them?" I asked.

"Yes, the goats I killed would invade my dreams. First, I saw them screaming in misery. Next, staring with vengeful eyes, they gored me with their horns and lacerated my flesh with their teeth. Then, a monstrous priest with a man's body and goat's head thrust my head onto the altar and severed it with my own chopper." Slapping his book shut, the man leaned back onto the tree. "I couldn't take it any longer and quit my duties as a priest to accept the life of a sadhu." My eyes wide, I listened. "In every religion," he said, "people interpret scripture and follow particular practices according to their level of realization. For those who seek the essence, the path is selfless service and meditation on God. For attaining higher material enjoyment and reducing sins, increasing piety is recommended. But for those who crave material boons, there are varieties of practices, such as the sacrifice you observed. The Vedas are said to be like a desire tree wherein we can find a path to fulfill whatever we seek. Kali is the merciful Goddess of nature and is worshipped in different ways by different kinds of people. But despite all they do in her temple, the Goddess Kali is a vegetarian."

I gazed into the river's current. In the West, I reflected, millions of animals were slaughtered behind the scenes, invisible to the eyes of society. Here, at least those eating meat witnessed the truth of what was required to provide for their diet.

Up until this day, I had been thinking that examining many paths would broaden my understanding of spirituality. But this incident gave me a deeper understanding that, without a mature guide, apparent contradictions in every tradition could seriously bewilder me.

As I walked along the bustling streets of Calcutta, my heart throbbed with anticipation for my next destination. Honking cars vied with one another for every inch of road. Trucks revved and roared, blaring their horns. Hundreds of bicycles and motorbikes clamored together. Sweating and straining, barefoot men tugged rickshaws, taxiing whole families. Oxen huffed, dragging overloaded wagons. Dogs, cows, buffalo, and sheep roamed about, not stopping for anyone, while a swarm of pedestrians pushed and shoved amid it all.

I arrived at the convent of Mother Theresa, a simple one story building, where a Catholic sister received me with a modest smile, "Welcome to the Missionaries of Charity," she said. "How may I serve you?"

Joining my palms in respect, I appealed. "Is it possible that I may have the honor of meeting Mother Theresa?"

"Follow me. We'll see if it's possible." She led me into a simple chapel. "This is our prayer room. Mother Theresa and the nuns perform worship here." I knelt down and offered a prayer. When I stood up, she led me out of the chapel and down a hallway. As we passed a dimly lit room, she exclaimed, "There is Mother performing her daily chores." I looked in and saw Mother Theresa scrubbing a large charred cooking pot with her own devoted hands. My heart melted.

"Mother," my guide said, "this is Richard, an American sadhu. He would like to meet you."

Mother Theresa greeted me with folded palms. "I pray to be forgiven for keeping you waiting, but may I first finish my service?"

"Of course, Mother," I replied.

The sister then led me into a small room, offered me a seat, and told me that Mother would come after washing the pots. In a few minutes, Mother Theresa entered the room and sat on a chair a few feet from mine. Although her aging form was shrunken and frail, I could feel her indomitable presence. Her face was furrowed with wrinkles from a life of austerity, yet her eyes twinkled with childlike innocence. Although activity swirled all around her, she still had time for this insignificant soul. From her tender voice emerged the words of her heart. "The greatest problem in this world is hunger. Not hunger of the stomach but hunger of the heart. All over the world both the rich and the poor are suffering. They are lonely, starving for love." Her gaze opened my heart to her every word. "Only God's love can satisfy the hunger of the heart. There is no other solution." She waved her hand in dismissal of her own work as meager. "Feeding the stomachs of the poor is not so difficult. Feeding the starving hearts of humanity with God's love—that is the great challenge. You see, our hearts must be pure to give that love." Her dedication to the mission of Jesus Christ was like an ocean, her every expression like a wave in that ocean. She continued, "Poverty is not only lack of a piece of clothing, but a lack of human dignity and the beautiful virtue of purity. Poverty is a lack of respect for one another." Pressing her heart she sighed, "When the impoverished people of Calcutta die in my arms, I see in their eyes a light of hope. I do not see this light in the eyes of many of the wealthy, powerful people of the West. Real wealth is in the hearts of those with faith in the love of God. The world is in desperate need of those who will give the poor-hearted this hope."

Other visitors entered the room just then. One British woman asked Mother, "Why do you wash the pots? Is there not someone else who can do this?"

Mother Theresa looked warmly on her interrogator. "Serving God and humanity is an honor, not a chore. Any type of service to God is a blessing. There is no high or low."

"But Mother," the woman's husband inquired, "where do you get your strength from?"

Mother Theresa held up her rosary. Then she said something I had heard many holy people from many traditions say. "All my strength comes from the Lord's Holy Names."

She turned to me and spoke. "If you are humble, nothing will touch you, neither praise nor disgrace, because you know who you are. God is our witness. Never be disheartened by any failure as long as you have done your best." Her words penetrated deeply.

Before departing, the British woman thanked Mother Theresa for her great work. "It is God's work," Mother Theresa replied. "I am only a tiny instrument." She then excused herself to scrub more pots.

Mother Theresa was born in 1910 in Macedonia from an Albanian family. At seventeen she dedicated her life as a nun and was soon after sent to Calcutta to serve as a schoolteacher and later principal at St. Mary's. But in 1948, a momentous event took place in her life—she heard her calling to serve the poor in the slums of Calcutta. In 1950, with only twelve assistants, Mother Theresa established the Missionaries of Charity. Over the years her selfless service has attracted thousands to assist her in "God's work."

At my request, the sister brought me to the shelter for the sick and dying. I felt so helpless to do anything for them, but I did perform some simple service, sweeping and carrying utensils. Soon after, Mother Theresa appeared. Her presence lit up the dismal room of misery and death with hope and joy. As she held the hand of a woman ravished by disease, she smiled tenderly. The woman was transformed, her eyes illuminated with a joyful sparkle as she smiled back at Mother Theresa.

The Mother then went to each and every bed, not out of duty but out of sincere affection. One emaciated man, coughing blood and rapidly declining, felt her hand upon his head. He looked up at her as if she were an angel who had come at his greatest hour of need. Bowing his head, he smiled. "God's love is with you," she spoke tenderly. "Remember Him in gratitude." To a dying woman, alone and rejected by her loved ones, Theresa offered comforting words. "If you sincerely want to love God, you must learn to forgive." The burden of the woman's heart was lifted. Mother Theresa's love for God included all people as well. In her humble, unassuming manner, she gave the miracle of hope and joy to everyone she touched. Hindu, Muslim, Jew, or Christian—all were treated with equal affection. At one point, Mother turned to me and said, "I see my beloved Jesus in each of these poor souls. My Lord is mercifully accepting my love through them."

"Mother," I said, feeling shy in her presence, "they see the love of Jesus in you."

Mother Theresa beamed back at me, "Isn't that a miracle of God's love?"

8

FTER LEAVING CALCUTTA, I made the long journey west across the Indian subcontinent to Bombay, where Goenkaji was teaching another course. It took me two and a half days to reach Bombay by train. On the train, I meditated on the picture of the blue boy playing a flute. Day by day a special attraction grew toward him and I wondered again when it would be revealed to me who this was.

Once in Bombay, studying with Goenka, I was again impressed with how he put his life into helping us to learn. When a teacher puts his or her life into the lesson like that, students can't help but be inspired to put their life into learning.

After the ten-day course, I had an overwhelming urge to stretch my legs and take a long walk around the city. For several hours, I walked with no particular direction. Suddenly, I found myself stuck at a red light in a crossroads of bustling traffic. As horns blared, a river of pedestrians flowed around me. There were men with suits, ties, and briefcases jumbled together with raggedly dressed street urchins and beggars, ladies in bright saris, hawkers peddling their wares, and elderly men dressed in traditional Gandhian attire. People with skin of dark brown, light tan, and those whose skin was bleached and splotched by white leprosy all hustled in the traffic along with several European tourists who wore jeans and mini skirts. Behind us were modern high rises side by side with Victorian bungalows and shanty huts. As the sun shone brightly in a clear sky, I looked upward and took note of a huge billboard painted with bold red letters that advertised a spiritual festival at Cross Maidan.

Cross Maidan is an expansive park in downtown Bombay. At the park, a gigantic *pandal* tent was erected. Entering, I found myself in a world of colors. Posters of Indian art hung from the red, green, and yellow-striped walls of the tent. Swirls of smoke rose from pungent incense sticks. My eyes then scanned over a long table of books. Suddenly, I was captivated by the cover of one in particular. My heart leapt. The picture showed the beautiful blue boy holding a flute. Enticed, I whispered, "That's him." *Yes, that's him*, I thought. Not knowing who he was, I had carried my picture of him all over India. Now that same person was again appearing before me. In bold red letters the title of the book proclaimed itself: *Krishna: The Supreme Personality of Godhead*. I softly cried out, "Krishna! His name is Krishna!" The long awaited mystery was now revealed. Eager to learn more about him, I asked if I could look through the book. A western monk with shaved head and white robes stood behind the table. Taken aback, he asked, "You speak English?"

"Yes, I'm from America." I eagerly reached out for the book.

"Really? You're not Indian? Are you a worshipper of Shiva?" He placed the book in my hands.

"I don't really know what I am, but I've lived with Shivaites."

"My name is Tusta," he said. "Here's a chapter I think you'll find interesting. It's about the relationship between Shiva and Krishna." I wondered why he was so surprised to learn that I was from America. I hadn't seen myself in a mirror for a long time and had not realized until now that, with my brown eyes and relatively dark complexion, long matted hair and river-stained robes, perhaps I had come to look just like an Indian mendicant.

Embracing the book to my heart, I wandered to a quiet place and, as a man parched from thirst drinks from an oasis of cool water, I read the Krishna book. It began:

"In the Western countries, when someone sees the cover of a book like 'Krishna' he immediately asks, 'Who is Krishna?'"

It went on to explain that Krishna is the Supreme Lord and that the name Krishna meant all-attractive.

"Because God possesses all wealth, power, fame, beauty, wisdom, and renunciation to an unlimited degree, He is all-attractive."

As I read, a young American woman draped in a yellow sari sat on the stage singing beautiful devotional songs. Her name, I would learn later, was Yamuna Devi. Absorbed in both reading the Krishna book and listening to her soul-stirring song, I was overcome with emotion.

As evening approached, the *pandal* filled to over 25,000 people. Eager to hear the speaker, I returned the book and sat in the rear corner of the massive crowd. On the stage, about twenty Western devotees chanted and danced, the shaven-headed men wearing the traditional robes of a sadhu, and the women wearing colorful saris. The whole crowd was anticipating the coming of the guru. To everyone's deep satisfaction, he soon appeared on the stage.

He was a regal man with shaven head and saffron robes and his body glowed. He walked with the grace of a swan and gestured with the confidence of a king. Still, his demeanor was meek and humble, as if he were seeing God everywhere he looked.

After welcoming the audience with joined palms, he sat on an elevated seat. At the far back of the crowd, I could barely see. I yearned to be closer but felt ashamed to step in front of anyone else. Up on the stage, I could see one devotee moving from side to side taking photos. The guru called him over and spoke in his ear. The devotee then gazed into the massive crowd, looking from side to side until he spotted the person he was looking for. Again and again, he signaled to someone in the multitude to come up onto the stage, but when nobody came, he finally descended into the crowd. Painstakingly, he tried to pass through the tens of thousands of people seated on the ground. To my surprise, he walked all the way to the rear and right up to me. Then with a calm smile, he announced, "Srila Prabhupada wants you to sit with him on stage."

Stunned, I mumbled. "How does he know me?"

He gave no reply, but simply took me by the hand and pulled me through the masses and onto the stage. There he presented me before the guru, whose oceanic smile flooded me with joy. Srila Prabhupada looked so familiar, but I didn't know why. Sitting cross-legged with back erect, he was dressed in the neatly arranged saffron robes of a swami. With a wave of his hand, he graciously motioned for me to sit near to him, so I took my seat on the carpeted stage. In awe, I looked up at him. His large, gentle eyes briefly studied mine with a glance that touched my soul. His complexion was bronze, his nose wide and rounded, and his drooping ears were like the ears of Lord Buddha. From his recently shaved head, short white hairs had grown out on either side, and two vertical lines of yellow clay representing the yogic path of devotion adorned his forehead. Two deep creases sloped down from the sides of his nose to the corners of his full, sculpted lips.

As the devotees jubilantly danced and sang, their robes clean and bright, I became aware of my own robes, tattered and stained by the mud of the rivers. Whereas the devotee men had freshly shaven heads and faces, I could not even remember the last time I shaved my face, not to speak of cutting or combing my hair. Having bathed in a river or muddy pond each day, I must have appeared filthy in their presence. While they sang and danced jubilantly, I sat in silence. Habituated to residing in secluded forests, now here I was sitting on a stage with tens of thousands of people looking on. Feeling self-conscious and extremely out of place, I was about to flee. But then Srila Prabhupada cast such an assuring, affectionate smile upon me that I instantly felt right at home. Why had this man called me up to sit with him? Me of all people?

As I pondered this mystery, Srila Prabhupada picked up a pair of finger cymbals and began to tap them together, each of his fingers moving with meticulous grace as a steady rhythm rang out. In a deep, resonant voice, his body swaying gently, he began to chant, "Hare Krishna, Hare Krishna, Krishna Krishna, Hare Hare, Hare Rama, Hare Rama, Rama Rama, Hare Hare."

I gasped. It was like a dream, to hear him chanting the very same mantra I had heard from the song of Mother Ganges. How often had I chanted this mantra since that day in Rishikesh when the river had revealed it to me! A tingle shot up my spine, shivers rushed through my limbs and my heart pounded like a kettledrum. Through tear-filled eyes I gazed up at Srila Prabhupada, whose eyes were tightly shut, eyebrows tensed. His lips arched downward as the mantra poured out from them. The massive crowd sang in response. The devotees on stage played traditional drums, cymbals, and gongs as the tent resonated with the sound of the mantra.

After the chanting, Srila Prabhupada cleared his throat and spoke into the microphone in a deep, resonant voice, explaining the meaning of the mantra.

"We are singing the Maha Mantra or the great chanting for deliverance."

He then described that the name *Hare* was an invocation for Radha, the divine energy or female counterpart of the Lord. "It is she that is the origin and giver of the love of God. *Krishna* is a name of God that means He is all-attractive. And the name *Rama* means the Lord is the supreme enjoyer and bestows unending bliss to those who offer Him their love." He went on to explain that transcendental sound vibration cleansed the heart of selfish desires and awakened our original, natural love for God, bringing about spiritual happiness.

"While chanting the Maha Mantra," Srila Prabhupada continued, "we are praying to the Lord, 'please engage me in your loving service, eternally'."

My mind flew back to the Himalayas and to that rock in Mother Ganges. I finally understood. These were the names of that beautiful blue boy playing the flute, the one who had appeared to me in the painting. And he was a form of God. All along, I had been chanting the mantra and meditating on the painting, having no clue of the connection. Now, Srila Prabhupada revealed very simply the sacred mysteries that I had pondered for so long. My mind soared in amazement as I observed the adventures of my quest unfolding.

Smiling, I redirected my attention to the words of Srila Prabhupada. He confidently explained how true religion was not the property of any sect, caste, or creed, but the nature of all living beings. Our nature, he said, is to love God, but this love has been forgotten since time immemorial. Such love of God must be unconditional to completely satisfy the self. "We are spirit souls," he said, "but in ignorance, we identify this temporary body with the self." He went on to explain how the cause of all suffering was forgetfulness of our relationship with God, and how this consciousness could be easily awakened by the chanting of God's names. In a voice brimming with compassion, he pleaded with the audience to take this message seriously.

"This process," he said, "which revives our dormant love of God, is called *bhakti yoga*."

As Srila Prabhupada was speaking, I heard a voice within my heart proclaim, *This is your guru.*

But my mind could not accept it. A battle ensued between my brain and my heart:

> *There are many saints and gurus I have met in the past, and I will meet more in the future. I can't be hasty. This is the most important decision of my life. I must be sure before committing myself to any particular path.*

My mind won the battle and, still confused, I dismissed the idea that I was ready to choose a guru.

After his lecture, as he was leaving, Srila Prabhupada stopped directly in front of me. Bustling crowds were gathered around us and my mind was exploding with excitement. I spontaneously fell to my knees and extended my hand to touch his feet. A thunderous voice shouted, "No one touches Prabhupada's feet." Struck with shame, I retracted my hand. But Srila Prabhupada looked deeply into my eyes. I sensed that he could feel the pain of my shame and felt responsible for the cutting words of his disciple. I felt a wave of affection pouring out from him. Then with a beaming smile, he gently spoke, "You may touch my feet." Feeling both relieved and honored, I placed the dust of his feet on my head. He rubbed my head affectionately and invited me to sit on the stage with him each morning and evening. His kindness left me speechless.

The next morning after the lecture, I waited in line with hundreds of people to receive breakfast, a popular Indian sweet called *halava*. Not having eaten in a day, I was hungry. Finally, after about an hour, I reached the front of the line where a leaf cup brimming over with fresh hot halava was placed into my hand. What a blessing! I could hardly wait. But out of the blue, my halava was snatched away. *What just happened?* My adrenaline rushed and stomach burned in dismay as I turned around. There I saw the same devotee who had brought me onto the stage the night before with my halava in his hand. His name was Gurudas.

"You're not going to eat this, are you?" he asked.

"I thought I would," I said, a little indignantly.

Right before my eyes, he handed my long awaited breakfast to someone else. Then grasping my hand, he pulled me away. Moments later, I was seated behind the stage where a calm American woman named Malati Devi put a plate in front of me. It was a feast with twelve varieties of sacred vegetarian food. Gurudas smiled, "This is better for your health. We just want to make you happy." Examining me, he boldly stated, "You're a devotee. Someday you'll understand."

Sitting beside me was an American devotee named Shyamasundar who struck up a friendly conversation. He was so easy to talk to and I had a strange feeling that I knew this man. Suddenly it dawned on me that this was the monk I had encountered at the Cosmos club in Amsterdam, the one who had ladled the fruit and yoghurt into my hands asking if I wanted spiritual food. When I reminded him about it, he laughed loudly, saying, "Oh, that was you. Everyone else had a bowl. I'm sorry about that." As we talked, his wife Malati brought more and more sacred food until I begged her to stop. Meanwhile their four-year-old daughter Saraswati frolicked in and out of the backstage. Her striking blonde hair, sparkling blue eyes, and unabashed enthusiasm was a wonder to the Indian people. I drank in the scene, eagerly breaking my fast.

It is said that a saintly person is so pure that he or she acts like a spotless mirror. When we come in the presence of such a mirror-like soul, we can see both the beauty and ugliness of our inner life. Our faith and doubts, virtues and sins, strengths and weaknesses are revealed. It is both a joyful and painful experience, one that I had in the presence of Srila Prabhupada.

One evening, as he lectured, the seriousness of his demeanor induced me to question my own sincerity.

How genuine is my motivation? Am I taking responsibility for my own life and that of others? Why have I not yet found a particular path? Is it fear of commitment or frivolity? What uncertain future is this life leading me into?

At the moment these thoughts were running through my head, from his high seat, in the presence of thousands of onlookers, Srila Prabhupada fixed his eyes into mine. Locked in his gaze, I felt the massive crowd blur into oblivion. It seemed that nobody existed except him and me. I could feel his eyes penetrating into the depths of my soul and silently speaking through my heart: *Do not waste precious time. Krishna is waiting for you.* I trembled in gratitude, but knew that I would soon leave. In my confusion, I felt it the honest thing to do.

The experience of those days with him had been incredible, but my faith was still like an anchorless boat on a stormy sea. My fear of commitment and a stirring in my heart to see more places and meet more enlightened beings impelled me to move on. *Yes*, I thought, *a deep conviction in both my intellect and heart must come before I can honestly accept a particular path or guru.* I believed that God would eventually reveal my destiny.

Overwhelmed by Srila Prabhupada's wisdom and compassion, I wanted to buy his Krishna Book before leaving Bombay. I had no money so, to afford it, I took to the streets of Bombay to beg. But I was too shy to be a good beggar. Pained and intimidated, I tried but couldn't raise enough. On the last day of the festival, a disciple brought me before Srila Prabhupada. He stood in the sunshine outside the tent. His head was slightly tilted upward, his back straight, and both his hands gripped the handle of his wooden cane, which he touched to the ground between his feet. His large eyes gazed into mine and his downward slanting lips highlighted his grave demeanor. "Yes?" he asked.

The disciple said, "This boy wants your new book so badly, he's been begging in the streets with the hope to buy it."

Srila Prabhupada was so touched that with his own hands he gave me a copy of the book. His eyes flooded with kindness and he patted my head and softly said, "Thank you very much."

Thank you very much, my heart echoed. I bowed my head in reverence.

III

Himalayan Pilgrimage

THE HIMALAYAS WERE CALLING AND I LONGED TO ANSWER. The next day I sat on the grimy concrete floor of a railway platform waiting for the next third-class ride toward the north. I settled in to read the book Srila Prabhupada had given me and was surprised to see that it had an introduction by George Harrison of the Beatles, who wrote:

> *"Everybody is looking for Krishna.*
> *Some don't realize that they are, but they are.*
> *Krishna is God. The Source of all that exists, the Cause of all that is,*
> *was or ever will be.*
> *As God is unlimited, He has many names*
> *Allah-Buddha-Jehova-Rama: All are Krishna, all are One…"*

I had been studying world religions, and felt I had so much more to learn. This ecumenical sentiment both pleased and surprised me, and I tucked the book into my bag for further examination in the future.

At the station, I met a man in his forties who was neatly dressed in white cotton pants and shirt, wore a white Nehru cap, and had a dark complexion with scars on his cheeks from a childhood bout with small pox. His name was Madhava and he worked as a supervisor for the railways. He persuaded me to join him on a trip to visit his guru. So, from Bombay we traveled a few hours east by bus to the holy site of Ganesh Puri. Upon arriving, he directed me, "Before meeting Guruji, you must be purified by bathing in the nearby hot sulfur springs." We approached three small ponds simmering with dark opaque water. Dozens of locals scrambled about shouting to one another while dozens more took their daily baths. Slowly, I submerged myself into smoking gray liquid that clung to my skin like oil, gradually adjusting to the burning heat and sour smell. Submerging myself up to my neck, the heat penetrated and revitalized my body and mind. Madhava then yelled out that I was now prepared to visit his guru.

After I dressed, he led me to a small brick temple. Passing through the arched entrance, I found myself face to face with a large, black and white photograph of a slightly heavy man with a shaved head who wore only a loincloth. He had a round face, prominent cheekbones, penetrating eyes, and white stubble covering his jaw. There Madhava informed me that this was his guru, Nityananda Baba, who had given up his mortal body ten years before. Here in his sacred tomb, or Samadhi, his spirit could be felt with vibrancy more real than life.

All around the Samadhi, which was lit with oil lamps, perfumed with mogra incense, and decorated with yellow and orange marigolds, Nityananda Baba's followers sang God's names in unison. To my surprise, they were chanting the Hare Krishna mantra, the very one the river Ganges had revealed to me in the Himalayas and which Srila Prabhupada had sung in Bombay. Chills ran through me.

Nityananda Baba is worshipped by millions of followers in the states of Maharastra and Karnataka. Madhava explained the details of his life, teachings, and miracles. In the latter part of the nineteenth century, while collecting wood in the jungle, a poor woman was attracted by the unusually loud cawing of crows in a densely wooded area. There she found an infant boy lying alone in the leaves. She entrusted the child to a barren woman who worked as a maidservant to a wealthy Brahmin. Even as a tiny boy, he was detached from the world, leaving his adoptive family at the age of ten to become a spiritual renunciant. Nityananda Baba traveled far and wide by foot, always eager to serve those in need and enlighten the hearts of whomever he met. In his latter years, he had settled here, at Ganesh Puri. While meditating at his samadhi, the chant in the background, I felt the overpowering presence of Nityananda Baba, as if to assure me that his blessings were upon me.

Several days later, I was led to a disciple of Nityananda Baba who was building an ashram nearby. Small but rapidly growing, the hall of worship was located just off the roadside. As the door opened, the mantra to Shiva, *Om Namah Shivaya*, reverberated in a slow hypnotic chant. Inside, a couple dozen disciples, both from India and the west, were chanting in unison. Stringed drones called *tambouras* made from hollow gourd vibrated intensely. As the chanting faded into silence everyone spilled out into a courtyard. I watched and waited. Then, as his disciples bowed down, their guru entered. He was sixty-three years old with dark complexion, deep brown eyes, short untrimmed hair and beard, and clothed in saffron robes. In his presence, his followers lit up with joy. I asked who he was. "Swami Muktananda," I was told.

Peering at me through his spectacles, the Swami addressed us through a translator. "When I was fifteen," he began, "I renounced my wealthy home for the life of a sadhu. I wandered to every holy place and at last met my gurudeva, Nityananda Baba." Smashing his right fist into his left palm, he exclaimed. "Baba crushed my pride like no one else could do." Here he was describing the very thing I had been wondering and worrying about, which path or guru to choose and why. The audience, myself included, clung to his every word. "*Shakti pat* initiation awakens a cosmic energy called kundalini from the base of the spine. The kundalini rises up the spine through the seven energy chakras to the top of the head where it merges into the supreme. The surest means of awakening the Kundalini," Swami Muktananda said, "is when a siddha guru, or perfected teacher, gives a mantra and transmits his or her shakti directly to a disciple." He concluded, "Become addicted to your mantra even more than an alcoholic toward his liquor. Never forget it."

On one occasion, as I stood with Swami Muktananda on the roadside, a vicious dog, howling insanely, baring its threatening fangs, came charging toward us. People shrieked and scattered. With a mere stare Swami tamed the creature and it meekly bowed its head. Blessing the dog, he turned to me and spoke through a translator. "I have noted you to be a sincere sadhu. If you wish, I will initiate you into shakti pat."

Images of Tat Walla Baba, the Naga Guru, and others who extended themselves in this way flashed through my mind. "Thank you, Swamiji," I replied, both startled and honored, "but I've vowed not to accept formal initiation from a guru until I'm convinced I will never leave his shelter." Nervously, I petted the dog. How part of me wished I could easily accept his generous offer. "I don't deserve your kindness, but I haven't yet made that decision."

"I appreciate your sincerity," he said, gazing into my eyes. "God will guide you." Then, like a confirmation to his blessing, the once vicious dog licked my hand again and again.

Madhava insisted that I travel to Goa, where the climate, he said, would be excellent for my health. He even offered to buy me a ticket by ship. It seemed like the arrangement of destiny so I accompanied him to the docks in Bombay and boarded a crowded boat that carried me 250 miles south along the coast of the Arabian Sea. After plying smoothly for the better part of a day, I reached my destination, a tropical paradise with endless beaches of soft sand and balmy air scented with sea salt. Starting in the sixteenth century, Goa had been the headquarters of Portugal's Asian empire. At that time, St. Francis Xavier, a Jesuit priest, converted tens of thousands of locals to Christianity. In 1961, Indian troops invaded Goa, defeating the Portuguese forces.

Arriving at the beachfront, I saw stretches of white sands, crystal seas, and scores of coconut trees. To pass the time, I traveled to Calangute Beach, a haven for Westerners who rented inexpensive houses there. Walking the beach, I passed men and women kissing and groping each other, heard rock and roll blaring, and saw drugs openly consumed. It was the same old scene I had left behind in Europe but it now seemed so alien, like something from a past life. Uninterested, I walked through the sand along the sea. I caught myself mentally criticizing them as if I were superior. I didn't want these thoughts, which exposed my own arrogance. I prayed to be purified from my own pollution of fault finding. But it was so hard. Living with the animals in the jungles was so much easier as they didn't so thoroughly expose my own shortcomings.

About a kilometer farther, I came upon drug addicts, all from the West, scattered along the seashore sticking needles in their arms. They had come so far, to one of the most beautiful places on earth, only to suffer the miseries of addiction. Quickening my pace, I arrived at a small mountain at the end of the beach. I climbed over its boulders, panting in exhaustion until I reached the other side. There, a tropical paradise lay before me. The plush white sands of the beach extended hundreds of yards. Groves of coconut trees swayed in the wind and not a single human being could be seen. This would be my home for the next week.

For seven days, I sat under a coconut tree absorbed in study, meditation, and prayer. With the exception of a few poor fishermen rowing their boats into the sea each morning, the place was deserted.

For my daily meal, I climbed a sloping coconut tree, shook down a fruit and, to open it, repeatedly smashed it against a rock. For my daily hygiene, I bathed in the sea, and for my bed, I stretched out on the sand under the starry sky.

One day, I took a walk inland. There, nestled in countless coconut trees, I found a few scattered huts made of mud and dry coconut leaves, all built on the sand. The inhabitants, most of whom had converted to Christianity, followed the tradition of their ancestors as fishermen with no assets but a rowboat, two oars, and a net. From sunrise to sunset the men labored in the sea under the burning sun, which blotched many of their faces with what looked like skin cancer, but hard work left them no time to dwell on such details. I thought how Jesus had made his first disciples from among fishermen and then ordered them to be the fishers of men.

On another day, as I was walking along the coastline, I found a tiny fish flapping desperately in the sand. A wave had washed it ashore. The fish's fear and desperation evoked my sympathy. He and I were not so different, after all, and I resolved to return him to his home in the sea. But each time I picked him up, he frantically flapped right out of my hand, so fearful he couldn't recognize me as a friend. Finally, I trapped him in my cupped hands and hurled him back into the water. Still, my sense of satisfaction was short-lived. The next wave washed onto the shore then receded back into the sea, leaving the same little fish once again flapping in the sand. Again I cast him into the water and again the next wave left him in the sand to die. The next time, with much difficulty, I held him inside my cupped palms, tread into the ocean up to my neck, and then hurled him in as far as I could. I returned to the shore and observed wave after wave washing in and out until I was satisfied that the little fish was safe.

Walking some distance, I came upon a group of fishermen dragging a net from their boat onto the sand. The net was filled with hundreds of such little fish flapping for life and doomed to the frying pan. What could I do? I stared soberly into the sea and walked by immersed in thought.

We are all like fish that have separated from the sea of divine consciousness. For a person to be happy outside his or her natural relation with God is like a fish trying to enjoy life outside of the water, on the dry sand. Holy people go to great extremes to help even one person to return to his or her natural spiritual consciousness, to the sea of true joy. But the net of maya, *or illusion, snatches away the minds of the masses, diverting us from our true self-interest.*

When I had first set out on my spiritual journey, my idea had been to learn as much as possible from various paths and teachers and then take from each path the practice that was most effective for me. This was a popular idea in the 1960s, but in India, I began to realize the superficiality of it. I had seen many spiritualists with this idea, but the depth of their realizations seemed vague. Those who impressed me as advanced had committed themselves to a particular path. I had come to understand that my traveling from place to place and teacher to teacher had its limitations. Part of my hesitation to accept initiation into one religion, I realized, had to do with a fear of division from others. Still, I knew I would need to choose in order to progress. Not doing so was becoming painful. But which path and which teacher were mine? How would I ever know for sure?

Already many great teachers have enlightened me with knowledge of different paths and experiences I didn't deserve. I see spiritual beauty in all of them. Which direction should I go at this crossroads in my life?

That night, I prayed for guidance and drifted into sleep. In the middle of the night, I awoke to a crescent moon that shone in the dark sky. Within the embrace of this crescent, a single star sparkled. It was the symbol of Islam, a sign of submission to God. I stared in wonder. My heart reassured, I accepted this as a sign that the mystery I had been contemplating would be revealed to me in due time.

2

FROM GOA I SAILED BACK TO BOMBAY and began my return journey to the Himalayas. I traveled by train to Delhi and then northwest to the town of Pathankote near the border of Jammu and Kashmir state. From there I journeyed east on the back of a truck to the Himalayan town of Dharmasala in Himachal Pradesh. Summer was approaching and the forest was bursting with blooming flowers of orange, yellow, violet, and white. Huge, ancient trees were cloaked in shining green leaves and a constant buzz of wildlife energized the atmosphere. High on a mountain ridge above Dharmasala reigned McLeod Ganja, a Tibetan refugee camp and the home to the Dalai Lama of Tibet.

In preparation for my pilgrimage to his mountaintop monastery, I read a book he had written entitled *My Land and My People.* I learned that Lhamo Dhondrub was born in 1935 in a simple Tibetan house made of stone and mud to a family of poor farmers. A search party of exalted monks was directed to this house by the Regent of Tibet, who had a vision revealing that this was the place where the next Dalai Lama had been born. When the child was only two, they came to the house in the guise of travelers seeking refuge. Around one monk's neck hung the beads of the previous Dalai Lama, which the child grabbed, claiming them to be his own. After several visits and consequent tests the committee concluded it had found the fourteenth incarnation of Chenrezig, the Bodhisattva of compassion who is believed to guide the Tibetan people spiritually and politically by reincarnating in each generation as the Dalai Lama.

The boy was conveyed to the monastery in Lhasa where he was groomed to be the head of state and spiritual leader of a nation. During the childhood years of his reign, Tibet flourished. But in 1950 the Chinese military invaded and, by 1959, the nation was torn by bitter agitation and violence. On the insistence of his people, who feared for his life, he had to flee from his beloved homeland. The Dalai Lama prayed in the temple of Lord Buddha and offered a shawl of white silk at the altar as a symbol of farewell with the intent to return. With a heavy heart, he shed his monk robes and in the guise of a soldier, he escaped the palace in the dark of night.

Through heavy snow, torrential rains, and bitter cold, he and his party trekked across the rugged mountains of Tibet like fugitives. All the while, his heart was breaking at the plight of his people. Struck by disease, exhaustion, and what he referred to as "unhappiness deeper than I can express," he crossed the border into India.

Gripped by this amazing story of exile, fate, and overcoming hardship, I was compelled to see the place where the spiritual leader of Tibetan Buddhism had made his new home. By the time I arrived in 1971, McLeod Ganja, nestled in the high, forested mountains and steep valleys of the Himalayas, looked like a Little Tibet. The refugees dressed in their traditional clothes and constructed wooden or brick buildings in the Tibetan style of architecture with dragons and other mythical beings carved or painted in rich colors onto their pillars and arches. Yaks grazed on the hillsides and a few scattered western pilgrims found secluded places to meditate. Just as in Tibet, many of the men were Buddhist monks. In the center of the village, the faithful circumambulated a large rectangular area surrounded by prayer wheels, all the while spinning the wheels and chanting the mantra, *"Om Mani Padme Hum."* I knew from my reading that the Tibetan Buddhists believed this mantra invoked the blessings of Chenrezig, the embodiment of compassion, and that all the teachings of Buddha were contained within it.

The people in McLeod Ganja were incredibly friendly. Glowing with smiles, they welcomed me wherever I went. Despite the hardships they had endured and despite being refugees in a foreign land, they seemed at peace. I saw no beggars or cheaters among them. Everyone looked content. One family welcomed me into their small home and served me a Tibetan noodle soup called *thupka* and traditional tea made with yak's butter and salt. This tea was especially effective at keeping a person warm during the cold Himalayan nights. My heart was so charmed by the people here that I often spent hours just watching them perform their daily chores as they grinned at me from ear to ear.

Not far from the Dalai Lama's house stood the temple of a magnificent deity of the Buddha sitting in the lotus posture. Both the monks and the common people worshipped this golden form of the Buddha by offering incense, bells, lamps, and gifts. The *puja*, or worship ceremony, fascinated me. The monks sat in two lines facing one another with the Buddha in the center. They read from scriptures inscribed on sheaves of unbound parchment leaves. Each leaf was placed on top of the previous as they recited ancient prayers in unison. At auspicious intervals, some monks blew long trumpet-like horns, others rang ritualistic bells, and others struck large gongs with wooden mallets and beat upon huge drums with sticks. As the vibration reached its crescendo, a high priest ceremoniously raised a scepter crafted of intricately molded brass. This *dorje* was a transceiver of spiritual energy. Decorating the walls of the temple were artworks called *tantras*, painted in vibrant colors, designed to aid enlightenment by depicting history and symbolism of Buddhism. The fragrance of burning oil lamps and sweet incense further lifted my mind as I sat with the monks meditating and chanting mantras.

I was particularly struck by the love and honor the people held for their Dalai Lama. For the Tibetans, he had the spiritual power of a pope and the political authority of a king. His photograph was prominently displayed in every shop and home.

One early morning while I was meditating in the temple, a tall elderly lama with a shaved head, maroon robes, and a strand of wooden beads draped around his neck sat beside me. He said that he had been observing me for several days and asked if I would like to ask any questions. We spent a couple of hours each day together. On one very special afternoon he invited me to join him for a personal audience with the Dalai Lama. The home of the Dalai Lama rested on a wooded hill surrounded by armed Indian military guards who, because he was under constant threat of death, were stationed for his protection. Passing through the security, I was ushered into a room where brightly colored paintings of Buddha and the great Bodhisattvas decorated the walls. A beautiful metal deity of Buddha sat on an altar decorated with flowers, brass lamps, bells, and other items of worship. Cedar scented incense perfumed the air.

Minutes later a door opened and the Dalai Lama glanced toward me, eyes sparkling with joy behind his brown-rimmed glasses. His large head was shaven and he had a square face, low rounded nose, and draped a maroon robe over a bright golden monk's shirt. Beaming a contagious smile, he sprinted across the room to greet me. Laughing aloud, he tightly gripped both of my hands and shook them again and again. His eyes twinkled with glee, as he spoke in a hearty voice. "You have come from far away. I welcome you."

We sat on two chairs across from one another. With a childlike curiosity he asked me about my life in America and why I had chosen the life of a sadhu. As I told my story, he listened to every word with rapt attention and concern. Whenever there was a trace of humor in my tale, his whole body shook with laughter and he clapped his hands together. We spoke for perhaps a half hour when I asked him about the condition of his people in Tibet. A wave of introspection then swept across his face and tears welled in his eyes. In the silence that now surrounded us, he whispered, "When I was a boy, my nation enjoyed freedom. We were a happy and united people, and our spirituality was flourishing." He paused for a long moment. In sober silence, he lifted a teapot to offer me a cup of Tibetan tea. I watched as the steaming tea poured from the spout into my cup. The Dalai Lama then returned the teapot to its place and lowered his head in deep thought, as if looking with his mind's eye, and feeling in his heart the strife of his people across the Himalayan peaks in Tibet. He added tenderly, "We owe a great debt to India for providing shelter to thousands of our people."

"The universal quality of religion," he went on, "is compassion to other living beings. To sacrifice for the good of others is true dharma." Seeing the immense sacrifice he extended for his people, his words struck my heart. "Meditation, study, and worship," he said, "give us the inner strength to live as kind and enlightened beings." His message invoked introspection and his personality inspired reverence, but his affection had made me feel to be his intimate friend. Smiling, the Dalai Lama graciously placed around my neck a white silken shawl embroidered with Tibetan mantras. "It is a tradition to offer this gift to all my special guests," he said. I felt undeserving of his time and kindness and bowed my head with gratitude. In his company, the virtue of selfless service was becoming more prominent in my mind. He was a person dedicated not only to his spiritual principles, but also to taking on the massive burden of serving the needs of his people who were either in exile or under subjugation. He had endured incomprehensible challenges and obstacles in his apparently hopeless struggle. Tolerating exile and threats, he served his people. In my mind, this is what the shawl represented. It was a special gift.

On a forested mountainside, I took up residence in a cave that overlooked a steep valley. There I survived on a food called *tsampa*, a dry powder made of roasted barley. When water is added, it becomes like porridge. Tibetan monks taught me how to survive on *tsampa*, as it does not spoil. Having thus simplified my bodily needs, each day I was able to come down to McLeod Ganja to learn from the people there. Nights, I returned to my cave. One night as I lay on the rock floor, a gigantic spider crawled along the wall just inches from my face. It moved its hairy black body slowly, lifting one leg at a time, until it disappeared into a hole about six inches from my face. As a small child, I had been terrified of spiders. Anytime one entered our house, I would run away from it, crying for my mother to remove it. This cave-dwelling spider was the most ferocious I had ever seen. *This is a test from God. I must overcome this fear,* I thought. From that night on, the two of us respectfully shared the cave. From where I meditated, I noticed cobras occasionally slithering about in the forest. At times, I had other roommates as well. One night, a huge scorpion fell from the ceiling. Inches from me, it wagged its deadly stinger from side to side. At that moment my only candle burned its last, and the cave became pitch black. I felt it unwise to move and so sat motionless in the darkness for a long time. In this state, I recalled fatherly Kailash Baba and how he taught me the proper consciousness around snakes and scorpions. Breathing slowly, I prayed to God to help me to overcome judgment, hatred, and fear.

One morning, in my cave, my mind drifted across continents and seas to my father in the Chicago suburb of Highland Park. Unsure about my own direction, I was nonetheless feeling that the greatest act of love I could offer him was to write a letter encouraging him to come closer to God in the way that would be most natural for him. With the conviction of youth, not yet knowing my own path, I wrote:

> *My beloved father,*
> *I would like to ask something very dear of you. Much of the compassion that you have is reflected from my beloved Grandpa Bill. I believe that the root of his compassion was his all-embracing faith in the Hebrew religion. Grandpa implanted within you the seed of love for Judaism. Please nourish this seed with all sincerity to attain the inspiration of*

*your faith and love for God. I feel that the sacred gift of meditation will
give you great insight to reach the depths of Judaism. Hebrew as well as
the other great religions can bring all of us closer to the Lord.*

*Please carry on the inspiration of your father and forefathers.
I believe this is what you truly want.*

Richard
Mcleod Ganja, Dharamshala, Himachal Pradesh, India
May, 1971

For the most part on my quest throughout India, I had had no
companion with whom I could reveal my heart. My associates either
spoke no English or were great, powerful sages far senior to me in age. At
times, I was lonely, but I learned to relish loneliness as a way to cultivate
my connection to God. Silent prayer became the medium through which
I could pour out my thoughts and feelings. The serenity of meditation
was my shelter from the restlessness of my mind and world around me.
While reassuring my family about my welfare, I was often impelled to
use these letters to open my heart, even to recipients who might find
my words difficult to comprehend. Sometimes, too, I would reveal my
heart onto a small writing pad. One sunny day, while sitting alone in the
solitude of my mountain cave, I wrote the following, to no one:

*In the mind of a hermit, in troubled times, when a man is tired and
weary, confused as to where he is going and what he has left to fall
behind, he doesn't know whether to cling to or to let go forever of those
things that still remain with him. Where to go for one who has forsaken
friend and home? What to do for one who wanders alone in the wilderness
of his own solitude? Should he break the walls that he has constructed
around himself or should he build them stronger and higher? He pleads,
"Oh Lord, is there a guide who can show me the way to you? Where
shall such a homeless man reside who believes that home is not in this
mortal world?"*

A reclusive mystic from Egypt lived a short distance from my cave.
From time to time, we shared soul-searching talks. He had a dark,
smooth complexion, large nose, thin lips, and an untrimmed goatee. His

black, introspective eyes were so intense they glazed over as if looking into another world. Outwardly calm, his mind was always working to find another missing piece of wisdom in the puzzle of life. An Egyptian master of the Oracle, a tarot-like science sometimes referred to as the *Metu Neter*, he offered one night to read my destiny. I agreed. Shuffling the deck and lining the cards into precise rows on a powder blue cloth in front of him, he commenced to enact a series of occult rituals from ancient Egypt. Then he guided me through an elaborate meditation that culminated in my selecting a card. Each brightly colored card was about six inches tall, three inches wide and illustrated with mystical symbols and mythical figures. For a good half hour he concentrated on the configuration before he finally broke the silence. He slowly rose from his chair, put both hands on the table and delivered his prophecy. "Neither your mind nor intelligence have the power to discern the spiritual path you long to know. Very soon, however, the divine power will direct you. Like a leaf in the wind, you will be led to the path you must follow." It was as if the cards knew everything about me and he was their mouthpiece. Placing his finger on a particular card, he fell silent. He closed his eyes and whispered, "You must persevere with patience. By a power beyond your own, you will recognize the very one you seek. Believe in this. It is your destiny. Your master will come to you."

3

I BADE FAREWELL TO THE HAVEN OF PEACE AT MCLEOD GANJA. I would never forget the joy and kindness I received there, but I felt driven to experience more of the holy places of India, to expose myself to even more practices and traditions in hopes that my destiny would indeed reveal itself.

From Pathankot, I took the train south into the state of Haryana, disembarking in Kuruksetra, the place where the Bhagavad Gita was first spoken and one of the holiest places in India. As I left the station, lugging my bag of spiritual books, I could hear from a nearby temple the Sanskrit verses of the Bhagavad Gita being recited through a crackling speaker.

Here, I immersed myself in reading the words Krishna spoke to his disciple Arjuna who was about to shrink from his calling in the face of insurmountable obstacles. The Gita had been spoken on a battlefield because life itself is a battle, where evil perpetually attacks good and our sacred ideals are destined to be tested. We would all be confronted by grave dangers and fearsome demons within and without. There was much to be gained from facing these aggressors with integrity and faith. Krishna's timeless call culminated in the practice of selfless devotion, determination, and spiritual absorption as the means to access a power beyond our own to overcome all fear—the power of God's love.

In that sanctified place, the Bhagavad Gita's message penetrated me so deeply that I felt as if Krishna were personally speaking to me on each page. I read several chapters every day, poring over my little Gita Press copy of the Bhagavad Gita, which was printed on cheap paper and bound in a white cardboard cover. I had read many spiritual texts in my travels, but none struck me as so highly practical.

Reading the Bhagavad Gita under the very banyan tree where Krishna originally spoke to Arjuna, I was struck by how powerfully it revealed the science of self-realization beyond sectarian or historical boundaries. It elucidated such intricacies as, how the soul is related to God, how that changeless soul is affected by material nature, how *karma* (the natural law of action and reaction) affects all of us, and how the imperceptible influence of time acts on creation. As a lonesome wanderer seeking truth, where danger, temptation, and fear could pounce on me at any moment, I found solace and direction in these immortal words. In Kuruksetra, the Bhagavad Gita became my handbook on how to live.

After a few days I left Haryana, and while I was traveling on a train winding through the Indian plains, we stopped for some time at a station. There I witnessed an ugly event. I saw a teenager being slandered and beaten by his employer on the platform. The teenager neither raised a finger nor said a word and was quickly dragged away. I asked a nearby college student what was happening. Shaking his head, he replied, "Because he was born in a lower caste, he's like a slave. Likely, he will not be given opportunities for a proper education or to marry anyone outside his suppressed caste and he will work slave labor for life. I know. I'm from a similar background, but I'm lucky. The government is fighting against these injustices and most educated, cultured, or socially minded people are battling against it as well. But it is still quite deeply ingrained in the minds of many." He explained to me that this caste system was actually a gross perversion of an ancient scriptural teaching, the *vedic varnashram*, which teaches that, just as the human body has a head, arms, belly, and legs, and each limb is meant to perform its function for the benefit of the whole body, in the social body, one is taught to accept responsibilities for the social and spiritual benefit of oneself as well as everyone in society according to one's natural inclinations and skills. The Vedic varnashram was meant to encourage, empower, and unify everyone. "However," he concluded, "this concoction of caste by birth and exploitation of the lower castes has corrupted a beautiful system."

My thoughts traveled back to the suppression of racial and religious minorities in America and Europe, and I reflected sadly on how the tendency to cultivate superiority and exploit others takes many guises, expressing itself in society, politics, philosophy, or even religion. It was becoming increasingly clear to me that I needed to follow a particular path if I wanted to truly know God, but I worried that such a choice could lead to narrow-mindedness. Attracted as I was to one of the most important religions in India, it heartened me that nothing in the true Hindu philosophy supported suppression of human beings on the basis of one's race, caste, sex, or birth, and that among saintly people, I had not witnessed any of this kind of prejudice.

In the beautiful Kulu Valley, in the state of Himachal Pradesh, I wandered through miles of pristine nature. I felt so close to God in natural settings. Two days before, upon seeing a single photo-poster plastered on a railway station wall, I jumped on a truck to Kulu. One day, while drinking in the fresh pine scent of the Himalayan air, I came upon a traveler from Colorado whom I had met previously in Iran. Back then, he had been on his way to India to study Tibetan Buddhism. "How has your quest gone?" I inquired.

Entering into a trancelike state, his eyes rolled upward. "God has incarnated." His eyelids fluttered and voice quivered, "I was blinded by the Divine Light by the mere touch of his finger. Rushes of ecstasy thrilled my limbs. Divine music filled my ears. I smelled ambrosia and tasted nectar. You must go immediately. The Lord of the universe has descended to earth."

Like a doctor giving medicine to a dying patient, he insisted, "The culmination of your long journey to India is waiting in Hardwar. Go now brother, do not delay. The Supreme Lord will soon travel abroad."

Intrigued, I journeyed south to the ashram in Hardwar. Entering the temple, I was puzzled by a large photo on an altar. It was the young guru, wearing a crown and peacock feather, playing a flute, and standing in the pose of Krishna. But he looked very different from the painting of Krishna I had purchased in Delhi. As my friend from Colorado had done, his disciples approached me and swooned. "The merciful Lord has come in the past as Rama and Krishna, now he has come again. When Guru Maharajji bestows 'the knowledge,' he opens your divine eye and you will know him as the Lord of the universe." As Guru Maharajji would soon be leaving for his first trip abroad, his disciples hurried me onto a bus to New Delhi.

Back in New Delhi, hundreds of Guru Maharajji's disciples crowded the ashram grounds waiting to get a glimpse of him. I sat in a corner and watched. An elderly disciple struck up a conversation with me and then introduced me to a group of *mahatmas*, a title for those empowered to bestow Guru Maharajji's "knowledge." The mahatmas decided that I must meet Sri Mataji, the holy mother of their Lord. She sat on a cushion surrounded by admirers who whisked her with yak tail fans and listened to her every word. To my surprise, she decided that I must have a private audience with her son before he departed, so a mahatma escorted me to his room. Guru Maharajji was a boy of only thirteen years old, slightly pudgy with hair neatly parted on the side. He introduced himself as Prem Rawat and explained that he was the successor of his father Sri Hansji Maharaja. From amid the bustle of disciples, Guru Maharajji brought me to a rooftop for a private meeting. There, away from the crowd, we paced together back and forth while he asked many questions about my life and described his forthcoming trip, his first abroad. When he asked if I desired to take initiation into the "knowledge," I explained to him, as I had to previous teachers, that I was careful about making such a commitment. As we conversed on the rooftop, the crowds below anxiously awaited him. Just then a mahatma poked his head onto the roof and announced that the time had come to leave for the airport. Guru Maharajji quickened his step. "I must go. If ever you decide to receive the knowledge," he said, "you may come to me personally in India, America, or London." With thousands looking on, we came down the stairs. I stepped to the sidelines as Guru Maharajji, with much fanfare, blessed his flock and departed by car. Watching from the background, I was grateful for his attention and believed he could be an accomplished yogi, perhaps from a past life, but when I looked inside myself, there was no inclination to accept him as Krishna, the Supreme Lord of the universe. "Who God is," I thought, "is a serious subject, not to be taken lightly."

During the course of my travels, I had become quite attached to the spiritual books I carried. I had gradually gathered a small library in a cloth bag. Except for this heavy bag of books, my only possession was a begging bowl and a branch used as a walking stick. Many times I considered reducing the weight of this burden, but every time I looked through the books, trying to decide which ones to give away, I found I could not part with a single one. Among them were the Bhagavad Gita, Bible, Upanishads, *Autobiography of a Yogi*, books on Buddhism, one by Shankaracarya, and the Krishna book personally given by Srila Prabhupada. Because each was special to me and I worried I might never find it again, I lugged this bag of books wherever I went, often exhausted from the load. Now, near Connaught Circus in New Delhi, I set the books down on a street corner. Auto rickshaws zoomed by spewing trails of black diesel smoke. Cars jammed the street, each trying to squeeze ahead of the other. Bicycle rickshaws, handcarts, and ox-driven bullocks moseyed by, while battered trucks blared their horns and blasted out clouds of carbon monoxide. Amid it all I waited for the traffic light to turn green.

Suddenly, a man stormed at me, grabbed the back of my neck with a vice grip and stuck a metal stick into the hole of my ear. He gouged me deeply, scratching away painfully. I shivered. Who is this man? What was he doing? Would he puncture my eardrum? He kept gouging and I was totally under his control, afraid to move. Next, he released my neck, yanked the metal out from my ear, and held it up for me to see. Attached to his stick was a big lump of earwax. I was delighted, as I could hear better than I had in years, at least in one ear. He then demanded one rupee as the price to clean the other ear. But I had nothing. He bargained but to no avail, leaving me with a dirty ear. I couldn't believe it. I had no idea how filthy my ear had been until I felt what it was like to have it clean, especially compared to the other one. With a rueful smile, I drew a parallel to the spiritual journey. *Perhaps,* I thought:

> *The dirty wax of egotism accumulated in the heart prevents us from clearly hearing the Lord's voice within. A guru, with the stick of knowledge, cleans our hearts. It's really ugly to see what may come out, but by following patiently, we keep cleaning.*

Another lesson I took from this experience was this:

> *Sometimes the Lord gives us a free sample of religious experience, but for more, we must pay a price with the currency of sincere dedication to the process of cleansing.*

My hearing was now like an unbalanced stereo system. I knew I had cleansing still to do, and on many levels. I waited on the street corner until the traffic light turned green, but when I reached down to lift my bag of books—it was gone. I was frantic. I searched the four directions, running here and there, asking everybody around, but to no avail. I had to come to grips with the reality that my books had been stolen. Standing on that corner, I lamented.

These precious books enlightened me with knowledge and inspiration. They were an irreplaceable treasure in my life. I received them from the benevolent hands of my teachers. My precious wealth has been ripped away.

Terribly sad, hopeless of their recovery, I walked away.

After taking a few steps, I became aware of how easy it had become to walk. The heavy burden that had troubled me for so long, the bag of books, was gone. Just as suddenly as I had felt despair, I felt liberated. Almost skipping, I reflected:

The nature of the mind is to interpret nonessentials essential. The mind creates artificial needs, believing it cannot live without them. In this way we carry a great burden of attachments throughout our life. Attachment is itself a great burden on our minds. We may never understand the extent of the burden till, like my books or the earwax, we're free of it. But if we find joy within, we can live a simple life, free of endless complications.

I had begun to develop an attachment to finding the right path and teacher by my own will. Paradoxically, I now understood that in order to truly find what I was seeking, I needed to be detached and sincere. Whatever obstacles I was to encounter along the way would serve, I hoped, to bring me to ultimate freedom.

4

YODHYA, THE BIRTHPLACE OF LORD RAMA, has been a place of pilgrimage for countless millions of devotees over millennia and I wished to join them. Long ago, the all-beautiful Lord appeared here in the role of a man to teach the world by His own example. As a son, he graciously accepted exile, sacrificing his right to the throne, all to protect the honor of his father. As a husband, he loved and protected his wife, Sita, to the extent of waging a war to protect her. As a student, he rendered menial services while eagerly learning from his teachers. As a friend, he showed tender love to all those who were in need. As a brother, his loyalty and love shone in the face of insurmountable temptations. And later, in the role of a king, Lord Rama treated every citizen without discrimination, like his own sons and daughters. All of these attributes were meant to teach us the responsibilities we have in our relationships and to endear our hearts to love the Lord.

Walking down a wide road lined with large temples and palaces, and seeing thousands of pilgrims swarming about, my first impression was that in coming to Ayodhya I had entered into a royal kingdom.

Each night I slept on the earthen bank of the river Sarayu. One morning, after my bath, I walked with great anticipation to the site of Lord Rama's birth. Little did I know I had stumbled onto one of the biggest sites of crisis in the world.

Were my eyes deceiving me? A place of pilgrimage worshipped by hundreds of millions, the sacred birthplace of Lord Rama, was marked by an abandoned mosque enclosed by coils of barbed wire fencing and patrolled by soldiers armed with rifles, bayonettes, and hand grenades. Outside the fence, about a dozen sadhus sat on a wooden platform chanting the Holy Names of Lord Rama. Confused, I inquired into what was happening here, but none of the sadhus spoke English. Finally, somebody gave me a pamphlet written in English. It explained that Janma Bhumi was Lord Rama's birthplace and that long ago a magnificent Rama temple stood here. But a Moghul conqueror built a mosque in its place and over the years, Hindus and Muslims had battled over ownership of the land. Finally, to subdue the bloody Hindu-Muslim conflict, the government had seized control. "Today, guarded by heavily armed military, no one is allowed entrance into the area," the pamphlet concluded. "That is why these sadhus have vowed to loudly sing the Holy Names of Rama constantly until the Hindus are given access."

Recalling similar tensions brewing in Jerusalem at the disputed Dome of the Rock, I faced the huge steel lock on the gate and reflected on worldwide politics and bloodshed. In my travels, looking for the love of God, I had discovered a unique beauty in all of the world's religions. But hateful aggression in the name of God is also a sad reality of this world. It is the way of those attached to external forms without understanding the essence. The essence is one, unconditional love of God. The symptoms of any true follower are faith, self-control, love, and compassion.

Looking through the barbed wire, I saw a wooden table at the entrance of the abandoned mosque. On it was a painting of Lord Rama. A soldier in full military attire marched toward it, leather boots stomping the dusty ground. He had a rifle with an attached bayonet slung over his shoulder and bullets strapped across his chest. Bowing down in prayer, he carefully placed a garland of marigolds around the painting. Under the circumstances, he was the temple priest. I watched in wonder.

It was in Ayodhya that I was given an English translation of the Ramayan, which I read daily on the bank of the Sarayu River. This ancient scripture recounts the life and teachings of Lord Rama. While I still had a tendency to meditate on the all-pervading, impersonal Truth, I was slowly finding my heart irresistibly drawn to the personal qualities of the Lord. Reading about the loving exchanges between Rama and His devotees drew my mind closer to the path of devotion. He was such a wonderful role model, teaching us how to be a spiritual person, but also active in the world of family and society. At the time of my departure, I thanked holy Ayodhya and prayed that I would never forget the treasured gifts I received.

My pilgrimage next led me southeast to Prayaga, praised as the king of holy places. This was home of the Kumbha Mela, the largest gathering on earth where up to twenty million pilgrims gather every twelve years to meet saintly people and take a religious purification bath. Prayaga is situated at the confluence of three rivers: the Ganges, Yamuna, and Saraswati. Six months earlier, I had declined invitations to come to Kumbha Mela in favor of staying alone by the Ganges in the Himalayas, but it had been a dream of mine to visit. Arriving on a sweltering summer morning, I asked a local man the way to the confluence. Pointing his finger, he directed me.

When I reached the river Ganges, I sat on her sandy bank and thought back to those first days of my life in India. I remembered sitting on that rock in Rishikesh while Mother Ganges taught me lessons that were to mold my life. I remembered hearing in her eternal song the Hare Krishna mantra that would become embedded in my soul. Now, sitting on that sandy bank in Prayaga, I knew that if I simply followed her current, I would come to her meeting with Yamuna and Saraswati at the confluence. It was this confluence that the Vedas declared to be the king of all holy places. I walked in that direction. It was high noon, and fine white sands blazed like fire, scorching my bare feet. Ever since that day I had offended the Naga Babas by wearing my shoes at their sacred fire, I had renounced shoes and walked barefoot. But that day, the sand was so unbearably hot that it seemed impossible to continue. The distance seemed endless. Finally, after over an hour, a beautiful sight rose before my eyes. The Yamuna River, descended from the Himalayas, having flowed through the plains of North India, was embracing Mother Ganges—Yamuna with her complexion of deep blue, Ganges with hers of white, and the transparent Saraswati joined them from below.

Sitting on the sandy bank, I gazed into the cloudless blue sky. There, a hawk, wings extended, soared the airways. His reddish-brown feathers shone in the sun as he hovered lower and lower, till he was just a few yards above my head, his glistening yellow eyes intently scanning the river. Suddenly he plunged headlong into the Ganges. There, a frantic underwater skirmish ensued until he emerged with a flapping fish, about a foot long, pierced in the grip of his talons. Squirming desperately, the fish was carried overhead and into a nearby forest. Looking on I reflected:

The unsuspecting fish, who knew nothing but a life in the river, went about its routine like any other day, but in an instant was ripped out of its reality to meet with death. Like that fish, we routinely live our lives hardly aware that, at the least expected moment, the yellow-eyed hawk of fate in the form of crises, tragedy, or even death, may wrench us out of our comfortable environment. We regularly hear of it in the news or see it around us but rarely take seriously that it could happen to us. Perhaps the lesson here is to guard against complacency and give higher priority to our spiritual needs. If the fish swam deeper, the hawk would not be able reach it. Similarly, if we go deeper into our connection to God, we will find an inner reality so deep and so satisfying that it lifts the consciousness to a place where we could deal with the effects of unforeseeable fate with a stable, detached mind.

On the bank of the three rivers, in the blazing summer heat, there was not a soul to be seen, so I left my few belongings on the riverbank and entered the water. After bathing, I was hit by a wave of enthusiasm to stay in as long as possible. After all, I didn't know if I would ever come to this magical place again. I ventured to swim across to the other side. It was about a hundred yards wide. The flow of the Ganges was forceful, the Yamuna gentle. As I swam, the force of the Ganges swept me to a bank where there was nothing and no one to be seen. I pulled myself out of the water and stepped onto the sandy bank. To my horror, I found myself being swallowed, seized by a power that sucked me downward.

Quicksand! It had appeared to be just like the soft sand I often slept on. But looks could be deceiving. Frantically, I struggled for my life, but in spite of my strongest endeavors, I sunk deeper and deeper. Already, my body had been sucked down past my knees, and I was gradually sinking deeper. Mustering all my strength, I squirmed doggedly, in vain. Mother Earth was literally devouring me.

I scanned all directions for help but found nothing. And then to my left I caught sight of a leafless bush. With a desperate lunge I grabbed on to it as my single hope of survival. It was a thorn bush. Gripping it tightly, I yanked with all my might. With bleeding hands, tugging and tugging on that thorny branch, I struggled to free my legs. Under the blazing sun, I squirmed for dear life. The razor-like thorns pierced my hands. My blood flowed from burning wounds. But what choice did I have? I could accept the agonizing pain, or surrender to the sands and an ignoble and ghastly death. Gasping in fatigue and soaked in sweat, I would somehow pry one leg free, only to have it sucked down again. With my next tug, the thorn bush with its rotted roots, sprung out from the sand. I silently screamed. Letting go of the useless branch and exhausted by my frenzy, I took a deep breath and relaxed. Amazingly, I discovered that if I was calm the quicksand was less aggressive. I laid my torso flat on the sand and found that I could almost float in that position. It was not a solution but it did give me some time. Inch by inch, in slow motion, I raised my legs. Finally, at a snails pace, I wormed my way back into the river.

I was free, or so I thought. Now all I had to do was swim across Yamuna's mild current. But that meant challenging the mighty current of the Ganges head on. No matter how hard I swam, Mother Ganges kept forcing me back toward the quicksand. Exhaustion was threatening to overtake me. I could no longer fight against the current. I toiled feverishly, but still I was moving backwards. My arms were fatigued almost to the point of paralysis; still I strained to keep body and soul engaged in a battle I was not winning. My destination was so distant I could barely see it. Struggling for survival, I prayed.

Suddenly, hope appeared. About two hundred feet ahead, a small fishing boat passed. There on the deck stood a shriveled man with a white beard wearing a red turban. Still chopping against the current, I screamed out to him again and again for help. *Will he hear me?* I continued crying out for help as my strength faded. Finally, he spotted me. Smiling, he waved his hand in a forward direction. Then, still smiling, he glided right past me, leaving me to drown.

Involuntarily swallowing more and more water, I now lost all hope. Even as my hopes died, I thought, *It is better to drown in a holy river than suffocate in that quicksand.* The same Ganges who, in Rishikesh, had taught me so many precious lessons and nourished me as a mother, to whom I offered my egotism in the form of my harmonica, and whose song awakened my soul, to her I now offered my life. Prayer was the only thing I had left.

Then something wonderful happened. Submerged under water, on the verge of death, a beautiful song awakened in my heart:

Hare Krishna Hare Krishna Krishna Krishna Hare Hare Hare Rama Hare Rama Rama Rama Hare Hare.

Just as the Ganges first revealed this mantra to me, she was revealing it again at the hour of my greatest need. Silently reciting this mantra, I resigned myself to die in a holy place. The mantra brought me into a state of peace beyond fear. Then, like the rising sun, a thought appeared in my mind. I thought, *Why did that fisherman wave his hand forward? What did it mean?* Suddenly, I understood. He was saying, "Do not fight against Mother Ganges. Go across her current by swimming with the current of the Yamuna." In my passion to survive, I'd not thought of that. That fisherman's wave saved my life.

As I was carried across the Ganges, I was seized by worry once more. I had left my passport and whatever little I carried alone on the other side of the river's bank. Now I was swimming in the opposite direction. Would my things be there when I returned? And then it occurred to me. *Why brood over such a trifle? Moments before, death was threatening my life and with only the passport of God's Names I crossed over and was saved.* Hours later, when I made it back to the other shore where I had left my things, evening was beginning to fall and hundreds of people were scrambling to take a bath. My belongings sat in their midst, unmolested.

Surrounded by the noisy crowds, I sat on the sandy bank. *In the morning,* I thought*:*

> *The sand scorched me like blazing fire, and later, was greedy to devour me. But now the same sand is cool and soft and gives me shelter. Like sand, a person influenced by circumstances can become viciously envious or affectionately kind. Our company and surroundings have a crucial effect on our consciousness. How important it is to be an instrument to bring out the inherent good of each other rather than the worst. So much wisdom is being whispered through every grain of sand if only I have ears to hear.*

As the soft sand glided through my fingers, I pondered my life and death struggle in the current of Mother Ganges. An affectionate mother may, at times, deal harshly with her child to impress a lesson that will not be easily forgotten. What was I to learn from today's ordeal? Perhaps we cannot always succeed by directly opposing a powerful force. I thought of the many trials I had faced on my path. If we do, our efforts will drown in failure. It is like swimming against the Ganges' current.

In such circumstances, it might be more effective to find a path of less resistance to accomplish the desired end indirectly. The summer sun was fading below the horizon and I recalled how earlier that day I witnessed a hawk rip an unsuspecting fish *out* of its home, the river. A little later, with no warning, the talons of fate had me gasping for dear life, *in* the same river. *Today,* I reflected, *the Lord has given me a startling glimpse of how far I am from my goal. It was not an easy lesson to learn. And hopefully it will not be easily forgotten.* I took a deep breath and looked up into the sky, there, far above all the smaller winging birds, I saw a hawk, with the confidence of an emperor, gliding effortlessly into the twilight.

5

THE MONSOON RAINS HAD COME. Billowing clouds of purple, indigo, and midnight blue were streaked with repeated flashes of lightning. Bass rumbles of thunder resonated across the sky. Although traveling in monsoon season was hard, I inhaled the moist, warm air and was thrilled. July was approaching and I wondered where to go for my next visa extension. There was a rumor that one could easily get an Indian visa in Nepal. Considering that it was not very far away, I decided to try.

On my journey northeast toward Nepal, I arrived in Patna, a bustling city of huge granaries, colleges, and political buildings in the state of Bihar. I meandered to the river Ganges and slept on the river's bank at the Collectory Ghat, where Mother Ganges looked as wide as a sea and was awakened by the rays of the rising sun and the sound of hundreds of people singing songs while preparing to take their baths. I lay there taking in this colorful display when suddenly I sensed an overpowering presence.

There, towering over me was a marvelous looking man with long white hair and beard. I felt to be face to face with a classical holy man of ancient lore. Three vertical lines called *tilak* were drawn on his forehead, the centerline was red and the other two white. Perhaps in his late seventies, he spoke no English but, pressing his hands together and bowing in greeting, gestured for me to follow him into his temple on the riverbank. Not bigger than a large hut, the gray stone temple looked very old. Its front was open to the river, and as we entered I saw a man who appeared to be in his mid-eighties sitting before an altar reciting prayers.

He greeted me in fluent English. "My name is Narayan Prasad, I hail from Patna." He began to tell me his story. "Now that my children are grown, I am retired from government service and come here each day to serve my guru." Taking my hand, he led me back to the same holy man who'd found me lying by the riverside. "This is my guru, Rama

Sevaka Swami, he is a great *bhakti* yogi." I knew by now that *bhakti* meant devotion, but I had no idea yet of the depth or true meaning of this tradition.

The Swami invited me to remain at his temple as long as I wished. He was to be the first sadhu who followed the path of bhakti yoga I would stay with. Like a loving father, he carefully considered my welfare. A gentle smile beamed from his aged face every time he looked at me. Although four times my age, he fed me with his own hands. Later, when I was ill, he prepared herbal medicines for me. He was a revered Swami and I a lost little soul, a Western kid struggling to find my way.

My heart was moved seeing the devotion of Rama Sevaka Swami. It was from him that I learned much about the behavior of an honest and genuine holy man. Simplicity and devotion poured from his heart in whatever he did. Each morning, he spent several hours alone chanting the names of Lord Rama on his wooden beads and performed his daily worship on the altar with great feeling. One day he explained to me the meaning of his name. "Rama Sevaka means 'one who serves Lord Rama' and the greatest service to Rama is to help others to know Him and love Him." He stroked his flowing white beard and became emotional. "I am indebted to you for allowing me to help you." Hearing this, even Narayan Prasad was overcome with emotion and had to struggle to speak the translation. As for me, I was only beginning to grasp the meaning of true devotion.

At night, as we all slept on the jagged stone floor of the temple, swarms of bloodthirsty mosquitoes tormented me. I felt I was being eaten alive. Their buzzing agitated my ears. Zeroing in, they stabbed into my flesh and sucked my blood. It was impossible to sleep. In distress, I looked over at Rama Sevaka Swami and a visiting sadhu. Even though mosquitoes swarmed around them and grew plump with their blood, they lay peacefully on the rocks, sleeping soundly. These two sadhus were completely oblivious to bodily suffering. I prayed to God that someday I might be so detached.

One evening, a visiting sadhu offered to cook for us. After begging alms in town, he returned and, while crouching on the floor, he started a fire with the fuel of dried cow dung paddies that heated a clay pot. He cooked *kitcheri* made with rice, mung, and some potatoes. His complexion was dark, his hair and beard matted, and he wore only a faded white loincloth. When he finished cooking, he offered the food first on the altar and then to us. I sat on the floor in a row with Rama Sevaka Swami and three other sadhus. As our cook heaped a ladleful of kitcheri on each plate, we chanted songs in praise of Lord Rama and prepared to eat. We ate with our fingers from a leaf plate. With the first bite, my mouth blazed. It was as if the cook had spiced the chili peppers with a little rice. I was sweating profusely; my nose ran, and tears streamed from my eyes. It felt like the remaining wax in my ears was melting. I despaired, for according to sadhu custom, one must complete everything on one's plate. At that moment, my only goal in life was to somehow finish my plate. The pain was excruciating and I hiccupped uncontrollably. I ate mouthful after mouthful of that blistering dish in sheer anguish. The others were enjoying it so much they never could have dreamed of my suffering. Just as I managed to choke back the last of my portion and feel the promise of relief, our generous cook came around to give seconds.

I blocked my plate with my hands. *"Puran, puran."* I am full, no more.

He smiled with the ladle brimming over, ready to fill my plate. *"Thora, thora."* A little, take just a little more.

I felt as if I were standing before death personified, pleading for my life. *"Puran, puran."* My hands protectively covered the plate.

"Thora, thora."

With a gracious smile, he performed the fateful deed: he dropped the contents of the ladle on my plate. My mind reeling, I somehow completed the fiery food and breathed a sigh of relief. Just then, I saw him returning with thirds. I knew I couldn't survive another plate. I wanted to run away but couldn't. The etiquette among sadhus is that no one gets up until all others have completed. He dipped the ladle into the pot and filled it with what looked like a ladle full of chilies.

Ever since I was a child, I had always felt bad when I caused other people sorrow. So intent was the cook on pleasing us that I didn't have the heart to reveal the pain he was causing me. My pulse was racing. What could I do?

In haste, I lifted my leaf plate and crumpled it into my hands.

He smiled and went on to the next sadhu. Amazed, I watched all the others thoroughly enjoying helping after helping. The cook pointed to me and bragged, "He likes my cooking so much he is crying in gratitude." I forced a smile and nodded in agreement, while reflecting on the philosophy of selfless service that was so much a part of these men's lives.

Yes, I'm crying, and it may as well be in gratitude, as he believes. To please others is not always easy, but it is part of my deepest nature to wish to do so. Enduring the burning pain of that food was a small price to please this sadhu.

That night the mosquitoes hardly bothered me—perhaps my blood was too spicy.

While in Patna, Narayan Prasad became a dear friend of mine. As it goes with friends, he was eager for me to meet a dear friend of his, a doctor who operated an X-ray clinic. One day, the doctor welcomed us into his office and invited us to sit around his desk. Although born a Hindu, he was disillusioned by prejudice against lower castes and, largely for this reason, had converted to Islam. He was now a scholar of the Holy Koran and accepted the name Mohammad. He continued to accept the teachings of the Bhagavad Gita, but did not want to be affiliated with a religion that discriminated against people on the basis of their birth. I challenged him. "But the Gita doesn't discriminate on the basis of one's birth. Many of the greatest saints of the Hindus were born of lower castes. The Bhagavad Gita teaches we are not material bodies but immortal souls."

Together we discussed the true basis of religion, examining the parallels of the Bhagavad Gita, the Bible, and the Koran. We continued to meet thereafter, and without bias or prejudice we enriched each other with dialogue. He didn't try to convert me to Islam and I didn't try to convert him either. Rather, with mutual respect, we shared our realizations. In our dialogue, I could feel the mercy of God flowing through each of the great scriptures, saints, and religions in a special way. I was becoming more and more aware that, no matter what one's path and no matter how narrow it became, in broadest terms, sincere devotion to God was the only way to overcome the strife and division of the world.

Sitting on the bank of the Ganges one day after a talk with Mohammed, I inquired of Narayan Prasad, "How is it that you have so much affection for someone from another religion in a country where there is so much conflict between the two?"

With a warm smile, he said something I have never forgotten. "A dog will recognize his master in whatever way he dresses. The master may dress in robes, suit and tie, or stand naked, but the dog will always recognize his master. If we cannot recognize God, our beloved master, when he comes in a different dress from another religion, then we are less than that dog."

As I had stayed longer with Rama Sevaka Swami than I'd planned, I hiked to the foreign immigration office in Patna to try for an extension. The office was nothing more than a small brick house with an old man behind a desk. There were hardly any filing cabinets. Most of the papers and records were piled high on the official's desk and floor. He searched through these piles for fifteen minutes before he found the application form. After filling out the application, I handed over my passport. He studied it for a moment, then in a flat, bureaucratic tone, said, "Your visa cannot be extended beyond the current expiration date."

His words left me dumbstruck. To leave my adopted Motherland would be unbearable. I pleaded with him again and again. But he stuck to his official response. It seemed hopeless. I prayed.

At that moment, I saw a painting of Lord Rama on the wall behind him. Meekly, I addressed the man. "Sir, in the country I come from, everybody eats cows."

His jaw dropped and eyes opened wide. "What? Killing our sacred cow? How horrible."

"Sir, in the country I am from, boys and girls often live together without marriage."

He shook his head in disapproval and clicked his tongue. "Uncivilized."

"I shudder to tell you this, sir, but no one in my country has ever even heard the name of Rama."

He could not believe his ears. Reaching across the desk, he grabbed my hands in his. "You must never go back to that horrible place."

"But if you don't extend my visa, I must go back to that place. I came to India to seek shelter in your beloved Lord Rama."

He pushed his chair back, jumped up and declared, "I am Rama's devotee. It is my duty to protect you." With these words, he stamped a new visa on my passport.

Each morning at Rama Sevaka Swami's ashram, five sadhus would gather in the temple to read in Hindi from the *Ramayana*, the story of Lord Rama. I could understand only a few words here and there but Narayan Prasad promised me that he would translate whatever was spoken after the session. For three hours, the sadhus sat in rapt attention as emotions flooded their hearts. Sometimes they shook in laughter; other times they wept with joy or sorrow. Still, at other times they sat motionless in suspense, fear, and wonder. I was starving to hear the story that affected them so.

When the discussion was complete, I begged Narayan Prasad, "Please tell me everything."

We strolled out of the temple and sat on the bank of the Ganges where he began the narration. "One morning, when Lord Krishna was a small baby, his mother Yasoda fed him milk from her breast. As she was doing so, she noticed that a pot of milk on the stove was boiling over, so after putting baby Krishna in a safe place, she ran to save it. Krishna did not like being put aside like this. To show that no one should have priorities above service to God, he displayed his heart enchanting quality of naughtiness by breaking a clay butter pot and eating the butter. Then, stirring up even more trouble, he entered another room where he climbed on top of a wooden grinding mortar. From this height, Krishna could reach up to steal more butter from a clay pot suspended from the ceiling by ropes. While eating to his full satisfaction, he fed butter to the local monkeys. Meanwhile, Yasoda searched for her child.

"Following his buttery footprints, she spied him feeding the monkeys while glancing fearfully from side to side. She smiled. As she tiptoed toward him, Krishna caught a glimpse of her and fled. Yasoda, overwhelmed by motherly love, chased after him, and Krishna, pleased to be conquered by his devotee's love, agreed to be captured. His little body trembled with thought of punishment. Tears fell from his eyes, pleas for mercy from his lips. He promised to not steal butter again. Because Mother Yasoda had household chores to do and wanted to protect her baby, she attempted to bind Him around the waist with a silk rope to the grinding mortar. But the rope was two inches too short, so she tied more rope to the original one. Still, it was two inches too short. Her friends, the *gopis*, or cowherd women, brought more and more rope. No matter what they tried, the rope was always two inches too short. Seeing his mother, smiling with uncontrollable affection and perspiring from her work with the rope, flowers falling from her hair, Krishna finally agreed to be bound by her love. In this pastime Krishna shows us that, although He is the supreme controller of all universes, He finds the greatest pleasure in being bound by the love of His devotees."

To my surprise, I found myself overwhelmed with joy, and begged Narayan Prasad, "Please tell me more."

"That's all we spoke today," he replied simply.

"But the talk was over three hours. Please say more."

"That's all that was spoken."

The next day, thrilled by the story about Krishna as a child and by the devotees' enrapt attention to the lecture, I was even more eager to hear. When the meeting ended, Narayan Prasad and I sat on the banks of the Ganges and once again he told me the same story of Krishna stealing butter. He would tell me no more, no matter how much I begged. With a mischievous smile he replied, "That is all that was spoken."

On the third day during the talk, the emotions of the sadhus were wonderfully vibrant with devotion. Sitting on the bank of Mother Ganges, I looked long and level at Narayan Prasad, my translator. "I must hear what was spoken today." He narrated the exact same story of Krishna stealing butter that he told before.

Upset, I challenged him. "Why are you doing this to me? Every day the talk goes on for three hours, but your story is only ten minutes. Why do you deceive me?"

"But that's all that was spoken."

Anger stirred in my breast. "Today, I listened carefully. Not once was the name Krishna or Yasoda spoken. Now please, please tell me."

He smiled and remained calm. "We only discussed baby Krishna stealing butter."

Tears filled my eyes. "Am I so unworthy that I am not permitted to hear?"

Seeing my distress, Narayan Prasad became sober. He gazed deeply into my eyes, "Seeing your sincere tears, I will now tell you the reason." He paused for several minutes then broke the silence. "The first night that you came here, Rama Sevaka Swami had a dream. Lord Rama appeared to him and spoke these words. 'This young boy is a devotee of Krishna, but he does not know it yet. You must not speak anything to him except the glories of Krishna. Vrindavan will be his place of worship. He will not believe you if you tell him this. But someday he will understand.'"

The Ganges flowed forcefully as Narayan Prasad put his hand on my shoulder. Tears welled in his eyes as he tried to pacify me. "My guru, Rama Sevaka Swami gave me an order. I am not to speak to you about anyone except Krishna. But all my life, I've been a devotee of Rama and although both Rama and Krishna are the same one supreme person who appeared in different forms at different times, the only story I properly know about Krishna is His stealing butter." He reached into his bag and pulled out a print of baby Krishna stealing butter and gave it to me. It charmed my heart. Still, I was unable to grasp what he said. Was I to worship Krishna, and in a place called Vrindavan? Because I could not understand it, I dismissed the idea out of hand. All I knew then was that I aimed to return to the caves of the Himalayas.

I had stayed several weeks at Rama Sevaka Swami's ashram, enchanted by his gentle manner and that of his followers. The day I was leaving, I bowed down to seek the Swami's blessings. He wanted to give me a gift, but what did he have to offer? Looking around, he noticed his own walking stick, and with a tearful smile, presented it to me. I was overcome with gratitude. Although it was nothing but a crude branch broken from a tree, it was a gift of love that meant more to me than all the fortune in the world. I accepted his sacred gift, and my eagerness to do so brought him joy. He spoke in a voice cracking with affection as Narayan Prasad translated. "The scripture tells us that the stick of a devotee's mercy can save one from the greatest dangers." The stick was to become my constant companion.

6

SUPPRESSING MY OCCASIONAL FEARS of what might lie before me, I pressed on. I felt that something special was waiting for me in Nepal. From Patna, I traveled by train to Raxaul, a town near the border between India and Nepal.

A truck driver, his hair and clothes soiled by the dusty roads, smiled through teeth stained red from chewing spices. With a wave of his hand he welcomed me to climb onto his cargo trailer. I found a place among the other passengers, mountain women dressed in long faded dresses with scarves wrapped over their gray hair and farmers in faded cloth traveling with their bleating goats and cackling chickens, and sat atop one of the many burlap grain bags piled up under our feet. We jostled along, ascending ever higher up the bumpy road.

The cargo area had no roof and was overloaded as much as humanly possible, so much so that we rode higher than the truck's cab. Although the conveyance was neither comfortable nor safe, there could be no better panoramic view of the Himalayas. As we climbed to greater elevations, verdant mountains and valleys stretched in all directions. Snow clad peaks presided over the horizons and at times soared above us. My lungs feasted on the fresh mountain air and my flesh thrilled to the touch of the crisp breeze. No one seemed to mind being lashed periodically by monsoon storms. Hours later, in the middle of the night, the truck dropped us off just outside of Kathmandu.

Exhausted and hungry, I continued on my way alone through the damp, black night. Dilapidated wooden houses loomed on either side of the deserted street. But something else seized my attention. From a distance I could hear the mad howling of dogs. With growing apprehension, I began to recollect warnings I'd been given from wandering sadhus about the wild dogs: how by night they roamed in crazed packs; how the pack would ensnare their prey in an ever tightening circle, ferociously attack, and rip their victim limb from limb; how they would then devour the corpse on the spot. Almost as soon as I'd had the thought, an outcast dog, foaming at the mouth, spotted me alone on the deserted street. He flung his head back and pierced the sky with a howl.

Seconds later, a pack of snarling dogs charged towards me. Were there six or eight? I was too shaken to count. But I did grasp the significance of the foamy white venom dripping from their snapping mouths. These beasts were rabid. Eyes bulging with rage, they closed in on me, howling madly all the while, intending to tear me apart. Their scrawny bodies were gaunt and nearly hairless. Their unearthly din petrified me. With foaming mouths and fangs dripping venom, they pressed in on me. To prevent an attack from behind, I pressed my back against a house, and in the darkness I prayed. *What shall I do?*

Then, as if shaken from a trance, I remembered the walking stick that Rama Sevaka Swami had given me. Wildly, I began to swing it back and forth. The horde fell back into a semi-circle around me, only a few feet away. As each frenzied dog lunged forward, I whacked its snout with the Swami's stick. With the full force of my skinny arms, I struck. Growling ferociously, yet another predator leapt at me. I whacked him as hard as I could. Each of my attackers, when beaten back by the stick, would fall back only momentarily, and then, unfazed, leap to the attack again. Howls filled the night. Again and again, the pack surged toward me, and again and again I managed to smack them down. But the more I fought, the more they escalated the siege. They could smell my flesh and blood. They could sense my exhaustion. There was no time to think. Every second I had to swing that stick with all my might. If even one dog were to get through, the horde would descend and instantly devour me. *Was this to be my fate? To end as dog food?*

My strength was waning. Sensing imminent victory, their snarling became more fierce and deafening. They closed in for the kill, so tightly now I nearly blacked out from the stench of their breath. Feverish, despairing, I helplessly prayed for mercy. I felt utterly alone and on the verge of being killed. Just then, glancing over my shoulder I noticed a closed door behind me. Was it locked? A single ray of hope broke through my nightmare. Quickly, I swung my shoulders around, twisted the knob, and pushed. The door gave way. I dove inside and slammed it shut behind me. Outside, the dogs vented their indignation by hurling their bodies against the door.

Inside it was pitch dark. Suddenly, a lantern flared up, revealing a family together on the floor roused from sleep. The men of the house, thinking me to be a burglar, sprang to their feet demanding to know who I was. But I couldn't speak their language. Lifting a sword, a man charged toward me. What could I do but sink to my knees and with joined palms beg for mercy?

When the host saw my supplications, he softened, and with arm stretched, pointed his finger to the door, demanding that I leave at once. But hearing the ferocious screams of the dogs, he paused and understood that for me to go outside would mean death. Still, he was apprehensive about this late night intruder and he stared long and hard into my eyes as if groping to size up my character and intentions. With only my expression, I pleaded for him to give me shelter. Somehow my silent plea reached him. He placed down his sword and offered me a seat. From this moment, he began to see me in a new light, accepting me as a sadhu who had come, under extraordinary circumstances, to bless his home. The other residents followed his lead and prepared for me fruit and hot sweetened milk, which I gratefully accepted. I spent the rest of the night as their guest listening to the pack of hungry dogs barking outside the door until dawn, their fury unabated.

I had once heard an old analogy from the American Indians, and it came to my mind now. Within every heart dwell two dogs, a bad dog and a good dog, both at battle with one another. The bad dog represents our debased tendencies of envy, anger, lust, greed, arrogance, and illusion. The good dog, our divine nature, is represented by forgiveness, compassion, self-control, generosity, humility, and wisdom. Whichever dog we feed the most through the choices we make and the utilization of our time will empower that dog to bark the loudest and conquer the other. Virtue is to starve the bad dog and feed the good dog. The pack of bad dogs that attacked tonight, foaming at the mouth with a lust to devour me, was a graphic visualization of what I was up against in my internal journey.

As I lay there in relief, my thoughts flowed gratefully to Rama Sevaka Swami. *If he had not given me that stick, I would surely have died tonight.* I recalled his words, prophetic and true: *"The stick of a devotee's mercy can save one from the greatest dangers."*

The next morning, when quiet prevailed and the dogs scattered for the day, I thanked my hosts profusely and left to visit a temple of Lord Vishnu. Here I heard a group of sadhus praising Janakpur, a holy place in the plains of Nepal where Sita, the consort of Lord Rama, appeared on earth. Their words invoked my spirit of adventure and at once I departed. From Kathmandu, I found passage on a rickety bus destined for Janakpur. Hours passed, the bus descended the Himalayan Mountains, and crossed the plains into a dense jungle where I saw a wild rhinoceros grazing on the foliage. Arriving in Janakpur, I first visited Vihar Kund, a small lake in an open, quiet area surrounded by old trees, quaint shrines, and an ashram, where I was brought before the guru Sri Vedji. He was an aged sadhu with white stubble covering his jaw and head. He was overwhelmingly kind and begged me to reside in his ashram with free meals of rice and dhal each day.

Sri Vedji explained to me why Janakpur was a holy place, known in the scriptures as Mithila, its glories sung in the spiritual epic *Ramayana*. King Janak, in preparation for a religious rite, was plowing the soil here when, out from the earth, the Goddess Sita appeared right under his plow. She became known as Janaki, the daughter of King Janak. Mithila was the first meeting place of Sita and Rama and the place where Rama broke the mighty bow of Shiva to win the hand of Sita in marriage.

By this time in my travels, the stories of God's incarnations on earth had become completely real to me. Seeing how enthralled I was, the kindly Sri Vedji presented me with English translations of two Indian classics, *The Ramayana* by Valmiki and *Ramacharitamanas* by Tulasidas. They were thick volumes, and every morning I rose, bathed in a nearby lake, performed my meditation, and began my study, reading from sunrise until sunset.

I found the Ramayana packed with adventure, romance, tragedy, heroism, horror, humor, and war. But there was more to it than this. All of these elements harmonized in a spirit of devotion to awaken the love of God in the heart of the reader. When I volunteered to do some chores, Sri Vedji just smiled. "Your reading, and accepting our food, is purifying my heart. What greater service can I ask you for?"

On an early afternoon, I sat on the main road, a dusty path, and did not see a single car or truck pass all day. This was not surprising since giant Nepalese elephants were the common form of transport in Janakpur. On the back of each elephant a large cargo box was secured by a rope extending around its belly. The driver, typically a small boy, sat on the elephant's neck, just behind the head, and held a stick. A heavy brass bell hung from the elephant's neck, clanging as it swung from side to side. Each elephant moved with a regal, confident gait. Elephant after elephant passed in this way, along with oxen and water buffalo pulling overloaded carts. Women strolled past carrying either baskets or earthen pots on the top of their heads, often balancing the load without hands. Even small girls effortlessly carried big loads in this way, maintaining perfect posture. As these girls carried their loads, they blissfully sang together the glories of Sita and Rama. The peaceful life these people lived soothed my heart. I prayed that Janakpur would never change.

Near a sacred lake in the heart of Janakpur sat many temples. Two of these temples were prominent: Janaki Mandir and Rama Mandir. One day in the courtyard of Rama Mandir, I came upon a sadhu in his fifties sitting on a raised platform beside the temple. With his long matted hair, beard, and mendicant's robes, he appeared peaceful and holy. Hundreds of people stood in line to receive his blessings. When they reached the front, he graciously blessed them with his open palm. Desiring his holy blessing, I too joined the line and approached him, bowing down like all the others. Surprised to see me, he motioned for me to sit beside him on the platform. I felt especially privileged.

While continuing to bless one admirer after the next, he inquired of me. "Where do you come from?"

"America."

"Why have you come from your rich country to the poverty of India?"

"In search of God."

He smiled at an old woman who lowered her head beneath his beneficent hand. "Why have you become a sadhu?" he asked through his smile.

"To seek enlightenment."

Hearing my words, his expression grew sour. His smile melted into a frown and his voice became ugly. Shocked by this reversal, I didn't know what to expect. "You are a fool," he hissed. "You are simply a fool. Do you hear me? A fool. A fool. An ignorant fool."

I knew that I was a fool. Perhaps he wished to enlighten me, so I inquired submissively, "Your Holiness, please instruct me how I can improve."

Flying into a tantrum, he screamed, "I have been living as a sadhu for thirty years. Do you know what I have attained? Nothing. In all my years as a sadhu, all I've gotten is some rotten rice and dhal." A woman stretched forth an infant to receive his blessing. "America is a land of riches," he shouted at me, while blessing the child with his palm. "America has the most beautiful women to enjoy. America has big comfortable houses and automobiles. America has fine clothes, food, and drink. America has the best movies and television." He closed his eyes and sighed. "Oh, how I long for the pleasures of America." His eyes blazed now upon me. "But you have given it all up, and for what? Rice and dhal, I'm sick of rice and dhal. You have come to this miserable place of poverty to search for God. You are a fool. There is no God. Do you hear me? There is no God. Go back to your great land to enjoy. If you don't obey me, you will lead a despicable life and be cursed with the misery."

As he spewed forth these words, hundreds of his admirers were busily worshipping him. They did not understand a word of English. The whole while he chastised me, his open palm was blessing these innocent, God-fearing people. They were begging him for God's blessings while he was decrying God's existence. They honored him as an enlightened being while he was speaking of the miserable futility of his life. In a daze, I walked away. My mind struggled to understand what the Lord had just revealed to me.

The man was right. America was a land of riches and comforts. But I had lost my interest in a merely comfortable life. Instead, I felt I was traveling a road that was at times easy and beautiful, at times hard, but all in search of a greater treasure than anything the material world had to offer. If this man wanted to enjoy material life, why didn't he get a job and be honest? Instead he posed as a saint to cheat the innocent.

There is always the real and the counterfeit. Hypocrisy in religion has crippled peoples' faith throughout history. A holy person cannot always be recognized by external appearance.

The Bhagavad Gita teaches that renunciation is not for a lazy man who does no work, but for one who works in a spirit of devotion.

I thought of all the people I had been meeting who lived their lives working in the spirit of devotion and I prayed that I could be one of them. I remembered the words I had heard Srila Prabhupada speak in Bombay: "Better to be a sincere sweeper of the street than a charlatan meditator." Then I thought about that poor man pretending to be a sadhu. *His bad dog is barking loudly, and he's daily feeding it enormous portions of rice and dhal.*

7

ONE DAY IN JANAKPUR, WHILE SITTING ALONE ON THE EDGE of a still lake in the early morning dawn, a peculiar looking sadhu sat down beside me. His opening words were startling. "Beware. There are scorpions in the guise of butterflies." Shaken, I asked why he was saying this. He stared at me intently and spoke again. "Don't open yourself up to demons in the guise of holy men or you may discover your life in ruins, only when it's too late."

"What are you talking about?" I asked, alarmed.

"Perhaps I'll tell you another time." Abruptly changing the subject, he introduced himself as Vasudeva and invited me to travel with him to a special historical place.

I consented. A handsome man in his early thirties, Vasudeva had the manners of an aristocrat and his speech rang with the distinction of the Queen's English. He wore white robes which, curiously, were immaculately clean. His long, jet-black hair was neatly combed. In all of my travels, I had never met such a well-groomed mendicant. He was learned in both spiritual and material subjects, and like many I had met in those parts, was a devotee of Rama. When my new friend invited me to travel by foot for three days to reach an obscure holy place, I agreed. We journeyed through countryside the whole way, each day receiving one of my favorite foods, some rice and dhal through begging. Whomever we met along the way was charmed by Vasudeva's gentle nature.

Vasudeva insisted on doing all the cooking in an open field or forest, finding two rocks to form a stove and balancing the pot between them, while I collected wood for the fire. He prepared the rice and dhal with the finesse of an artist sculpting a masterpiece. As we walked along on pilgrimage, we discussed many subjects. Vasudeva seemed to know about everything.

But something puzzled me. Behind a mask of cheerfulness, I sensed that this man was tormented. Yet he strained to hide his suffering and hold back his tears, and my affection for and curiosity about him grew. Strangely, one night while we were traveling together, sleeping in a cow shed to escape the rain, I had a horrible nightmare of being attacked by ghostly beings. I wondered why.

After three days we reached our destination: a historical rock in an abandoned field. That evening, as the wind began to gust, we could taste and smell the humidity rising and knew that the monsoons were brewing an imminent downpour. We searched around for a shelter and found a small stone structure abandoned long ago. We entered and flushed out several bats that were hanging from the ceiling. They hastily flapped outside. The house consisted of nothing more than one room about ten feet by ten feet, with two openings for what were once a window and a door. The walls were crumbling. Moss and cobwebs were the only furnishings. Once inside, we sat silently as thunder shook the earth, winds lashed the trees, and a torrential rain poured down. Vasudeva gazed at me through tear-filled eyes. He asked if he could pour out the storm in his heart. Honored that he would confide in me, I consented.

Vasudeva shared with me that he had been born to a well-to-do family in Calcutta and received a Ph.D., becoming a popular, celebrated professor. Having met other devotees, he, too, became devoted to Rama at this time. "One day, two distinguished persons visited my office, bringing gifts and food that they claimed were sent by their guru. After several such visits, they invited me to meet the guru, so I did."

The guru knew everything about his life down to the most private details and was able to read Vasudeva's mind. Astounded, he accepted the man's invitation to visit him regularly. I listened intently, fascinated as ever to learn the story of how a person comes to accept a guru.

"One day," Vasudeva continued, "the guru revealed his mind. 'I've been carefully examining you,' he said. 'You are young, popular, and intelligent. I need your help. I wish to initiate you into our rites.'" Vasudeva choked back a strong emotion as he recalled these words. "I told him I would think about it." His voice trailed off and he buried his head in his palms, as if trying to bury untold miseries from the past. In desperation he looked up at me. "Richard," he sighed, "I don't want to pollute your mind with my horrible story, but I'm going mad. I must tell someone. May I continue?"

"Please do."

He stared out the window hole. A lightning bolt highlighted the anguish of his face. Finally, full of despair, he spoke. "I commenced to do research on this man and, to my horror, discovered that he was the leader of a powerful sect, a master in the black tantric arts." His eyes now penetrated mine. "Do you know about black tantrics, Richard?"

"No," I admitted.

Vasudeva shuddered and his voice trembled. He explained that tantric mysticism was extremely powerful, and could be either beneficial or sinister. "There are the white tantrics who use their powers to serve humankind. Then there are the black tantrics who use their powers to exploit people's lives for their own diabolical purposes. They gain terrible influence through unspeakable sacrifices, tantric sex rites, and yoga. This guru was an extremely powerful black tantric, endowed with the power to control people's minds and manipulate their lives. In my research, I was appalled to find that at the time of the rites of initiation, he seized control over that soul for many lifetimes to come. I never went back."

"But Vasudeva, if you got free, why do you still tremble and quake to think of him?"

"That was only the beginning," he went on. "Daily, the guru's disciples harassed me in my office, in my home, or at any event I attended. I could not escape them. One day, five of them barged into my office and surrounded my desk. I felt like a hostage. The next moment, the guru stood before me to claim my soul. He warned me, 'It is too late; I have claimed you as my own. Surrender to me and I will award you the pleasures of fame and fortune beyond your belief. But if you refuse, I vow to torment you till death.' Boiling over with disgust, I refused his command. Cursing me, his eyes blazed with vengeance as he stormed out."

Vasudeva sighed. "One evening when I returned home to my widowed mother, I found that she had fallen into his trap. Shaking with anger, she scolded, 'Why have you offended that religious man? You must become his disciple.' I was shocked. I tried to explain his cruel machinations, but she would not listen. The guru and his henchmen had effectively controlled her. After some days, she threw me out of my own house, saying she would not be a party to my offenses. What was happening to my world? Then, under the sect's powers, the president of my college fired me."

Outside, lightning struck a tree and cracked off a huge limb, crashing it down on our rooftop. We sat speechless. An explosion of thunder that seemed to shake the universe followed the devastating lightning bolt. Vasudeva paled. With a faltering voice, he continued. "Homeless and jobless, I was haunted by the black tantric's disciples wherever I went. They even influenced the police, who refused to protect me. What could I do but leave Calcutta? By his supernatural powers, this black tantric knew where I was at all times and dispatched his followers to harass me."

Any job he landed, they convinced the employer to fire Vasudeva and any room he rented, they convinced the landlord to evict him. He even went to a newspaper to tell his story, but the reporters would not believe him. "My life was in tatters," he said.

At that moment, a large toad hopped in through our doorway. His amphibious eyes gazed into mine. I wondered if he could be a secret agent of the black tantric and shuddered at the thought. Vasudeva seemed to read my mind. "Are you sure you want me to continue?" he asked.

Thunder rumbled in every corner of the sky. "I don't know any more, Vasudeva," I admitted. I was frightened, but it seemed important that I hear the story. "What happened after that?"

"This evil yogi was incensed by my determination and resolved to murder me. With black rites and mantras, he created an invisible weapon that separates the soul from the body. In other words, it slays the victim. But the killing of the body is the least of it. In that interim period between life and death, the black tantric gains control of the subtle body covering the soul. As the sinister weapon struck, my body and mind were paralyzed with pain. I felt ghastly beings in ethereal forms haunting me. Begging to be saved, I chanted the name of God. As long as the Name was in my mind, the invisible weapon could not end my life. For a full day and night, that weapon tormented me. I knew if I ceased to remember the Name for a moment, I would meet a fate worse than death. I chanted ceaselessly. The weapon was powerless to kill me in the presence of God's Name. If an evil tantric weapon cannot kill its victim, it must return to slay its sender. The black tantric was struck dead, killed by his creation. God's Name had saved me."

Hearing this spooky tale, a wave of shivers rushed my body from head to toe. I leaned forward to hear more.

"This evil mystic still exists; he just doesn't have a gross body. Now he controls his disciples from the astral plane, dispatching them to wherever I hide, to seek revenge. They hunt me down at all times. I cannot settle in any one place because within a matter of weeks, they terrorize me."

The furious storm outside was beginning to subside. In the emerging silence Vasudeva sighed. "It is for this reason, contrary to my will and nature, that I have become a homeless mendicant. I know that if I genuinely surrender to God he will protect me, but until that day comes, I must run and hide in the guise of a holy man."

Crickets began to sing. Vasudeva looked deeply into my eyes. "I'm sorry to tell you all this. I've kept it to myself for years, but I had to speak to someone. Richard, I have no one to blame, it's ultimately my own doing."

I couldn't understand how he could blame himself and asked him to explain.

Modestly, he attributed his present troubles to past-life karma. "I don't know what I've done to deserve my miserable lot in life," Vasudeva concluded, "but I know that it's justified. And I know that if I sincerely pass this test and surrender to the Lord, He will deliver me."

Vasudeva's trembling hand now held mine as he made one last appeal. "Because you are my friend, I must advise you to abandon me lest you get implicated. If I don't see you in the morning, I will understand. My brother, as you search for your path, please be cautious. You are exposing yourself to powerful beings and not all are holy. And please pray for me."

We sat in silence. I could not speak a word. I knew from what I'd already observed in India that many gurus had strong powers, including the power to sway followers to do whatever they asked. I was more terrified of what my companion had revealed to me than I had been of the pack of rabid dogs. The dogs I had at least been able to see and fend off. But how does one fend off the invisible forces of evil that could attack an unsuspecting person trying to follow a spiritual path?

Vasudeva then lay down on the dirt to sleep, with his arm as a pillow. But sleep was far from my mind. I gazed through the hole in the wall. There were stars emerging from the parting clouds, but no moon. Next to me, Vasudeva tossed anxiously in his sleep. *Am I willing to be implicated in the harrowing complexities of his life?* The thought caused me to shiver. *I can think of no other way to help him except to pray. That is all he asked of me.* As he tossed, turned, and groaned in his sleep, I walked far away into the night praying that the path I was taking would be a safe one, and that he, too, might find safety and peace.

My path continued to be rife with experiences both dark and light, each experience offering me a window into the different worlds that might await me were I to take certain turns and not others.

Most of the sadhus who greeted me upon my return to Janakpur were old enough to be my grandfathers. I was praying in the Janaki Temple when, to my surprise a young Nepalese student by the name of Vishnu Prasad approached me. Well-dressed, with a round face and pious demeanor, he was so fascinated to see a Western youth who had taken to the life of a sadhu that he invited me to his home in the village of Brahmapur. His home there was like a beautiful ashram, the wealth of the family evident in bright furnishings, carpets, brass vessels, and flower gardens. As I entered, Vishnu's mother and father cordially greeted me and served me a sumptuous meal of spiced vegetables in aromatic sauces and rice glistening with clarified butter. I happily spent several days there.

Uncles, aunts, and cousins all lived under one roof, but I never heard a single voice rise in anger. They had nothing but respect for one another. In the morning, the children respectfully touched the feet of their parents, and the parents, in turn, offered blessings. No matter what their age, the children, even the teenagers, were naturally obedient to their elders and the younger children showed honor to the eldest son as the representative of the parents. Having been brought up in 1960s America, I experienced this teenage respectfulness as a pleasant kind of culture shock. Moreover, every inch of the home was immaculately clean—except me. I felt like a disheveled mendicant in a haven of class and refinement. My body looked quite beaten down and, taking note of this, the family gave me a medicinal balm for my bruised, cracked feet. Although they offered me my own room with a comfortable bed, I chose to sleep in the garden under an ashoka tree. Each morning and evening, the family members would gather together for worship ceremonies in their small temple of Lord Rama in the center of the home where, during the day, the women performed various devotions.

I found nothing but happiness in their home. In the evenings, I sat with Vishnu Prasad in a pleasant garden among the marigolds, roses, and flower-bearing trees. Tara Prasad, his father, sometimes sat with us. A wealthy man with a wife and children, his purity of character was impressive, more so than many of the ascetics I had encountered. *Spirituality is a matter of the heart,* I pondered. The more I grew to love Vishnu Prasad's family members, the more of a friend he became to me. From these gentle souls I learned much about the traditions of family life in the East. Most importantly, my realization that true spirituality comes in many forms was confirmed.

However, I could not stay too long in these comfortable surroundings, for I had chosen the life of an ascetic. When it was time to go, the whole family saw me to the gate. They were crying as I turned and walked off down the brick path and so was I.

Now, more than ever before, the path I was choosing struck me as strewn with unseen dangers. In my passion for truth, which admittedly I couldn't fully explain, I had left the comforts of home, and continued to renounce comforts along the way, pressing on despite fears that arose at the uncertainties awaiting me.

From Janakpur, I traveled back to the Kathmandu Valley. Just below the hill of Bodhnath, seven miles east of the city, in a grove of flowering trees, I meditated. Opening my eyes, I looked up into a magnificent rainbow arching over the entire Himalayan valley that glowed against an indigo backdrop of monsoon clouds. I took a deep breath, drinking in a breeze of cool, earthy air. Soon, stomping footsteps nudged me out of my dreamy state and drew my attention to a European tourist marching through the field and carrying a large bag of groceries. Well over six feet tall, blond, with muscles bulging from beneath his T-shirt, he had the physique of a bodybuilder. Suddenly, from out of the forest, a gang of brown monkeys surrounded him. Although each monkey was only a fraction of his size, they knew how to find his weakest point and attack. They snarled and bared their teeth, threatening him with intimidating gestures. While holding the groceries in one of his massive arms, he hoisted a sizeable rock in the other and, whooping like a warrior, threatened to pulverize the little bandits. But the monkeys were unfazed and only snarled louder. They took small leaps toward their target, succeeding in attacking his mind. Paralyzed with fright, the hulk could only tremble like a scared child. Finally, one of the little monkeys stalked right up to him and seized the grocery bag from his hands. He didn't even resist. While the monkeys clustered around the bag to devour the groceries, they paid him no heed. Reduced to a bundle of nerves, the he-man slipped away.

Seconds later, a skinny little Nepalese boy of about eight years old appeared on the scene. The gang of monkeys had just begun feasting on their booty, but stirred with apprehension upon seeing the tiny boy. The child skipped toward them with a stone in his hand. The gang of bandits screeched, terror in their eyes. Suddenly, they abandoned the food and fled in all directions. The little boy collected up the groceries and sat down to dine. Meanwhile, the monkeys anxiously watched from a distance. I was amazed. What had just happened here? That playful boy was hardly the weight of one bicep of the Herculean European. The monkeys were unfazed by the threats of the giant because they sensed fear in his mind. But they feared the child because he had no fear of them. What did this mean for me, and my ever-narrowing path to God? I thought of the pack of wild dogs and of Vasudeva's frightening tale of the evil black tantric. I considered my fear of coming under the spell of an unscrupulous guru were I to choose too hastily. But I could see how fear could block my progress.

> *We are vulnerable to defeat when our minds succumb to fear. The foreigner was unfamiliar with monkeys, but the Nepalese tot had lived around monkeys all of his life. So we fear what we don't know. Through knowledge of our spiritual nature and sincere faith in God, we can overcome all fear. Please, Lord, bless me with such courage as I find my way to You.*

As I pondered these thoughts, the smiling boy ran up to me and offered some bananas from the grocery bag. The monkeys chattered with excitement, marking me as a prospective victim. They made me realize that I had more in common with that European than I would like to think. Feeling I had a long way to go on my path to reach the innocent, fearless faith of this child, I politely declined.

While wandering in the forests, I came upon Sita Rama Baba, an extraordinary soul whom I fondly remember as the standing baba. A bearded man of sixty-two with large brown eyes and a rugged complexion, Sita Rama Baba wore a simple, one-piece pullover of burlap from neck to ankles. When I asked him why he wore only burlap, he replied that the coarse, itching texture of burlap kept him always in an uncomfortable condition. This, he said, helped him to always seek comfort in remembering Rama. Even more amazing to me were the wooden splints he kept tied around his ankles. Strange as his appearance was, he immediately treated me with the love of a father for a son.

Like yogis I had met in the Himalayas, Sita Rama Baba followed extreme vows, far beyond the vow of celibacy. He vowed to always stand on his feet and never sit or lay down. That is why he wore wooden splints around his ankles, to support his body. For almost fifty years, he had observed this penance. Along with his begging pot and prayer beads, he carried a rope and a wooden plank that he would hang from a tree branch like a swing. At night, he would lean on this and sleep standing up.

He also followed vows to never sleep inside walls and, besides being a vegetarian, never ate grains or beans. I witnessed the severity of this dietary vow. Wandering mendicants typically subsist on the inexpensive foods that people give easily in charity, foods such as rice, dhal or *rotis* (unleavened wheat bread), all of which contain grains or beans. We wandered together. Every day, Sita Rama Baba would blissfully beg rice and dhal for me, collect wood, and build a fire under an improvised stove made of rocks, all the while standing or squatting. When the food was cooked, he lovingly offered it to a picture of his beloved Lord Rama with prayers and mantras, and then gave it all to me. But I was curious, what did *he* eat? During my stay with him, I never saw him eat anything more than a handful of cheap peanuts given to him while begging. That's all he could collect that wouldn't violate his diet. Yet he was so happy to take pains to feed me nicely. He would explain that to show love for God, one must affectionately serve His children.

One day, when Sita Rama Baba received a few vegetables while begging door to door, I was overjoyed. Finally, here was something for him to eat besides raw peanuts. My heart sank, though, when he served my meal, and I saw that he had cooked all of the vegetables into the rice and dhal and kept nothing for himself. He was joyful. Fascinated, I scrutinized him, but I found nothing artificial about him. He was utterly sincere in his devotion.

I once asked Baba, "Why do you follow such difficult vows?"

Meekly, he replied, "It helps me to be focused on my spiritual practices. But I am happy." And amazingly, he really was.

Early one morning, before the light of day, I sat under a tree in the forest while contemplating this amazing person. I could not understand his strange vows. They seemed excessive and even unnecessary. But still, he had attracted my sincere love and trust. It is said that artificial austerity makes the heart hard. But his heart was soft and filled with humility, compassion, and devotion. Lord Jesus said, "You can judge a tree by its fruit." Although his appears to be a strange tree, the ripened fruits are sweet.

In Sita Rama Baba's company, a question brewed in my mind. Most of the yogis I had encountered meditated on God as an impersonal force while he and others meditated on the Lord as an all-loving person. Rama Sevak Swami served Lord Rama in such a personal way. Srila Prabhupada, too, expressed such genuine love for Lord Krishna, as an all-attractive person. Did this contradict the beliefs of those yogis who strove to merge their souls into a supreme impersonal oneness? Did it conflict with the practices of Buddhists who strove for a perfection of a quality-less nirvana? As a child, I had naturally prayed to God in a personal way, but as I studied philosophies, I found more and more leanings toward God being an all-pervading existence. While strolling together down a forest path one day, I inquired of Baba, "Is God ultimately impersonal or a person?"

Coming to an abrupt halt, his bushy brown eyebrows tightened and his face, marked with the deep furrows of a rugged life, cringed. He sighed, "How could our Lord have less personality and form than we have? He has everything without limit." He shook his head, "This misunderstanding breaks my heart."

His reaction struck me. I was becoming more aware of this fundamental disagreement over the ultimate nature of the Supreme Lord. Was He an impersonal, disembodied force or was He the Supreme Person? In a way, it was the same question I'd asked myself as a child trembling during thunderstorms: Who was God? Was he comforting like my parents, or as formless as the wind? I was wrestling to reconcile this philosophical issue, and knew the answer would help me choose my path, but I couldn't find the missing piece in the puzzle. I had been meeting wonderful souls who held both opposing views.

Days later, as I left Sita Rama Baba, I contemplated that how much one loves God is not something that can always be measured by looking at external forms. On one hand, I found holy people working jobs and raising families, and on the other, I found this eccentric hermit of the forest. But what they all had in common was their humility, a deep focus on spiritual practices, and an unquenchable thirst to serve.

8

I NEXT ROAMED ON TO SWAYAMBHUNATH, which lies three kilometers west of Kathmandu. Surrounded by a vast expanse of rice paddies, this beautiful hill is crowned with the Monkey Temple, an ancient Buddhist temple covered by a wide dome called a *stupa* and said to be built two thousand years ago. The eight eyes of Buddha on the base of the spire observed the four directions. These eyes were about to see something amazing.

For no apparent reason, one morning I had an urge to walk to Kathmandu, so I left my reclusive abode on the mountain, wandered on foot to the city, and meandered through the streets and markets for a short time. Then I began to walk back to Swayambhunath through a long stretch of rice paddies. With its rich greenery and snowy Himalayan peaks piercing the skies, Kathmandu Valley is like a heaven on earth. As I walked along the narrow bank that enclosed the swampy paddy fields, tiny raindrops began to fall. Dark blue monsoon clouds thickened in the sky, obscuring the sun and promising to send down torrents.

As the drizzle grew to a light rain, I looked around for a shelter but saw not a single tree. Nothing but rice paddies stretched in all directions. Then, at a distance, I beheld the figure of what appeared to be an elderly man carrying an umbrella over his head. Hoping to share his umbrella, I scurried along the thin paddy border to catch up with him. The path was narrow and slippery, so I could not walk beside him; instead I nestled in behind. Struggling to keep under the umbrella, I repeatedly slipped down toward the soupy mud of the paddy. Meanwhile, the umbrella carrier never once turned around. Perhaps he was intimidated by my intrusion, or maybe he was concentrating on not falling into the pools of mud. In this anonymous way, we two strangers walked along together through the deserted and soggy fields for some time. Two men alone in a vast paddy field, we shared a single umbrella as the monsoon poured down torrents.

Ten minutes later, when the storm subsided, I offered thanks to the stranger. He turned around now for the first time to have a look at my face. Our eyes met. We were thunderstruck. Our mouths dropped open and our eyes filled with tears. How could this be? For a moment, we stood motionless in a place outside of time.

The umbrella dropped into the mud. "Gary!" I cried.

"Monk!"

Under the monsoon sky, hearts bursting with joy, we embraced. "We're together again!" I said.

There we stood, alone in a vast Himalayan valley, thrilled by the mysteries of life. From the time of our sad farewell on the Isle of Crete, we had walked our respective paths. Inseparable childhood friends, we'd been separated by destiny and today that invisible puppeteer had pulled us together in an isolated rice paddy in Nepal.

Reeling from joy, we strolled through the paddy fields toward the place Gary was staying, all the while exchanging our experiences since parting. Slipping and sliding on the narrow paddy bank, Gary walked in front and I close behind.

"Did you ever make it to Israel?"

He turned to me and stroked his beard, which had grown several inches since we last parted eleven months before. "After you left Crete," he explained, "I worked on a fishing boat for my passage to Israel. I worked on a kibbutz for a while. Then with some money in my pocket, I set out for India."

"How did you get here?"

"I took the Magic Bus." He paused for a moment and began walking again. He described the cheap bus for down and out travelers that ran from Europe to India. After returning from Israel, he had boarded in Istanbul, crossed the Middle East, and got off at the end of the line in Old Delhi.

"And what brought you to this uninhabited rice paddy?" I asked him.

"The sweltering heat of Delhi was too much," Gary told me, still trembling with excitement. "So, with some friends from the Magic Bus, I came up to Kathmandu Valley and found a little house in the countryside."

We approached the village and left behind the narrow boarders of the rice paddies. I walked side by side with my old friend. A water buffalo trudged toward us on the sodden path, so we stepped aside to let her pass.

"Monk," Gary continued, "I came to India with a hope to find you, but seeing the hundreds of millions of people in this vast land I concluded it was impossible. I knew you would never be in the hangouts where travelers make the scene. I figured you were in some cave or secluded ashram. I never thought I'd see you again." Gary stopped and turned, his eyes widened. "Nobody will believe this story. Nobody."

It was August of 1971. Almost a year had passed since we'd parted in Crete. By my appearance, Gary could see that I had adopted the life of a sadhu. The arduous journey across the Middle East, the time spent in the company of enlightened yogis, and the many months in seclusion had left me as a seasoned ascetic. For good reason, Gary was hesitant to bring me to the place he was crashing with his friends.

What happens when a Nepalese village home is rented to hippies of the West? As we entered the little structure, rock and roll music blared, men and women danced seductively, and opium pipes were passed around in a cloud of smoke. Gary introduced me to his friends, all of whom I greeted politely. To say I could no longer identify with this scene was an understatement. I just stood on the sidelines and watched.

After some time, I took Gary aside, escorting him to a quiet place in an open field where we sat under a banana tree. A blanket of hovering clouds released a mist of cooling droplets. We breathed deeply the fresh mountain air, a welcome relief from the opium cloud inside. Although I feared being judgmental, I spoke openly to my friend. "Gary, you have traveled across the world to come here. This is a land of spirituality. Yet you have brought the hippie culture of the West with you. You could live like this in Chicago. You're just doing the same old things and more in a different setting. How will you grow? What will you gain?" I pleaded with him in earnest, "Please, my brother, while you're in this part of the world, try to experience the wealth of spirituality here. If you agree, I'll take you to the holy places and teach you the life of a sadhu."

Gary looked far away into the horizon. "Let me think about it."

"Come on, Gary," I pressed. "Don't you remember when you begged me to go to Europe with you? I dropped all my plans and did it. Now I'm pleading with you to come to the holy places with me." I loved my friend and it pained me to see that he came so far and was missing this precious opportunity.

The next day, Gary said goodbye to his friends and entered into the school of spiritual mendicants. Together again, we began exploring the meaning of life by meeting new people in new places. But this time we followed traditions that were long ago established by enlightened beings. Day by day, I taught my old friend how to survive in India as a spiritual seeker. How amazed he was to learn the method for hitchhiking in India—jumping into the window of a moving third class train. I also shared with him the art of begging for simple food and dressing like a sadhu.

An elderly swami informed us about a pilgrimage to Amarnath, a famous cave situated high in the Himalayas of Kashmir. He said that any soul fortunate enough to complete the rigorous pilgrimage would be awarded great spiritual merit. Gary was ripe and ready for the adventure and so was I. We set off.

On the road again from Kathmandu, we returned to India riding in the back of a truck to Raxaul and then on to Patna, where I introduced Gary to Rama Sevaka Swami. Swami was thrilled to see me again and still carrying the stick he gave me. Gary looked on in wonder, amazed by the kind of friends I was keeping.

From Patna we traveled west by train. Gary was especially eager for a tour of Varanasi from a sadhu's perspective. While there, we visited the famous temple of Kasi Viswanath in the early morning. Brass bells were ringing, hymns were chanted by the temple priests, and swirling pillars of incense smoke rose and dissipated into the air. I prayed, *My Lord, I long to know You and to love You. Please, show me the path I must follow.* Something happened to me at that moment. I was overwhelmed with a feeling of hope, that if I only humble myself before the Lord, everything would be revealed. I felt that His hand was reaching out to me and that something very special was about to happen in my life.

It was at the railway station in Varanasi that we squirmed into a train of compressed human bodies crushed limb to limb in the sweltering heat of the monsoon. The whistle blew as the steam engine pumped up bellows of smoke and hissed out steam. The heavy steel wheels ground forward, the train lurched, and we were on our way.

The monsoon storm was furious, converting an agricultural field into a muddy lake and paralyzing the engine. Hours passed in stagnancy. In the extreme heat, striving to set aside my physical discomfort, I longed to hear the whistle blow, signaling movement.

Nearly two days later, the train inched out of the fields, and before dawn, halted at an unknown station. Gary and I escaped through a window and onto the platform for temporary relief before the journey continued. The fresh air was glorious. The dimly lit crowded railway platform looked dirty and rundown. To us, though, it was like a paradise, a place where we might find water to drink, air to breath, and space to move our limbs. But while we were stretching, the whistle blew, the steam hissed, and the train jerked forward. Frantically, we ran alongside and tried to jam our bodies back in through the window, but couldn't penetrate the masses inside. Window after window and door after door, we tried to claw our way in. Finally, the train disappeared down the tracks, leaving us behind.

We stood there, stranded in an unknown place, not knowing how long it might be until another train came through. Gary looked at me and asked, "Now what?"

9

I T WAS ABOUT FIVE O'CLOCK IN THE MORNING and dawn was just emerging. Not knowing where to go or what to do, I stood with my friend on a railway platform, which bustled with the crowds who came off the train and the hundreds who wrestled to get on. Amid it all, a strange comfort arose in my heart. It was similar to that feeling I had while praying in the temple of Kasi Viswanath, a feeling that something special was about to happen in my life. There appeared to be a jovial mood in the crowd. Gary and I looked at each other and, remembering the flower that had determined our route through Europe, decided to stay put for the time being. After some time the station became quiet.

I saw some sadhus sitting some distance ahead in a circle on the platform. I gestured to Gary to wait and I approached them.

"Excuse me," I inquired, "Where are we?"

Saying nothing, a sadhu stared up into my eyes as if he had been waiting for me. Rising to his feet, he broke the silence. "This is Mathura, Lord Krishna's birthplace. And today is Janmastami, Krishna's birthday."

On their invitation, Gary and I walked with them to the place where the Janmastami festival was being celebrated. As we approached the main gate, one elderly sadhu turned to me. "Do you know about Lord Krishna?"

"Not very much," I admitted. I knew little more than he was the blue boy in my picture, that his name appeared in the mantra Mother Ganges had let me hear, and the story of how he broke the clay pot and fed butter to monkeys as a child. "Could you tell me more?"

His face lit up with enthusiasm as he repeatedly rubbed his beard and began. "Krishna is our name for the one God of creation. He is without beginning or end, unborn, and undying. The Lord resides in his Supreme Abode, but by his sweet will, he has taken birth in this world many times and in many forms throughout human history, all to show us the way out of suffering and into spiritual happiness." The sadhu pointed into a huge courtyard teeming with throngs of pilgrims.

"In this spot, Lord Krishna first appeared on earth five thousand years ago. Come. Please join us in the celebration."

What I saw inside spurred my curiosity. A massive mosque towered over a tiny underground temple for Krishna. "Is there some reason there is a mosque at Krishna's birthplace?" I asked our self-appointed guide.

"Previously this was the site of the Adi Kesava Temple, one of the greatest monuments in the world, but in the seventeenth century the Mughal Emperor Aurangzeb destroyed it and built a mosque in its place."

"Why?" Gary asked.

The sadhu shrugged his shoulders to convey his helplessness. "I suppose this was his way of showing the superiority of his religion and his power over the subjugated Hindus." A hopeful smile crept back onto his face. "But there is a plan to build a majestic temple for Lord Krishna just beside the mosque. Soon it will rise. Anyhow, this place is sacred regardless of what man does to it. Now let us go in and celebrate."

The mood inside the courtyard was indeed one of celebration. Thousands of worshippers stood in line to enter the small underground temple of Lord Krishna, and legions more gathered above. In every direction, people were celebrating. Hundreds danced and chanted to live music played with drums, flutes, and cymbals; Elderly scholars claimed their places and lectured to their followers; and on a makeshift stage decorated with bright colored cloth, strings of flowers, and painted backdrops, stage actors in extravagant costumes relived the story of Krishna's advent. Meanwhile, priests poured oblations of clarified butter into a sacred fire while chanting mantras from the *Vedas*, or ancient Sanskrit holy books. Smiling and singing, devotees tossed colored powders on one another as they roamed about from one event to another. We even saw Hindus with clay markings on their foreheads and bearded Muslims wearing their traditional caps laughing and dancing together—absorbed in the festivities. The recluses celebrated too, sitting on the sidelines softly chanting and fingering their prayer beads. During the festivities, lectures, songs, or conversations, I frequently heard devotees say the word Vrindavan. I could sense how dear this place called Vrindavan was to them.

We spent all day absorbing the wonderful sights and sounds of the birthday celebration. As midnight approached, swarms of people streamed through the lanes that led to the Yamuna River, crowding into the Dwarkadish Temple near its banks. According to the scriptures, it was at midnight that Lord Krishna appeared in the city of Mathura. Now everybody waited for that moment. Although the temple was already packed with thousands, a steady flow of thousands more managed to stream through the door. The police tried to control the crowds in vain with long bamboo sticks.

Neither Gary nor I had ever seen such massive crowds. To get a better view, we climbed up two pillars in the temple hall and looked down upon this astonishing scene. We scanned the multitude, which vibrated in anticipation. When the clock struck midnight, the doors of the inner sanctum swung open to reveal the altar of Krishna. A tumult of joy rose like a tidal wave. Enthralled, the people in the crowd were oblivious to being shoved and crushed. Old and young, male and female, rich and poor, all merged together with palms joined in prayer and eyes glossed with devotion. Small circles of villagers sang their own special songs, while everyone else laughed, cried, danced, and exuberantly called out Krishna's holy names. For Gary and me, clinging to our pillars, the eagerness of these pilgrims was astounding.

At about three in the morning, we found a place to sleep on the bank of the river Yamuna. We were told that this particular place, Vishram Ghat, was where Krishna personally took rest on occasion. The next day, as we strolled through the lanes of Mathura, four well-dressed young men rushed out from a tea stall to greet us. "We are proud to see foreigners in our city," the leader said. "Would you care to meet our revered guru?"

"Sure," Gary replied. "We'd love to meet him."

"Come, my friends," the man said, leading us back into the tea stall. "Long ago our guru renounced the world's pleasures to realize the highest truth. Guruji is a scholar who can answer any query you may have. We are among hundreds of his faithful disciples in this area. Excuse me while I go and call on him."

Minutes later, the guru appeared. He was a man of forty or so with a shaved head. His movements were meticulous. Speaking refined English, he articulated for us, in a pleasing accent, the scriptural importance of Mathura City. To our joy, he invited us to spend our nights at his temple. We followed him into a small temple honoring Lord Shiva. In the middle was a Shiva Lingam, just behind it an iron trident planted upright in the ashes of a sacred fire pit. The swami carefully saw to our needs, bringing us a vegetarian dinner and answering whatever questions we asked.

When night set in, the swami offered Gary a straw mat on the floor to sleep and invited me to share his wooden bed. To sleep on the same level as this revered guru was an honor I did not deserve. I mused on how his many disciples would have given anything to be in my position that night. The swami lay down beside me. Then, in the quiet of the night, I felt his hands massaging my body.

"Why are you doing this?" I asked.

"This is our custom to show hospitality for guests."

Not wanting to be ungrateful, I said nothing. Slowly his hands crept toward the private parts of my body. My mind swam in a whirlpool of apprehension. Confused, I pushed his hands away. After a few minutes, his hands snaked downward again. Again, I pushed them away. "Please do not massage me. I don't like this."

He whispered into my ear, "I am giving you God's blessing. It is not me that is doing. I am simply God's instrument. You must not resist."

The room was dark and hot. I lay there in anguish. *What if I disappoint him? He might punish me.* I thought of Vasudev and his unfortunate experience with a corrupt guru. *Or he may have yogic powers.* Each time the man tried to grope me, I pushed his hands away. *Was this really a custom for showing hospitality?* His aggression increased with each failed attempt.

Now he was panting with passion and becoming more forceful. He wouldn't take no for an answer. Incited, I was on the verge of smashing him with my fists, but I restrained. How could I fight a swami? Is that what a sadhu should do? And what would his disciples do to me if I did? Perspiring profusely in the sweltering humidity of the monsoons, I lay there and prayed to be saved from this horrible situation. Then I made up my mind. Shoving him away, I jumped to my feet. Infuriated, he embraced me tightly, but I wriggled my way out, pushed him away and fled. Gary, meanwhile, slept peacefully through the whole ordeal.

I rushed into a deserted lane in the late night and was free. From a safe distance, I spied on the swami through the open entranceway, making sure he did not offer any of his "hospitality" to Gary. Like a watchdog I stood guard, ready to come to Gary's aid if required. Standing in the shadows of night, drenched by a monsoon downpour, I remained awake until dawn. In every spiritual path, there are those who are true and those who are false. Saintliness is not determined by one's title, dress, hairstyle, or place of residence. This man, for example, had the title of swami, a shaved head indicating he had renounced worldly pleasures, and the robes of a sadhu. He was a scholar of scripture, the high priest of a temple, and the guru of many disciples who revered him. Yet he'd tried to exploit me to satisfy his own carnal desire. Real saintliness should be understood by a person's behavior. Exerting one's spiritual authority to exploit the innocent is a grave injustice. I prayed that this incident would not create doubt in my mind toward the sincere devotees. Gary continued to sleep peacefully through the night without incident, oblivious to the storm that raged both inside and outside the temple of Shiva.

In the morning, Gary was shocked to hear my description of what had happened. A guru ravaged by lust? Our idealistic innocence was once again challenged by the real world.

Despite having been stranded in Mathura, we were still determined to make our pilgrimage to Amarnath in the Himalayas. But that day, while taking my morning bath in the Yamuna River, I felt an intense pulling to visit the nearby village of Vrindavan everyone had been talking about. For reasons I could not explain, I longed to go to Vrindavan alone, as a solitary pilgrim. Gary agreed to meet me there the next day, at which time we planned to resume our journey to Amarnath.

IV
Forest of Grace

1

VRINDAVAN. ANTICIPATION FILLED MY HEART. With each step I trod on the eight mile stretch, I was thrilled. Lining the asphalt road were huge tamarind trees and spacious fields. A bullock cart overloaded with straw passed slowly by, its wooden wheels creaking, while the team of oxen strained, snorting foam from their nostrils and clacking their hooves over the asphalt. A jalopy of a bus approached from behind and halted. The door swung open, and the driver, beaming a semi-toothless smile, beckoned me to climb aboard for a free ride. How could I refuse such hospitality? The driver wore the visible markers of a religious life: a shaved head with a tuft of hair at the back and sheet of cloth wrapped around his waist. When we arrived in the town of Vrindavan, I asked him where the river was, and he pointed the way.

A few steps later, a farmer stood blocking my path, his palms pressed together in supplication. Gleefully, he exclaimed, "Welcome to Vrindavan. Whoever comes here is Lord Krishna's special guest." Clasping my hands, he effused, "I am a *Vrajabasi*, a resident of Vrindavan. It is my duty to make you happy. Let me arrange food and accommodation for you."

"Thank you very much, but I'll be happy to sleep on the bank of the river and beg for food."

Casting his head down, he grew desperate. "Please accept my humble service. If you do not, how can I show myself before my Krishna?"

His humility was too difficult to deny. I instantly loved this Vrajabasi, feeling him to be a family member welcoming me home. He arranged my stay at the ashram of an old blind swami and departed.

That afternoon I left behind the crowded ashram to roam into one of the lush forests of Vrindavan. As I walked, I pressed my feet into the soft, fine sands, strolling among ancient trees whose trunks swirled upward, each one cloaked with white, orange, and yellow flowers, and shining green leaves. A sweet lowing attracted my eyes to a herd of white cows grazing on the shrubs. With wide glistening eyes, they gazed at me as if they had always known me. Strangely, I felt the same for them. I walked on. A startling, protracted caw rang out, and I turned to see a peacock, the plumes of his brilliant tail fanned out and his iridescent neck, moving gracefully back and forth. Next, a deep resonant *'mmm'* drew me to a huge white bull that loped along the pathway chewing lazily on scattered shrubs. Looking up into the trees, I saw a flock of bright green parrots with curving orange beaks and bright red eyes. They chattered to one another, took note of me, and then soared off into the sky. Monkeys with brown fur, pink faces, and green eyes swung from branch to branch like mischievous children, all the while screaming, *"Cheee cheee."* Through the treetops, I could hear the rumbling of monsoon clouds. Perfumed by blossoming flowers, the breeze carried a cool mist that caressed my skin.

But of all of the lovely sights and sounds, it was the song of devotees chanting hymns that most lifted my heart. Small girls balanced clay water pots on their heads as they sang "Radhey, Radhey" and danced down the sandy pathway lined with forest, shrines, ashrams, and thatched houses. I followed the children until we reached a clearing. There, I beheld the river Yamuna, winding with a gentle majesty through the forest.

Wooden rowboats plied along, transporting ladies dressed in colorful saris, men with white turbans casually wrapped around their heads, and talkative children whose skinny, restless legs splashed in the water. Lining the riverbank were medieval domes of intricately carved red stone, under which Vrajabasis gathered for shelter from the sun and rain, all the while chanting Krishna's names. As temple bells resounded in the distance, my heart swelled with surprise and gratitude. After more than a year of wandering, I felt that I had finally found home again.

I saw a sadhu sitting in the hollow of a tree near the riverbank whom, I was told, was a hundred and ten years old. He wore only a burlap loincloth and his matted hair wrapped his head like a crown. His aged face drooped with folds of skin and he had to lift his heavy eyelids with his fingers in order to see. With a stroke of the hand, he beckoned me. I soon discovered that he was a *mauni baba*, one who has taken a vow never to speak, and his only means of communication was a piece of broken slate and a clump of chalk. As I squatted down beside him, he scratched two large words on the ten-inch slate: "People think." Then he erased the words with his bare fingers and continued writing, "that the people," he erased again and wrote, "of Vrindavan"—erase—"are crazy,"—erase. "It is true"—erase. "We are crazy"—erase. Then he wrote in big letters, "for Krishna." This, too, he erased, then wrote, again in sections, "If you stay here you will become crazy, too." Then he smiled, as if he knew something I didn't.

The next day, Gary and I met again. With huge festival crowds congesting the town, Gary longed to escape to a quiet place in the Himalayas, but the mystical forest of Vrindavan was pulling me and I decided to remain a few more days. Gary would go on ahead, we agreed, and in five short days, we would meet at the Brahma Ghat in Hardwar to carry on our pilgrimage to Amarnath. Sure we would see each other soon, we said goodbye easily.

In those few days, I saw no foreigners in Vrindavan. Indeed, it appeared that Vrindavan's charm was hidden from the West. I rejoiced, for I had observed that when Westerners frequented any place in India, commercialism tended to spread like an epidemic. Affected by the atmosphere, a longing to learn about Krishna awakened in my heart. Since that day they had been stolen from me on a Delhi street corner, I no longer had any books to refer to. When I asked a local man where I could find books in English about Krishna, he directed me to the Ramakrishna Hospital.

Reaching the neatly-kept one story building, I entered and inquired about books. Nurses and housekeepers stared curiously. They brought me to the director of the hospital, Shakti Maharaja, a disciple of the famous yogi Sri Ramakrishna. Just then, a mutilated woman was hurried in. She had been hit by a bus right outside the gate and was a bloody mess. The staff frantically assembled to save her. Preoccupied by the crisis, still Shakti Maharaja turned to me and asked, "How may I help you?"

I knew it wasn't good timing, and was myself stricken by the crisis, but asked anyway. "Maharaja, do you have any books about Krishna in English?"

He stared at me in disbelief, "This is a hospital, not a library. Come back if you're sick."

"I'm sorry. I will go."

He reached out and touched my forearm. "No, stay," he said. Offering me a seat, he promised to return in a few minutes. When he returned, he drew a map and explained, "You should go toward the temple of Madan Mohan. Everyone knows where it is. Close by is the ashram of Swami Bon Maharaja. They will have English books."

I followed the map, walking along various roads and pathways. On top of a grassy hill overlooking the Yamuna River was one of the most beautiful sights my eyes had ever beheld. An intricately carved temple of red sandstone, it was an octagonal spire that rose about sixty feet into the sky then tapered and again, widening at the top to form a huge, flowerlike disk. This was the 450-year-old temple of Madan Mohan. It evoked more than just the power and reverence of a grand religious monument, but a feeling of intimacy that touched my soul.

Climbing down the hill and through a narrow lane, I approached the ashram and, unlatching the gate, entered a quaint courtyard. To my right was a temple of Krishna, to my left a small temple of Lord Shiva and a flourishing garden of *tulasi* bushes. Tulasi, in the botanical family of basil, is widely considered sacred to Hindus. A young Bengali sadhu appeared from the kitchen dusting flour from his apron. "I welcome you," he said, introducing himself as Gopesh Krishna. Little did I know then that in years to come this simple cook would become the guru of that mission. He led me into a small office where he offered me some water and an English book about Krishna before returning to the kitchen.

I read for several hours. Then, returning the book to the bookcase, I set out for the Yamuna. But at the main gate I encountered a man in his mid-twenties with sparkling blue eyes and white skin. He had a shaven head and clad in saffron robes. "My name is Asim Krishna Das." He smiled. "Welcome to Vrindavan."

Offering me a seat, he excused himself for a moment and returned with a plate of fluffy rice and spiced vegetables. Eating eagerly, I asked him how he came to live in India. He told me that his given name was Alan Shapiro and was from New York. He had traveled through Europe and Israel, and ultimately his search for spirituality brought him to India. In the Punjab state, he said, he met a saint named Mukunda Hari who advised him, "Go to Vrindavan, there you will find everything." Asim smiled. "His words were prophetic." As I was leaving, he offered, "If there's anything I can do to serve you; that will be my greatest joy."

The following day I roamed alone in the forest and eventually returned to the riverbank just beneath the hill of Madan Mohan Temple. I was to leave early the next morning for Hardwar, where Gary was waiting for me. When night fell, I offered my farewell to the land of Vrindavan. But my mind was divided. Lying down to sleep on the earthen riverbank, I thought, *Vrindavan is attracting my heart like no other place. What is happening to me? Please reveal Your divine will.* With this prayer, I drifted off to sleep.

Before dawn, I awoke to the ringing of temple bells, signaling that it was time to begin my journey to Hardwar. But my body lay there like a corpse. Gasping in pain, I couldn't move. A blazing fever consumed me from within, and under the spell of unbearable nausea, my stomach churned. Like a hostage, I lay on that riverbank. As the sun rose, celebrating a new day, I felt my life force sinking. Death that morning would have been a welcome relief. Hours passed. At noon, I still lay there. *This fever will surely kill me,* I thought.

Just when I felt it couldn't get any worse, I saw in the overcast sky something that chilled my heart. Vultures circled above, their keen sights focused on me. It seemed the fever was cooking me for their lunch, and they were just waiting until I was well done. They hovered lower and lower. One swooped to the ground, a huge black and white bird with a long, curving neck and sloping beak. It stared, sizing up my condition, then jabbed its pointed beak into my ribcage. My body recoiled, my mind screamed, and my eyes stared back at my assailant, seeking pity. The vulture flapped its gigantic wings and rejoined its fellow predators circling above. On the damp soil, I gazed up at the birds as they soared in impatient circles. Suddenly, my vision blurred and I momentarily blacked out. When I came to, I felt I was burning alive from inside out. Perspiring, trembling, and gagging, I gave up all hope.

Suddenly, I heard footsteps approaching. A local farmer herding his cows noticed me and took pity. Pressing the back of his hand to my forehead, he looked skyward toward the vultures and, understanding my predicament, lifted me onto a bullock cart. As we jostled along the muddy paths, the vultures followed overhead.

The farmer entrusted me to a charitable hospital where the attendants placed me in the free ward. Eight beds lined each side of the room. The impoverished and sadhu patients alike occupied all sixteen beds. For hours, I lay unattended in a bed near the entrance. Finally that evening the doctor came and, after performing a series of tests, concluded that

I was suffering from severe typhoid fever and dehydration. In a matter-of-fact tone, he said, "You will likely die, but we will try to save your life."

Taking the thermometer out of my mouth, he read it and pronounced, "No solid food for the next week. Your diet will be glucose water only."

With those words, he departed. Overcome by fever and nausea, with no strength in my body and teetering between life and death, I lay there. There was little money to treat the patients in this charitable ward, so we received only the crude basics. Once a day, the doctor made the rounds, giving a few minutes to each patient. Nurses appeared from time to time, but not a single one spoke English. Other patients wailed in agony all night long. The first night I was there, one man died. And death would have been a blessing to an emaciated old man in the bed next to mine. Silently bearing his miseries, he would lean over to pass red urine in a small pot kept on his bed. He coughed blood constantly, often spraying my face. One sweltering night, as I lay immobilized in anguish, patients throughout the room howled, moaned, and screamed in agony amid a stench of sweat, mold, and excrement. *Why am I here? Why did I leave my home and family and friends in Highland Park? And what about poor Gary? He'll never know why I didn't meet him.* Placing my life in the hands of God, I prayed, *I am yours, please do with me what you will.* All night long, I softly chanted the words that had begun to bring me solace in the most troubled moments. "Hare Krishna Hare Krishna Krishna Krishna Hare Hare, Hare Rama Hare Rama Rama Rama Hare Hare."

The next morning, having somehow heard news that I was ill, Asim came to visit me. Accompanying him was a beautiful old man whose eyes glistened with spiritual love. "This is one of the greatest saints in all of Vrindavan," Asim said. "His name is Krishnadas Babaji." Babaji wore only a simple white cloth around his waist. It extended just above his knees. Another piece of cloth draped around the back of his neck and hung over his chest. His head and face sprouted bright white hairs. With indescribable compassion, the elderly Babaji gazed upon me. Then, reaching out, he patted my head and burst out, "Hare Krishna!" Every day they both came to bless me. And every day, Babaji filled my heart with a healing joy and his laughter sprang from the bliss of his soul.

One day two young doctors in training came to my bed and took turns firing off a litany of questions. But I had one question for them. "What disease does that man in the next bed have?"

One of them stared blankly and replied, "Contagious tuberculosis." He added, "Please be careful, sir. If you inhale his cough or if one drop of his blood falls in your mouth, you will catch it, too."

"What, then why is he kept in a crowded room?"

"It is our policy. No one is quarantined unless the laboratory tests return positive. Unfortunately, our laboratory is closed because the technician is sick with tuberculosis. Therefore no quarantines are permitted." Lifting his umbrella, he strutted toward the door, and turned to me. "It is certain that the man beside you has the contagious germ, so please be careful. It was pleasant to meet you. Good day, sir." A few days later, the poor soul died before my eyes.

One day, sitting on my hospital bed, I wrote these words to my family:

Where there is faith, fear cannot exist. May you all be blessed with good health, happy lives, peace of mind, and love for God.

Richard
Vrindavan, September 1971

After about ten days, the doctor released me with the instruction, "You must not travel for one month." Pointing his finger into my face, he warned, "The way you sadhus travel, you will not survive. Stay in one place and eat simple rice." The news that I was not to leave troubled me. My first thoughts were of poor Gary. What had he thought when I did not meet him in Hardwar? After tearing him away from all his friends, now I had abandoned him alone in India. Would we ever meet again? But part of me was happy to stay and discover what more Vrindavan held for me.

2

KRISHNADAS BABAJI AND ASIM KINDLY brought me to their ashram to recuperate. The whole first day I rested. The next day, early in the morning, Asim asked if I would like to meet his guru. I eagerly consented. In a courtyard of *tulasi* trees, I first saw the man—a stately figure in his seventies—sitting on a wooden chair, eyes closed, chanting on prayer beads. This was Swami Bon Maharaja. Clean-shaven and with short white hair, he wore a simple T-shirt and the saffron lower cloth of a *sannyasi*. When he heard us approach, he slowly opened his eyes. "Please come," he said, gesturing for us to sit on the ground near him. Smiling, he asked my name. "Ah, yes, Richard. I am happy to welcome you as our guest. It is no accident that you have come to Vrindavan. Do you know what is Vrindavan?" His warm manner was compelling.

"I will be most grateful if you explain."

He placed his prayer beads on a nearby table, raised his forefinger, and spoke in flawless English. "Beyond our temporary material existence is the spiritual sky or *Brahman*. This is the destination sought by those who worship God as impersonal. Within the spiritual sky, there are spiritual planets where the One Supreme Lord resides in His various forms. Vrindavan is the highest realm of the spiritual world." He began to recite ancient Sanskrit verses to verify his words. The rhythm of his words entranced me. "Five thousand years ago," he said, "the Supreme Lord Krishna descended into our world and manifested His own abode, Vrindavan. Those with pure *bhakti*, or devotion, can still see Krishna performing His pastimes here." He paused, looked deeply into my eyes and said again, "It is not by chance that you have come here, Richard. We welcome you back home to Vrindavan and to our ashram."

Faithful disciples began to file through the quaint wooden entrance gate offering their love. A middle-aged woman approached Bon Maharaja and handed him a golden flower. He turned back to me. "You may stay with us as long as you like, Richard. You will be my special guest," he said. He nodded in the direction of the temple where Krishnadas Babaji was pacing back and forth chanting on beads. "You see Krishnadas Babaji over there?" I nodded. "You stand to gain great spiritual benefit if you spend your mornings with him. He is a *paramahamsa*, perfected soul, who is absorbed in *kirtan*, the chanting of God's Names, day and night." The swami's eyes filled with tears as he praised the elderly Babaji. "His devotion is an inspiration to all of us. Stay with him in the mornings and you will learn the essence of bhakti yoga. In the afternoons, feel free to roam through the forests of Vrindavan and experience the divine atmosphere." He told me that there would be no pressure on me. He said that for residents of the ashram there were strict rules, but added, "You are my special guest and may come and go as you please. Please be comfortable and happy." Between his fingertips, Bon Maharaja twirled the flower. "Each morning, I sit here in this courtyard. You are always welcome to come and talk with me."

I bowed in gratitude. "Thank you."

In my sickly condition, I felt his generosity to be a lifesaving gesture. Asim, too, smiled at the kindness I was receiving.

Education was an important mission for Bon Maharaja, who established a college in Vrindavan. He himself was highly educated and distinguished in character, the pride of an orthodox Brahmin family from East Bengal.

Asim explained that when he was only twenty years old, Swami Bon Maharaja met his guru, Bhaktisiddhanta Saraswati. Upon hearing his powerful message and seeing his spotless character, Bon Maharaja offered his life to the path of devotional service. Bhaktisiddhanta Saraswati boldly declared that no one should be categorized on the basis of race, nationality, or caste, that we are all eternal souls, not the temporary body. He taught that people must be respected according to their personal qualities, not their birth. Boldly exposing the modern perversion of the caste system, he faced plots to end his life. Bhaktisiddhanta Saraswati emphasized the spirit of genuine devotion, or bhakti, and dismissed mundane superficialities and pseudo spirituality. At the young age of twenty-three, Bon Maharaja took the vows of a *sannyasi*, lifelong celibacy, and began to preach throughout India. He was among the first of Bhaktisiddhanta's disciples to be sent to England and Germany in the 1920s.

Each morning as the sun was rising, Asim and I met in the courtyard to speak with Swami Bon Maharaja. Afterward, when Asim left for the college to assist his guru, I hurried to the temple. There, from eight o'clock until half past noon, Krishnadas Babaji sat every day alone on the floor absorbed in singing devotional songs. I sat by his side. His eyes radiated with spiritual emotion, and he often struggled to restrain tears. While chanting, he played a two-headed clay drum called *mrdanga*. Although his voice was simple, it was saturated with a devotional power that penetrated my heart.

Every morning at 4:30, Babaji was given the honor of leading the assembly of monks in prayer. As prayer grew to *kirtan*, or congregational chanting, everyone danced in joyous abandon. While beating his drum, Babaji, who was small, thin and old, would dance out from the Krishna temple and into the courtyard as the rest of the devotees trailed behind him. Entering into a small temple of Shiva, he sang loudly as twenty monks leapt high, bells clanging. Then, leading the procession around the tulasi garden and back into the temple, Babaji performed a grand finale that electrified the normally grave monks, who went wild with bliss. This was how every day began in the ashram. At seventy years old, Krishnadas Babaji was like an inexhaustible volcano, erupting with devotion each time he sang the glories of the Lord.

Babaji seemed never to stop chanting. Once when I had dysentery, I raced out to the latrine in the middle of the night and heard his strong, simple voice chanting the Maha Mantra from inside his room. Did he ever stop chanting God's Names? Anytime I awoke at night, I would quietly wander to the window of his room. In the seclusion of his personal love, he chanted Krishna's name day and night. No one in the ashram could determine when he slept.

Except for his outburst of "Hare Krishna" in the hospital, Babaji never spoke a word to me and I assumed he spoke no English. One morning I rose late and took my bath at the well. With a rope, I lowered the bucket down, filled it with water, and hauled it up. Crouching down on a rock near the well, I scooped the water from the bucket with a brass vessel and poured it over my body. Suddenly, I heard a voice. "Where were you this morning?"

I looked around to trace its source but there was no one around except Krishnadas Babaji. I continued my bath. Again the words boomed out,

"Where were you this morning?" I searched for the source but again saw only Babaji. I looked at him quizzically. Maybe he knew who was speaking.

Looking straight into my eyes, he said in English, "Why do you not answer my question?"

"Babaji," I blurted out, "I didn't know you spoke English."

"That does not answer my question."

From that day on, although his most prominent words consisted of "Hare Krishna," he spoke to me in fluent English. This impressed me. In India in the early 1970s, most people who knew a word of English, even if they didn't know what it meant, were proud to show it off, especially to foreigners. But Babaji Maharaja, who spoke fluent English, never spoke a word of it until it was required to help someone. Not a trace of arrogance could be detected in him. Perhaps this was the reason he was empowered to chant the holy names constantly.

Previously, I had thought that silent meditation was the path of stalwart spiritualists and that chanting and dancing was for sentimental people with no deep philosophical realization. Krishnadas Babaji shattered this misconception. I could not deny the power of his knowledge, detachment, and love. His path was bhakti yoga, devotional service to Krishna. Clearly the method for awakening that love was his chanting of God's holy names.

Babaji was loved all over Vrindavan. In many temples, whenever there was a special function, Babaji was invited to lead the *kirtan* and sometimes he took me along. One day, we entered a crowded temple where hundreds of people were chanting. Krishnadas Babaji chose to sit quietly in the rear, happy just to observe. As soon as somebody noticed him, the kirtan stopped and the guru of that temple came forward and placed the *mṛdanga* drum around Babaji's neck, the entire congregation begging him to lead the chanting. With his first beat of the *mṛdanga,* the crowd melted in gratitude. When I witnessed this outpouring of love for Babaji, I understood the saying that it is only when one has no desire for adoration that one is truly qualified to receive it.

On the day of Ekadasi, a fast day observed twice a month, Krishnadas Babaji would spend the entire night under a sacred tamarind tree chanting Krishna's names from sunset to sunrise. Joining him, I was amazed. The old man showed no symptoms of fatigue, while I struggled to stay awake. For Babaji, this all-night fasting and meditation, I realized, was not a discipline but simply the natural outpouring of his love for Krishna.

As the sun was rising, Babaji exclaimed, "Five hundred years ago, under this tree, Lord Chaitanya revealed his love to the world."

"Babaji," I asked, "please tell me about Lord Chaitanya."

His eyes beamed. Intoxicated by his all-night chanting, he explained, "Lord Chaitanya is Krishna, the Supreme Lord, who descended five hundred years ago to distribute love of God in the easiest possible way. Ages ago, his appearance was predicted in the scriptures. Although God Himself, he assumed the role of a devotee just to teach us by His own example." Babaji's voice soared with enthusiasm. "The personification of ecstatic love, he wept tears of compassion for all beings. 'In this age of quarrel and hypocrisy,' he taught, 'the essential medicine to cure our spiritual disease is the chanting of God's holy names.' Lord Chaitanya taught that God has revealed many names through the ages and has invested His potency in all of them. Love of God is the inherent nature of the soul and is dormant within everyone. But we have forgotten. Chanting God's name reawakens that love from within the heart." Lifting his fist, Babaji boldly cried out, "Lord Chaitanya rejected all sectarian boundaries and gave one and all equal opportunity to spiritual perfection."

His words struck me as so simple and true. I longed to learn more.

"What is the best way to chant?" I asked.

His eyes glazed with emotion and, closing them, he sang a Sanskrit verse and explained, "Lord Chaitanya taught that one should strive to be more humble than a blade of grass, more tolerant than a tree, and to offer all respect to others while expecting none for one's self. In this way, one can chant the Lord's names constantly." He stroked the grass on the ground between us. "You see this grass? It is happy to serve everyone, even by remaining in the most humble position under our feet. Whenever it's stepped on, it comes right back up, to serve. We can learn from this humility." He bowed his head toward the tree behind us. "You see that tree? It tolerates the burning summer sun while giving us shade. It tolerates the bitter cold while giving wood to keep us warm and it may stand for months without a drop of water, while giving us juicy fruits to quench our thirst, all of this without complaint. We should learn tolerance from the tree. Lord Chaitanya taught that we should aspire to be the humble servants of the servant of the servant of the Lord. Only in this way can we taste the nectar of the Holy Name."

Then Babaji stood up and, with a hearty laugh, rubbed the top of my head and strolled away along the riverbank. I remained, staring into the deep blue water of the Yamuna. Still wide from the monsoon rains, she flowed quietly through the forest and fields of Vrindavan. *His words are like precious jewels,* I thought, *and because he so sincerely practices them in his life, they deeply penetrate my heart.* At that moment an upsurge of peace sprung from within me. I felt I was just where I needed to be.

3

FROM HALFWAY ACROSS THE WORLD, I could feel the anguish of my parents, helpless as they were to communicate their feelings to me. In the year and a half I had been traveling, it was very rare that I stayed in a place long enough to send my family a note with a return address. So it had been a long time since I had had any news from them. In a recent letter, I had shared my experiences in Vrindavan and included a return address. I awaited their replies.

One afternoon, Asim Krishna handed me three letters. Sensing the content, I brought them to the bank of the Yamuna. The first letter was from my father. Tears from his eyes had washed away words and whole passages. Just holding the paper in my hands, I could feel his pain. *What have I done to my father and mother, who have dedicated their lives to my welfare?* In every line, my father pleaded for me to come home. "Every day," he said, "seems to last forever in guilt and worry. What horrible things have I done to you that you have rejected me?" he wrote. "How can I live knowing my son to be living in jungle caves, alone with no money?" It was signed, "your brokenhearted father." Gazing out across the graceful current of the Yamuna, I felt my heart breaking with his. Then I opened the second envelope. It was from my mother. She longed to know, "Why are you in a foreign land for so long? Haven't you found what you're looking for yet? What are you wearing and eating? How is your health?" Throughout she reiterated her love.

The third letter was from Larry, my younger brother and dear friend. Larry was an honest and simple person, so I knew that whatever he said would be true. He described the perpetual worry into which I had cast my entire family. Of my mother he wrote, "Don't you understand a mother's love? Mom is in a state of confusion. She helplessly worries day and night about your safety." Then he described my father's condition. "Our father's hair is graying. He has aged years since you abandoned us. He stares blindly at a wall lost in grief. Thinking of you, all alone living in caves and jungles, he cries. Do you want to kill your own father? Is this your idea of religion? Maybe you don't care if he lives or dies, but we love him. If you don't come home, you will be held responsible for his death."

My heart pounding, I silently prayed for guidance. As I gazed into the gentle, flowing waters of Yamuna, my whole life played before my mind's eye. I felt so grateful for my family's affection and hated to cause them pain, but this burning in my heart for God's love was stronger than anything else. I could not expect them to understand. I recalled my readings about great persons who, in their dedication to God, had borne the suffering of breaking loved ones' hearts. Upon hearing the call of God, Abraham was willing to sacrifice Isaac, his beloved son. Hearing his calling at Gethsemane, Lord Jesus accepted crucifixion while his mother Mary wept bitterly beneath the cross. His apostles, too, left everything behind to heed His call. Hearing that same inner call, Prince Siddhartha Gautama left his loving family in tears as he disappeared into the forest to travel the path of becoming the Buddha. When the inner voice of God called for him, Sankaracarya, the greatest proponent of the path of non-dualism, left home, breaking his poor mother's heart. And for our sake, Lord Chaitanya left his widowed mother in pools of tears. *These saints and avatars are great,* I thought, *and I am small. Yet a calling, this longing for the Divine, has overcome me.* I spent the day on the bank of the Yamuna praying for my family and praying for guidance.

The next morning in the temple courtyard, I sat at the feet of Bon Maharaja and presented him the letters. Tears welled in his eyes as he read them. For a long time, he stared across the courtyard, lost in thought. Then he turned to me and spoke. "Long ago, when I was about your age, I accepted a life of renunciation. This caused my father and mother unbearable pain. It was a great test in my life. To break the hearts of your loved ones is often a price you must pay to accept a life of exclusive devotion. But you will see, in the passing of time they will understand and appreciate your life. In fact, they will be proud of you. In the meantime, there is no restriction in a sadhu meeting his father or mother. You must search your own heart."

In my reply to father, I wrote:

My Dear Father,

On receiving your last letter dated September 14, 1971, a painful sensation melted into my heart. Listen to what I say, not with ears, but with your tender heart: Each man must choose what he believes to be the most sacred path to follow in his life. If a man does not follow what he truly believes in, his life will have little meaning. With all my heart and all my soul, I believe that the highest purpose in life is to live a life devoted to the one God who lovingly rules over us all. We are servants of the same Lord. I believe that the root of all man's quarrel and sufferings is his forgetting that highest truth.

Since ancient times, there have always been politicians, businessman, soldiers, etc., and along with these there have always been those treading the path of truth and living a religious life. But today, everyone has become so engrossed in satisfying his material hunger that God has been all but forgotten.

Is it not true that the noblest man is he who is humble, honest, righteous, and respectful to all fellow beings? This is religious life in its truest sense. I believe that this is the life that I must lead. Please trust that all I am doing is striving to lead a life free of malice. For a man of my temperament to enter into the business world would result in a life of no meaning or satisfaction. For when a man fights his own inner nature, he ruins himself. At present I am rather unsettled.

Please, I beg you to give me a little more time to secure my convictions. At that time we will arrange to unite once more.

I will keep in touch with you. In America, many parents of sons are suffering the great pain of separation to the army for 2 to 4 years, where their son endangers his life for a cause rooted in hate. I pray to you only to have faith that what I seek is for the good of all.

Bless you my loving father, Bless your tender heart.

I will soon tell you my plans, very soon.

Richard
Vrindavan India
Sept. 30, 1971

To my mother, I wrote a letter describing my eating habits and what I was wearing, assuring her I was in fine health, and trying to explain my choice to search for the meaning of life. I thanked her for her loving concern and wished her peace.

I knew they could not comprehend my calling. My naive words certainly perpetuated their grief. But I had a simple faith that God understood my heart and would extend his loving hand to help them.

4

A T NIGHT, I LAY ON THE ROOFTOP OF THE ASHRAM gazing into the starlit Vrindavan sky. Peacocks carried on a dialogue and the night guards protected the village by loudly calling out to one another the names of God.

But of all the sounds of the Vrindavan night, the one that most captivated my ears was the melody of the Hare Krishna mantra floating in the breeze from far away. Alternating voices of an old man and woman sang through an amplified speaker all night, every night. These sounds, the guards, the peacocks, the old man and woman singing, created a spiritual symphony that stirred my heart. I thought back to the aged sadhu who had written me a message with a piece chalk on his broken slate. Was I becoming crazy for Krishna here in magical Vrindavan?

Traditionally, devotees circumambulate holy places like Vrindavan as an act of worship. One night, a mystical force drew me from the rooftop and onto that dusty pathway that wound around the town. Guided by the moonlight, I roamed along a riverbank path that led into the forest. From a distant place, a sound drew me. As I came closer, my anticipation soared. Could it be the same song sung by an old man and woman that had been charming me to sleep each night? I yearned to find its origin. The closer I came, the louder the mantra grew. Yes, it was that same song. Soon I found myself in a quaint temple of Hanuman, the divine monkey who personifies ecstatic devotion, where a man and woman in their late seventies were sitting on the floor chanting, their eyes shut in intense absorption. They were clothed in worn white cloth and appeared to be farmers. It was about one o'clock in the morning and I joined them in chanting the familiar melody. When we later parted ways, they invited me to return for lunch the next day.

The next afternoon, I stepped from the dusty footpath into Hanuman's temple. Not knowing why, I was brimming with anticipation. Hardly a minute had passed when an Indian man in his mid-twenties approached. "Maharaji wants to meet you now."

"Me? I asked, pointing to my own chest, "Who is Maharaji and how does he know me?"

"Oh, he knows all about you."

"Will you be so kind to tell me about Maharaji?" I asked.

"Not now. Maharaji is waiting for you. We'll talk later."

Taking my hand, he led me into a sunny courtyard where a round man beaming a beatific smile sat cross-legged on a wooden bed, a faded checkered blanket wrapped around his body. I drew closer. His face, framed by white stubble, glowed with an otherworldly joy. His squinting eyes seemed to penetrate through the windows of mine and into the mysteries of my life. This was Neem Karoli Baba. While I was living in the Himalayas I had heard of his extraordinary qualities. His followers affectionately addressed him as Maharaji.

As I approached, he was speaking in Hindi to a few Indian disciples who sat on the ground in a semicircle around him. Seeing me, he broke into a contagious smile and welcomed me. He raised his index finger and spoke to me through a translator. "You have forsaken wealth and comforts in search of enlightenment and with great struggle have come to India. Now you travel alone and cry for God while your family, far away, cries for you." With a gracious swoop of his hand, he motioned for me to sit with the others. "Have no fears," he said, so serious that his brow furrowed and lips tightened. "Rejoice to bear all difficulties. Krishna has heard your prayers and brought you to Vrindavan. By chanting the name of Rama and Krishna, everything is accomplished. But," he said, shaking his head, "people are creating a hell by their addiction to criticizing and fighting. Do not judge others or fall into those egoistic ways."

He seemed to know everything about me and spoke just the words I needed to hear. I was both charmed and amazed. "But almost the whole world has fallen into that trap, how do I avoid it?" I asked.

His eyes twinkled as he smiled. "Love everyone, serve everyone, and feed everyone. Serve like Hanuman without selfishness and greed. This is the key to realizing God."

Assuming the mood of a playful child, he put his hand to his mouth as if eating and invited us to take the sacred food.

As we entered the special hall for a meal, I expressed to my guide how eager I was to hear about his guru. He obliged. "I'm from a village near Nandital in the Himalayas and from childhood I've loved Maharaji." We sat in lines on the floor. A devotee placed leaf plates in front of us and filled them with scoops of wonderful food. My host was dressed in a buttoned down white shirt and pants, his wavy black hair oiled and neatly combed. After reciting a short prayer, he related some memories of Neem Karoli Baba. "Maharaji is a *Siddha Purusha,* a perfected being. I have personally witnessed his knowledge of past, present, and future. Actually, he always knows where I am and what I'm doing." He sipped from his clay cup of a cooling yoghurt drink called *lassi.*

"Let me tell you something else," he added. "Maharaji is sometimes in two distant places at the same time. This has been documented. We are always expecting him to appear or disappear at the least expected moment. He's unpredictable. At any moment he may appear or disappear, chastise or praise, speak in riddles or profound truths, or instruct someone to renounce the world or get married. But the one thing we know for sure is he always brings out the very best in us and carries us closer to God." He smiled with pride. "Neem Karoli Baba, although a grave yogi, can be so charming in his playfulness. Just like Hanuman."

I was served steaming *halava,* farina sautéed in butter and steamed in sweet syrup. The delectable aroma filled the room. As we ate it, Neem Karoli Baba appeared in the doorway. Noting us relishing our food, he smiled with joy. I rejoiced, too, seeing his sweet mood. He personified everything he taught us. "Love everyone, serve everyone, and feed everyone." Just like Hanuman.

The next day, I returned and found Maharaji surrounded by a few followers reciting the story of Hanuman's devotion from the *Ramayan.* Transfixed, Neem Karoli Baba trembled, tears streaming from his eyes. For the next few weeks, I spent an hour or so each day sitting at Maharaji's feet. He didn't give formal lectures while I was there, but rather he spoke casually with his followers or sang *kirtan.* I was fascinated by how he would respond to questions with brief but concise wisdom such as, "Just serve every creature in God's creation with humility, respect, and love." Or, "Just sing the names of Rama and everything else will be attained." One day he turned to me, his eyes seeming to search my soul. Then, shooting up a single finger, he exclaimed, "Ek, Ek, Ek. God is one."

At that time, I was not aware that people from the West knew of Neem Karoli Baba until the arrival of a celebrity well known in my generation, Baba Ram Dass. One day, while I sat at the feet of Maharaji, Ram Dass and a small entourage of Westerners unexpectedly turned up at the ashram. This icon of the 1960s counterculture, formerly the controversial Professor Richard Alpert of Harvard University, had, together with Timothy Leary, popularized LSD as a means of expanding consciousness.

Upon entering, Ram Dass meekly bowed his graying head in the lap of his guru as a small child might. Affection poured from his guru's heart as he playfully tugged the graying beard of his disciple and patted his head like a puppy. Laughing, Maharaji said, "We were waiting for you." How beautiful it was for me to see a distinguished Harvard scholar and powerful social icon enjoy being treated like a naughty little boy. Maharaji beamed a smile upon all of us then waved his hand exclaiming, "Jao, prasadam. Go, take lunch." Maharaji must have mystically known of their unannounced arrival, as an amazing feast had been prepared in larger quantity than usual that day.

I had the pleasure of bringing Ram Dass and his entourage to some of the holy places in Vrindavan. One day, we attended a kirtan and talk given by Anandamayi Ma, who had an ashram in Vrindavan. She remembered me from our meeting in the Himalayas, and as she gave her lecture to a large audience, she looked toward me and nodded, then reconfirmed the spiritual direction I was heading with the words, "Whenever you possibly can, sustain the flow of the Holy Name. To repeat His Name is to be in His presence. If you associate with the Supreme Friend, He will reveal His true beauty to you." When the program ended, Ram Dass and I fell into a soul-searching discussion. But night was falling, so he invited me to continue our talk the next day at his residence.

I arrived early at the Jaipur Dharamsala, a guesthouse on a noisy lane lined with cloth shops and food stalls and congested with bicycle rickshaws honking loud rubber horns to scatter the foot traffic. Baba Ram Dass opened the door, morning light beaming on his welcoming face. I looked beyond him into the room, which resembled not the residence of a distinguished professor but that of a simple sadhu. Graciously, he led me to the only piece of furniture, a wooden bed.

After offering me a seat, he too sat cross-legged, spreading out his flowing white robes. We faced each other. His graying hair streamed from his balding head and draped onto his back and shoulders. A breeze from the nearby window slightly whisked his peppered beard. His large blue eyes glowed and the faint wrinkles in their corners creased deeply as he smiled. Speaking no words, we simply looked into each other's hearts through the channel of the eyes. Those moments seemed timeless. That long gaze we shared affected my vision in such a way that at times he looked like an innocent child and at other times like an ancient, stoic sage.

I reflected on a verse from the Bhagavad Gita: "As the eternal soul passes in this body from boyhood to youth to old age, the soul similarly passes into another body at death. The self-realized soul is not bewildered by such a change." A sublime peace filled the room. Perhaps half an hour passed in this way before Ram Dass took a deep breath, slightly shrugged his shoulders, and broke our silence with the invocation, "*Om.*"

"Could you tell me something about your spiritual journey?" I asked him. I was eager to learn how he had come to India and how he had met his guru.

Ram Dass shifted his weight on the wooden slab of a bed, as if readying himself for the narrative. "A few years back," he began, "I came to India. I brought with me a supply of LSD, hoping to find someone who might understand more about these substances than we did in the West. In my travels I met an American sadhu, Bhagavan Dass, who guided me to Neem Karoli Baba. That was in 1967. I was grieving the death of my mother. Maharaji saw into my heart and consoled me with unimaginable compassion. Without my ever having said a word about my life, he could read my heart and tell the confidential details of my past. His powers, combined with his love, wisdom, and humor, transformed my life."

"I had a similar experience when I first met him," I said. "He seemed to know everything about me."

Baba Rama Dass smiled. "One day Maharaji asked me, 'Where is the medicine?' At first I was confused but Bhagavan Dass suggested he was asking for LSD. Intrigued, I held out three pills of pure LSD and to my astonishment he swallowed them all. I was prepared to clinically monitor his reactions, but nothing happened—nothing. His consciousness is beyond LSD!"

Having myself witnessed the powers of Himalayan yogis, I laughed in wonder.

Ram Dass sat cross-legged with back erect. His palms rested upward on his lap. "I couldn't separate myself from Maharaji's association, and so I stayed as long as I could. Accepting me as his disciple, he gave me the name Ram Dass, which means servant of Lord Rama. Months passed in his extraordinary company. As influential as I was in America, Maharaji forbid me from bringing anyone to him." Ram Dass shook his head in disbelief. "He had no inclination for anything material, neither money, fame, or followers. I'd never seen anyone like him." Apprehending anew the love he felt for his guru, his voice began to tremble. "When I sit with Maharaji, I feel that I have unconditional love for everyone in the world." In that same year, 1971, Ram Dass published his story in the classic *Be Here Now*.

As the day passed, a sense of brotherhood grew between us as we shared the realizations and inspirations we had gained on our spiritual journeys. Before parting, I confided in him a concern that had come to weigh heavily on my mind. "Mother India has become my spiritual home. I have so much still to discover. But I fear that my next visa extension will be denied and I'll be forced to leave."

Baba Rama Dass closed his eyes and submerged into deep thought. Despite the commotion from the busy street outside, the room was serene. I closed my eyes as well and drifted into the tranquility of meditation. Five minutes passed. When I opened my eyes, I found Rama Dass gazing at me with a gentle smile. He said softly, "You may have to leave the geographical boundaries of India. However, you never have to leave Bharata, the spirit of India within."

5

DYSENTERY, AN ALL TOO COMMON MALADY for foreigners in India, soon struck me down again. Weakness, nausea, and repeated dashes to the latrine became my daily reality. Without the selfless care of my friend Asim, it would have been far more difficult. He often reassured me, "Bhakti means to serve with love and devotion." While I lay on the floor, Asim brought boiled rice, yoghurt, and flea seed husk. Each time he visited, he would share his love for Krishna and Vrindavan. In this way, my sickness became just another episode that helped to cement our friendship.

Early one morning, I had regained my health and Asim invited me to join him on a journey into the inner villages around Vrindavan. He told me that Vraja was the name for the whole area around the town of Vrindavan, and that Krishna had performed His pastimes in this area. Vraja consists of about eighty miles of forests, fields, and villages, and over 5,000 temples of Krishna—some the largest in all of India and others quite quaint. "You'll be fascinated by the Vrajabasis' natural love for Krishna." His blue eyes widened with enthusiasm. "Shall we go?"

A few minutes later we were bouncing and creaking along in a dilapidated local bus. Fields of golden wheat and mustard, its yellow flowers bending in the wind, stretched out on all sides. Every so often, poor farmers on the side of the road would flag down the bus and climb aboard. Their clothes were ragged, some of them suffered cataracts, skin diseases, or untreated infections. But they were blissful as they sang devotional songs, clapped their hands, and danced on the moving bus. Old women with wrinkles creviced into their dark, leathery skin spontaneously rose to their feet, raised their arms, and danced while shyly covering their heads with tattered saris. They beamed with the exuberance of children.

In the villages, the Vrajabasis, although poor, smiled radiantly and greeted one another with "Jaya Radhey," the name of the compassionate, feminine aspect of Krishna. They loved God not just as the Supreme

Creator but also as an intimate neighbor in their village. The women drew water from a well and carried it on top of their heads in round, clay pots, smiling at me as they passed chanting "Radhey, Radhey." From their clay stoves the pungent smell of burning, dried cow-dung paddies drifted in the air. The men of the village shaved their heads each month as an offering of devotion and spent their days herding cows, plowing fields with their oxen, or selling their wares along the footpath. The skinny children, eyes sparkling, jumped about, playing with sticks and balls. Everybody, man, woman, and child smiled at me and called out "Radhey Radhey" as I passed. I observed hundreds of villagers coming to the temples with offerings of milk, butter, and sweets, some praying and others singing and dancing for the pleasure of their Lord. Walking through this other world, I reflected, *The religion of these people is not reserved for Sundays or holidays but is intrinsic to every aspect of their daily lives. It is utterly spontaneous.*

One afternoon Asim and I were relaxing on the hill of Madan Mohan Temple overlooking the river Yamuna. Sitting in the grass as black bees hummed a meditative drone around us, I stretched my legs and leaned back against a boundary wall of red stone. There I revealed my mind. "Asim," I asked, "could you explain your understanding of deity worship?" I told him of how, in my travels through India, I'd found almost everybody worshiping the carved image of the Lord. The Yogis and Shivaites worshipped the Shiva Lingam or statues of Lord Shiva, and the Buddhists made elaborate offerings to the Deity of Lord Buddha. "Some people from Western religions condemn all this as idolatry," I said. "But Christians offer prayers to statues or paintings of Jesus as well as to the Holy Crucifix." I told him about how, when I was in Italy, I had visited the Convent of Saint Damiano in Assisi where Jesus spoke to Saint Francis from the wooden crucifix on the altar and ordered him to restore His church. "And Jews offer articles of veneration to the Torah, while Muslims, too, who condemn idol worship, bow repeatedly to the Ka'aba in Holy Mecca." I knew there were differences in explanations as to the meaning of these forms of worship, but I saw the common idea they shared, to focus on a form or sound that connects our consciousness to the divinity. I wondered what Asim's impressions were as they related to Krishna worship.

At that moment, Krishnadas Babaji strolled by and erupted into his trademark and blissful, "Hare Krishna." We bowed in joy as he passed.

Although it was I who'd asked him the question, I realized that Asim was giving me the gift of coming to some of my own conclusions. "You know," I went on, "when I see the unbelievable devotion of devotees like Krishnadas Babaji, while they worship the deity, I can't dismiss it as idol worship. When I see such high moral and spiritual character, I can't dismiss these people as idolaters. They seem to be experiencing love of God in their worship. Didn't Jesus say you could judge a tree by its fruit?"

Asim smiled with the reassurance of an elder brother, then leaned forward and prompted, "Yes, go on."

I told him how, when I first saw deity worship in India, it had repelled me a little, striking me as strange and superstitious. "But after spending so much time with holy people who naturally accept their deity as a form through which to communicate with the one God, I have come to accept deity worship as beautiful. Now I want to understand the scriptural philosophy behind it. Can you help me?"

Asim sat up near a patch of tulasi bushes, rubbed his chin in deep thought and took a moment before replying. "Really, I'm not qualified to explain these things, but I'll share what I heard from my guru and what I've read in the Vedic Scriptures." As the bees moved from flower to flower, collecting nectar, I drank in his words. "God is unlimited and independent," Asim began. "To say He cannot appear in the deity form is to limit Him. The Vedas also condemn idol worship. Historically, there were traditions in both East and West where people concocted forms and worshipped them out of superstition with no clear conception of the one God. Quite often, they had selfish or evil motives. It is this type of idolatry that has been condemned through the ages. In the age of the Bible and Koran, it was common among non-believers. But this is not the type of deity worship approved of by the Vedas. Legitimate deity worship, according to the Vedas, is a science in which the Lord is called with devotional rites to appear in designated forms. In these forms He accepts our devotional offerings, all for the purpose of purifying the worshippers' body, mind, and words by fixing in us the remembrance of the Lord. The aim is to please the Lord through surrender and love."

A butterfly with iridescent purple, red, and yellow wings fluttered by and landed on Asim's thigh. He sat still, appreciating its beauty. "Just look," he said, his voice overflowing with happiness. "Creation is a gallery of art with a masterpiece wherever we look. I long to meet the artist. Everything emanates from the Lord. All material elements are the Lord's energy. By His will He may choose to appear in His own energy as a deity to help us focus our minds and senses in loving servitude. Just as electricity manifests in a light bulb to radiate light, so God can permeate the deity with His presence. Electricity is invisible to the naked eye and the bulb by itself gives light only when the electrical energy infuses the bulb with its presence. Then we can see and feel the light. In a similar way the Lord may appear in the tangible form of a deity to help us see and feel His presence and reciprocate with our love." Smiling, he asked me if he had made sense.

I nodded, a feeling of calm permeating my heart.

That year, after an abundant monsoon season of rains, Vrindavan was filled with lush forests and pastures. It was autumn and the days were warm while the nights grew cold. I watched in fascination as the residents of Vrindavan were preparing to celebrate one of their holiest festivals. Followers on the path of Bhakti celebrate God's love with the joy of their own love and the festivals are rich with sponateity. Wherever I wandered, everyone anticipated the full moon night of October. According to the scripture, *Srimad Bhagavatam*, this was the night when Lord Krishna performed the *Rasa* dance. Profusely glorified in art, poetry, and drama, the Rasa dance, I would learn, is one of the deepest revelations of spiritual love. The whole of Vrindavan was buzzing with excitement, and the markets bustled with devotees who were purchasing decorations for their temples, ornaments for their deities, and food for the feasts. On this night, all of the five thousand temples in the region arranged to host a celebration. Just before sunset, a group of disciples assembled around Bon Maharaja in the courtyard to hear him explain the meaning of the *Rasa* dance.

"This is not like any worldly dance wherein people try to satisfy their material senses," he began. "While the *gopis* live as cowherd maids, they embody the highest expression of the soul's love for God, for pleasing the Lord is their exclusive aspiration. This dance represents the most perfect intimacy between the soul and God, free of any tinge of selfish desire but charged with the fullest bliss. On this night, when Krishna called them from their homes with the sweet song of His flute, the gopis forsook everything they had and risked dangers and social rejection all to satisfy the Lord. When they reached Krishna, the Supreme Lord, He admitted that in the span of creation He had no power to sufficiently repay the gopis for their pure devotion. But in reciprocation He expanded Himself to dance simultaneously with each gopi in their eternal spiritual bodies, for a night of endless joy." Bon Maharaja turned his face toward the sinking sun and the rose colored light glinted in his eyes he concluded, "In a few minutes, we will celebrate, praying to someday follow the lead of the gopis."

In the tulasi garden of Bon Maharaja's temple, the devotees had worked all day constructing a throne by weaving together thousands of tiny fragrant flowers. Now, as the time for celebration arrived, they ceremoniously carried the deities from the altar to the throne amid offerings of sweets and savories. The moon rose in the east, full and golden. In Vrindavan, this *Rasa Purnima* moon is celebrated as the most beautiful moon of the year. Devotees welcome it with songs composed specially for this occasion. As the moon climbed higher, its golden light illuminated the four directions. All the while, Krishnadas Babaji sang with deep emotion while everyone else blissfully chanted in response.

Joining them, I fixed my mind on the enchanting vision of Radha and Krishna in the moonlit flower forest of Vrindavan. As the moon ascended still higher, it spread its silvery hue on every leaf and flower. Mother earth seemed lit up by its touch. Bathed in the sweetness of that pearl moon, everyone was beaming—the deities, the forest, and we who worshipped. In this way, we sang late into the night for the Lord's pleasure.

How deeply my time in Vrindavan was affecting my heart. In the sweetness of those moments, I thought how unconditional spiritual love for God was a higher experience than attaining mystic powers wherein one could perform supernatural feats or even liberation wherein one was freed of all sufferings and anxieties. In spiritual love, like that of the gopis, a devotee fully gives his or herself for the pleasure of the Lord and can fully relish the intimacy of God's love.

On another such moonlit night, as the night birds crooned in the temple garden, Swami Bon Maharaja, sitting back on his wooden chair, gazed at me intently. "I have been carefully examining you,

Richard." He paused to prepare me for what was to come. "Tonight I would like to initiate you as my disciple." He held up a string of prayer beads carved from the wood of tulasi. "I have sanctified these for you. Are you willing to accept?"

A chilly breeze whisked across the courtyard. My mind swung between gratitude and pain. I was honored to be asked by him, yet I dreaded the thought of disappointing him. I couldn't accept without sufficient conviction. "I am indebted to you," I replied in a frail voice, "for all the inspiration you've showered on me. But I have vowed not to accept initiation from any guru until I have confidence that I will remain faithful throughout my life. I believe it would be an act of disrespect toward your holiness for me to make such a commitment without appropriate sincerity."

Tears welled in Bon Maharaja's eyes as he patted my head and spoke. "I'm pleased by your sincerity. I will put no pressure on you. You must follow your heart. The members of the ashram would like to call you by a spiritual name, so if you permit me, I'll give you a name, not an initiation name but an affectionate name. You may use this name until you decide to accept initiation." I nodded in agreement. "We'll call you Ratheen Krishna Das. Ratheen Krishna means Krishna who is the charioteer of Arjuna and Das means you are His servant."

I bowed my head in gratitude.

"There is one problem." His eyes narrowed. "Everyone is complaining about your long, unkempt hair. Why don't you shave your head like the other ashramites?"

I pleaded, "To me, shaving the head represents surrendering to a mentor. Until that decision is made, I will not do it superficially."

"Then will you at least cut it shorter? Our guests do not appreciate it."

"If it pleases you, Maharaja, I will cut it shorter." My desire to please him overshadowed any other concerns.

That night, out of curiosity, I looked into a mirror. It had been a long time since I had last seen my reflection or used a comb for that matter. Hanging halfway to my waist, my mane was quite matted. The next morning Bon Maharaja instructed Asim, "Bring our Ratheen Krishna Das to the barber."

Asim chuckled while leading me toward the barbershop, a warped and rotting wooden shack hardly big enough for four people to sit in.

As I took my seat on a heavy wooden chair, the barber gawked at my matted locks. He was a skinny little man in his mid fifties, bare-chested, and wore only a checkered cotton cloth around his waist that extended to just above his knees. "How to cut such hair?" he muttered. He desperately attempted with every variety of scissors he had, but none could penetrate. Finally, he called an open-air conference in the lane with other local barbers. "How to cut such hair?" they repeated again and again. After much deliberation, they decided to call for a gardener.

The gardener arrived—a muscular, heavy-set man with a thick black mustache wearing loose cotton clothes soiled with a mixture of dirt and sweat. He evaluated my head for some time and then left for his storehouse to fetch the proper equipment. He returned with a rusted set of loppers used for cutting bushes. The tool was shaped like a gigantic pair of scissors. My haircut was becoming an elaborate project, and the gardener, the self-acclaimed foreman of the site. Pointing his stubby finger, which was caked with dirt under his uncut nails, he dictated orders. "Grab his hair and pull backward," he said to his assistant. "Pull harder—harder. Yes, now hold it as tight as you can." Canvassing a passerby, he instructed, "You hold this sadhu down on the chair, and don't let him move." Then he ordered the barber, "You grab the bottom of the cutter with both hands and push up. I'll push the top of the cutter down." With great seriousness, the four men assembled, each in his strategic position. The gardener and the barber strained, groaned, and perspired, using all their body weight as they pushed the cutter from both directions. Dozens of passersby stopped to gawk at the spectacle. A few more even joined in the effort, each one pushing his weight into the bush cutter. Whatever came of this one big cut would be my new hairstyle. There would be no second cut.

Everyone in the crew was moaning and sweating in the struggle to penetrate my hair. Little by little, I felt the blades biting into my locks as hundreds of hairs snapped out from my scalp. The whole while, my friend Asim laughed so hard that tears streamed down his cheeks.

Finally, after a very long few minutes of pushing and tugging, the two blades of the bush cutter snapped together. It was done. Strewn on the floor like trash was my precious hair. It had once represented my revolt against war, prejudice, and the superficialities of society, all my ideals that I held sacred. Now the barbers trampled it beneath their sandals with no mind. What little remained on my head hung to just below my neck. It was perhaps the sloppiest haircut in modern history. But it was done. The gardener and the barber proudly held up a mirror. "It is complete. Please see. Please see." With joined palms, I thanked them. But I preferred not to see.

Back at the ashram gate, two interesting Americans appeared. One was David, a sincere and intelligent man who had recently acted as a personal secretary and friend of Alan Watts, the famous author of books that blended Eastern mysticism and Western logic. David and I instantly bonded and shared many hours of soul-searching conversation. David, like Asim, spoke from his heart and was an excellent listener.

One day, five of Bon Maharaja's prominent disciples arrived from East Bengal. Their leader, Jagannath, served as both the principal of a school and the head of his town. He was tall, well groomed, and walked with the poise of total confidence. Yet he was humble and respectful to all. Although he was older than my father, we became close friends. One morning, Jagannath and his companions saw David with a camera in hand. "Sir, please take our group photo," one said, while they all posed in front of the temple.

David turned to me and whispered. "There is only one more shot in the film. It's my last roll. I was saving this shot for something special. What should I do? They're posing." We decided to pretend to take their photo by imitating a clicking sound as they posed. Then, without thinking twice about this deception, we went about our duties.

The next day, I was taken aback to see Jagannath standing alone, silently crying. "Why is he in such distress?" I asked his friend.

He sizzled me with his stare. "Because of what you did."

"What did I do?" I replied, bewildered.

"Yesterday you pretended to take our photograph while we posed. This was duplicitous. Shame on you for insulting us."

I darted over to where Jagannath stood and begged forgiveness, but he said nothing. The next day, again I pleaded for him to excuse my foolishness. He fixed my eyes in his sad stare. "You are a devotee of Krishna," he said. "How could you treat another human being with such indignity? Don't you know that Lord Chaitanya taught us to be humble like a blade of grass and offer all respect to others? Duplicity is a terrible disease." Tears welled in his eyes as he turned his head away from me. Gazing skyward, he said, "I trusted you as a devotee but you have disappointed my expectations. Therefore I cry. I cry for you, my friend, because you know so little. A real devotee would never treat anyone so cheaply." Then he embraced me and walked away.

Pacing to the riverbank, ashamed of my insensitivity, I tried to make sense of all this. *In ordinary society,* I reflected:

> *Such an insignificant transgression would be hardly noticed. But in a devotional culture, soft-heartedness and integrity are held sacred. What really is the culture of devotion? It is so very subtle, but it fertilizes the field of the heart so that the seed of true love may grow.*

I had passed more than two months in the pleasant company of Asim, Krishnadas Babaji, and Bon Maharaja. Bon Maharaja never pressed me to initiate. However, there was one monk at the ashram who could not tolerate that I had refused initiation. One day he called me to his room and with scorn written on his face, preached fire and brimstone. "Look at you," he chastised. "You gave up material life to live as an ascetic. But until you take initiation from a guru, you have no spiritual life." His eyes narrowed to slits and his voice quivered. "Do you know what happens to one who dies not having either material or spiritual life?" I looked at him in silence. "Do you know?"

"No," I replied timidly.

He sprung up from his seat and pointed his finger into my face. "He becomes a ghost. I'm talking about you. You're living as a ghost. If uncertain death comes, you will suffer miserably for thousands of years, wandering as a ghost." He stared at me. "Why do you take our guru's mercy so cheaply? You must surrender or leave."

Saddened, I looked down to the floor and replied, "I'm sorry. I will go." Walking out his door I gathered up my cloth bag and begging bowl and proceeded to leave the ashram. On the way out, I noticed Bon Maharaja sitting in the courtyard, so I prostrated myself at his feet and asked for his blessings to leave.

His eyes shot open with surprise to hear my words. "Why are you leaving us?"

"Maharaja, I wish not to offend you." I went on to paraphrase the sermon I had just heard.

His expression soured with disgust. "Who has spoken this nonsense?" he asked. I informed him. Then, with the tenderness of a loving father, he spoke these words. "I never thought such things about you. You are a sincere devotee. I love you like my son. You have not offended me. Rather, you bring me joy. I welcome you to stay here as long as you wish. I assure you, there will never be such pressure again."

I was grateful for Bon Maharaja's kindness. Still, considering this episode, I felt it was time to move on. I did not wish to disrupt his disciples' minds. After all, I was still searching, and residence in the ashram *was* for dedicated disciples. In respect for the affection and wisdom Swami Bon Maharaja always showered upon me, I remained a few more days. Then, receiving his blessings, I departed for the forests of Vrindavan.

6

To LIVE IN THE LUSH FORESTS OF VRINDAVAN! The river Yamuna beckoned me to her banks where once again I could live the life of a homeless wanderer, sleeping under a different tree every night. I had only the clothes on my back, two pieces of unstitched cloth, one that I wrapped around my waist to cover the lower part of my body and one that covered the upper part. Solitude was again my welcome companion.

Often I slept at Chira Ghat near an ancient kadamba tree. Aspirants to pure love of God had come since time immemorial to this holy site to hang token garments as a prayer-filled symbol for Krishna to steal away the cloak of their ignorance. The kadamba tree is considered especially sacred in Vrindavan and its blossoming flowers bring everyone joy. The kadamba flower, a bright golden ball about the size of a strawberry and covered with hundreds of tiny golden trumpet shaped petals, has an intoxicatingly sweet fragrance. Because these flowers resemble Sri Radha's golden complexion, kadamba trees are very dear to Lord Krishna. Each night I would kneel under the tree at Chira Ghat and pray for humility and devotion. Then I would stretch my body on the riverbank, feeling the cold soil beneath my flesh as I drifted into sleep. My bedding was the sacred earth, my blanket the starry sky, and my waking call the distant ringing of temple bells.

Every morning at four o'clock I would awaken in the darkness, bow down on the riverbank in gratitude, and wade into the sacred waters for my bath. November was approaching, and the Yamuna had turned frigid. Often I stood shivering, submerged up to my neck. I recalled lyrics from a song that I had loved in my childhood: "The river Jordan is chilly and cold. It chills the body but warms the soul." *Yes*, I reflected, *enduring difficulty for a meaningful purpose is a sublime pleasure*. Dunking my entire body under the water again and again, I meditated on purifying my body, mind, and soul. Then I stood quietly under the still-starlit sky praying for a pure heart. This was my first meditation each day. I felt so close to the Lord. Afterwards, I would climb back onto the riverbank, disrobe to my loincloth, wring the water from my dripping garments, and put them back on. Sitting down on the riverbank, I would again meditate on the Hare Krishna mantra while fingering prayer beads made of the wood of tulasi. Each day began this way, an experience I prayed never to forget.

One evening, as twilight dimmed into night, I sat under the sacred kadamba tree and composed a letter to my father. It had been two weeks since I had made the riverbank my residence.

> *My dear Father,*
>
> *My long search has led me to Vrindavan. I have at last found something that attracts my heart as pure truth. It has taken until now to find the conditions I have been seeking. In the past couple weeks I have realized the great jewel that is to be learned in Vrindavan. Believe me when I tell you that I am not here for any pleasure or leisure. I am here with all earnestness and sincerity to carry out a mission that I cannot neglect. You know that in all my life I have never willfully hurt you. Please believe the importance of this journey to my life.*
>
> *Love,*
> *Richard*
> *Vrindavan, October, 1971*

One quiet afternoon as I walked along the bank of the river Yamuna, little barefoot boys wearing shorts and little barefoot girls in cotton blouses and skirts frolicked, laughing with wild abandon while playing cricket with sticks and balls. Other children herded cows, buffalo, goats, or sheep with slender sticks. Women passed with baskets of grains balanced on their heads, covering their faces with their saris out of shyness as I passed. To my right, under a tree, Krishnadas Babaji was sitting, softly singing the Lord's names. Taking note of me, he patted the ground, inviting me to sit. There we watched as a boatman ferried people across the river. Then Babaji whispered, "Under this tamarind tree is a favorite meeting place for Radha and Krishna."

Intrigued, I inquired, "Babaji, everyone around here loves Radha so much, please tell me about Her."

His eyes filled with tears at the mere sound of Radha's name. Closing his eyes, he leaned forward. "The scriptures and saints teach us that God is one, yet the one Lord has both a male and female nature. Krishna is the male principle and Radha is the feminine potency. In the spiritual world, the one Lord presides in these two forms. The love between Krishna, who is the beloved, and Radha, the lover, is the divine origin of all love."

"Babaji," I asked, "how does this love between God's masculine and feminine nature relate to the love people share in this world?"

Krishnadas Babaji answered, "Under the veil of illusion, or *maya*, we forget the ecstatic love for God, which is intrinsic to our souls. Love in this world is only a reflection of it. We are searching for real love in so many ways, forgetting that it is within our hearts." Babaji looked so meek. Raising his white eyebrows, his voice faltered. "Krishna longs to be conquered by the love of His devotee and by the supreme grace of Radha we can realize that love. She is the compassionate nature of the Absolute and the fountainhead of all spiritual love."

The mystery of Radha, the female energy of God, had both fascinated and eluded me. After all I had experienced, after all I had read, after all the sadhus I had met, nothing had prepared me for the hidden truth of yoga's greatest mystery: the mystery of bhakti, or devotion. And now I was learning that the keeper of this mystery was Radha. For the first time it began to dawn on me that these saints of Vrindavan had penetrated into the deepest, most confidential aspect of the spiritual journey.

The secret? That beyond worldly pleasures and beyond the liberation of oneness with God, is an eternal dance, an endless night of love, and the intoxication of one's very soul. And the one capable of giving entry to this unbearably sweet realm was Radha.

It was their yearning to connect with Radha that allowed these yogis of Vrindavan to demonstrate such intense and genuine humility. By casting aside all interest in yogic powers, they seemed to be drowning in an ocean of divine love. My mind and heart were charmed by this rich theology known as bhakti, the yoga of unconditional love. It seemed to put so many of my mind's questions, both asked and yet to be asked, in a comprehensive perspective. Although still apprehensive about committing myself to one particular path, I felt a yearning brewing in my heart to follow the path of Bhakti.

After Krishnadas Babaji blessed me, stood up, and walked away along the riverbank, I sat there staring into the river and contemplated on this secret of the feminine divinity. In the Christian church, the adoration of Mary, the Mother of Jesus, inspired both divine love and embittered factions. And the mystery of Mary Magdalene gave rise to secret orders, veiled symbolism, and intrigue. Many Hebrews saw Shekinah as the female aspect of God or the bride of the Sabbath, as did certain students of the Kabbalah. And within Islam, there were followers of the Sufi sect who honor the divine feminine in their reverence to Fatima. Now I was finding how from the Vedic, ancient scriptural perspective, Feminine Divinity had always been accepted as truth.

As I looked out onto Mother Yamuna, I pondered on how the nourishing, compassionate side of spirituality is often overruled by the elements of power and control. It impressed me how important it was to pay attention to the feminine aspect of the divine.

About the same time I left the ashram, so did my friend Asim. I supposed he felt stifled by the constant demands on him there and was impressed by how my lifestyle was simultaneously so strict yet so free. We often met to explore Krishna's forest home together. One sunny afternoon while Asim and I talked under the shade of a banyan tree, we were struck by an overpowering presence. Turning, we discovered someone sitting right beside us. Where had he come from? His features looked simultaneously aged and youthful. A single garment made of white cotton covered his upper and lower body. Semi-matted locks of hair reached below his neck. He had large eyes and a round, bearded face, and beamed a boyish smile. "Anyone who enters Vrindavan," he said, "is immediately connected to Krishna. Others worship God as a great king, but here in Vrindavan..."—he gazed around and stretched his hand toward the forest—"...Krishna is at home. Here we love him as a friend, as a child, as a lover."

We looked into the forest and, from a distance we saw an animal that looked like a wild, bluish cow hidden in the trees. Everything seemed so magical. We were wonderstruck. "In the beginning," the man continued, "we learn to love God as the all powerful creator, destroyer, and savior. But God is also the sweetest and most perfect lover. The scripture tells that in Vrindavan, playful Krishna is the essence of all beauty and sweetness." Then, rising to his feet, this sadhu, who had mysteriously appeared as if out of thin air, said, "Come, I'll show you places you will never forget."

We followed eagerly behind as he strolled through the woods, along the riverbank, and from temple to temple. As we roamed, the local people and temple priests offered him honors. "Where did he go?" Asim asked suddenly. I looked around. The man was gone and we were abandoned in an ancient temple. Asim inquired of an elderly priest, "Do you know that sadhu who was with us?"

The priest's eyes widened and his mouth opened in awe. "Oh, you don't know?" He led us out of the crowd into a secluded chamber and whispered, "That was Sripad Baba. No one knows his age or where he resides. He is a homeless mendicant and mysteriously wanders in a God-intoxicated trance."

Almost every day when Asim and I were together, Sripad Baba would mystically appear. How did he find us? Never did he bother to greet us. Never did he bother to say goodbye. It seemed that his power was such that he was always there with us, either visibly or invisibly.

Sripad Baba seemed to know about every hill, rock, stone, pebble, or grain of dust in all of Vrindavan and its surrounding area. We wandered with him for many days and often throughout the night. One freezing winter night, as I lay resting on the riverbank, I observed Sripad Baba standing shoulder high in the frigid waters offering prayers until sunrise.

One morning in an alleyway, an elderly widow dressed in a white sari greeted us. "I've observed you wandering the forest with Sripad Baba. Now you come with me." Each step she took was laborious, her back hunched as she braced her overweight body into a bamboo cane. She hobbled along toward her home and told a story of Sripad Baba's obscure past. Asim translated her Hindi for me. "Long ago, when Baba was a child in school, he and his friend enjoyed flying kites between their classes." Halting, her shriveled face puckered as she poked her cane onto the walkway, frowned into our eyes, and raised her voice. "The teacher slapped their faces and scolded them." Her body and voice now trembled. "The poor little boy was shocked; he couldn't understand what he had done wrong. He wondered why he should continue studying if his teacher, who had mastered all of the very subjects he sought to

271

learn, still did not know how to love. At that moment he renounced both school and home to search for God." Turning a skeleton key to open the door of her brick hut, she glanced at us over her shoulder. "Eventually, he became the disciple of a saint in Vrindavan."

One night, together with four others, Asim and I stole away with Sripad Baba to a secluded forest. It was about nine-thirty and night had already fallen. Beside me, on the bank of the Yamuna, sat a sadhu with a hand-carved sitar strapped to his back. Sripad Baba introduced him as a master of the instrument, a pupil of the same teacher as sitar legend Ravi Shankar. "Now, though, he is a sadhu."

With a refined bow of the head, the sitarist greeted us then closed his eyes. The sky appeared as black as ink behind the silver moon, each star radiated a special glow, and all of these light-filled jewels above our heads danced on the river Yamuna's sparkling current. Nearby, hidden among the branches of a kadamba, night birds crooned and, from a distance, peacocks cawed as night-blooming jasmine perfumed the mild breeze. From all of this tranquility emerged the sweet sound of the sitar. Long, weeping notes of an ancient *raga* harmonized with the symphony of the Vrindavan forest, each note expressing, to my ears, the musician's yearning for God.

An overwhelming experience came upon me while listening. I felt so far from Krishna. I couldn't find a trace of love in my heart. Bereft, I longed for that love, cried for that love, begged for that love. Suddenly, all of creation seemed irrelevant in the absence of that love. The sitar, too, wept and cried, perfectly articulating my aspirations.

7

VRINDAVAN WAS FULL OF MIRACLES for me both great and small. One afternoon, while meandering alone along a forest pathway, I found myself face to face with a charging bull. A cloud of dust billowed around his huge body and he was fuming white foam. He stared at me in rage, opened his mouth wide, and let loose a chilling roar. Wildly pounding the earth, his hooves prepared to trample me. Before I could even react, he halted, cocked his head down and then threw it upward in a swooping motion, jabbing his horn into my belly. I gasped. I was hurled upward and flew headlong over the bull's body then crashed to the ground. As I lay there, he impatiently scraped the earth with his hooves, snorting through his nostrils and prepared to attack again. Writhing in pain, I thought I was a dead man.

Just then, a thin, neatly dressed elderly man wearing a Nehru hat appeared on the path. He shouted some words in the local language, which induced the bull to lower its head. To my relief, the animal strode quietly away. Extending his hand, the strange man lifted me up. "Are you all right?" he asked. "That bull was too much angry."

Relieved, I took inventory of my physical condition. To my amazement, there were no injuries and my pain had vanished. As I took my first step, I cried out. A thorn had pricked deeply into my foot, causing me more discomfort than the horn of the bull. I reached down to extract the thorn reflecting that perhaps this was Krishna's kindness—a token thorn to replace the bull's horn. "I'm fine," I replied. "Thank you for saving my life."

"I did not save you, Baba." The old gentleman smiled. "Krishna saved you. I was only His instrument." His voice wavered with emotion. "All Krishna wants in return from us is our love." He turned me around, examining me for wounds and sweeping the dirt from my clothes. "Where do you come from and why are you here?" He asked. I explained my situation, and the old man, noting the position of the sun, announced, "I am late for a meeting. You may join me if you wish."

Together we passed along the sandy pathways of the forest. He removed his hat from his neatly combed white hair and said, "I'm taking you to the home of a rare saint and scholar. He is unknown to the public, but the spiritually elevated souls of this area revere him. I believe in English you would call him a saint among saints." We came upon a flat rock that served as a bridge for crossing over an open sewage canal. Thick black sewage bubbled and gurgled in this three-foot wide moat. Choking from the stench, I carefully crossed over it. Just then, a family of hogs dove into the moat and reveled about, slurping and gulping down the putrefied black nectar. Faces dripping with fecal matter, they snorted in joy.

Minutes later we were surrounded by a natural haven of greenery, aromatic flowers, buzzing bees, and trilling birds. After some distance we spilled out into a courtyard with a small *kutir*, a hut for worship. "Please come," my guide said, pressing my hand into his. Inside, sitting on a wooden plank, was a sadhu. Both his head and face were clean-shaven in what I now understood as an expression of detachment from selfish pursuits. A small tuft of hair remained at the back of his head to represent servitude to God. I was to learn that he was over eighty years old. With a soft smile, he placed his joined palms to his forehead and bowed his head. "We welcome you into our family." This was Vishaka Sharan Baba.

An assembly of five elderly sages sat at his feet, eager to hear his every word. Vishaka Sharan Baba gazed toward me and spoke. My guide, who everyone called Punditji, translated his Hindi into English. "If one begs for God's love like a starving man for food, the Lord will bestow that rarest treasure." He took my hand. "Please let me feed you."

The satisfaction of his company drew me down that sandy pathway every afternoon at about four o'clock. Upon my arrival, Vishaka Sharan Baba, with his own hands, would offer me a straw mat to sit on and some flat homemade bread, or *rotis*, with *gur*, a sugar cane extract. This was the fare of the poorest people in Vrindavan. His followers exalted him and were eager to arrange for his meals, but he refused. Longing to feel humble, even in his old age, he begged door to door. Whatever he received, usually coarse rotis and gur, it was his joy to share with me. Although over four times my age, a saint among saints, and recognized scholar, he treated me with a compassion that left me speechless.

Vishaka Sharan Baba had first come to Vrindavan as a sadhu in 1918 and he remained for the rest of his life. Little is known of his past, as he rarely discussed it. In the Himalayas, I had lived among holy men who practiced severe indifference to the world, and I witnessed varieties of supernatural powers. Vishaka Sharan Baba neither displayed such miracles nor tortured his body. He was just absorbed in loving service. When he spoke of Sri Radha's love and Lord Krishna's pastimes, he was like an innocent child, unaware that he had the authority of a spiritual king. In his shyness he hid his ecstasies and served in an ordinary way. His presence drew an affection from my heart that I could not fully understand.

On one occasion, I asked Vishaka Sharan Baba. "Please tell me whatever you feel I need to hear."

Sitting on his wooden plank, he closed his eyes and, entering a trance, a stream of words so relevant to my concerns, questions, and longing to embrace Krishna flowed from his mouth and I listened while Punditji closed his eyes and translated for me.

"Lord Krishna's body is purely spiritual. His form is eternal, full of knowledge and bliss. The Vedic scriptures and the visions of millennia of saints all concur in describing His form in the spiritual world. Although His beauty is indescribable to the material senses, the scriptures give as close a description as is humanly comprehensible. He is the reservoir of all beauty.

"His complexion is bluish like a newly formed monsoon cloud, with the exception of His palms and soles that are like pink lotuses. His eyes, which see everywhere, are the shape of fully blossomed lotus petals. His nose is soft like the sesame flower, His lips reddish like the bimba fruit, and His teeth like rows of pearls. His cheeks and forehead possess the beauty of full moons. His ears, which hear everything, are decorated with bejeweled earrings shaped like sharks. His hair, like radiant black silk, cascades luxuriously around His moonlike face and is ornamented by a string of tiny flowers, jewels and a peacock feather. His neck gently swirls like the conch shell and His every limb is softer than fresh butter. Yet He may act with the power of a thunderbolt.

"He is unlimited and supremely independent. Through His energies all material and spiritual worlds are pervaded and He expands to personally reside within the heart of every living being as our constant friend and witness.

"He oversees the material creation, sometimes as a strict father. But in the highest realm of the spiritual world, Krishna is the supreme enjoyer. He shares His bliss with everyone through His playful pastimes, humorous words, and mischievous pranks. When He poses with three graceful bends and plays His flute, He mesmerizes our hearts with His all-enchanting love."

In a state of bliss, Vishaka Sharan Baba went on as I listened, fascinated.

"And Sri Radha, the Lord's feminine counterpart, has a complexion like molten gold. She is the supremely compassionate Mother of all beings and Her beautiful attributes enchant even the mind of Krishna. But I feel unqualified to even begin to describe them. Her love is the all-pervading reality that charges the spiritual world with endless bliss."

His enchanting description then shifted into an erudite analysis of these most personal forms of God, a perfect salve for my analytical Western mind. "One might think that such a description of God is anthropomorphic or trying to impose humanlike qualities upon God. But to the contrary, it is humans who, in minute degree, have been blessed with qualities that originate in the Lord. As it is written in the Holy Bible, 'man is made in the image of God.'"

His conception of the one God was so highly personal, not just in an allegoric or symbolic way but as a spiritual truth far beyond our sensual or intellectual purview. The only way to access God, for him, was through sincere devotion. I found myself gradually gaining a deeper appreciation of these people's reasons for chanting God's names, serving others with such humility, and praying to the deity.

One afternoon I found Vishaka Sharan Baba and the sages gathered around an old wooden radio with an arched top, metal knobs and a protruding antenna. It was probably made in the 1930s. As the crackling of static boomed out, my friend who had saved me from the bull translated the news for me. "India and Pakistan are at war." His face clouded with grief. "The cruel war is raging, bombs are dropping, and thousands of troops are battling; no place is safe. The government has declared a blackout, cutting electricity, to protect us from night bombings." His attention was drawn again to the crackling voice of the news. "America is warning all American citizens to leave India at once." I now felt more like an Indian sadhu than an American, so it hardly registered that this might apply to me.

Still, news of the war would certainly intensify the worry of my parents. To assure them of my safety I composed a letter on December 7, 1971, my twenty-first birthday.

My family,

The wars on earth are but a manifestation of the battle within man's mind.

We enter into the battle zone the moment we forget the Lord.

Today there is war in Vietnam, in Israel, and now between India and Pakistan.

As long as we are prisoners of our mind's passions we are in each of these battlefields.

But be assured that I am safe.

Be kind,
Richard

While the Vietnam War afflicted my colleagues across the globe in America, I now found myself in another battle zone. Why another war? With the partition of India in 1947, a split with Pakistan had been created, and West Pakistan and East Pakistan were formed on opposite sides of India. On December 3, 1971, West Pakistani warplanes attacked Indian soil in retaliation for India aiding an East Pakistani party that supported autonomy from West Pakistan. Full-scale war began between India and West Pakistan. A bloody war ensued, with aggressive battles on the land, air, and sea that left thousands dead and many more injured. After fourteen days, West Pakistan would surrender in defeat, and East Pakistan would become the independent nation Bangladesh.

While the war was still raging, Vishaka Sharan Baba and these old sages gathered around their radio and listened to the evening news broadcast. Tears of sympathy filled their eyes when they heard of the bloodshed. After switching off the radio, they immersed themselves in discussing the Lord and soon enough began bubbling over with joy. At the same time, they were both blissfully absorbed in a spiritual reality beyond birth and death and also distressed by the human suffering surrounding them.

Vishaka Sharan Baba and his followers were teaching me the virtue of balance. It was an art that required maturity and realization. Through them I saw that to be sensitive to the troubles of the world and the plight of others on the material plane did not mean that one had to neglect the spiritual plane. On the contrary, I saw how loving God naturally awakened the qualities of an ideal human being, one with compassion for all.

8

PACK OF HUGE ANGRY MONKEYS, GROWLING AND SHRIEKING, surrounded a recently born calf who trembled with helpless, weeping eyes. She mooed for her mother. While walking through the village I happened to come upon the scene. As I searched for a suitable stick to help, the mother cow released a powerful cry and frantically galloped to the site. With her horns and her fearless love, she scattered the monkeys away. Now, with eyes glazed by affection, the cow tenderly licked her baby, until the calf was pacified enough to suck milk from her udder.

While I observed the scene, I recalled Lord Chaitanya's teaching that we should chant God's name in a humble state of mind, like a baby calling out for its mother. Coming from a background where humility was often taken to be a weakness, I seriously questioned what real humility is and how it works, not knowing that I was about to come upon an unforgettable lesson on the subject.

One day, Sripad Baba led Asim and me to an ancient temple. Looking inside, we saw a cavernous hall of red stone with a towering ceiling. The temple had been abandoned long ago. In the semi-darkness, monkeys were sleeping and huge black bats hung upside down from the border of a dome high above, stains of their excrement spotting the slab floor. We walked past the temple, moving along a crumbling footpath that abruptly came to an end. Bordering the footpath was an open sewage canal about two feet wide. Sripad Baba prompted us, laughing, "Come on, I want to show you a very special temple." We stepped onto a single rock used as a bridge to cross the moat. Once on the other side we found ourselves in a quaint home where children jumped and played while the mother squatted on the floor cooking over a small fire. *What kind of temple could this be?* I wondered.

To my surprise, in a common closet I beheld an incredible sight, an altar enthroning deities of Radha and Krishna. They stood about two feet high, Krishna of black stone and Radha of shining bell metal. They looked ancient. Oddly, the family seemed indifferent to the radiant deities gracing their home. But as we drew closer, we noticed an old man in torn cloth fanning the deities of the Lord, his eyes filled with tears of devotion. A small, thin man in his seventies, he had soft eyes. His head and face were shaved and he looked incredibly frail. Hurrying out of the closet, he bowed to the feet of each of his guests. On his knees he welcomed us again and again with tears of gratitude.

"I am your obedient servant," he faltered. "Please bless me." He gestured toward the deities in the closet. "Please meet Radha and Krishna. Krishna called you here today because you are His dear friends, but as for me, I am only a tiny servant. My only fortune is to serve. Please allow me to serve you." This was my first encounter with Ghanashyam.

As Sripad Baba told him how we had traveled so far to reach Vrindavan, Ghanashyam thrilled with wonder. "Krishna has called you to cross oceans and continents from a faraway land," Ghanashyam said. "He has been waiting so long for you, and now you have come." His voice cracked, "Yes, now you have come." Ghanashyam's small aged face looked so gentle and frail. His small misty eyes, rounded nose, thin lips and delicate wrinkles gave him an expression of permanent melancholy. The tone of his soft voice echoed with the same feeling. But underneath it, his heart and soul overflowed with such ecstatic love that it filled the lives of whoever came near him. Seeing us standing before his deities, Ghanashyam was overwhelmed with joy.

I began to spend more time with this devoted man. Every morning at nine, I was drawn down that shambled footpath to this closet room temple. I found his company irresistible. Whenever I arrived, he extended the same affectionate greeting, "I am your obedient servant." And he meant it. He gave everything without expectation of anything and loved doing so. I longed for this quality in myself.

One morning, as Ghanashyam and I sat alone, I asked him how he first came to Vrindavan. He bowed his head. "My story is of no importance," he said. Then he gazed up in wonder. "But Krishna's mercy upon a sinner is worth hearing." Softly, he began to tell me how he was raised in an affluent family. "When I was a young man, my family made pilgrimage to Vrindavan. It was here that the net of the Lord's grace captured my heart. I had no power to go away." As he narrated his story, Ghanashyam shrunk in meekness. He told of how his family was aghast by his resolve to give up a promising career and stay in Vrindavan. "They threatened to cut me off from our wealth, but I was unmoved. Krishna had stolen my heart," he said. Sleeping on the ground and daily begging for dry bread from the homes of the Vrajabasis, he never once hankered after his former wealth. Instead, he said, "I felt grateful to serve Krishna in his sweet home."

Ghanashyam's dark eyes moved about like a timid child. "For a long time my heart yearned to worship a deity. Then came a day I will not ever forget. While sitting under a tree in a nearby garden, I etched with my finger the name 'Sri Radha' in the dusty ground. The whole of that day, I worshiped the impression of Her written name in the soft dust with flowers, songs, and prayers. Finally, at sunset, I erased Radha's Name with my hand."

Ghanashyam fell silent. Gazing at his beloved deities, he struggled visibly to restrain his emotions, and, after a long pause, resumed his story. "While rubbing the ground, I saw something gold where Her Name had been. I was intrigued. 'What is this?' I thought, 'Let me come back when no one is around.' Early the next morning, I dug with my hands in that spot where Radha had been present in her holy name."

Ghanashyam now lost the battle he'd been waging to restrain his feelings. Tears streamed down his cheeks as he related, in a trembling voice, the tale of his love. "That golden object my fingers had been led to was the top of the head of my Radha. Her deity appeared to me from the earth. And, standing beside Her there, underground, was a black deity of Lord Krishna. At His base was written His name, 'Gopijana Vallabha', the Beloved of the Cowherd Girls."

His high voice cracked. "But I had nothing, nothing. What could I possibly do for them?" Ghanashyam gazed lovingly toward his deities and murmured, "I do not know why they did so, but they put themselves under my care. So I have cared for them day and night. In the beginning, passersby would donate some food for me to offer. For a long time I worshiped them under a tree. Then, the forefathers of this family, feeling sympathy at seeing Radha Gopijana Vallabha without a home, offered their closet as a shelter. I've worshiped them here for over fifty years."

As the weeks passed, I gained much inspiration studying the character of Ghanashyam. "I am your obedient, I am your obedient," he would say while trying to give me everything he had. Together we sang for Gopijana

Vallabha or fanned them with peacock feather fans. Every day he insisted that I eat the Lord's prasadam, three Vraja *rotis*, or simple breads. Vraja rotis are the most common food for the people of Vrindavan. Although from an ordinary perspective, a Vraja roti is nothing but a dry, flat piece of coarse unleavened bread, for those with faith it is a priceless blessing. Grown in the soil of Vrindavan and cooked and offered to Krishna by the hands of a devotee, the Vraja roti is considered a holy sacrament. With gratitude, I ate the Vraja rotis of Ghanashyam.

One afternoon, while bathing in the river, I happened to see a familiar sadhu. Expecting to receive the customary blessings this Baba always offered, I was blindsided by the harsh reprimand he served me instead. "Because of you," he shouted from the riverbank, "Ghanashyam is starving."

"I don't understand," I cried out.

He glared at me. "A Vrajabasi brings him three rotis every day. That is his only food. And every day you eat all of it. How selfish!"

"What?" I gasped, while climbing up the riverbank. "This cannot be. Please believe me, I never knew."

The next day Ghanashyam sat me down on the floor of his simple dwelling and lovingly served me the Vraja rotis. I pushed the leaf plate away. "I am not hungry today and will not eat."

Hearing my words, Ghanashyam was stricken with sorrow. "You must eat. This is Gopijana Vallabha's food. He saved it only for you." I refused. With joined palms trembling, he pleaded, "Is it because of my sins that you will not accept my service? Please eat my rotis."

My heart was breaking. I pleaded with him. "Ghanashyam, you're starving because I'm eating all of your rotis. I can get rotis anywhere, but you never leave here."

"But I have so many *rotis*," Ghanashyam insisted. "There is no shortage." Again he set the plate down in front of me. "Please, I beg you to eat and enjoy."

Again I pushed it away. "If you have more rotis, show them to me."

"No need, no need." He spoke quietly, in a high pitched voice that shook with desperation.

"I refuse to accept your only food until you show me more."

He raised his voice to meet my challenge. "No need, No need. They are in that room."

I jumped up and searched the room but found nothing in it. "Ghanashyam, there are no rotis here. You have been starving because of me. Please, please you eat these rotis."

Ghanashyam's eyes filled with tears as he revealed his precious heart. "You are Gopijana Vallabha's friend, but I am only the servant of His servants. My only happiness in life is in serving devotees. I beg you to enjoy these rotis." With palms folded in prayer, he pleaded, "I beg you, do not deprive me of the single thing I live for." I cried on witnessing his selfless love. For the pleasure of dear Ghanashyam, I ate all his rotis.

The next day I came two hours later than usual, assuming he would have eaten his rotis by then. Ghanashyam rejoiced, "Krishna Das, Ratheen Krishna Das, you have finally come. Gopijana Vallabha has been waiting for you." I could not believe what I saw. The rotis were still on the altar. Ghanashyam explained, "My Lord will not honor my offering until he has the company of a friend. Krishna has saved these rotis only for you." With these words, he placed all the rotis before me to eat. "Only when you eat will Sri Radha accept me as Her servant." Again I was defeated.

One day a well-wisher presented Ghanashyam new clothes. He shyly looked away from them and poured out his heart. "This body accepts only the worn remnants from devotees." Ghanashyam only wore used cloth previously worn by a sadhu. He considered it priceless.

Another night, I found Ghanashyam sitting alone singing beautiful *ragas* and playing a small harmonium. Absorbed in devotion, he was unaware I had entered the room. Although I could not understand the language of the song, the sweetness of his devotion revealed everything. Sometimes his voice lilted with joy. At other times, it mourned in feelings of separation from his beloved. I had been told that in his youth he was a court musician in the palace of a king. He was so absorbed in his singing that an hour passed before he noticed my arrival. Discovering me, he radiated with joy. "Krishnadas, you have come." He asked if I would help him to put his deities in a bed for the night. For fifty years, he had done this every night, but now in his old age, he was too weak to lift them. I felt honored to oblige.

As I was departing, he inquired, "Krishnadas, where will you rest tonight?"

"On the bank of the Yamuna, where I rest every night."

He held my hand and stroked my head like a worried father. "But it is the freezing winter. You must sleep here tonight."

"But, Ghanashyam, I sleep there every night."

"Tonight you sleep here, please."

He slept on the floor of a narrow hallway outside of the closet. The family used it as a thruway in the house, stepping around him. As I lay on the floor, Ghanashyam placed his only blanket over me.

I could not allow this to happen. Snatching up the threadbare blanket, I handed it back to him. "This is your blanket. You must use it."

"No need, no need." He sighed in a high voice, refusing to take the blanket.

"You are an old man, and I am young. You must use it." I again handed him the blanket.

But he jumped back, "No need, no need."

An argument ensued. When he insisted, I threatened to return to the riverbank. I dropped the blanket and stormed toward the door.

"No need, no need." He picked up the blanket. "I will use the blanket."

So I lay down beside him, curled up to keep warm on that cold winter night, and fell asleep. Some time later I awoke, wondering why I was so warm. I looked over at Ghanashyam, who was lying on the floor trembling from the cold like a leaf in a windstorm. There was no blanket on him. I realized that he silently placed it over me after I fell asleep. Quietly, I covered him with it.

As soon as the blanket touched him, he leaped up and shouted, "No need. No need. You are Krishna's friend. You must enjoy good sleep."

"Then I will go to the Yamuna," I cried out, while again storming to the door.

Again he agreed to accept the threadbare blanket, but later in the night I awoke feeling nice and warm. There was my dear Ghanashyam, his frail old body violently shivering in the cold. I tried again to place the blanket upon him. "No need. No need."

Ghanashyam loved to serve everyone he met. In fifty years, he never left the area around that small temple except to bring water to his Lord. Indeed he could not dream of leaving his deities to whose service he dedicated his life and soul.

Early one morning, while on my way from the river, I was surprised to see the aged form of Ghanashyam in a lonesome alleyway, stumbling and falling. I rushed to help him. With great pains, he struggled to carry a bucket of water that he had collected from the Yamuna to bathe his deities. After every few steps, he stood limp in exhaustion.

"Ghanashyam, please allow me to carry the bucket."

With a stern glance he replied, "No need, no need."

I could not bear to see him toil in this way. "Please, please, I am young. With no difficulty I will have it at your temple in five minutes. You are very old and weak. It will take you half an hour. Please let me take it."

That innocent smile of little old Ghanashyam radiated from his face as he pleaded, "You are Gopijana Vallabha's young friend. You should enjoy. I am his old servant. My life is to serve. You go now and enjoy Vrindavan. That will make me happy."

His humility simultaneously melted my heart and worried my mind. "Please, I will be most happy to carry your bucket." I gripped the handle of the bucket and pulled, Ghanashyam's entire body tensed like a tree. Freezing with determination, he grasped that handle with all of his strength. He clenched it as a man helplessly hanging from a cliff clings to the rope that separates him from death.

His eyes searched mine in desperation. "I am a poor old man. My only wealth is my service." His eyes grew red and swelled with tears. "If you take away my service to the Lord, you will take away my life. Please allow me to live. Please."

My heart sank. What else could I do? I gave him his life back, and his bucket. But when he noted my anxiety for him, he consented to our carrying it together, side by side, asking me every minute if I was all right.

One night, Ghanashyam suggested that I visit Varsana, a nearby village that was the home of Radha, he softly cried out, "Krishnadas, your life will never be the same after you feel the atmosphere of Varsana." Seeing my enthusiasm, he shyly added, "When you go, please tell Sri Radha that Her tiny servant Ghanashyam wishes to see Her."

My heart was deeply affected by this little old man who lived in obscurity. He was not a learned scholar, a famous guru, or a mystic yogi. But he was a true saint, his humility was an expression of his love for God.

At one time I had thought, like many in the West, that humility was an act of self-effacement, a weakness that revealed a lack of self-confidence or self-care, even a negative obsession that could lead to a sense of inferiority or depression. But I was discovering, in the company of people like Ghanashyam, that true humility was the opposite of that, for it connected us to an inexhaustible power beyond our own, the power of grace. True humility is a universal pride in the greatness of God and a genuine appreciation for the virtues of others.

Real humility, I was finding, did not mean I ought to be cowardly and shrink from challenges, but propelled me to strive with all my resources to overcome challenges with integrity, respect, love, and gratitude, to be as much as possible an instrument of the divine.

In real humility there is a deeper principle than our sad need to feel superior to others. That higher principle prevents us from being arrogant and condescending toward those we feel are inferior. It protects us from being envious towards those who are more accomplished. When one is humble, one feels grateful and gives credit to the Lord and all those who have ever offered help. With a humble heart one can easily admit mistakes and open one's heart to learn. Becoming humble is not the act of killing the ego but of liberating the real ego, which is eternally vibrant with love for God and others.

The most profound mystery, I was finding, is that to the degree one possesses these exalted characteristics, he feels himself to be very small, a part of God and the servant of all. To selflessly serve others was Ghanashyam's heart's only joy. Ghanashyam Baba was one of the happiest and wealthiest men I had ever met, a simple man who simply loved God.

Above: The author with B. K. S. Iyengar
Below: The cremation ghats at Varanasi

Above: Meeting U.S. President Barack Obama
Below: Meeting the President of India, Smt. Pratibha Devisingh Patil

The author was rejected at the border of India, but promised the immigration officer to do something good for the people of India if he let him pass. Persuaded, the officer granted passage. Today, Radhanath Swami has fulfilled his promise by establishing the Midday Meal program (www.radhanathswami.com/activities/midday-meal/), which feeds thousands of children in the slum schools of Mumbai (*top*), and the Bhaktivedanta hospital (www.radhanathswami.com/activities/bhaktivedanta-hospital/) (*bottom*).

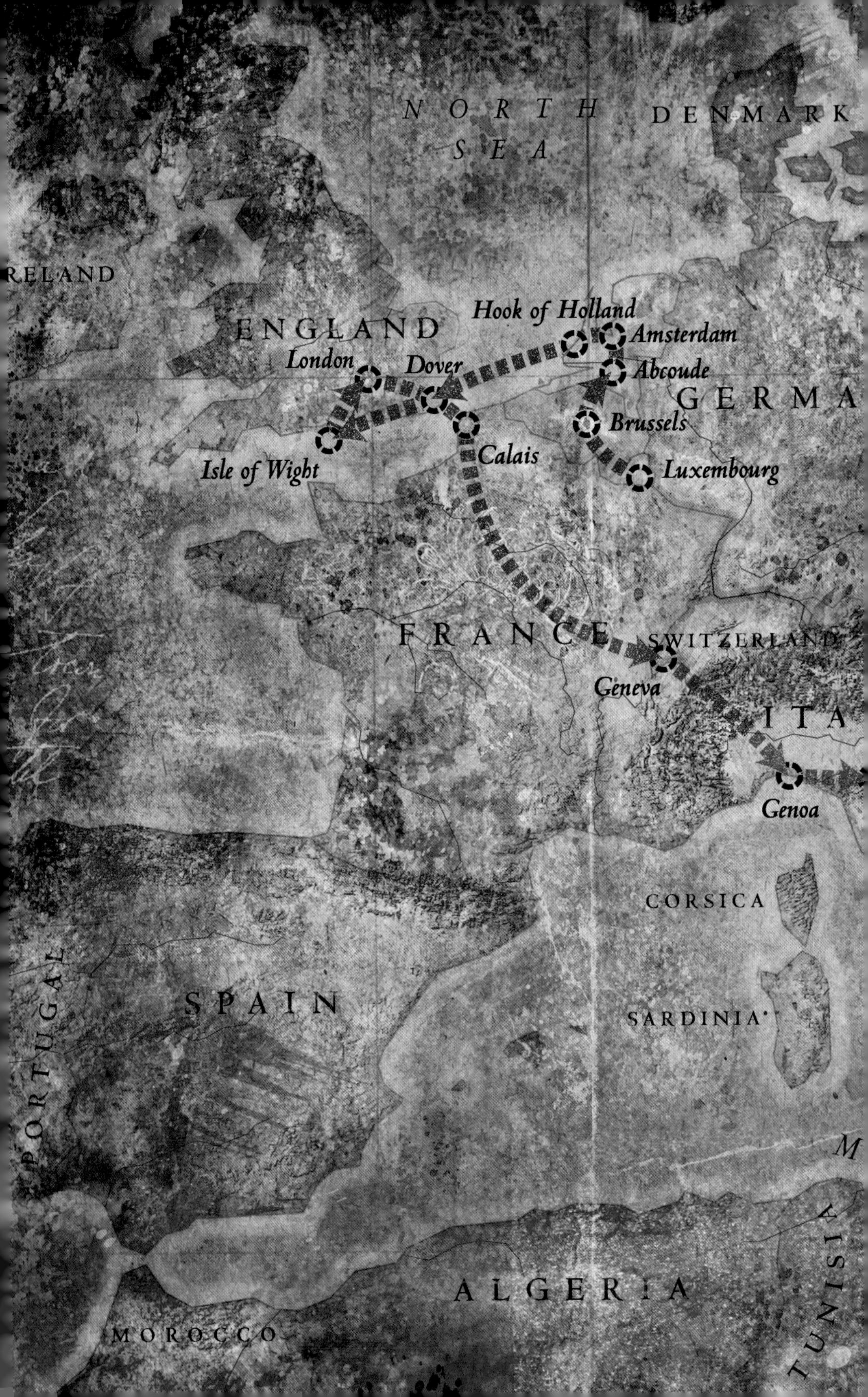

NORTH SEA
DENMARK
RELAND
ENGLAND
Hook of Holland
Amsterdam
London
Dover
Abcoude
GERMA
Brussels
Calais
Isle of Wight
Luxembourg
FRANCE
SWITZERLAND
Geneva
ITA
Genoa
CORSICA
SARDINIA
SPAIN
PORTUGAL
ALGERIA
TUNISIA
MOROCCO

CHINA

TIBET

HIMALAYA

Indus River

MOUNTAINS

Manali
Pathankot
Dharamshala
Lahore
Hussainiwala
Firozpur
Debra Dun
Uttar Kashi
Dev Prayag
Rishikesh
Haridwar
Kurukshetra
New Delhi
NEPAL
Pokhara Valley
Kathmandu
Swayambhunath
Bodhnath
Pashupatinath
Vrindaban
Mathura
Ayodhya
Agra
Ganges River
Janakpur
Raxaul
Sarnath
Patna
Yamuna River
Prayag
(Allahabad)
Varanasi
Bodh Gaya

Bhmati River

INDIA

Ca

Ganeshpuri
Bombay

ARABIA
SEA

Goa

BAY
OF
BENGA

9

A BLACK SNAKE SLITHERED OUT FROM UNDER THE ROCK where I sat, flitting its shiny tongue. Under the graying sky of evening, as mosquitos buzzed around the bank of the river, my mind stirred. *Fear is a dominating force in life. Fear of disease, failure, disappointing others, or economic ruin. Fear of enemies, thieves, cheaters, or a multitude of other possibilities including doubt in ones direction in life.* Feeling a mosquito biting into my ankle, I realized that any one of these tiny insects could kill me with malaria and I wondered about the whereabouts of that snake. *Certainly,* I thought, *I must be realistic to protect myself, but too much fear could either stifle my progress or consume my mind with anxiety.* In the arms of her mother, a baby is relieved of all fear. This faith, whether born of scientific or philosophic knowledge, or simple trust, brings peace. *Real faith,* I thought, *comes through direct experience of a higher reality or through the company of those who have attained that faith.* The following adventure highlighted this truth, and became another signpost on my inner journey.

One day, Krishnadas Babaji, Bon Maharaja, and Asim recommended that I visit Varsana. I recalled the night when Ghanashyam asked me to do the same. Ghanashyam never asked anything from anyone. That was his nature. In his own affectionate way, I considered, he was leading me deeper into the mysteries of my path. A path that was gradually unfolding. They directed me to stay with a reclusive sage who resided in the remote, rolling mountains of Varsana. This was a town dedicated to Radha thirty kilometers from Vrindavan and full of lakes, gardens, palaces, and palatial temples. To reach the sage, I first climbed a wide staircase that swirled up a mountain and led to a temple replete with domes, spires, and arches. My breath was taken away. The path led me through this temple and into a flower-filled mountaintop garden, then through yet another palatial temple. Minutes later, I found myself on an earthen pathway, meandering through a forest inhabited by monkeys, peacocks, and exotic trilling birds.

As I walked, I meditated on the Hare Krishna mantra. The atmosphere, charged with spiritual grace, seemed to embrace me and the mantra filled me. Blessed from both without and within, I fell into a beautiful state of consciousness. It was there, alone in Radha's forest, that a profound glimpse of spiritual love awakened within me. I felt my heart flooding with intoxicating nectar. Closing my eyes, which were full of tears, I felt Radha and Krishna showering Their love upon me and calling me to meet them within my heart. I shivered. The forest where I stood now seemed to be in another world billions of miles away from Earth.

In gratitude, I continued slowly uttering the Hare Krishna mantra. I sensed that this was only a glimpse of divinity that would soon recede, and it created in me a longing for more. That afternoon, in Radha's forest, I realized that this longing for spiritual love, invoked by the mantra itself, was a fuller, deeper experience than anything I had ever encountered.

Winding along the trail through this enchanted forest, in a state of joy, I approached the sacred mountain of the sage. It was now almost evening by the time I gazed up at the steep climb before me. Straining, I scaled the crude red rocks that served as steps to the sage's dwelling.

At the top I found a deserted-looking temple crumbling from age. For some time, I sat alone until curiosity lured me into one of the ruins. As I approached the entrance, a long snake slithered by only inches away and disappeared into a hole in the wall. I entered deeper, my eyes straining to adjust to the dark. When they did, I discovered a wooden altar holding a single faded picture. Mud plaster crumbled from the walls, revealing spots of bare brick. From the shadows, a soft voice emerged.

"You have been called here from far away. I welcome you." I turned. Sitting in the ruins in a dark corner was a man with shaven head, his large, round belly contrasting with his slender limbs. Except for a loincloth over his groin, he was naked. Perhaps forty years in age, he looked utterly aloof as he gazed into a world that the eyes can't see.

I introduced myself and asked, "Could you please tell me about this place?"

He drifted into deep thought and closed his eyes. "You have entered Man Garh, the mountain of angry love. In this forest, Sri Radha feigns anger toward Lord Krishna to express Her unique love for Him and He comes here to plead for that love." His eyes searched deeply into mine. "Love conquers the beloved Lord. It is His own sweet will to be conquered. And when Radha is pleased by our sincerity, She, too, blesses us with God's love." Patting the dirt floor with his palm, he said, "Come, sit down if you please."

Speaking distinguished English, he introduced himself as Radha Charan Das, the sage I had been seeking. "But people call me Ramesh Baba," he added. We talked a bit and went outside. The sun was setting, and the sky glowed gold and crimson over the hills and valleys. As the stars emerged in the still sky and the air turned cool, about a dozen children from a nearby village assembled on the roof of the ruins. Small, skinny, and dressed in tattered clothing, they surrounded Ramesh Baba as he played a harmonium and sang classical ragas. When he opened his mouth, heavenly sounds streamed. The small children sang along with him, rising to their feet and dancing wildly as the music grew in tempo. One boy beat a native drum with two tree branches, while another struck a metal gong with a wooden mallet and others jingled hand cymbals. From that lone mountaintop, under the starlit sky, they danced and sang the Lord's praises, their high voices ringing. As their enthusiasm reached a crescendo, the Baba rose from his seat to dance in a graceful trance. After the chanting swelled to its tumultuous conclusion, Ramesh Baba sat down to sing a slow, soul-stirring melody that culminated in breathtaking silence.

A boy of about seven pressed his small hand into mine and led me away to the rooftop where he and his playmates had made an altar, nothing more than a straw hut tied together with twine. Inside was a painting of Lord Krishna embracing a calf. The child's pitch black eyes glistened in the moonlight. Smiling proudly and in a voice peaking with enthusiasm he declared, "This is my God." He spoke with a certainty that left me awestruck. Playfully dropping my hand, he ran off to join his friends. I stood speechless. He had spoken from a heart that bore no malice, envy, or conceit, exhibiting the type of faith that rare souls aspire to gain through a lifetime of spiritual practice and scrutinizing scriptures. I remembered the words of Lord Jesus. *"Unless one becomes like this child, one cannot enter into the Kingdom of God."* In the presence of that child, I felt like an agnostic at best. Humbled, I stood gazing at that picture and prayed. *My Lord, will I ever be blessed with such faith?*

Sakhi Sharan Baba, the only other soul residing on the mountain, told me about Ramesh Baba's earlier life. Ramesh Baba was born in Allahabad, the place of the Kumbha Mela. As a child he earned distinction in his study of Sanskrit and philosophy, and at the age of twelve his voice won him the national award at the All-India Competition for Music. Despite his promising future, a spiritual craving prompted him to run away from home to live as a sadhu. Each time he did so, however, a family member captured him and brought him home again. In his teens, he was such a powerful scholar and preacher that thousands flocked to hear his lectures. "But he gave all that up to reside in this lonely place," Sakhi Sharan said.

One quiet night, as we sat by the flickering light of a lantern, I asked Ramesh Baba why he had abandoned such a successful career as an orator. His eyes rolled upward with a grimace of disinterest. Baba was not at all inclined to talk about himself. "Because you have asked," he said, "it is my duty to respond." He cast his eyes down, "Thousands of followers were attending my discourses, but my heart yearned for the love of Sri Radha. She called for me." Baba stared into the lantern's flame, his round face illumined by its glimmering golden light. "So," he continued, "I abandoned my growing fame as a preacher and came to Vrindavan, where I found my guru at the Govardhan Mountain. Then I came here. That was in 1950. I was sixteen. At that time, this place was a jungle inhabited by wild animals, this mountaintop a hideout for murderers and thieves. For twenty-one years, I have remained here, meditating on the name of Sri Radha."

Over the years, Ramesh Baba became one of the most revered saints of the Vrindavan area. He was the only son of a widowed mother who later moved into a cottage at the foot of the mountain to be near her son. She lived the life of a renounced widow, choosing a simple life, absorbed in worshipping the Lord.

Since there was no electricity, plumbing, water, or food on the mountain where Ramesh Baba lived, Sakhi Sharan and I would carry buckets down the front of the steep mountain to gather water from a pond. It was a strenuous climb, and so taxing in the heat of the sun that we had to stop and rest every few steps. After leaving the water on the hilltop at noon, we would climb down the backside of the mountain to the small village of Manpur where we begged door to door for food. In one home, the mother blew on a conch shell, summoning her family to hasten home from the fields where they were working. Soon the family had gathered, and sang a beautiful kirtan to celebrate our arrival. The father played the harmonium and led the chant while a small child of no more than ten skillfully played upon a two-headed *dolak* drum. Yet another child accompanied the others with hand cymbals. All the household women clapped and sang blissfully. After twenty minutes of chanting, they placed a scripture before my begging partner and requested that he lecture. Sakhi Sharan Baba spoke for about fifteen minutes in the local Hindi language as the family listened in rapt attention. Then the mother filled our begging bowls with thick coarse Vraja rotis and we returned to the mountaintop where we shared them with Ramesh Baba, who sat on the dirt floor.

But in this world, a price for being honored and loved is also to be envied and hated. A deadly gang of criminals, the local mafia, was spurred by those who despised Ramesh Baba's growing popularity and his loud chanting of the Lord's names. One quiet night as I sat on the rooftop with him, I caught sight of the thugs, wielding guns and knives, stalking up the mountain. They stormed right up to us. I knew that in such remote places there was little regard for life or law. With savage stares they sized us up, making it clear that they were ready to slash our throats on the spot. The leader was filthy and disheveled, big, strong and violent. He had a black scarf wrapped around his head, and had a thick mustache and rotten teeth.

"We are the law in these parts," he raged. "Stop this chanting or you will die. To kill you will be like squashing a mosquito."

Baba just sat peacefully, utterly indifferent, until the gang left. On another night, a follower of Baba's from the nearby village described the death threats his family received. I was aware that murders in these isolated forests were not at all uncommon. But Ramesh Baba was not disturbed. "I am chanting God's name in kirtan according to the saints and scriptures," he told me. "If the Lord is pleased with me, I do not mind what they do." Baba carried on with the kirtan, unfazed. I realized that such conviction was a quality I needed to cultivate in order for my heart to be a proper vessel to receive what I prayed for. Yes, he had an ideal he was willing to live and die for.

Under the starlight, we slept on a cement platform just outside of the temple. One night, I took note that Ramesh Baba laid on his back with a three-foot stick by his side. Curious, I sat up. "I have never seen you sleep with a stick, Baba. Is there a reason you have one now?"

His voice was calm. "Yes, the villagers sent news that a man-eating leopard is in the area. It has already massacred some cows and villagers." Then, knitting his eyebrows, he raised the stick. "This evening the leopard was seen climbing our mountain. I'm keeping this stick for protection." He spoke as nonchalantly as one might talk about the weather.

Wonderstruck, I asked, "But what will that small stick do to protect us from a wild leopard?"

"Nothing, Krishnadas. Only the Lord can protect us." He yawned deeply and closed his eyes, drowsily finishing his thought. "However, our duty is to show Krishna that we are doing our part." Encouraged by his faith, I slept well that night. And the Lord did protect us.

I stayed with Ramesh Baba on several occasions. During the hot season, Baba's mountaintop was burning, sometimes reaching 115 degrees Fahrenheit. The winters were equally extreme, with temperatures often dipping to frigid. Despite the severity of the seasons, with neither a fan to cool him in summer nor a heater to provide warmth in winter, Ramesh Baba was peacefully absorbed in chanting, meditating on Krishna day and night. Given that there was no plumbing, responding to nature's call meant walking into the forest with a small container of water. Squatting down, we would first evacuate and then cleanse ourselves with the water we'd brought. We completed the process by taking a full bath in the pond. In fact, throughout my travels in India this was the sadhu's way of eliminating wastes from the body. Enthusiastic hogs, the local sanitation department, often appeared to devour the meal of waste.

On an autumn afternoon, suffering a bout of dysentery, I squatted in the bushes in response to the screaming call of nature. Already feverish and completely exhausted by the disease, I was horrified to see an enormous snake crawl out of the bushes and slither toward me. It was about six feet long and two inches thick, yellowish with green spots. I recognized by its triangular head that it was poisonous. The reptile fixed his stony stare on me, crawled right on top of my squatting bare feet, and stopped, resting its chilly body. I dared not move. Holding my breath, I contemplated: *Death may come at the least expected moment. Is this the inglorious way I must die?* Unlike Ramesh Baba, who'd had no fear of death, I did. The pounding of my heart and reeling of my mind showed me how very far I had to go to be yet surrendered to the Lord.

I thought back to the powerful current of the Ganges as it had hastened me toward my death. Here I was again. With all my heart and soul, I softly chanted again and again, *Hare Krishna Hare Krishna Krishna Krishna Hare Hare, Hare Rama Hare Rama Rama Rama Hare Hare.* Then, just as on that day when I was being pummeled by the Ganges' current, I gradually began to feel peace through the inconceivable power of the mantra, and detachment arose. I found myself able to view the snake, not as an enemy, but as a brother. In the presence of the Lord's name, all fear had dissipated. I rejoiced. Minutes passed. The serpent stared into my eyes. Then, slowly turning its head, it slithered back into the bushes. Humbled, I reflected:

> *Today the Lord has revealed to me what a tiny child I am on the spiritual path. When a child is in danger, his only means of protection is in appealing to his mother or father. And today the mother and father of this tiny child have come in the form of their holy names to give me shelter.*

Each night Ramesh Baba and I shared rotis on the dusty floor. One night, as his form shimmered in the lantern's light, he inquired, "Which place in America were you brought up?"

"A small town near Chicago," I replied.

He stopped chewing and a tear of compassion welled up in his eye. "Oh, Krishnadas. Chicago is the place where cows are killed." Taking a deep breath, I closed my eyes, sadly remembering the stench and cries of the stockyards we used to pass in the car when I was a boy. Isolated as Ramesh Baba was on that solitary mountaintop and not having heard world news in decades, how did he know this? But it was true. In the past, the Union Stockyards on the south side of Chicago comprised the largest slaughterhouse operation in the world and processed most of America's meat. It moved my heart to witness Ramesh Baba's compassion for the cows 10,000 miles away.

Ramesh Baba became my lifelong friend and great inspiration. He lived and spoke what he believed caring nothing for public opinion. I found it fascinating that he lived in similar conditions to the sages of the Himalayas while never leaving Vrindavan. He was a strict ascetic and profound scholar who spent his life begging and crying to be an instrument of Radha Krishna's gentle love. When he sang and when he served, that love was evident. *Yes,* I pondered, *the path of bhakti is very deep. Kind souls like Ramesh Baba and others I have met are leading me deeper into my journey and kindling the fire within my heart to find my guru.* I sincerely believed now that this teacher would be revealed to me when I was ready.

10

CHILDREN ADORNED WITH DAZZLING CROWNS, sparkling jewelry, and scintillating costumes performed the pastimes of Krishna on stage. Trained in the minute details of drama, they sang, danced, and acted for an audience of over a hundred enchanted locals who sat in a garden. Such theater was performed simultaneously all around Vrindavan and Asim and I would sometimes attend. On this particular day, Krishna and his cowherd friends pretended to be tax collectors and blocked the path of Radha and her cowherd girls, who carried clay pots of butter on their heads. Asim translated the local Hindi for me.

The sweet little boy playing Krishna said to Radha, "Before you can pass, you must pay taxes for the beauty, charm, and sweet love that you possess. The tax will be the pots of butter on your heads."

The beautiful child playing Radha's friend Lalita replied, "Why should we pay taxes to you? My Radha is the Queen of Vrindavan. You should pay taxes to her for all the grass your cows eat every day."

Through playful dialogue filled with humor, joy, and spiritual emotion, the players captivated our hearts, their classic stories enhanced by song and dance. In every encounter, Sri Radha's love won over playful Krishna. I had learned in the course of my travels how the essence of Yoga meant, simply, to be absorbed in the Supreme. It struck me how many ways there were to be absorbed.

Dawn cast its first light on a spacious courtyard behind a medieval sandstone temple. A brick wall ten feet high and covered with leafy, flowering vines that hosted droning bees bordered the yard. Birds hidden in tree branches began their chorus to welcome the rising sun. The enclosure was a sanctuary where devotees prayed quietly. Previously, Krishnadas Babaji had explained to me that in the center of the courtyard was the samadhi, or tomb, of a renowned saint named Rupa Goswami. He and his elder brother Sanatan had at one time ruled Bengal under the king as prime ministers. These young aristocrats were handsome, scholarly, and owned palaces of fabulous wealth. Although charitable in every way and loved by all, they longed to give society the greatest of gifts, the love of God. With this conviction, they gave away all they had in charity and moved to Vrindavan where they slept under the forest trees. Under the inspiration of Lord Chaitanya, the brothers composed vast literatures to illuminate the world with the inner secrets of spiritual love while they personally exemplified those teachings. For almost five centuries they had inspired countless followers. I had become so attracted by Rupa and Sanatan's devotion, I couldn't hear enough about them.

I knelt down before Rupa Goswami's tomb and prayed silently. Above the earth where the saint's body was enshrined was a small, square room made of sandstone that had a domed roof and was crowned with a spire. In my readings from religious books of various faiths, I had learned of how a saint's presence is especially powerful at his tomb, but nothing could have prepared me for what was about to unfold on that day. I suddenly experienced an invisible energy, mystical yet real, that poured out from the samadhi. It was as if a spirit that possessed limitless grace were embracing me and filling me with love. I felt weightless, beyond the body and mind. My limbs shivered and skin tingled as waves of gratitude thrilled my heart. Looking down at the dusty ground, I felt so small and unworthy of such an intimate experience. Was this another glimpse into the divine love that I yearned for, spurring me on to crave for more? I felt it was. My Lord was nudging me onto yet another step forward toward my destiny.

I suddenly knew, with certainty, that bhakti was the path I would give my life to and that Krishna's name would, in time, reveal His love to me. All the reservations that had prevented me from committing my whole heart to this path were now gone. But I understood that I would have to follow sincerely, under the shelter of an authentic teacher or guru, to whom I believed Krishna would bring me.

Bhakti. The path of devotion. My path had been revealed. Finally, I accepted.

I had now been in India for one year. I continued to learn the lesson that along with everything wonderful came an equal number of challenges. Months before, I had dutifully trudged to the immigration office in nearby

Mathura, to apply for a visa extension. The agent sent my application on to New Delhi, assuring me that in the meantime, the receipt of my application would serve as my legal visa until the official reply.

The autumn was giving way to winter, and there was still no reply. At least that's what I thought. Unbeknownst to me, a letter had been delivered to an ashram where the recipient lost it and never informed me. The letter, it turns out, had stated that I must report immediately to the office in Mathura. Unaware of any of this, I failed to report. Time passed. As a result, the immigration agent in charge of my case was outraged, feeling that I had defied his authority. I, in the meantime, went about my life unaware that anything was wrong.

One day, a temple priest hurried out to the street where I stood. His face was solemn. "A government agent is hunting you down," he said. "He believes you defied him."

"What are you talking about?" I blurted, bewildered. What could I have done to warrant such attention?

"In the morning, he came here searching for you. He screamed like a mad dog, threatening that when he found you, he would severely punish you." The priest's face twisted in disgust as he lowered his voice. "I know this man. He is cruel and corrupt. We fear him more than the local criminals, for he has the power to do anything."

"What should I do?" I inquired. My heart was pounding.

"Be careful."

Everywhere I went, people told me that the agent had been there searching for me. Dozens of Vrajabasis and sadhus prayed for my protection.

In those days, along with Sripad Baba and Asim, I would sometimes visit the second home of an affluent woman from Delhi named Yogamaya. She had a small two-room apartment where nightly she hosted devotees to perform kirtan while she cooked for everyone. One such night I met a man from New Delhi called Engineer. A mechanical engineer by profession, he was a tall, middle-aged man with neatly combed black hair and a trimmed mustache, and like everyone else at Yogamaya's place, he was a gentle soul and a sincere devotee of Krishna. After hearing my case, he assured everyone that through his connections he would try to normalize my immigration status in New Delhi. Everyone at the house insisted that the two of us leave at once.

Under the cover of night, Engineer and I crept along the small lanes of Vrindavan to reach the bus station. As we stood in line to purchase our tickets, a voice resounded like a crash of thunder. "Arrest him!" A hush fell over the bus station. Before I could understand what was happening, a hand seized my neck and slammed me against a brick wall.

I was face to face with the government agent. "You defied me," he blasted. "Now you are mine." His eyes flashed with rage. Engineer tugged at his sleeve trying to explain the miscommunication, but the agent was not a man to listen to reason. He was a man of force. He struck Engineer across the face again and again and then pinned him against the wall next to me. "You dare to challenge my authority," he screamed. "If you speak another word, you too will be beaten and arrested." Women screamed, men gasped, and children cried. Two police constables flanked him holding clubs to prevent anyone from interfering with him. As Engineer cowered against the wall, the agent gripped my neck and dragged me away. The local people looked on in horror, crying, "He's a sadhu. Do not hurt him. Do not hurt this boy."

The agent yanked me along and shoved me into the bus bound for Mathura. At the door of the bus, he turned to the two constables. "Away with you. I don't need your help. This culprit is all mine now." He rammed me down into the front seat and sat beside me. I got a good look at him now. He was built like a warrior with disheveled hair and short beard. Shaking my shoulders, he screamed into my face. "I'll whip you, starve you, and make you wish you were never born." Spittle shot from his lips. Wiping his spit from my face, I thought, *I'm in the hands of a sadist. This man is mad. What can I do?* I closed my eyes and softly chanted the mantra. The overcrowded bus jerked forward.

We drove along for a while when, suddenly, chaos erupted in the rear of the bus. A fight had broken out between two farmers. My captor seized this opportunity to display his prowess. He lept up from his seat, he ordered the bus driver to watch over me, as if I could go anywhere with the bus speeding down a highway. Roaring, the agent rushed to the back of the bus knocking everyone aside. At the rear, he dove into the brawl and mercilessly thrashed the two farmers. Meanwhile I thought to myself, *The next few seconds may be my only chance to escape.* Inwardly, I cried out for direction.

An idea popped into my mind. I sprang from my seat and rushed to the driver, crying out "Pani, pani, pani"—meaning I had to pass urine. With a wave of his hand, he ordered me back to my seat. But to his dismay, I didn't leave. Instead I jumped up and down, holding myself like a little boy screaming out with the pangs of a bursting bladder, "Pani, pani." Again he ordered me to sit. At that moment, I took note that the driver was barefoot. This was my only possibility to escape, and it was passing. What I did next should be understood as a radical measure in a time of great emergency. I squatted down beside the driver's seat and passed urine onto the floorboard of the bus, carefully aiming it so the stream would ricochet onto his bare feet. Feeling my warm urine sprinkling upon his feet, his eyes flung wide in shock and his mouth gaped open. Utterly bewildered, he slammed on the brakes, cranked open the door, and screamed, "Do it outside."

I ran like the wind. To my surprise, the bus drove off. I guess that bus driver wanted to be rid of me forever. In a field I watched from behind a bush. Fifty yards down the road the bus came to a screeching halt and backed up. I could just imagine my captor smacking the driver for setting me free. The agent burst out into the darkness of night and searched frantically up and down the road with a flashlight in hand, but all he found was an isolated highway. Frustrated, he stomped back onto the bus and returned to Mathura. Meanwhile, I slinked through fields, forests, and back alleys to reach Yogamaya's house.

Engineer was there. He had already narrated my capture to the devotees. They, in turn, had been praying and chanting all night for my protection. They did not know what else to do. When I entered the doorway, everyone leaped up to greet me.

"How did you escape?" They asked in unison.

"By Krishna's mercy." I was ashamed to describe my unconventional methods.

Later, other passengers who were on the bus related to me the events that followed my escape. As the agent had blazed with rage, an old widow ridiculed him. "You boast to be such a big tough man? Ha ha ha! But now you've been defeated by that skinny little sadhu." Everyone in the bus roared with laughter. Utterly humiliated, he publicly declared to avenge the wrong I did to him. From that night on, he dedicated his time to hunting down his prey—me. The Vrajabasis gave him wrong leads.

Meanwhile, I learned every back alley in Vrindavan, daring not to step on a main road. I lived like a fugitive with an obsessed agent of the law hot on my trail.

One morning, at four thirty, as I prayed in the Radha Raman Temple, I presented my case before Krishna. "If I try to leave India with an invalid visa, I will never be allowed to return. If I stay, it is only a matter of time before I'm apprehended and then deported from Vrindavan forever. Please do to me whatever you wish."

In the darkness of the early morning, I left the temple and paced along a narrow lane. Suddenly, an eerie howl rang out in the dark. I hesitated in my step, horror struck, and the fangs of a beast plunged into my right leg. Gripped by formidable jaws, I was dragged to the ground. Then it was over. I looked back and saw only darkness. The creature had disappeared into the night just as quickly as it had appeared. My leg burning with pain, I limped forward in the shadows, lost my balance and stumbled into a canal where I lay in thick black sewage. I hauled my body up out of that mess and hobbled on to the Radha Vallabha Temple where I was warmly greeted by the chief priest and his son, Radhesh Lal Goswami. They arranged for me to bathe. In their affectionate company, the pain in my leg began to seem irrelevant.

Later that morning, as I sat with Ghanashyam and two other sadhus in his temple, Ghanashyam noticed my bleeding leg. Startled, that lovable old man raised his eyebrows and asked in a high pitch, "Krishnadas, what happened to you?" I explained. They shook their heads in grief. An elderly sadhu gasped, "Any mad dog that bites like that has rabies. You must immediately take treatment."

Dejected, I replied, "Better that I die in Vrindavan than get sent away."

Their bodies swayed restlessly and they looked to me like beggars pleading for food. "Rabies makes you raving mad. We insist you must take proper treatment."

The free medical stall was a wooden shack right on a main road. With the agent hunting for me, it was especially dangerous for me to be there, but I took my chances anyhow. Dozens of poverty-stricken people stood in line. Flies swarmed, buzzing and biting. The doctor had a terribly limited supply of medicine. I carefully observed as he gave a diseased person an injection, swished the needle in a cup of alcohol, and then used it for the next person and the next person and the next. Then came my turn. The doctor analyzed my wound and frowned in dismay. He exclaimed, "You must have rabies. Can you identify the animal that bit you?"

"Doctor, it disappeared in the night," I answered. "I don't know what it was."

He made me lie on my back on a bare wooden table. Scrambling through a metal box, he lifted out a huge needle. It was tarnished and bent. Before my eyes, he sharpened it with a file. Slowly, he drew the serum into the syringe. "Forgive me, but I must inject you in the stomach. This will be very painful." The doctor pushed the dull needle into my stomach, but it would not penetrate. He tried again and again, struggling to dig it deeper as I lay there squirming. Visibly frustrated, as dozens of impatient sick people waited in line, he cried out, "If I don't get this serum in, you will die. In an emergency sometimes we must abandon conventional techniques." In a passion, he thrust that needle down into my stomach with great force and my entire body bounced from the table. It was excruciating. Finally, the needle penetrated. I felt like it was ripping me in two. The doctor slowly pushed the serum through the muscles and into my bloodstream. My stomach swelled in agony.

I was desperate to get out of that place and never come back. As I staggered away, he announced, "You must return for the next thirteen days to receive these injections."

I knew it was not possible for me to survive another such ordeal. "It's not possible for me to return," I said.

"If you don't, you will go mad with uncontrollable convulsions and die."

I explained my complex situation. "If I come on this main road every day, I'll surely be imprisoned."

As we spoke, he grew affectionate and assured me, "I am a government doctor. I will write a letter with a government stamp. You take it to Delhi and they must give you a valid visa."

The next day my stomach was bruised with purple and green swelling. There would be no reprieve, however. The same painful ordeal had to be repeated for another thirteen days no matter what. The poor doctor was earnestly trying to do the best he could with what he had. He promised to have a better needle when I returned. As he'd instructed,

I boarded a third-class train to New Delhi. When I reached the Home Minister's Office, I was given over to a high-ranking official, as mine was a special case. The official gravely read the doctor's note, which stated that I had rabies and would die without proper treatment. The doctor went on to request urgently that I be granted a valid visa so that he might continue my treatment.

Done reading, the immigration official looked sternly into my eyes. Then he spoke. "I will not be able to sleep at night if I know that I am the cause of your death." He called for my files to be brought in, and with great care, regularized my immigration status. "Now you are completely legal. There is no longer any problem." With these words, he stamped my passport with a fresh visa.

I returned to Vrindavan feeling that I had passed through another necessary purification to prepare me for my destiny. I was not to be bothered by the government agent again as he was now under investigation and soon to be fired for abuse of power. I was free to stay in this place I loved and had an overpowering sensation that something wonderful would soon unfold for me here.

One chilly night, during the last days of November, I sat alone under a kadamba tree on the bank of the river, where I carefully listened to the quiet, swishing song of Yamuna. The moonlight glimmered on the surface of the water while birds of the night filled the air with soothing sounds. My mind became a projector and the river a cinema screen on which I observed the events of my life. I witnessed the joys and sorrows of my childhood and the senseless escapades of my teens. I saw Gary and myself, charged with the energy of youth, leaving our homeland to seek meaning. We had roamed Europe seeing the sights, making friends, and soaking in every possible experience. The one constant through it all had been a longing for God, which became an obsession. Where did this longing come from? I didn't know.

Searching, I had studied religions and philosophies and, from childhood, had prayed in synagogues and later in monasteries, cathedrals, mosques, and temples. Gazing into the current, my mind flowed back to that fateful sunset on the island of Crete where I resolved to embark upon my pilgrimage to India. Life-changing lessons had greeted me as I crossed the Middle East. While studying the Holy Koran, danger and disease perpetually hovered over my head. As I looked deeper into the river, my mind's eye beheld the panoramic beauty of the Himalayas. I envisioned the great *rishis*, mystics, ascetics, yogis, and lamas from whom I had so eagerly learned. They had all been so kind to me and in my heart I thanked each of them. Then I witnessed the miraculous reunion with Gary in that rice paddy of Nepal. I wondered where he was now and why we'd been separated again. On that riverbank, I heard again all the unceasing prayers that I had offered on my arduous pilgrimage, praying that my spiritual path be revealed. I recalled how Lord Rama had appeared in Rama Sevaka Swami's dream and said of me, "This young boy is a devotee of Krishna and Vrindavan will be his place of worship." At the time, I had disregarded those words, but now, having resided in Vrindavan for about five months, I had a sense of sincere surrender and had finally accepted devotion to Krishna as my spiritual path.

Still, emptiness lingered within. I knew that I must accept a guru to whom I could fully dedicate myself. This necessity was emphasized both by tradition and by the words of scripture. To harmonize one's life in the service of a guru's teaching was the path that enlightened souls had followed since time immemorial. Gazing into Yamuna's dark current, I prayed for direction.

It was now late at night. With these thoughts in my mind, I lay down to sleep on the riverbank only to be haunted by a strange dream. I found myself in a comfortable house in America surrounded by people chattering on about frivolous topics while a television droned in the background. I awoke with a start. *Why did I leave Vrindavan?* I shouted. Confused, I rolled about on the riverbank sobbing into the darkness, *why did I leave Vrindavan? Why did I leave Vrindavan?* Gradually, I recognized the Yamuna flowing by and the nearby kadamba tree. *I am in Vrindavan.* I was exulted. "I am still in Vrindavan," I said aloud. I pressed myself to the cold earth beneath me feeling that I never wanted to leave. After regaining my composure, I reflected. *This cold, dusty riverbank in Vrindavan is many times more precious to me than a palatial mansion in the country of my birth.*

Later in the morning, as I walked along a narrow lane, I stepped around a cow stretched out lazily in my path. When I looked up I saw a Western monk dressed in saffron robes eagerly approaching and waving his arms as he called out, "Richard. Richard." It seemed

I knew this person. As he drew nearer, I saw that he was a devotee I had met nine months earlier at the Hare Krishna festival in Bombay. I had never seen one of these Western-born disciples of Srila Prabhupada in Vrindavan. I was delighted.

"Srila Prabhupada is coming tomorrow," he exclaimed. The sun was about to set. Chattering birds frolicked in the sky. The cow rose lazily from its slumber and, clacking her hooves on the footpath, strode away with a gentle moo. A strange feeling of excitement rushed through me as he continued. "Did you know that Srila Prabhupada is a resident of Vrindavan? He's returning after spreading the culture of devotion all over the world." Patting my back, he smiled, "Prabhupada will be so happy to see you here. We were all wondering where you could be. Please, come."

11

I T WAS NOVEMBER 26, 1971. I stood on the side of a road as an Indian-made bus rattled into Vrindavan. It came to a halt, the door swung open, and out stepped a small elderly man dressed in saffron robes and carrying a wooden walking stick in hand. Srila Prabhupada, I would learn, was Vrindavan's ambassador to the world. From the four directions, both young and old rushed to greet him. Seeing the man who had once showed such kindness to me, I melted with joy.

What followed invoked cheers from the locals. Out from the same bus came forty Krishna devotees, women and men from a mix of nationalities and races, European, American, Latin, African, Asian, and Indian. It was the first time in history that such a large group of foreigners had come. As they got down from the bus, priests and pilgrims marveled in joy, children smiled in fascination, while farmers looked on in disbelief.

Krishna is worshipped by hundreds of millions of Indians and Vrindavan is their holiest place of pilgrimage. The hearts of the people of Vrindavan swelled with pride to witness people of races they had never seen before sharing what they held most dear. A ceremony began during which dignitaries, including the mayor, government officials, priests, and religious heads, welcomed Srila Prabhupada back home. That elderly sadhu, who had departed from Vrindavan penniless, with only a dream, had now returned as a world-renowned teacher.

Srila Prabhupada was born Abhay Charan to a deeply religious family in Calcutta in 1896. I had read while in Bombay that, in 1922, the young Abhay met his guru, Srila Bhaktisiddhanta Saraswati. At the time of their first interaction, Srila Bhaktisiddhanta told him, "You are an educated young man. Why don't you teach the message of Lord Chaitanya throughout the world?"

Abhay couldn't believe what he was hearing. They had not even met, yet this sadhu directed him in a life mission. At that time, Abhay was actively involved in Mahatma Gandhi's independence movement.

"Who will listen to our message?" Abhay countered. "How can we spread Indian culture if we are under British rule?"

Srila Bhaktisiddhanta replied, "Whether one power or another rules is a temporary situation. The eternal reality is that we are not these bodily designations but the soul who is eternal and full of bliss. Real welfare work, whether individual, social, or political, should help a person to reestablish his eternal relationship with the Supreme Reality, Lord Krishna."

Hearing Bhaktisiddhanta cite from scripture with both logic and compassion, Abhay was convinced. In his heart of hearts, he accepted Bhaktisiddhanta Saraswati as his spiritual master and entered into that order with all his life and soul.

"My old friend," someone boomed out. I turned to find a smiling white man, slightly hefty with flashing green eyes, shaved head, and white robes running toward me with raised arms. It was Gurudas, that boisterous soul who, nine months before in Bombay, had brought me onto a stage to first meet Srila Prabhupada. He embraced me. "We meet again, and in this holy place." Later that day, he led me through a series of lanes, through the arched gateway of a medieval temple and into a small room where he told me more about the life of Srila Prabhupada.

"In 1954, Srila Prabhupada came to reside as a renunciant in Vrindavan. In this small room, where we sit today, he lived a secluded life for six years, preparing for what was to come." As I pressed my body against the earthen floor, my eyes scanned the tiny room. A slender green lizard of about eight inches with a long wagging tail let out a croak then raced across the clay-covered brick walls. A low table and a wooden bed with criss-cross rope for a mattress were the only furnishings. "Right here," Gurudas continued, "he translated the Sanskrit scriptures into English."

I nodded, encouraging him to tell me more.

"In 1959, he took the vows of a swami and was awarded the title A.C. Bhaktivedanta Swami," Gurudas said. "At the age of sixty-nine, in 1965, he left his home in Vrindavan to fulfill his life's mission. With less than seven dollars and a complimentary ticket, he boarded the Jaladuta, a cargo ship to America. He sailed over rough seas, suffering two heart attacks and his seventieth birthday on the voyage, before arriving alone, docking first in Boston and then sailing on to New York City."

A cool winter breeze drifted in from the courtyard outside while, as part of a ceremony, temple bells clanged and priests used wooden mallets to bang on brass gongs. *Bong bong, bong bong, bong bong.* While crowds of people thronged the temple courtyard for the ritual, Gurudas continued speaking. "Arriving at the New York Harbor, Srila Prabhupada didn't know a single soul. He struggled alone, living on the Bowery and the Lower East Side until gradually, his loveable qualities and vast knowledge attracted sincere seekers of the counterculture. He transformed the hearts of many American and European youth. In 1967, I became his disciple in San Francisco. We affectionately called him Srila Prabhupada, which means 'at whose feet great masters sit.' After only a few years abroad, he had established a worldwide movement, and now, for the first time, he's bringing a group of his eager disciples back to his home, Vrindavan."

I shook my head in wonder at Srila Prabhupada's journey. Though I, too, had traveled through foreign lands alone with no money and knowing no one, I had been nineteen years old and in good health when I started. He began his journey at the age of seventy and traveled through foreign lands with no money, knowing no one— and all to be an instrument of the Lord's compassion.

That evening, I returned to the temple to hear Srila Prabhupada speak. In an overcrowded hall, with rattling ceiling fans spinning overhead, I sat on the floor waiting. Through the windows could be heard a chorus of trilling and warbling birds as the assembly sang devotional hymns. Upon Srila Prabhupada's entrance, a tranquil silence descended on the room. Disciples bowed, old friends embraced him and guests stood in awe. He was dressed in the saffron robes of a swami, perfectly clean and neatly arranged. He sat cross-legged at the far end of the hall on a red upholstered dais. The sunset shone through many windows, bathing his dark golden complexion with soft rays. His deep brown eyes, although old and wise, glittered with the innocence of a child as they gazed affectionately at each and every member of the audience. He was quite small in stature, perhaps five feet and five inches, but his presence was immense. With his hands in a prayerful gesture, he bowed his head to welcome us then cleared his throat. He spoke with a deep voice into a microphone.

"The basic principle of the living condition is that we have a general propensity to love someone," he began. "No one can live without loving someone else. This propensity is present in every living being. The missing piece, however, is where to direct our love so that everyone is included and can be happy." He paused and looked out at the audience thoughtfully. "At the present moment, human society teaches one to love his country or family or his personal self, but there is no information on where to direct the loving propensity so that everyone will be happy."

His voice cracked with heartfelt emotion. I sensed that he was not just teaching, but pleading with each member of the audience to understand the urgency of the message he carried. Here was a man who deeply cared and the entire audience clung to his every word. "We have failed to create peace and harmony in human society, even by such great attempts as the United Nations or our economic and scientific progress, because we have missed this point." Closing his moist eyes and briefly entering into a trance, he seemed to be feeling the suffering of the entire world. "That missing point can be found in awakening our original love for Krishna. If we learn how to love Krishna then it is easy to immediately and simultaneously love every living being. It is like pouring water on the root of a tree—all parts of the tree are nourished. Or supplying foodstuffs to the stomach—all parts of the body are nourished. When we are situated in that position we can enjoy a blissful life."

I was so intensely focused on my spiritual search at that point in my life, and the urgency with which he begged us to revive our lost love for God affected me profoundly.

The devotees invited me to stay in a house with them but I felt awkward. I preferred resting under the trees on the bank of the Yamuna. But each day, after my early morning bath and meditations, I walked in the quiet dawn to hear Srila Prabhupada's morning lecture. Although I was somewhat skeptical about his disciples—thinking it odd, for example, that some carried cameras and tape recorders, something I had never seen any sadhu do—I was becoming more and more impressed by Srila Prabhupada's knowledge and personal qualities. He had an art of explaining even intricate philosophical points with simplicity and ease. And after the class each morning, Srila Prabhupada would personally take us on a tour of Vrindavan. While walking with him, I saw the same places I had seen many times, but in his company

I experienced realizations like never before, as if a deeper level of reality was being revealed. When he told the story of a place, it was as if I could see with my eyes what he described. After lunchtime, I would sit in his room for several hours as he informally conversed with guests. Feeling extremely shy in his presence, I asked no questions but was content just to listen.

One such afternoon, while sitting in his room, I found myself the target of a leading disciple's rebuke. "This meeting is for guests only," he said. "Please get out of here. All devotees are to perform their duties now. That's the rule." Although I did not have a shaved head like all the other male disciples, I was the only Westerner in the room. Evidently, this man did not see me as a guest.

I held a lock of my hair between my thumb and forefinger and shook it gently. "But please see. I am not a devotee."

Visibly annoyed, the disciple looked to Srila Prabhupada for direction. I anxiously awaited the verdict, wanting very much to stay. Srila Prabhupada lifted his eyebrows, smiled at me and laughed heartily. "He is not a devotee. Let him stay." The disciple left in defeat. Then, with a serious but modest expression, Srila Prabhupada said to me, "I appreciate your eagerness to hear." My heart was melted by the intimacy of the exchange.

Another day I happened to meet Krishnadas Babaji on the road. "Hare Krishna!" he greeted me, and after returning his greeting, I informed him that Srila Prabhupada had come. His face lit up. "Wonderful. Please take me to see my dear good brother." Together we strode through the lanes, hurrying around honking rickshaws and water buffalo sleeping on the road. After climbing a flight of steps, we entered the door of Srila Prabhupada's room. Sitting on the floor behind a low table, Srila Prabhupada was speaking to a dozen guests. When we entered and the eyes of these two great souls met, their faces blossomed with joy. Krishnadas Babaji erupted into smiles. "Hare Krishna," he exclaimed.

Srila Prabhupada beamed with a bliss I'd never seen on any human face. A broad smile radiated and his eyes gleamed with tears. He, too, cried out, "Hare Krishna" and leaped from his seat to greet Babaji. Both rushed to embrace, tears of happiness filling their eyes. Srila Prabhupada then escorted Babaji to sit on the same cushion as he. For the next hour, they filled the room with laughter as they conversed in their native Bengali language, oblivious to all others in the room. Sitting only a few meters away, I observed, bubbling over with excitement. What an incredible spiritual relationship these two men had. Never had I seen such love and honor between two human beings. I felt I had received a glimpse into the spiritual world.

Only a couple of days passed when several of Srila Prabhupada's disciples pressured me to make a commitment. "It is wrong for you to be living in Vrindavan," they said. "You should join our movement and travel with us." Although I was accustomed to dealing with such pressures, I was not happy with it. If ever I were to commit myself to a teacher, which I wanted to do with all my heart, the decision would have to be impelled by deep faith and inspiration, not by anyone's pressure.

One afternoon I rushed to a garden where Srila Prabhupada was scheduled to speak, but I was late. I found myself amid grazing cows. Leafy trees swarmed with sweetly singing birds and a crowd of native Vrajabasis gathered under the warming winter sun. Srila Prabhupada was just departing and hundreds of people lining the path bowed to him as a gesture of respect. I was among them. As I lifted my head from the sandy earth, I found his feet, covered by simple canvas slippers, planted just inches from my face. On my knees, looking up, I was face to face with him. His demeanor was grave.

"How long have you lived in Vrindavan?" he asked.

My mind squirmed, fearing he too would chastise me for living here. I replied, "About six months, Srila Prabhupada."

His large dark eyes gazed down into mine. It was as if nothing else existed but that gaze. I felt that he knew everything about me—my strengths and weaknesses, virtues and faults, all I longed to achieve and all I prayed to be rid of. I was speechless. Perhaps a minute passed in this way. Then, before my eyes, his face blossomed into a munificent smile. "Very good," he said, rubbing my head affectionately. "Vrindavan is such a wonderful place."

In his glance and in this briefest of exchanges I experienced the love of an eternal friend, a benevolent parent, and of God. Turning slowly, he walked away down the path, his wooden cane tapping the ground with each step. I closed my eyes and pondered.

He is such a busy man, with tens of thousands of people the world over waiting for a moment of his time. Why did he stop for me? I have nothing to offer, I am just a penniless nobody who sleeps under a tree.

That small gesture had a profound impact on me, more than many of the miracles I had witnessed. It was an impact I could neither understand nor explain. *Perhaps*, I thought, *the miracle of being an instrument of kindness is the most powerful of all.*

For some time, I had been troubled by a fundamental philosophical dispute over whether God was ultimately impersonal or personal. On the one hand, I had heard some yogis and philosophers profess that ultimately God is impersonal and formless, but that he accepts a temporary material form as an *avatara* when He descends into the world for the benefit of all beings. After accomplishing His mission, He again merges into His formless existence. All form and personality, according to the impersonalists, is a nonpermanent product of material illusion. In the final state of liberation, the soul sheds its temporary identity and becomes one with God, merging into the all-pervading spiritual existence.

On the other hand, I had heard other yogis and philosophers profess that God is the Supreme Person, that His spiritual form is eternal, full of knowledge and bliss. At the time of liberation, the soul enters into the kingdom of God where it eternally serves the all-beautiful Personality of God in pure love.

I often pondered this apparent contradiction. *How could they both be correct? God must ultimately be one or the other. Either He must be ultimately impersonal or personal.* Out of respect for my beloved teachers, it had been difficult for me to think that any of them were wrong. Some attacked the opposing point of view while others refrained from argument by keeping the subject vague. I found that many spiritual teachings were similar until they came to this point.

What is the goal I should aspire to? I wondered. Should I strive to transcend dualities to become one with an impersonal, formless God? Or should I strive to purify my heart to serve a personal Lord with unconditional love in His eternal abode?

One afternoon, a guest asked Srila Prabhupada this very question. "Is God formless and impersonal or does He have form and personality?" The chattering of birds, screeching of monkeys, and honking of distant rickshaw horns were silenced by the anticipation in my heart. I sat up with attention, eager to hear his answer. Srila Prabhupada slowly leaned forward, his face perfectly relaxed and full lips curved downward at the edges. Sitting cross-legged on the floor, his elbows rested on the low table in front of him and his hands were clasped together under his chin. With a grave gaze, he quoted from the Vedas and explained, "We must first understand the inconceivable nature of God. The Supreme Lord is simultaneously personal and impersonal. It is an eternal truth that He is both formless and that he has an eternal, blissful form."

I felt a warm, peaceful sensation flood my chest. With one hand Srila Prabhupada stretched his index finger upward. "The Lord's impersonal, all-pervading energy is called *Brahman*. And *Bhagavan* is the personal form of God, who is the energetic source and never under the influence of illusion. Take for example the sun. The form of the sun as a planet and the formless sunlight can never be separated, as they exist simultaneously. They are different aspects of the sun. Similarly, there are two different schools of transcendentalists who focus on different aspects of the one truth. The impersonalists strive to attain liberation in the Lord's impersonal, formless light, while the personalists strive for eternal loving service to the Lord's all-attractive form. There is no contradiction.

"Similarly, the soul is part and parcel of the Lord, simultaneously one with God and different from God. Qualitatively we are one with God, being eternal, full of knowledge, and full of bliss. But quantitatively, we are always but a part, just as the sunray is but a tiny part of the sun and yet has the same qualities as the sun. We are both one with God and different from God. God is the independent controller, but when the soul misuses his God-given independence, he forgets his relation to the Lord and falls into illusion and subsequent suffering."

Leaning back against the wall, he tilted his head slightly and gazed directly into my eyes. "The two schools, personalists and impersonalists, both approach different aspects of the One God." He went on to explain how Krishna, His form, qualities, personality, and abode were unlimited, and that all the true religions of the world worshipped the same One God. He had simply revealed Himself in different ways at different times.

How beautiful. With these simple and intelligent words, Srila Prabhupada had harmonized two apparently opposing views. As I listened to him, tears of appreciation welled up in my eyes. *Yes, now it all makes so much sense*, I thought. A dilemma that had confused my progress was now completely removed. A spontaneous, joyous smile stretched across my face. Srila Prabhupada reciprocated with a smile, too, one endowed with both wisdom and serenity.

One guest asked him, "Are you the guru of the world?"

Srila Prabhupada meekly bowed his head and cast his eyes toward the floor. "I am everybody's servant," he said. "That's all."

I found a special charm in this exchange. Srila Prabhupada was so unpretentious, so free and comfortable in all that he did and said. I recalled the humility of dear Ghanashyam, who had lived in a hallway outside a closet for fifty years. Srila Prabhupada was a learned scholar, eloquent orator, and powerful yogi who had founded a worldwide society with thousands of followers. Dignitaries came to honor him daily. Still, that natural spirit of humility was present—"I'm small. God is everything." Paradoxically, that humility empowered him with unlimited confidence and determination.

After the meeting, I stood up and offered Srila Prabhupada a rose. He smelled it and graciously bowed his head. Departing from the house, I wandered back to the Yamuna, elated. Prabhupada's words had put the puzzle of personalism and impersonalism together, piece-by-piece. And in so many other ways, he had impressed me deeply. *But who is this amazing man?* I wondered. *What is he like as a person?*

12

IN DECEMBER, THE DAYS WERE GROWING SHORTER and, by late afternoon, the temperature dropping. As I wrapped a cloth over my head and started down the pilgrim's path to the river Yamuna, the life of the forest stirred around me. Birds and peacocks warbled their evening songs, farmers returned from the fields, and Vrajabasi women clad in orange, green, and yellow saris glided along the path with huge pots of water balanced on their heads. Suddenly I spotted a familiar figure ahead. It was Shyamasundar, the devotee who had fed me spiritual food in Amsterdam and taken such an interest in my well-being in Bombay. Even from behind, I recognized this tall American who served as Srila Prabhupada's personal secretary. His right hand was buried in a bag of beads and he was chanting as he advanced toward the river. I quickened my pace to catch up and shouted his name.

He turned to look and a smile of recognition flashed across his face. "Ah, Richard. Or what do they call you now?"

"Some people call me Krishna Das."

He wrapped his long arm around my shoulder and pulled me close. "So Krishna Das, I hear you've been living in Vrindavan for a while now. It's so great to see you again." We stood for a moment on the path exchanging pleasantries. Something told me that this man, in time, would come to own a special corner in my heart. It seemed as though I had known him forever. "Srila Prabhupada likes you very much," he volunteered. "He often asks about you."

"You are very fortunate to be so close to him." I said, elated. "And every day too, I can't even imagine..."

"Yeah," he laughed modestly. "Sometimes I pinch myself to see if I'm dreaming. You know, I've been around him for nearly four years now and he just seems to get younger and more beautiful every day. He's always fresh, I've never even seen him sleep."

"Do you remember the first time you saw him?" I asked. I was eager to hear as much about Prabhupada as I could, and to understand how others had decided to change their lives so radically to follow him.

On the riverbank, sitting cross-legged, Shyamasundar rocked slowly back and forth. "It was in Haight-Ashbury, San Francisco, January 1967. My friends and I had put together this big rock and roll dance at the Avalon Ballroom. We called it a Mantra Rock Dance. Everyone was there to welcome 'The Swami' to the West Coast—the Grateful Dead, Janis Joplin, Jefferson Airplane, Canned Heat, Quicksilver, and Moby Grape, they all played. Even Allen Ginsberg, Timothy Leary, and Ken Kesey were there. All the hippie heroes came." Shyamasundar became excited and his body rocked faster. "Picture this scene. The whole place is pulsating with strobe lights and rock and roll, packed with wild, longhaired kids, most of them on acid. Then, about midnight, Srila Prabhupada walks quietly onto the dark stage and sits down cross-legged on an elevated seat. The place falls silent. Srila Prabhupada begins humbly chanting the Hare Krishna mantra. A spotlight finally locates him, and gradually the crowd joins in the chanting. Then, one by one, the rock groups come on stage to join him, and the rest is history. For two hours, Prabhupada led the most incredible kirtan you can imagine. When he danced with his arms upraised, he won the hearts of thousands. Or as he put it later, 'I have turned hippies into happies.'"

I tried to imagine Srila Prabhupada living in Haight-Ashbury, the world capital of the hippie culture. Gary and I had spent some time there in 1968. From what I remembered, it was like a universe unto itself filled with peace-loving hippies, starry-eyed seekers, drug dealers, junkies, tourists, entrepreneurs, and Hells Angels roaring up and down Haight Street on their majestic chrome-plated Harleys. I just couldn't imagine the elderly saint from Vrindavan living there. "How long did he stay?" I asked.

"Four months. He lived with us American kids. We could hardly understand what the Swami was telling us. All we knew was that we were in love with him, this beautiful person sitting in a small apartment above a Laundromat who was happy to meet anyone who came to see him. And what really got me was that he was always joking. Sometimes he would lie back and laugh so hard that all of his teeth would show and tears would roll down his face."

The riverbank was beginning to grow dark and chilly, the air filling with wood-smoke from village cooking fires. I suggested we walk along the river to Kesi Ghat.

We both rose to our feet and he dusted off his backside. As we walked along, Shyamasundar continued, telling me how Prabhupada won the hearts of the Beatles, and especially George Harrison, and how devotees became such close friends with the superstars, residing in John Lennon's home for months. "How could that happen, if not by divine providence?" he asked.

All I could do was smile.

"And Prabhupada didn't want anything from these guys. He just wanted to give them the secret of life. In the first meeting with John and George, Prabhupada saw into their hearts. And he was so charming, telling them very simply that Krishna is the Supreme Person and describing what He looked like, what He said and did, how much He loved music and singing and dancing. And then, he promised them, they could meet Krishna face-to-face."

Stopping in my tracks, I couldn't believe I was hearing about the Beatles while walking along the bank of the Yamuna River in Vrindavan. I just had to laugh.

Shyamasundar stopped for a moment, excited to tell this story. A tear streamed down his cheek as he stuttered. "I remember before their first meeting, George whispered to me outside Prabhupada's door that he was really scared, more so than going on Ed Sullivan or meeting Elvis. But when he bowed down and Prabhupada greeted him heartily, it was like watching two ancient friends reunited, taking up where they left off. On the way out after that first meeting, George turned to me and said, 'Yeah, Prabhupada is the real thing.'"

It had been over a year since I had last listened to rock and roll music. Ten thousand miles from home, in a village in India, it had been the farthest thing from my mind. Still, I relished the idea that George Harrison of the Beatles was taking his spiritual life so seriously. I was feeling him to be a brother, sharing my cherished ideal. *What a small and wonderful world*, I thought.

As I sat on the steps at Keshi Ghat with my new friend, I observed meteor showers to the north. Shyamasundar looked up, and began telling me about Srila Prabhupada's visit to Russia. In those years, because of the Iron Curtain, nobody could get into Russia. But once again, Krishna paved the way to facilitate His devotees' desire.

"We had no plan, no proper food. We stayed in tiny, ill-lit rooms, and there was an overall depressing atmosphere of fear and repression and gloom. What were we going to do for five days?" Shyamsundar went on to say that he had been wandering around Red Square when he met the son of the Indian ambassador and a young Russian man named Anatoly, who came back to the hotel to meet the guru.

"For three days and nights, Anatoly stayed at Prabhupada's side and absorbed, like a sponge, everything Prabhupada taught him. Prabhupada was full of charm and humor, but also precision, as he taught Anatoly the entire Krishna consciousness process. Then we left Moscow, Prabhupada and I together. But from that seed, now Krishna's teachings are spreading like wildfire, underground, behind the Iron Curtain."

Looking upstream, into the horizon, I recalled growing up in America, indoctrinated with fear of the Russians. As schoolchildren, we had air-raid drills and were trained to duck under our desks in the event of a Russian bomb attack. In fact, several of the wealthier families in my neighborhood built fully stocked nuclear bomb shelters in their back yards, anticipating such an attack from Russia. Yet in the height of the Cold War, Shyamasundar and Srila Prabhupada were in Moscow blissfully teaching the path of bhakti yoga to a Russian.

"Why has Srila Prabhupada brought all you Western devotees to India?"

Shyamsundar looked thoughtfully into the distance before answering. "Prabhupada has often told us that real religion in this country is waning. Instead of God, he says, people want television and cars." I thought of the false guru I had met in Janakpur whose highest ambition was to be a rich American. "So I think he came back here and brought some of us along to say to the Indian people, 'Just see. These Western boys and girls have everything, TVs and cars, more than you will ever have—and they were not happy until they found Krishna. You have something they want, Krishna, so you should export Krishna.'" Prabhupada has often said that with India's philosophy and America's wealth, the world can really prosper. He calls us Western devotees his 'dancing white elephants'!"

I laughed and considered the brilliance of synthesizing Eastern philosophy with Western wealth and technology. I realized I had been so immersed in searching for God in my own life that thoughts of how to bring spirituality to others were far from my mind. I asked, "And how are the people of India receiving all of you?"

"Here in India, wherever we go, there are festivals of joy to greet us. But sometimes Srila Prabhupada is criticized to the point of death threats for giving initiation to Westerners, ignoring the caste system, or for engaging women in priestly duties." This impressed me. During my travels in India, I had witnessed oppression to the lower castes and women, and it had saddened me. Srila Prabhupada's courage to fight against it inspired me.

Shyamasundar continued, "Srila Prabhupada is truly a revolutionary." He bent down to splash some river water on his face to refresh himself and then stood up and stretched. "Krishnadas, it is really a pleasure to meet with you tonight. Is there anything else I can do for you?"

"What can I say?" I rose to my feet. "I'm just so grateful." I placed my hand on his shoulder, "But I've taken so much of your time. I'll see you in class tomorrow."

Shyamasundar smiled. "Thank you. You're right. I had better be getting back." He reached down and took my hands in his. "Srila Prabhupada will be very happy to hear that you and I met."

As I watched him hasten away, I felt immense gratitude and, along with that, a sense of blooming curiosity.

13

I N THE PRECIOUS, QUIET MOMENTS JUST BEFORE DAWN, it was natural to feel close to God. Rising from the bank of the river, I left for the morning lecture.

"Everything is potentially spiritual," Srila Prabhupada began, as if picking up from my own waking thoughts. "Everything is the energy of the Lord. Material consciousness is to forget an object's relationship with God. Spiritual consciousness is to see everything in relation to God and utilize everything in devotional service." Prabhupada tapped the microphone to make his point. "Let us take this microphone, for example. If it is used to sing songs about mundane passion, it is material. If, however, it is used to sing the glories of the Lord, it is spiritual. It's all a matter of consciousness. We want to use everything for a spiritual cause. Bhakti Yoga is the art of transforming material energy into spiritual energy through a spirit of devotion."

Like an earthquake, his words shook my world. *This concept is revolutionary,* I thought. *It challenges the very core of my idea of detachment.* I had assumed detachment meant to give up everything and live with nothing but the barest minimum to survive. When I honestly searched deep into my heart, I had to admit that in a subtle way, I was proud of the way I had been living in India and even thought it superior to the way people lived in the West. *But perhaps this idea of detachment is just another product of self-deceiving ego, inducing me to feel superior to others.* My reality was shaken. It was easy to think of the beautiful natural surroundings in Vrindavan and the temples to the deities as spiritual. But a microphone? I thought of how I had judged Prabhupad's Western followers for carrying cameras and tape recorders.

How foolish it was of me to look down on them, feeling that I was better because of my ascetic lifestyle. I now understand that detachment is only sacred to the degree it fosters humility, respect, and love.

In a few words, Srila Prabhupada had just crushed my illusion. My ego felt battered, and yet I was thankful.

It is said that a saintly personality can be softer than a rose or harder than a thunderbolt. This morning, one guest made excuse after excuse to defend his immoralities and spiritual weaknesses. Srila Prabhupada listened, then his voice rose like thunder, "If you are weak, rectify it. If you have no determination, you have no character. What makes you different from an animal?" The man shrunk like a punctured balloon. Bowing down, he promised to do what he knew was right. When required, Srila Prabhupada could be very strict to emphasize the urgency of a person's predicament. Like a scalpel in the hands of an expert surgeon, his strong words cut only to heal. Or as he himself explained, "A spiritual teacher is required to have the courage of a British General and the heart of a Bengali mother."

Srila Prabhupada went on to say, addressing us all in a pleading tone, "When a drop of water falls from the clouds, it is transparent. But in contact with dirt it loses its transparency. Through filtration we can bring it back to its original quality. Similarly, our consciousness is originally pure, but in contact with material energy it has lost its transparency. By chanting the names of the Lord, we can revive our natural, blissful state." He explained how we must rise above sectarianism and understand that God had many names and had invested divine powers within all of them. "The name Krishna means all-attractive," he said. "He is all-attractive because He is the reservoir of all beauty, knowledge, strength, wealth, fame, and renunciation. Possessing a particle of these qualities makes a person great. God is great because He is the origin of all of these opulences and possesses them without limit. This is what is meant by the Supreme Personality of Godhead."

He went on to explain that it was a natural process. The more we hear about Krishna, the more the soul's dormant attraction to Him is awakened. The path of bhakti is centered around hearing about Krishna and chanting His Holy Names. As our love awakens, so does our enthusiasm to serve. Often I had heard the words "God is great," but this explanation of *how* He was great thrilled me. Chills ran through my body.

That evening, I sat on the hill crowned by the ancient Madan Mohan Temple. Overlooking the river Yamuna, I read a prayer written by Srila Prabhupada when he was stranded on that cargo ship in the middle of the ocean on his voyage to America. Seventy years old, he had endured consecutive heart attacks on the trip. He had only seven dollars in Indian currency and did not know a single soul outside of India. After thirty days at sea, he approached the Boston Harbor where he composed a personal prayer to Lord Krishna. Years later his followers happened to find it in an old trunk.

In the solitude of that mountaintop, the leaves of the trees rustled in the wind and in the distance I heard the lowing of cows and boatmen calling out to each other. I meditated, in the stillness of my mind, on a few verses from what are now called the Jaladuta prayers, which read as follows:

My dear Lord Krishna, you are so kind upon this useless soul, but I do not know why you have brought me here. Now you can do whatever you like with me.

But I guess you have some business here, otherwise why would you bring me to this place?

Somehow or other, O Lord, You have brought me here to speak about you. Now, my Lord, it is up to you to make me a success or failure as you like.

O spiritual master of all the worlds. I can simply repeat your message; so if you like you can make my power of speaking suitable for their understanding.

Only by Your causeless mercy will my words become pure. I am sure that when this transcendental message penetrates their hearts they will certainly feel engladdened and thus become liberated from all unhappy conditions of life.

O Lord, I am just like a puppet in your hands. So if you have brought me here to dance, then make me dance, make me dance, O Lord, make me dance as you like.

I have no devotion, nor do I have any knowledge, but I have strong faith in the holy name of Krishna. I have been designated as Bhaktivedanta, one who possesses devotion and knowledge, and now, if you like, you can fulfill the real purport of Bhaktivedanta.

Signed, the most unfortunate, insignificant beggar,

A.C. Bhaktivedanta Swami,

On board the ship Jaladuta, Commonwealth Pier,

Boston, Massachusetts, U.S.A.

18th of September, 1965

From the hilltop, I gazed down toward the Yamuna as she wound across the plains. As I meditated on Srila Prabhupada's prayer, my thoughts drifted to the parallels between my arduous journey from America to India in search of teachers, to receive knowledge about God and Srila Prabhupada's incredible voyage from India to America in search of students, to impart knowledge about God.

Perhaps God, I thought, *reveals true love to the world through the lives of those who love Him.* In Prabhupada's prayer, I found humility springing from the heart of a man who had forsaken everything for the spiritual welfare of others. An aged man who was seriously ill, penniless, and alone in a foreign land begging God for only one blessing: to be used as an instrument of God's mercy.

Early the next morning, awakened by distant temple bells, I lay on the riverbank for a long time gazing at the morning star and remembered the prayer I'd read the night before. Today was Srila Prabhupada's eighth and final day in Vrindavan. As was my custom, I bathed in the frigid waters and then stood in prayer, submerged to my shoulders. The soft moonlight shone on the silhouettes of distant temple spires. Silence covered the ether like a feathery blanket. Solitude was my only companion at this hour. Trembling in the cold, I pressed my palms and fingers together and prayed to Sri Radha and Krishna for guidance. Then I climbed onto the riverbank, squeezed the water from my clothes and put them back on, all the while quaking from the cold. I sat down to chant the holy names of the Lord on wooden prayer beads, preoccupied with Srila Prabhupada's departure from Vrindavan later that day.

An hour later, I was striding through the dim lanes of Vrindavan, eager to attend Prabhupada's last talk. Along the way, interspersed with the quiet of dawn, temple bells and gongs rang, the faithful sang, and shopkeepers were opening for business. Arriving, I took my seat on the floor. The hall was brimming over with disciples and guests softly chanting the Maha Mantra while a clay drum and hand cymbals kept a rhythm. In the chill of the winter morning, some were bundled with wool shawls, hats, or sweaters. A sweet fragrance rose from burning sticks of sandalwood incense while a bittersweet feeling rose from the assembly. No one wanted to see Srila Prabhupada leave Vrindavan.

As Srila Prabhupada entered, the kirtan rose in volume and tempo only to fade into a silent hush as he took his seat upon the dais. The rays of the rising winter sun came through the window and bathed his form in light. Outside, the parrots sang their elaborate songs. To this avian symphony Srila Prabhupada added the chimes of brass finger cymbals. Then, closing his eyes, he sang a beautiful devotional prayer, "Jaya Radha Madhava Kunjabihari, Gopijana-vallabha Girivara-dhari." As he sang of the love between the Lord and his loving devotees, I listened to the voice of my heart. *Srila Prabhupada's love for God is conquering me.*

Srila Prabhupada's singing flowed through my ears and streamed down into my chest. I felt that all of the events of my life thus far had been conspiring to bring me to this point. From my very core welled a spirit of acceptance that, yes, God had revealed my guru. I felt my soul rising and swirling on an enormous wave of faith that was plunging me into an ocean of gratitude. In this unfamiliar state, joy flooded my heart.

I thought back to my first meeting with Srila Prabhupada in Bombay. At that time, a voice in my heart had proclaimed, "This is your guru." But I was neither convinced by nor ready to accept what that voice commanded, so while my mind had done battle with my heart, I dismissed it and carried on with my search, a search that eventually brought me to Vrindavan and to Krishna. Now my heart and mind were harmonized by a power infinitely greater than either one. *Yes, Yes,* I could hear my heart rejoicing. My quest, which had begun half a planet away in Highland Park, Illinois, had finally delivered me to the feet of my guru. In that moment, I realized that there could be no greater goal in my life than helping Srila Prabhupada to spread God's love to the world. How I longed to be even the smallest instrument in that compassionate mission.

Gradually, other thoughts arose. I recalled the Egyptian mystic in the Himalayas who had prophesied: "You must persevere with patience, for by a power beyond your own, you will recognize the very one you seek.

Believe in this, it is your destiny. Your master will come to you." His prediction had come to pass.

My Lord had revealed a seed of faith in my master and I seemed to be swimming in a sea of euphoria. But within the span of a few earthly moments, I had to honestly face my own reality.

Can I really remain faithful to my guru's teachings? There are endless temptations in the world. To disgrace him would be an act of unthinkable ingratitude. And, too, though I am coming to respect them, his Western disciples are so different from me. Can I live among them? I have great faith in him but little in myself. Am I honestly qualified to be his disciple?

Tears welled in my eyes, my limbs tingled, and my heart pulsated with a warm feeling as I concluded that I was not qualified, but was determined to prepare myself with the passing of time.

As the morning sun warmed the world from a chilly winter morning, I drifted along in the sizeable crowd that was gathering outside to bid Srila Prabhupada and his followers farewell. Moments later, the flow of the crowd pushed me in such a way that I found myself standing right before him, gazing into his deep brown eyes, and he into mine. A mystical feeling overwhelmed me, it was as if the Lord Himself were gazing into my soul through Srila Prabhupada's eyes. Everything else seemed to disappear. He stood calmly waiting for me to speak. With a choked voice and my emotions swirling in gratitude, I shyly said, "Srila Prabhupada, I wish to offer you my life."

Countless time passed in the silent moment that followed. Then he graciously touched my joined hands with his fingertips and gently smiled. His eyes, moistened with affection, were like those of a father welcoming home his wayward son after untold years of separation. In his gaze, I encountered an endless sea of wisdom that stretched beyond time. I felt a love deep, yet personal, giving me a comfort I had never before known. With a slight nod, he said, "Yes, you are home."

A surge of gratitude pushed tears through my eyes and, struggling to restrain my bursting emotions, I bowed. Srila Prabhupada tilted his head, handed his cane to my friend Shyamasundar, and stepped into his car, smiling and bowing his head to his friends and admirers. With many cheers, waves, and tears we watched as the entourage drove off into the horizon.

I stood motionless, gazing into the clear morning sky. Today, I felt that the sun of faith had risen from the shadows of my mind. It was a sun that I believed would never set.

An outpouring of gratitude sprung from my heart. For this blessing, I had endured dangers and hardships. For this treasure, my whole journey had been taken. For this precious moment, my soul had ached and yearned. God had revealed my path. The fog of doubt and apprehension had cleared and I now found myself before a fully enlightened spiritual master to whom I could dedicate my life. That for which I had offered thousands of prayers and shed countless tears to attain was now revealed. And how sweetly it was done.

My joy knew no bounds. In his divine person, Srila Prabhupada embodied the teachings I'd discovered at the heart of every tradition I'd scrutinized. I experienced the timeless love and the wisdom of galaxies of saints flooding from his lips and drowning my every doubt as he spoke. He delivered a message that had been preserved through the ages by an unbroken line of masters who teach us how to realize our intimate relation with the all-attractive Beloved. In my heart had awakened a faith that this humble saint, so small of frame, was actually fully in love with Krishna, and that Krishna, the Supreme Lord, was fully in love with him.

During my travels, it had not been my practice to compare my teachers as if one were better than another. I simply absorbed, like a sponge, their teachings and the experiences I had with them with faith that God would reveal my path and guru. In Bombay, Srila Prabhupada first planted the seed of our relationship in my heart, like a spiritual conception. It remained hidden, gestating, while I found my way to Krishna's birthplace in Vrindavan and made it my home. Now, nine months from the time of that spiritual conception, it had taken birth in this holy land. Looking back into the events of my life, I began to recognize how the invisible hand of my Lord had carried me along.

I could see every stage of my life as being a beautiful blessing. I looked back at the times of joy and sorrow, pride and shame, successes and failures, and how they all led me forward on my path. I recalled those who had showered me with affection, like Kailash Baba, and those who despised me or plotted to destroy me, like the assailants in Istanbul. They were all part of a beautiful plan. As the water of a river finally finds its place in the sea, my life's calling finally brought me to the feet of my Krishna and my beloved guru. With tears of gratitude I could feel my Lord proclaiming, "I am here, it is I who have brought you here, and this is he to whom you belong."

Lost in thought, I walked back to the small room in the ancient temple where Prabhupada had resided for six years as a recluse. Sitting on the floor in the tiny space where Prabhupada would cook, I gazed out the window and couldn't believe what I was seeing. Only a few meters away from Srila Prabhupada's hermitage was the Samadhi or tomb of Rupa Goswami, the very place where I had a life changing revelation and where my spiritual path was finally revealed.

I returned to my place on the riverbank and savored the experience of that unforgettable day. The night grew late. Under the quiet of the moonlight, I reflected on my fascination with rivers throughout my journey. Each one drew me to her banks where she nourished me with wisdom and provided me a sanctuary. Searching into the waves of the Yamuna, with my mind's eye, I could also see that creek in Gettysburg, the stream in Luxembourg, the canals in Amsterdam, the Thames in London, the Tiber in Rome, and the beautiful Ganges. Each had whispered to me at critical junctures and times of need.

Now, gazing into her gentle current, I meditated on how the Yamuna River began her journey in the Himalayas where she flowed through forest dwellings of yogis and sages, and eventually, by a power beyond her own, Yamuna was irresistibly drawn to Vrindavan. In a similar way, I thought, arriving in India, I began my journey in the Himalayas where the river of my destiny carried me through forest dwellings of yogis and sages, and eventually, by a power beyond my own, I was irresistibly drawn to Vrindavan, the land of bhakti, and to the feet of my guru.

In the moonlight, I looked down into the river and saw the silhouette of my own reflection. All along, the Lord had been trying to show me, through the river of life, who I really was. As I lay down on the earthen riverbank, I remembered how I had prayed to my Lord in my bedroom in Highland Park and I smiled. "Yes, all along You have been listening."

14

IT WAS APRIL OF 1972 AND ALMOST FOUR MONTHS had passed since Srila Prabhupada's departure from Vrindavan. Since he'd left, I had been absorbed in my spiritual practices in quiet forests and in spending time visiting the people and temples I had come to love so dearly.

I hoped to stay forever, but, my visa was soon to expire and the day of my departure from Vrindavan and from India drew closer. It seemed like so long ago, while enroute to the Himalayas, that I had found myself mysteriously stranded here on the day of Lord Krishna's birth. What I had longed for—my spiritual path and my beloved guru—had been revealed here.

In the final days before leaving, I bowed my head to the forest and all the temples and people who captured my heart. I counted each moment that remained as an undeserved fortune.

One morning, just days before my departure, I was sitting with Ghanashyam and some of our friends in his closet-room temple, where they showered me with kindness and gifts to help me remember Vrindavan. A devoted Australian woman named Radha Dasi, who was a follower of Sripad Baba and the only other Westerner in Vrindavan beside Asim and myself, painted different scenes of Vrindavan in a notebook as a gift to help me feel at home while away.

On the day before my departure, Asim and I visited a place very dear to us, Govardhan Hill. For millennia, pilgrims and saints had circumambulated this mountain and honored even the smallest stone from its ground, for here the most intimate pastimes of love had been enacted between Radha and Krishna. When only seven years old, Krishna had effortlessly lifted this mountain and held it, with a single finger, like an umbrella to protect his devotees from a devastating rain, for seven days. Amid tranquil forests, lakes, cows, and hundreds of devoted pilgrims, we walked the fourteen miles around Govardhan Hill feeling both joy and sorrow, for the next day I would be gone.

Returning to Vrindavan village, I roamed about to the places I treasured most. Collecting dusty soil at each place, I sprinkled it into a small cloth pouch so that I could bring Vrindavan with me wherever I was destined to be. I prayed to Krishna, *Wherever life takes me, please allow me to always keep You in my heart.* That night, on the bank of Yamuna, I sat in the starlight chanting my mantra.

At sunrise the next morning, Asim accompanied me to the Vrindavan railway station where we boarded a train to Mathura. Once on board, we shared our hearts and our favorite food, Vraja rotis and gur. My eyes teared thinking how I would miss this food of the poor farmers. "I don't know when I'll ever see Vraja rotis and gur again."

Asim smiled and handed me a cloth bag. "Please open it." It was filled with a couple dozen thick Vraja rotis and a lump of gur.

At the Mathura railway station, we disembarked and stood waiting for the train that would carry me out of India and into Nepal. There on that railway platform, I bade farewell to my friend and brother. Together we had shared unforgettable experiences. As the train lumbered into the station, I struggled to control my emotions. I couldn't believe I had to leave the place I loved so dearly, the place where Krishna had answered my prayers. Tears streamed down my face. Asim clasped my hand in reassurance. He smiled through his tears and spoke a blessing. "Krishnadas, wherever you remember Krishna, you will find Vrindavan. I will be praying for your return."

I could not speak, for already I was overwhelmed by the grief of separation. With joined palms, we exchanged *pranams.* "Thank you for everything," I said softly and climbed aboard. I bade farewell to Vrindavan, my spiritual home, as the locomotive chugged away.

I traveled on to Kathmandu wondering if there would be something waiting for me at the American Express Office. There was. Although I had written to him that I could find my way back on my own, my father, eager to see me, had wired a three hundred and fifty dollar money order for my airfare. At the Indian Embassy in Kathmandu, I was issued a new two-week transit visa for India where I would catch my plane and fly from New Delhi to Belgium, and then on to the U.S.

Prior to my departure from Kathmandu, I took a nostalgic walk to Swayambhunath and gazed out at that fateful rice paddy where I had been reunited with Gary. I missed my old friend. So many dramatic events had unfolded in my life since our paths diverged, and I longed to share them with him. *I am still living as a homeless wanderer. Is he?* It would take another miracle for us to meet again.

I then wandered along the bank of the Bagmati river to Pashupatinath. Sitting on the riverbank in the moonlit night, I recalled the tears of longing I had shed here a year before and the many blessings I had received since that night. In the morning, I bade farewell and, solitary wanderer that I had become, boarded the back of a truck to the Pokhara Valley, one of the most beautiful of routes back toward India.

The valley was surrounded by snow-clad Himalayan peaks. I found a place to stay in a cave hidden on the face of a steep cliff, high above a river. For the next seven days, I rowed a canoe to the center of Phewala Lake where I performed my meditations from sunrise to sunset. During that week, I hardly saw a soul except for an occasional farmer or fisherman. On the seventh day, two days before my Nepali visa was to expire, I spoke softly to the mountains, sky, and water, "I say goodbye to you, beautiful Pokhara. Tomorrow I must depart." After rowing to the shore, I laid the oar across my canoe, and in the last light of day walked across the fields.

In a remote forest, as I crossed a dark, lonely road and began the descent back to my cave, a bus jostled by. With my first step down the cliff, I suddenly heard a strange scream. Curious, I turned. The bus momentarily halted about twenty yards away then drove off. Out from the growing darkness a ghostly figure scurried toward me. *Am I being attacked? Should I flee?* As the shadow advanced, I strained to make out who this was. Step by step, the silhouette was becoming clearer. *Could it be? My God, it is.*

"Gary!" I leaped in the air and dashed to meet him. Wild with joy, grateful beyond words, we embraced. Stunned, we could only repeat, "It's God's will."

Behind Gary was another familiar form running in from the dark. Who could this be? Impossible. It was our friend Hackett from Brooklyn. It had been at Hackett's home that I received Gary's call, the call that catapulted my journey. The words Hackett had spoken on hearing that we were going to Europe now rung in my heart: "I'll track you guys down in heaven or hell, mark my words." Sure enough, he'd tracked us down 2,700 feet above sea level in the heaven of a Himalayan valley. Now, nearly two years later, the three of us stood mesmerized under the stars on that remote mountainside in Nepal.

I invited them to spend the night with me. They followed behind as I climbed down the steep cliff and onto the plateau outside my cave. My two friends stood amazed to see my residence, a primitive cave in the wall of a cliff, in the middle of nowhere. Together, we sat on the stone floor. As hospitality, I offered them chipped rice and creek water with some of my remaining Vraja rotis and gur. Without utensils, they resorted to eating with their bare fingers.

Putting down his wooden bowl, Gary said, "We left Kathmandu on the bus this morning on our way for a trek in the mountains." He scratched his head, still staggered by our reunion. "Monk, or Richard, or what is your name now?"

"Some people call me Krishna Das."

"Well, Krishnadas, I was sleeping on the moving bus and just as I opened my eyes I caught a glimpse of the headlights momentarily flashing on you as you were climbing down a cliff. I screamed out for the bus to stop and jumped out, in the middle of nowhere." Gary grinned. "No one will ever believe this."

Hackett couldn't contain himself. Dropping his bowl to the floor he exclaimed, "I'm an eyewitness and even I don't believe it." His eyes flashed in thought. "I guess you're right. There must be a God."

We fell silent at the wonder of it all. From our little shelf high above the river, we stared dreamily at silhouettes of mountains far across the valley. Finally, I broke the silence. "I'm very sorry to say it, but I have to leave tomorrow at sunrise."

Still, we had the whole moonlit night before us. Hackett was dead tired from the arduous bus journey, so despite his struggle to stay awake, he soon fell asleep. Gary and I, meanwhile, had catching up to do. Gary told me about how he, too, had lived as a sadhu, visiting ashrams and holy places, and I told him about Vrindavan. When he considered my present predicament, he grinned. "Who can understand you, Krishnadas? You now have money that your father sent you and still you choose to live in a forest cave. Amazing."

I hadn't even thought about this until he mentioned it. "Yes," I admitted, "it's been so long, Gary, I've forgotten how to spend money."

In that mystical place overlooking the river valley, we shared the experiences and realizations of our respective quests. All night long, we gazed out across the valley, watching the moon spread silvery light on the nearby mountains. Below us, the song of the river sounded steadily.

Over the years, Gary had witnessed the transformations of my life. As small children, we played together, went to school together, got in trouble together. As teenagers, we rebelled against the social norms and entered the counterculture. In Europe, we explored the arts and cultures of new places. He had watched as my spiritual yearnings gradually shaped my destiny. We traveled together as my calling drew me to prayer in synagogues, monasteries, and cathedrals, and meditation in caves and mountains. From a cave in Crete, I left to follow that inner call. Then a year later in a rice paddy in Nepal, he found me as a hardcore renunciant seasoned by a life of asceticism with yogis and lamas. At that time, I was still longing, still searching for my path and my guru. Tonight he found his old friend fixed in dedication to a path revealed by the One God. The Lord had led me to my beloved spiritual father, Srila Prabhupada, whose divine grace attracted my faith and love. Now with a whole heart I was striving to develop humility, love for Krishna, and a genuine spirit of service to mankind.

As the sun was rising, a tear streamed down Gary's cheek and dropped into his beard. He whispered, "I'm happy for you, my brother. God has fulfilled your prayers." Gary smiled. "It's been an amazing journey."

I closed my eyes and took a deep breath. It was time to say goodbye again. We gave each other bear hugs and wished each other safe travels. Smiling, I turned and climbed the steep hill toward the road.

"My brother," Gary called to me.

From halfway up the mountain cliff, I grasped onto a rock for support and looked down at the plateau where Gary stood. A lost look covered his face and tears welled in his eyes. Rubbing his beard, he called out, "I wonder if we'll ever meet again?"

I looked on the Himalayan cave that had given me shelter and listened to the enchanting song of the river below. With tears of gratitude, I called out to Gary, "I believe we will, if we continue to follow the inner call."

At the New Delhi Airport, I boarded an Air India flight to Aston, Belgium. Dressed in the robes of a mendicant and carrying for my baggage only a cloth bag around my shoulder and a metal begging pot, I was a strange sight among international tourists and businessmen. An Irishman seated next to me in economy class puffed incessantly on one cigarette after another. The smoke burned my eyes and suffocated my breath, but the smoker seemed not the least concerned. The challenge of returning to the West had already begun.

Seeing the hostess serving meals sparked my memory. In my bag was a treasure that could transform this airplane into a spiritual oasis—my dear brother Asim's gift of Vraja rotis and gur. They may have been old and dry, but they were utterly delectable to me. On that flight, 35,000 feet in the sky, I jubilantly ate my Vraja rotis and gur while absorbed in remembrance of my spiritual home.

From Belgium, I hitchhiked to Holland to visit the first friends Gary and I had met in Europe. Traveling to Kosmos' place in Abcoude, I learned from his mother that he had moved to Amsterdam. When I arrived at their apartment unexpectedly, Kosmos, Chooch, and their friends leaped up and rushed to the door to greet me. Loud rock and roll music blared as some drank beer while others puffed on marijuana. In the cloud of smoke, men and women lay in passionate embraces.

My heart was sinking.

Just two days before, I had been living with sages in a holy forest in India and now here I stood in the midst of this party scene in my sadhu robes with my prayer beads and begging bowl. Disoriented, I contemplated, *what has happened to my dear friends?* Then I remembered my encounter with Sean in Connaught Circus and it dawned on me. *The real question is—What has happened to me?* We spoke for a couple of hours, then I politely bade them farewell.

Entering into the streets of Amsterdam, the entire environment seemed so foreign. How people dressed and related to one another seemed strange. Evening came, so I checked into a youth hostel where I was given the bottom bed of a bunk in a common room. *Maybe while I lie quietly in bed,* I thought, *I can adjust my mind to these drastic changes.*

Only a day before, I had been in a quiet holy place on the banks of a sacred river. Now I was in Amsterdam. Weary from my journey, I drifted into sound sleep. Suddenly, in the darkness of the night, my bed began to rattle and shake. As I bounced about, I wondered if this were an earthquake. Then I understood. From the bunk bed above came the sounds of passionate moans and groans of a young man and woman. I was not ready for this cultural adjustment. *Where am I? Why am I here? Where is my sleeping place at the bank of a holy river?* I slipped out of the hostel and walked the streets until morning. When morning came, I sat in a small park to eat my remaining Vraja rotis and gur. Later that day, I wrote a letter to my parents explaining that I wouldn't be flying home right away. I needed a little more time to readjust to the Western world.

Back in Amsterdam, I ate a diet of peanuts mixed with yoghurt. I didn't know how to be a vegetarian in the West, but I did like my simple diet very much.

One night, I visited the Cosmos. This was the nightclub where I first met that strange looking man with a shaved head and ponytail who poured the ladle of runny fruit salad into my palms. And that same man, Shyamasundar, had appeared again in Bombay and Vrindavan to become my dear friend. I marveled at the twists and turns of my life, feeling myself to be completing a circle.

It was about eleven o'clock on a Saturday night when I left and inadvertently found myself walking along a main street rowdy with hundreds of American sailors and flashing with neon lights. On both sides were overcrowded discotheques, pubs, nightclubs, and brothels. Live music blared from all sides and the smell of liquor and burning animal flesh filled in the air. I still wore the garb of a sadhu. A heavily perfumed prostitute with shiny red lips and thick mascara grabbed my hand to drag me away, but I resisted. A gang of drunken sailors surrounded me. They yelled, "What kind of freak are you?" and shoved me back and forth to one another. While one pinned me across the chest, another howled with laughter. "Have a drink buddy," he said and poured a gallon pitcher of cold beer over my head. What planet had I landed on? Finally, they released me.

Now I found myself roaming aimlessly in a jungle with predators more intimidating to my mind than the leopards, elephants, and serpents of the Himalayas. Wandering desperately in that vast city I found myself on a narrow lane in the red light district. Brothels lined both sides of the street and rats scampered in the shadows. From inside picture windows, prostitutes posed in various states of undress trying to seduce customers. A sign over one storefront advertised in large letters, "Sex Shop." To the left of the sex shop was a garage door with a smaller door carved into it. Above it read a sign, "Radha Krishna Temple."

Could this be? I knocked. Opening it, a smiling devotee exclaimed, "Please come in and make yourself at home." After taking a shower, I sat down to recover. Sweet spiritual music played softly. Religious art with scenes of Radha and Krishna in Vrindavan decorated the walls. Musk-scented incense filled the air. "Have some hot milk," said the devotee. The steaming milk was lightly flavored with banana and cardamom. In great relief, I looked around. I felt I'd come out of a vast desert and entered an oasis. And then, on the wall, I saw a painting of Srila Prabhupada, gently smiling he seemed to be once again welcoming me home. Silently, I thanked him for making the trip from India, on that cargo ship, so many years back. As a result of his efforts, hundreds of such oases were later to be established throughout the world.

From Amsterdam, I went to London where I spent some time in an ashram near the British Museum. Then I boarded a flight to New York. On reaching the U.S. immigration desk, I was greeted by a female officer who scrutinized every page of my passport. She called someone on the phone and then stamped one of the pages. As I walked forward, two big men in business suits stepped in front of me. They looked frighteningly official as they flashed a badge in my face.

They confiscated my passport. "We are federal agents. Come with us." They led me to a private room and stared me down. An agent declared, "You're being held for smuggling illegal narcotics into the United States. If you voluntarily surrender and cooperate with us, your punishment will be reduced."

"I have no narcotics," I replied meekly.

"We know for certain that you do. Surrender them or we'll find them." He slammed his fist against a hardwood table. "I warn you, don't make us angry."

They thoroughly searched my bag. Finding the small pouches filled with my collection of Vrindavan dirt, they elated. Dangling it in my face, an agent challenged, "What is this?"

"It's dirt from a holy place."

He carefully examined the dirt, rubbing it with his fingers and smelling it. Disappointed, he closed the pouch and put it aside.

One of the agents frisked my body. Suddenly, his eyes lit up as he slapped his hands together in a fit of excitement. "I found it. I found it. The dope is here." He felt a hard lump at the base of my back. "What is this?" he shouted.

"It's my loincloth." They had obviously never seen a sadhu's loincloth.

"Strip off your clothes," they demanded. I took everything off except the loincloth. "What's that?" shouted an agent. Taken aback, the leader mocked, "It sure ain't Fruit of the Loom." They examined my loincloth, which was stained by hundreds of baths in muddy rivers and ponds. "Put your clothes on," they said. Then, with an official politeness, one agent explained that the stamps from Afghanistan, Pakistan, and Nepal on my passport were red flags for narcotics import. He apologized, "We're sorry for the inconvenience, but please understand, it's our duty to protect America." Handing me my passport, they escorted me through U.S. Customs to the door.

I had left home as a teenage student going for a summer vacation to Europe and returned two years later as an ascetic following an ancient spiritual path. By the time I returned, my family had sold our home in Highland Park and bought an apartment in Miami Beach, Florida. From JFK, I caught a domestic flight to Miami. My father, on crutches with a broken leg, came with my little brother Larry to the airport. They found me sitting on the floor, meditating with closed eyes, holding nothing but a faded cotton bag and metal begging pot. My father, choked up with excitement, burst out, "Son, thank God, you're finally home."

I jumped up to greet him. His eyes welled with tears as he wrapped his arms around me in a tight embrace. He sighed, as if years of pain were finally being lifted. Thrilled, little brother Larry, now seventeen, smiled as we shared a brotherly hug. He stared at me as if I were some kind of a returning hero.

As we entered our new apartment, my mother ran to the door and cried out, "Richard, how we missed you." She wept tears I will never forget, embracing me and kissing my forehead. "You've become so thin," she said, and then went on. "Look, I'm learning vegetarian cooking just for you." There on the kitchen counter I saw a small library of vegetarian cookbooks. Hoping only to please me, she immediately served us a dinner of soup, salad, stir fried vegetables, a baked casserole, rice, and apple strudel for dessert.

The phone rang, and it was my elder brother Marty calling from his college in Arizona to welcome me home as well. I was overwhelmed at the lengths my parents would go to in order to make me happy. As difficult as my choice had been and would continue to be for them, they strived to understand and accept my way of life. I sincerely tried to express my love for them while upholding the ideals I held sacred. Although our lives were worlds apart, the affection and respect we shared remained prominent. Through the practice of devotion to God, I was coming to learn that preserving loving relations in this world required much forgiveness, tolerance, patience, gratitude, and humility. An essential virtue of humility is to accept others for what they are, despite differences. I contemplated again how the tendency to judge others is often a symptom of insecurity, immaturity, or selfishness, and I yearned to rise above it. *Everyone is a child of God. God loves all of His children. If I wish to love God, I must learn to love those whom He loves.*

We all knew that I wouldn't be home for long. While my mother had a beautiful room prepared for me, I chose to sleep on a cement patio that extended from our fifth floor apartment. From there, in the quiet hours before the dawn, I gazed out past a vacant swimming pool toward a bay lined with palm and eucalyptus trees that swayed in the breeze. As I meditated, the faint song of the sea whispered from a distance, I felt the patio transform into my cherished rock in the Ganges. While quietly chanting the divine mantra I had received from the river, in my mind's eye I could see the river Ganges flowing effortlessly into the same sea that now spread out before me. I felt Vrindavan, my Guru and my Lord to be indescribably present, beyond time and space. I took a deep breath of the salty air, and gratitude filled my heart. I smiled, folded my palms, and whispered, "It has been an unbelievable journey and you *have* answered my prayers. Wherever I remember you I feel at home."

AFTERWORD

Nearly four decades have passed since I set off on my journey to the East. Over the years, I have realized that whether living in a holy place in India or a congested city in America, if we harmonize our lives in a spirit of devotion to the Lord, we can realize our eternal home.

Shortly after returning to my family, I chose to live in an ashram in America. Two times I was offered initiation from my guru but I declined, feeling I was still undeserving. Neither would I cut my hair nor shave my head like all other monks until I felt absolutely ready to commit myself to initiation. In the spring of 1973, we celebrated the appearance day of Lord Chaitanya, the incarnation of Krishna for this age, and fasted till moonrise. I secluded myself in a dark attic, the closest thing I could find to a cave, and vowed to chant one hundred thousand names of the Lord on my wooden prayer beads. After about six hours, a special inspiration sprung from within. I prayed, "My dear Lord, on your birthday what gift can I offer you?" Another hour passed as I meditated on the Maha Mantra. While chanting "Hare Krishna… Hare Rama," my question seemed to echo in the background. "My dear Lord, on your birthday what can I offer you?" As I chanted the very last of the one hundred thousand names, a voice within my heart called an answer to my question. "Offer your hair."

I knew what that meant. In the past I had resolved to only sever my hair when I was ready to accept the vows of initiation from a spiritual master. I believed that this was the voice of the Lord confirming that I was now ready to take that vow which I had refused to accept repeatedly from many great souls on my path. So, in the summer of 1973, I took the formal vows of initiation. At that time Srila Prabhupada lovingly offered me the name Radhanath Das—servant of Lord Krishna who is the beloved of Radha.

To help me remember the special day, a friend gave me a framed photograph. Neither he nor I were prepared for the stunning reaction it would invoke. My body shivered and mouth dropped. I could not believe what I was seeing. It was the same back cover photo from the pamphlet that I had been left with at the Randall's Island Rock Festival in New York. That was the day before I received the fateful call from Gary. The day before destiny pulled me away from the life I knew and into the realm where everything had to change. Weeks later, while crammed in the back of a van while hitchhiking in England, I had looked at it for the first time and been struck by the personality in that photograph, thinking, "If anyone in this creation has spiritual bliss, it's this person." I lost the pamphlet after that day and never had another thought about it. Now, for the first time I made the connection. The person in the photograph was my guru Srila Prabhupada. I couldn't believe it. Destiny had led me in a full circle. At the very onset of my spiritual quest, the Lord had cryptically revealed who my guru was to be and the path I was to follow. The mystery was only disclosed on the day of my initiation.

For the next six years I resided in an austere monastery on a secluded mountaintop that one had to trudge a three-mile muddy footpath through a forest to reach. The snow-blanketed winters were frigid there and we had no heat. To bathe, we used a rock to break a layer of ice, then dipped in the icy water. Our sanitation system was to climb down a hill with shovel in hand and bury our waste in the mud. In this place, I found myself living a similar life as Ghanashyam, day and night serving the Lord's deity form, trying intensely to follow spiritual disciplines and also tending cows.

After years spent there in meditation on my guru's compassion, I developed a deep longing to share the gifts I had received with others. For the next eight years, I served as a lecturer in colleges and universities, mainly in Ohio and Western Pennsylvania. Professors invited me to speak on topics such as philosophy, religion, sociology, interfaith, the Bhagavad Gita, and I also taught courses on vegetarian cooking.

My beloved gurudeva Srila Prabhupada departed from this world in Vrindavan on November 14, 1977. That day is forever etched in my heart. In separation from him, I felt myself cast into emptiness. As relentless tears washed away all of my patience, my heart cried out, *Where to go now, my dearest friend and guide has left me alone in this world of conflict and confusion? How will I carry on without his love, his smile, and his wisdom?* Now I had to realize his presence was within my heart. My sincerity would be tested by how I followed his sacred instructions to love Krishna and be an instrument of that love in my life. But, for one who follows sincerely, the guru is always present to guide and protect the disciple. Service in separation is a test of our gratitude and love and that separation, I found, is also the sweetest union.

In 1982, the society of devotees urged me to accept the vows of a Swami, a celibate monk exclusively dedicated to God's service. Extremely apprehensive, I resisted because I felt that the honor and distinction that comes with being a Swami was a burden and distraction. Besides that, I felt unworthy. However, appeals and pressures came repeatedly. *What should I do?* I prayed to Srila Prabhupada and the Lord. In the months that followed, my seniors and the voice of my guru within revealed that the primary consideration should be how I could best serve the Lord. In May of 1982, I accepted the vows of *sannyasa*. Conferred upon me at that time was the title Radhanath Swami.

In 1983, I returned to India for the first time in eleven years. I traveled by airplane from London to New Delhi. The same trip that took me over six months when I hitchhiked was completed in less than nine hours by airplane. The speed and safety of an airplane, though, could not compare with the life-changing experiences I'd had on the overland route. In India, I at last made pilgrimage to my most cherished home, Vrindavan. The unbounded joy of returning was mixed with the dismay of finding that almost all of my dear friends had passed away. I roamed from one hermitage to another only to receive the news that another friend was gone.

I rushed to see one dear soul in particular, praying that I was not too late. Near the ancient ruins of a sandstone temple, I witnessed a sight that melted my heart. Sitting all alone on the stone steps was a personality whose glories were hidden from the world but ever shining in my mind; it was dear Ghanashyam. His aged body had aged even more since I'd seen him last. His tiny form was now so thin and frail it appeared that a strong breeze could knock him down to the ground. His tearful eyes gazed downward while he was slowly chanting Radha and Krishna's names. Gently, I sat right beside him. I wept in joy whispering,

"Ghanashyam Baba, do you remember me? I have remembered you every day of my life."

Looking into my face he squinted his childlike eyes trying to make out who this intrusive stranger was. After long seconds passed, he broke the silence with an astonished whisper, "Krishnadas?" Suddenly tears burst from his eyes and streamed down his cheeks. Trembling with emotion he cried out, "Krishnadas, is it really you?" His shaking hand stroked my cheek as he gazed deeply into my eyes. Every muscle of his aged face tensed with feeling as he cried out, "Yes, it is you. Krishnadas, it is you." With great difficulty he bowed his head onto the ground in gratitude to God. He rose slowly and timidly held my hand. His voice cracking, he rejoiced, "Come Krishnadas, Gopijana Vallabha has been waiting so long for you. Please come." Ghanashyam slowly led me a few steps into that alleyway that I dreamed of so many times and into his tiny closet temple. What a feast it was to both my eyes and soul; to be once again face to face with Radha Gopijana Vallabha and Their dearest Ghanashyam. He then proceeded to offer me his Vraja rotis and practically everything else he had. For hours I sat in a trance of gratitude. I was home.

But my duties at the universities soon called me back to America. The next year I returned to Vrindavan, elated with the prospect of seeing dear Ghanashyam. Shivering with anticipation, I crossed the sewage canal and entered the house. But Radha Gopijana Vallabha's intimate closet temple was now nothing more than a closet for storage. The deities were gone. For over sixty years that simple closet had been a glorious temple for the Lord who appeared from the earth to accept the service of dear Ghanashyam. Now it was cluttered with brooms, cleaning buckets, underwear, and utensils. Just then the mother of the house interrupted her cooking to see what I wanted.

"Where is Radha Gopijana Vallabha?" I inquired.

"They found another home."

"Where is Ghanashyam Baba?" I cried out.

Whisking her hand up toward heaven, she replied, "He has gone to Krishna."

In a daze, I walked outside. There, I looked up into the Vrindavan sky and wept. I whispered, "Ghanashyam you will forever dwell in the small closet of my heart. There, I will ever find warmth under the blanket of your humility and be nourished by the Vraja rotis of your selfless love."

One day in 1985, I was guiding about twenty devotees around Govardhan Hill in Vrindavan when, unprepared for a shocking surprise, I found myself face to face with my old friend Asim. Elated, we embraced in gratitude. In our last days together, fourteen years before, we had also circled Govardhan Hill. It was as if we were meeting exactly where we left off. He was so proud that I was now a Swami. Finding a quiet place, we sat together.

In the years since I had seen him, Asim had received a PhD in Sanskrit from Columbia University. In the academic world he was Alan Shapiro and assisted prominent scholars the world over in Sanskrit research. But still Vrindavan was his home.

Asim smiled, "Wait here, Swamiji." A few minutes later he returned with a cloth bag. An uncontrollable smile captured my face for I knew what was in it. Marveling at the sweet will of the Lord we gazed at the beauty of Govardhan Hill and celebrated our reunion with a feast of Vraja rotis and gur. Our precious friendship continued until, by the Lord's will, he passed away in 1998.

My work as a swami began to include more and more travel, as I began to lecture to a wider and wider circle of people.

In the summer of 1988, while in Los Angeles, a friend agreed to drive me up the coast to Big Sur to meet with a special friend, Father Bede Griffiths, a Catholic monk and author of several books that bridged the wisdom of Christianity and Hinduism. He had invited me to give a seminar in a monastery of Benedictine Monks. We sped up Highway 1 with the windows open, savoring the Pacific breeze. At a gas station, my friend stopped to fill up the tank. From a phone booth on the roadside I completed a call. Hanging up the phone, I noticed something peculiar. Right under my nose, the telephone directory was open to a page with the letters "Lis" on the top of the page. My long lost friend Gary's last name happened to be Liss. I scrolled my finger down the page on a whim and was shocked to find the name Gary Liss. *This can't be. I haven't seen him since 1972 in that cave in Nepal. It's been seventeen years.* The address read Malibu Road in Malibu Beach. Looking up, I discovered a street sign directly over the phone booth. *Malibu Road*, it read. Gazing across the street and down the block, I saw a small house with the identical address. I reasoned that there must be thousands of people with the name Gary Liss in America. We had been warned to reach Big Sur by nightfall, and so, letting my rational mind override my excitement at the slim prospect of seeing my old friend, I noted the address and resolved to return and investigate when I could.

A year later in the summer of 1989, returning from India, I borrowed a car and drove alone from Los Angeles up to Malibu Beach. The mystery thickened. Where the small house had once stood was now nothing more than a vacant lot. I asked a neighbor, "What happened to that house?"

"They tore it down last month."

"Do you know the name of the person who lived there?"

"No, I'm sorry."

Perplexed, I just stood there wondering what to do. Behind the empty lot was a tennis court and behind that was a beautiful home right on the beachfront of the Pacific Ocean. With my shaved head and saffron robes, standing in a vacant lot in the posh neighborhood of Malibu, I certainly must have stood out. Suddenly, from out of the house came a middle-aged, well-groomed man with a thick neck and huge muscles that bulged from his arms and chest. The bodybuilder stared at me with suspicion as I did him. He strutted across the tennis court in my direction. *Maybe I shouldn't be standing here*, I thought. As he came closer, though, I recognized that behind all those big muscles and years of aging was someone very familiar. Blissfully, I called out, "Gary, it's me, the sadhu from the cave. Do you remember?"

"My brother, it's you," he cried out. "I can't believe my eyes."

The invisible hand of the Lord had brought us together again.

Eighteen years had passed and we both looked so different. I was still about 120 pounds, but my long locks had been replaced with a shaven head and I wore saffron robes of a swami. Gary's long hair and beard were gone. He was clean-shaven, his short hair neatly parted. His once skinny body was now rippling with huge muscles. It was strikingly obvious that we had taken very contrary paths. A sense of apprehension stirred in both of our hearts. *Do I have anything in common with this person anymore?*

Gary asked, "What do you call yourself now, Richard, Monk, Krishna Das or what?"

"People now call me Radhanath Swami, but you could just call me Swami."

"Well, Swami," he said, "a lot has changed in the past eighteen years. Don't expect me to be what I used to be."

"Please, Gary, let's catch up on all those years."

It turned out that he had torn down his old house on the lot we were standing on and was about to construct a new one. He invited me into the elegant home on the seashore that belonged to his aunt and uncle. Here we spent hours and hours catching up.

From India, Gary told me, he had hitchhiked through all of Africa, South America, Central America, and then north through Mexico. He had spent almost seven years as a hard-core traveler until he finally returned to the U.S. Inspired by Mahatma Gandhi, Gary decided to become a lawyer. While preparing for his law degree, he struggled to restore the ill health brought on by traveling by focusing on bodybuilding. In the years that passed, he graduated law school and got married, but in the meantime, he happened to become a regional champion bodybuilder. When later he was offered a position as a physical trainer at the prestigious Malibu Gym, he opted to make that his career. Since then, he has made his living training the affluent people of Malibu, Hollywood, and Los Angeles.

"Gary," I exclaimed, "I never could have believed that you would end up living on Malibu Beach as a physical trainer for the elite. The mysteries of life never cease to amaze me." In the opulent oceanfront home, we talked throughout the day and night, the song of the waves crashing upon the shore in the background. I sat cross legged on the carpeted floor, leaned back against the wall and noted, "Gary, although your body and social position have changed in every way, I find that the same goodness, loyalty, and spiritual searching still live within you." All barriers of apprehension between us crumbled that night as we shared our thoughts from long ago. It was as if that cave in the Himalayan jungle had transformed into a luxurious home on Malibu Beach. It now seemed as if only moments passed since our last meeting and we bonded on a higher level than ever before.

After hearing my story, Gary had tears in his eyes. "Swami, I've thought about you thousands of times. I knew you would be doing something like this. I'm remembering that fateful evening in Crete when that voice called you away. After all these years, you're still following that inner call. Amazing."

Memories swelled up like waves and then receded into the ocean of our grateful hearts.

"Swami," Gary said, "our lives are totally opposite. What do we have in common? I'm a physical trainer and convince people that they'll be happy with a healthy, handsome body. But you're a swami and convince them that they'll be happy if they realize that they're not the body at all, but an eternal soul."

I had to smile, and replied, "Because the Lord is in everyone's heart, the body is a temple of God. Gary, we can harmonize our talents. You teach people how to improve the temple and I'll try to teach them what to do inside."

Gary, glowed with joy, "That's it; our journey now has a new beginning."

Over the years, I felt a great debt to the land and people of India. Often I would remember when I was a penniless boy in desperation at the Indian border and I made a promise to that Sikh immigration agent. "Someday, I promise to do something good for your people," I had said.

In 1986, I returned to make my permanent residence in India. I was feeling that where there is great need, there is a special opportunity to serve. With this in mind, I settled in downtown Bombay. As a service to my guru and to the beautiful people of India, I was fortunate enough to help in establishing several temples as spiritual educational centers, ashrams to cultivate pure living, and a hospital that treats patients with both conventional and alternative methods of medicine with the aim of giving better quality of life to the body, mind, and soul. The hospital also reaches out with free medical camps in both the ordinary times and emergencies like terrorist acts, earthquakes, and tsunamis. Along with my lifelong friend Ramesh Baba and his followers, we offer an annual eye camp in Vrindavan and perform six to seven hundred cataract surgeries each year. Over the years we've had the opportunity to develop schools for academic, moral, and spiritual education, an orphanage for downtrodden children, a farm to demonstrate environmentally sustainable farming and cow protection, as well as kitchens that are currently feeding nutritious lunches to 150,000 undernourished children daily in schools in the slums. Considering the rise of immorality and sectarian hatred, in several primary and high schools we offer courses in value education to combine students from Hindu, Muslim, Christian, Jewish, Jain, Buddhist, and Parsi communities, teaching universal ethical values with stories and analogies from all the world's great religions. And to help inspire integrity-based leadership for the future, we hold weekly cultural programs at about thirty colleges in the area.

But I must confess that this is all but an insufficient token in comparison to the treasures I have received from the people of India, both the saints and the ordinary people. They have blessed my life with Krishna, my beloved guru, and endless opportunities to serve them and share this blessing with the world.

In 1989, my mother and father visited me in India for the first time. It was a life changing experience for them. They fell in love with the Bombay devotees, who have remained some of their dearest friends. When my beloved mother passed from this world in Chicago in 2004, my father and brothers requested that I deliver the eulogy and carry her ashes to India. They said, "She took such pride in what you're doing there and she had such love for your people."

During the ceremony, on the bank of the Ganges, with almost two thousand devotees sincerely praying and chanting, I placed her ashes into Mother Ganges. With tears of gratitude, I remembered how thirty-four years before I had accepted the Ganges as a mother. As the ashes merged into the flowing current, I prayed with a tearful whisper, "Today, the mother of my physical birth and a mother of my spiritual birth have united, and in this beautiful current they are flowing together to reach the sea. I pray, my dear Lord, please carry mother's soul into the sea of your eternal grace."

This moment was deeply symbolic for me. Yoga means union with our spiritual essence and religion is to bring us back to that same essence. Bhakti Yoga is the science of transforming material into spiritual. By harmonizing our relationships, talents, and property in devotion to the Lord, our spiritual love awakens. In this way the physical body and the spirit soul are united in purpose, and the love we share in this world reaches the eternal spiritual plane. The Bhagavad Gita reveals this mystery to be the perfection of Yoga and the fulfillment of life.

As I look back, I am forever grateful for the journey I traveled and to all the people who helped me to grow on the way. Never could I have imagined where the invisible hand of destiny was leading me. Through it all, I have come to realize that if only we cling to our sacred ideals, not being diverted by either successes or failures, we may find that amazing powers, beyond our own, are there to test us, protect us, and empower us.

I pray that this simple story of mine may inspire all my readers with hope. Our true home awaits us at the end of life's perilous journey. It is a place of lasting peace, beckoning us to persevere until we, too, reunite with our lost love.

AUTHOR'S NOTE

Over the years many people have pressed me to write this story. I resisted, considering it inappropriate to write a book about myself, until something happened to change my mind. In May of 2005 my lifelong friend Bhakti Tirtha Swami called me. He was dying and wanted me to be with him. Bhakti Tirtha Swami was an African American who rose from the ghetto of Cleveland to become a world spiritual teacher whose admirers included, among others, Nelson Mandela, Muhammed Ali and Alice Coltrane.

I arrived at a modest home in rural Pennsylvania where Bhakti Tirtha Swami was passing through the last stages of melanoma cancer. He looked up at me from his bed with a beaming smile and said, "I want to die in your arms. Please stay with me." For the next seven weeks I sat at his bedside, talking about mysteries and miracles and enjoying stories from the Sanskrit devotional texts.

Nobody knew me better than Bhakti Tirtha Swami. He knew the details of my quest and also my hesitation to write about them. One day he clasped my hand, gazed into my eyes and said, "This is not your story. It is a tale about how God led a young boy onto an amazing journey to seek the inner secrets that lie within all of us. Don't be miserly. Share what has been given to you." His voice choked up and a tear streaked down his ebony cheek. "Promise me," he said, "here on my deathbed, that you will write the story." A few days later, on June 27, 2005, he passed from this world. This book is my attempt to honor his wish.

ACKNOWLEDGEMENTS

I offer my sincerest gratitude to all the friends who have helped to make this book a reality, starting with Joshua Greene for being an affectionate brother and guide and for offering his expertise and insights into all phases of this project. His inspiration is a priceless gift. To Dr. Marguerite Regan and her husband David Carter for their invaluable contribution to the manuscript through their research, writing and editing skills, love and humor, and for their attempts to teach me how to write. To them I am forever grateful. And to their guru Tamal Krishna Goswami who showered his blessings on this work. My thanks go to Kyra Ryan, a gifted editor, who drew from my memory the details that were long forgotten, and whose expertise and insight shaped the manuscript into what it is today. I am indebted to her for her sensitivity and wisdom.

My sincerest gratitude to Satsvarupa das Goswami, Sacinandana Swami, Giriraja Swami, Niranjana Swami, Devamrita Swami, Bhakti Vijnana Goswami, Shyamasundara, Gurudas, Gaura Vani Buchwald, Radha Vallabha, Yajna Purusha, Gadadhara Pandit, Kaustubha, Raghunath Cappo, Atmananda, Steven Rosen, Kristin Dornig, Arish Fyzee, Gary Liss, Vraja Lila, Jambavati, Jay Gurupada, Namamrita, Shyamasundari, Balarama, Kishori Lila, and my kindhearted Godsister Rukmini Devi for their invaluable encouragement and suggestions.

My heartfelt thanks to the congregation of Radha Gopinath Temple in Mumbai, India, especially to Rajiv Srivastava, Narendra Desai, Kushal Desai, and Hrishikesh Mafatlal for their enthusiasm to help in every possible way. My thanks go also to Govinda, Gauranga, Gaura Gopal, Gaura Govinda, Radhey Shyama, Chaitanya Charana, Radha Kunda, Jagannath Priya, Radha Gopinath, Devananda Pandit, Shyamananda and Sanat Kumara for their input. To Jagannath Kirtan for making the maps, Gopinath Charan for his photos, and Arjun Mehra for creating a website.

It has been a pleasure working with my dear friend Raoul Goff of Mandala Publishing who put his expertise as well as his heart into this publication, along with Arjuna van der Kooij, Ashley Nicolaus, Jake Gerli, Chris Maas and Rasikananda.

The affection of my father Jerry Slavin, late mother Idelle, and two brothers Marty and Larry with their families and their eagerness to see this book published has made the effort all the more meaningful.

Finally, I extend my sincerest appreciation to you, the reader, who have so kindly opened your heart to allow me to serve you in this humble attempt.